Million Dollar Consulting

The Professional's
Guide to Growing
a Practice

Fourth Edition

Alan Weiss

New York   Chicago   San Francisco   Lisbon   London
Madrid   Mexico City   Milan   New Delhi
San Juan   Seoul   Singapore
Sydney   Toronto

> This book is dedicated to educators everywhere.
> Theirs is the noblest of all callings

1 2 3 4 5 6 7 8 9 0 DOC/DOC 0 1 0 9

ISBN: 978-0-07-162210-3
MHID: 0-07-162210-1

Product or brand names used in this book may be trade names or trademarks. Where we believe that there may be proprietary claims to such trade names or trademarks, the name has been used with an initial cap or it has been capitalized in the style used by the name claimant. Regardless of capitalization used, all such names have been used in an editorial manner without any intent to convey endorsement of or other affliation with the name-claimant. Neither the author nor the publisher intends to express any judgment as to the validity or legal status of any such proprietary claims.

This publication is designed to provide accurate and authoritative information in regard to the subject matter covered. It is sold with the understanding that neither the author nor the publisher is engaged in rendering legal, accounting, or other professional service. If legal advice or other expert assistance is required, the services of a competent professional person should be sought.

—From a declaration of principles jointly adopted by a Committee of the American Bar Association and a Committee of Publishers.

McGraw-Hill books are available at special quantity discounts to use as premiums and sales promotions, or for use in corporate training programs. To contact a representative, please e-mail us at bulksales@mcgraw-hill.com.

CONTENTS

PREFACE

I'VE WRITTEN 32 books, but *Million Dollar Consulting* remains my all-time best-seller. Who even dreams that a business book will be constantly on the shelves for almost 20 years?

When my agent first offered the book, then titled *Confessions of a Consultant*, no less than 15 publishers turned us down. McGraw-Hill wasn't enamored of the concept either, but instead asked for a different approach that led to *Million Dollar Consulting*.

What I've learned consistently from that time to this is that it's better to move when you're 80 percent ready and make up the other 20 percent while you're moving than it is to wait until you're 100 percent prepared. The delay in waiting for that final 20 percent is dysfunctional and adds little value in the eye of the beholder (or buyer). You'll find this refrain in the pages that follow.

Mark Twain said that even if you're on the right track, if you just sit there, someone will pass you by. This book is about movement and progress, and the changes from the previous edition (about 40 percent) respect the changes in our society, economy, technology, and profession.

A few reviewers, while overwhelmingly positive overall, have taken me to task for not writing about building large practices, with scores of employees, that represent a significant equity stake for one's retirement. In effect, they are unhappy that I didn't write a book I never intended to write!

This book is for the entrepreneur who wants to build a blazingly successful solo practice. It is as simple as that. Once you're successful with that practice, you have further options, but not before.

Real wealth is discretionary time, being able to do what you desire when you desire to do it, whether it's watching your kids' soccer games and dance recitals or creating a new client proposal. You can always earn more money, but you can't make more time.

My way has been to consistently earn seven figures a year, provide tremendous value to clients, lead the good life, work smart and not hard, and generate the money required for both retirement and living well now, today, in the present.

The philosophy behind *Million Dollar Consulting* is unchanged. However, since its original publication in 1992, I've met quite a few more million dollar consultants who have read my work. Many have worked with me in the Million Dollar Consulting® Colleges, the Million Dollar Club, and the Private Roster Mentor Program.

I'm pleased to invite you now to join our company.

ALAN WEISS,
East Greenwich, RI

ACKNOWLEDGMENTS

FOR THE FOURTH EDITION

I'm pleased to publicly express my gratitude to Betsy Brown, the editor who first obtained the original *Million Dollar Consulting* in 1991; to editor Mary Glenn, who supervised editions two and three; and to Knox Huston, who is responsible for this newest edition. Every one has been a pleasure to work with.

Thanks to my agent, Jeff Herman, for his representation over the years. He is my first and only agent, and exceptional.

I want to thank technical genius Chad Barr of CB Software, who guides me in cyberspace.

Thanks to Koufax and Buddy, who carry on the tradition of L. T. Weiss in a wonderful way.

FOR THE THIRD EDITION

I'm pleased to publicly express my gratitude to Jarvis Coffin, CEO of Burst! Multimedia; Keith Darcy, executive vice president of IBJ Whitehall; Marilyn Martiny, director of solution selling at Hewlett-Packard; and Lindsey Matheson, COO, and Joe Zammit-Lucia, CEO, both of Cambridge-Pharma Consulting.

Thanks to my agent, Jeff Herman, for his representation over the years, and to Mary Glenn, senior editor at McGraw-Hill, for supporting this third edition.

This is my first book without my longtime friend and colleague,

L. T. Weiss, and I want to send him my love, which I'm sure he can clearly hear.

FOR THE SECOND EDITION

Once again, my sincere appreciation goes to the clients of Summit Consulting Group, Inc. In particular, I'm indebted to Lowell Anderson, CEO of Allianz Life; Barbara Schisani, senior vice president at Merck Medco Managed Care; Connie Bentley and Matt Galik, CEO and vice president, respectively, of Times Mirror Training Group; and Paul Cottone, CEO of Mallinckrodt Veterinary.

My thanks to the finest editor I've known through seven books and four publishers, Betsy Brown, senior editor at McGraw-Hill. I'm appreciative of the technology contributions from Rebecca Morgan, Darek Miliewski, Terry Brock, and Marlene Brown, all of whom are "bilingual," in that they can work with the latest technological marvels while still speaking passable English. And the book simply wouldn't have been completed in the midst of a very heavy consulting, speaking, and writing schedule without my crack research team, Claire McCarthy, Laurie Marble, and Paul Dunion. And thanks to Phoebe Weiss for proofing and invaluable office work.

My love to my wife, Maria, who keeps us both young.

Finally, my deepest gratitude and respect to L. T. Weiss, my collaborator and best friend for 10 years, for unerring editorial assistance through seven books.

FOR THE FIRST EDITION

I am indebted to the many clients of Summit Consulting Group, Inc., who, over the past nine years, have allowed me to practice, develop, and hone my craft. Their trust at first amazed me and now exhilarates me.

In particular, I want to thank Fred Kerst at Calgon, Rick Haugen at Allergan Optical, and Mike Magsig of Cologne Reinsurance, three of the finest chief executive officers I've had the pleasure to work with and learn from. I also very much appreciate the longstanding working relationship I've enjoyed with Del Macpherson, Jim Jones, and George Rizk of Merck, who know how to work hard and laugh harder. All three are admirable people in America's "Most Admired Company."

I owe a great deal to Ben Tregoe for giving me 11 years of fine (and not so fine) tuning all over the world. Ben cofounded Kepner-Tregoe in a garage and built it into a business staple. To this day, his remains the best mind I've encountered in this business.

My thanks go to Bill Howe, principal of Kenny, Kindler, Hunt, and Howe, for 10 years of irregular lunches in the finest restaurants in New York and 10 years of regular commonsense "smacks in the head" that kept my ego from becoming an entry in the Rose Bowl Parade.

Finally, common sense *is* hereditary, and I inherited 100 percent of mine from my wife, Maria, and from Danielle and Jason, who claim to be my kids. I am humbled by the fact that although they have seen my act many times, they continue to tolerate it and help me to improve it.

And for the second consecutive book, my appreciation goes to L. T. Weiss for his unerring editorial assistance and judgment.

PREPARING TO BE A MILLION DOLLAR CONSULTANT

The State of the Art

Most art is in the eye of the beholder

Do not seek to follow in the footsteps of the men of old; seek what they sought.

Matsuo Basho (1644–1694)

CHAPTER 1

WHAT IS A CONSULTANT?

ART AND SCIENCE

An attorney is a person who has graduated from an accredited school of law, passed a bar examination in the state in question, and deals with matters requiring legal opinions and actions. A doctor is a person who has graduated from an accredited medical school, passed state examinations in appropriate areas of expertise, and is licensed to practice medicine in conformance with certain regulatory laws and ethical practices. A certified public accountant is a person who . . .

You get the idea. Most professions have a clear definition. They require formal certifications and have specific, enforceable limitations. A teacher needs education courses and a college degree. A bus driver needs a driver's license. A manicurist must be state certified to work on your nails in a salon. But there are no such constraints on the consultant.

Anyone, at any time, and virtually anywhere can be a consultant. There is only one other calling I know of that has as much influence over the public and requires as few formal qualifications, and that's astrology. In fact, I have found that more licensing is required to be a palm reader on the Boardwalk in Atlantic City than is needed to become a consultant.

At the Ritz-Carlton Hotel in Naples, Florida, where I was holding a Million Dollar Consulting® Graduate School, I told senior management that I had 12 world-class consultants in the room to work on some hotel challenges. We weren't asked for hospitality experience, or references, or client lists. The reaction was simply, "Wow, we're lucky to have you."

Later, a woman in the class told me, "When you said there were a dozen world-class consultants present, I looked around to see who they were!"

The horrible news about consulting is that there is no barrier to entry. The great news about consulting is that there is no barrier to entry.

The Institute of Management Consultants (IMC), for which I once served as a board member, has been doing its level best to try to establish a recognized certification process for a couple of decades, but this is unlikely, in our lifetimes, to attain the state sanctions accorded to other professions. Membership in that organization is static or declining and represents less than 1 percent of actual solo practitioners and less than 0.5 percent of those who call themselves consultants.[1]

Yet consulting is a profession that can earn its practitioners wealth far in excess of what can be earned in fields with rigid qualifying criteria. And this wealth is not only in the form of financial success. It also includes a dramatic learning curve, experiences of a broad and diverse nature, and the potential to provide value to clients that can have an impact on tens of thousands of people at any given moment.

One Percent Solution: tools for change®—Improve by 1 percent a day, and in 70 days you're twice as good. Wealth is not money, but discretionary time. You need to make the money necessary to have maximum discretion as to how you spend your time, the antithesis of the corporate grind.

In view of this peculiar situation, I would like to begin by establishing a definition of a consultant. This is not a definition for the ages, or one that will be acceptable to everybody. However, it is sufficient to serve as a working definition for the remaining chapters, and it serves to establish what a consultant *is* and what a consultant *is not*.

A consultant is someone who provides value through specialized expertise, content, behavior, skill, or other resources to assist a client in improving the status quo in return for mutually agreed-upon compensation. *A consultant improves the client's condition.*

---

[1] Sources such as Kennedy Information in Peterborough, New Hampshire, and my own work with IMC, Society of Advancement for Consulting® (SAC®), and others result in an estimate of about 200,000 individuals working full-time in a solo consulting practice. Double that number when you consider others who are between jobs, part-time, subcontracting to others, and so forth.

Consultants may be internal —working for the organization full time—or external. The latter group is hired on a situational basis. Those situations may last for a day or a year, but most are (and should be) of fairly brief duration. There will be more about timing in later chapters.

The most important part of my definition for those of you who are seeking to build consulting practices is the notion of bringing something of value to the equation that justifies a fee above and beyond the client's normal business investment.

Too many consultants do not market well because they fail to identify their value proposition: how is the client improved after the walk-away? *This is never about methodology or input; it's about business results and output.*

Consulting is not synonymous with implementing, delivering, instructing, or executing, although consulting may include any of these activities. Many and perhaps most of the people working for the big consulting firms (Deloitte or Boston Consulting Group, for example) with thousands of employees are not consultants at all. They are actually implementers, specialists in outplacement or technology, who are the management equivalent of plumbers or electricians. That's right—most consultants really aren't.

A client who hires an outside instructor to conduct programs that the client has developed or purchased elsewhere has no more hired a training consultant than the client who hires part-time office help has hired a typing consultant. A great deal of the confusion that exists in the marketplace and among consultants ourselves is caused by an overly encompassing use of terms.

Some trainers are *also* consultants, and some professional speakers *also* consult, just as some Web site developers *also* consult on search engine optimization. But merely being a site developer, a speaker, or a trainer does not de facto make one a consultant any more than being a consultant makes one a trainer, a speaker, or a programmer.

Only consulting can achieve the final bridge to unconscious competency and the application of new skills to the job.

There are many large training firms that have not been successful in crossing over into consulting and many large consulting firms that have not been able to develop a training function. Although these are compatible, they are two separate disciplines that require separate skills. Thus, try as they might, with advertising, promotion, and attempts to manage public perception, historical training firms such as Wilson Learning, Forum, Kepner-Tregoe, and dozens of others have had little success as consulting firms (no matter what they've put on their business cards), and major consulting firms usually subcontract training assignments to others.

The fact is that consultants must deliver value-added to the client. If the consultant isn't bringing anything to the endeavor that the client doesn't already possess, then why make the investment?

The value added that the consultant brings to bear usually falls into one of six basic categories:

1. *Content.* This is the most common consulting value, largely because most people enter consulting coming out of a field they already know well. (They didn't go to school to become a consultant nor did they begin their careers that way.) Their comfort, experience, and relationships usually lie within such a field. Consequently, there are retail-store display consultants, textile consultants, shrink-wrap packaging consultants (whose job, no doubt, is to ensure that no one opens a package of batteries or paper clips without dislocating a finger), and a plethora of similar content experts. Whatever the industry or pursuit, its work, or *content*, provides the basis for someone to consult in it. Although content consulting is often the province of those who break from organizational life to go out on their own, it is also the realm of specialized firms. Any expert witness in a legal case is a content consultant, acting in that capacity.

2. *Expertise.* Many consultants have a particular expertise that transcends industries and is applicable to a wide variety of environments. For example, Bain & Co. tends to specialize in strategic planning. Its clients are diverse, having only one thing necessarily in common: the value added they are seeking is help with strategic planning. Bain can adapt its approaches to various areas of content. The type of firm doesn't matter. Bain can apply its expertise and formulas equally well to any type of business, whatever its exact nature. Many consultants who strike out on their own after working for a larger consulting firm include expertise as their value added because they have been so intimately exposed to those areas of expertise during the course of their work. (No, this is not illegal, unethical, or even uncomfortable. Ideas cannot be patented, and indeed, there is nothing new under the sun. The basic analytic problem-solving skills we all use today were first postulated by the Greeks two millennia ago.)

> *One Percent Solution: These first two categories are the difference between content and process. Pay heed. This distinction will be critical as we discuss your success in consulting. For the solo practitioner, process expertise is far more valuable than content expertise.*

3. *Knowledge.* In my definition, knowledge is largely experiential. People who have knowledge are the ones who have "been there before." A bank board on which I served chose to hire a former regulator as a consultant because he had vast knowledge of the rules and procedures the regulators would be enforcing in a stricter banking environment.[2] Engineering consultants are often hired out of this same need. In general, knowledge is a broader category than expertise, just as engineering is a broader discipline than the specific pursuit of calculations of projected shareholder value. Moreover, knowledge includes an understanding of *process* as opposed to *content*. That is, the consultant understands the process of time management irrespective of content or the process of decision making regardless of the environment. This is often referred to as *process consultation*. It involves form as well as substance.[3]

4. *Behavior.* The value added in this case is interpersonal. These consultants may facilitate groups to achieve conflict resolution or teach others how to make presentations and interact with an audience. They are virtually never behind the scenes, as the others may be, but are hired specifically to be onstage. They possess a set of interpersonal competencies that enables them to resolve conflict, enhance brainstorming and creativity, focus on critical issues, listen to customer or employee feedback, and so on. Their utility is in the overt role they play, which, for any number of reasons, management itself cannot assume. Sometimes an objective third party is required, and sometimes specific behaviors must be applied. Many people who specialize in these areas have found themselves naturally drawn to them because of previous successes in dealing with such issues. Mediators and arbitrators come to mind as consultants in this field.

5. *Special skills.* Some people have highly developed, well-defined skills that can be in great demand. These are often talents and innate abilities. For example, image consultants, who are able to improve one's wardrobe and grooming, bring to bear an instinctive sense of style and impact. (Contrast this with shareholder-value specialists, whose approach can be reduced to formulas, matrices, and calculations.) An image consultant may know nothing of the content of the client's work and may not have

---

[2] Note that these terms have considerable overlap. The former regulator could also be seen as a content expert or a contact expert. The key, and the reason for the separation at all, is that the client's perception of what he is hiring (buying) and the consultant's perception of what is being offered (the value) are both critical to successful marketing.

[3] See Edgar Schein, *Process Consultation* (Reading, Mass.: Addison-Wesley, 1987), and my own book, *Process Consulting* (San Francisco: Jossey-Bass/Pfeiffer, 2002).

precise expertise or knowledge (e.g., about where to get the best buy on clothes or how to arrange a closet), but nonetheless has a talent for creating a certain look. Consultants in this area have a gift, or specialized talent, that the client usually cannot acquire independently or finds cost-prohibitive to acquire. "We are translating this program into French-Canadian. Find someone who knows the particular idioms and cultural norms and who can put it into conversational language that doesn't appear to be an insensitive translation from English."

6. *Contacts.* Basically, consultants who are called in to help because of their contacts are lobbyists of one stripe or another. Whether they are truly consultants is a question I don't propose to debate here. I've included the category primarily because a great many people entering consulting do so on the basis of being able to introduce clients to key contacts in public or private life. While consulting fees are paid for this work, it is the role that is least able to fulfill the definition I provided earlier. Those who enter the field as so-called introducers are advised to broaden their scope into other areas fairly rapidly if they are serious about making it big as a consultant. Former presidents have always struck me as a good example of someone in this capacity who never chose to or could not leave it. They are hired for their name value only, and appearances at events or memberships on boards have never been dictated by any intrinsic expertise or ability other than having been the president. Calling them consultants is courtesy, not accuracy.

Digression: What about Coaching?

Coaching has become an entity unto itself of late, which leads me to ask, "Was there no coaching before the advent of 'life coaches' and 'coaching universities'?" (I'm also curious about those universities. Who certifies the certifiers?)

Consultants have always had to coach their clients and continue to do so. I believe that coaching is a subset of consulting. In fact, since you've already bought this book and probably can't return it, let me provoke you still more: a true consultant who understands organizational dynamics and change management will always be a better coach than someone who merely focuses on changing a client's behavior in isolation. Don't be lured by what's become the coaching "industry," which has tried to create qualifications for entry that are, in my opinion, completely arbitrary.

Consultants bring one or more (and in more cases than you would suspect, *all*) of these competencies to bear to help a client move from the status quo to an improved position. If I were moving an operation to South America for the first time, I might need *content* to understand the nature of the competition for my goods and services in the new locale, *expertise* to provide the requisite language skills to my transferring managers, *knowledge* to gain the proper licenses and tax permits, *behavior* to help with the advance work in preparation for our arrival and in dealing with the local press, *skills* to assist in the acculturation process (what we should do to assimilate as rapidly as possible), and *contacts* to build relationships with local governmental and business leaders.

I've previously suggested that there are several hundred thousand independent consultants in the United States. In addition, there are thousands of consulting organizations, from tiny practices to the Deloittes and McKinseys of the world. It is folly to attempt to make sense of that panoply in any conventional manner, because huge organizations such as International Business Machines (IBM) and General Electric (GE) often prefer to use the lone wolf for one assignment and Deloitte for another just down the hall. (Over the past couple of years, IBM and Hewlett-Packard also have established their own quite successful consulting operations; in the former's case, it has become the top contributor to corporate profits.) Consequently, it's probably more useful to view the market in terms of the values the consultant brings to the client rather than in terms of an arbitrary category or size.

There's one more point to be made from the perspective of the consultant, which I've found over the years (and through more than 1,000 participants in my private mentoring program) to be true of all entrepreneurs. Three paths must converge for you to be successful:

Market need. You must have an existing need or be able to create one. Akia Morita created one for the Walkman. Now the iPod and the iPhone, two of the most successful new products ever launched, have exploited that previously created need. But needs such as sales ability and strategy formulation will always exist.

Competency. You must have the skills to meet that need or be able to develop them, and the buyer must perceive that you possess them. Fortunately, we can all become lifelong learners, although I'm not about to learn quantum mechanics no matter what market need may develop.

Passion. You have to love what you do and be perceptibly enthusiastic.

Note that two of the three are not enough. The greatest competency and passion will fail if the market need isn't there, and the most compelling need and highest passion will succumb to poor skills. You must develop in all three areas, but be aware that you can't learn passion—you have to feel it.

> *One Percent Solution: Where those three paths converge, you have branding opportunities that draw people to you and make high fee levels acceptable to the buyer because of your perceived value.*

HOW ORGANIZATIONS CHOOSE CONSULTING HELP—HOW TO BE "DISCOVERED"

There is more logic in the Internal Revenue Service tax code, or in the myriad pieces of billing information you get from the phone company, or in any Rube Goldberg invention for catching a mouse than there is in the selection process for consulting help.[4] (My estimation is that approximately 50 percent of consultants don't really know what they're doing, but that about 90 percent of potential buyers don't know that until it's too late.) Consequently, it is difficult and even foolhardy to try to market against a consistent buying habit unless you are in a highly specialized area such as government, in which requests for proposals (RFPs) are uniform and the only way in which the customer will do business.[5]

These are the major ways in which organizations go about securing the services of outside consultants:

1. *Word of mouth.* This is probably the most comfortable method for many buyers, particularly at middle- to upper-management levels. If a trusted colleague can endorse someone who's done the job for her, the client saves a great deal of time and minimizes the risk. If the colleague is in the same industry—even as a competitor—so much the better. (I've received hundreds of calls from potential buyers who have been referred to me by satisfied clients.) This technique is what I call *passive marketing* because it is out of your hands. However, deliberately gathering the names of a client's colleagues and obtaining permission to use the client as a reference can help you respond much more effectively to some of the other selection methods used by prospective buyers. My concept of *marketing gravity* relies heavily

---

[4] We are dealing with new business, not the continuation of existing business or the expansion of current business within existing clients. The notion of repeat business will be dealt with in Chapter 4.

[5] And even here there are exceptions. For example, if you can qualify as a "sole source" for a particular service, you can circumvent the entire ponderous competitive bidding process.

on creating a brand and a buzz that will bring people to you. [See *How to Establish a Brand in the Consulting Profession* (San Francisco: Jossey-Bass/Pfeiffer, 2001) and *How to Market, Establish a Brand, and Sell Professional Services* (Fitzwilliam, N.H.: Kennedy Information, 2000).]

After successful engagements, million dollar consultants always ask the client two things. First: What other people do you know who can use these same services and approaches? Second: May I use you personally as a reference? *Greatest catalyst*: Peer-to-peer recommendation from one buyer to another. That is the platinum level of marketing.

2. *Repute.* This is slightly different from the first method, in that the potential buyer may not have actually spoken to anyone who is familiar with your work but may have heard of you through a third party, from publicity, or as a result of casual conversation. This method is often—and unfortunately—popular with top executives, who feel safer acquiring the services of a "name" firm or individual so as to justify the investment (and not have to think too analytically about the actual intervention). Reputation in the consulting business is like reputation in the entertainment business: sometimes the biggest stars are the flops, living on repute and little else, and sometimes the unknowns are powerful surprises, living on talent and little else.

Greatest catalyst: A commercially published book. This is the gold standard.

3. *An outstanding and manifest body of work.* A track record of success, intellectual property, visibility in key areas of interest to clients—this is the art of blowing your own horn. *And if you don't blow your own horn, there is no music.* The Internet has wonderfully accelerated the ability of consultants to make their work known. The combination of newsletters, blogs (and some other, but not all, "social media"), Web sites, hard-copy publishing, speaking, interviews, product sales, and so forth creates avenues to race down with news of your value and your successes. In a world where people are searching for 15 minutes of fame by slogging through deserted islands on television reality shows, you can certainly build a career by riding in triumph down Main Street. Success breeds success, *if* it's manifest. This is the silver standard.

Digression

All-star gaffes, or the "lead standards":

- *No answer at the consultant's phone number*
- *An answering machine with a stupid message*
- *E-mail that is not a private domain, such as AOL or Yahoo[6]*
- *Lack of letterhead, envelopes, and/or business cards*
- *No brochure, company descriptive material, and/or press kit*
- *No Web site, or one that is always "under construction"*
- *Proposals with typos, poor grammar, and misused words*
- *Being late and/or unprepared for initial meetings*
- *Talking instead of listening*
- *Poor attire, battered briefcase, cheap pen, etc.*

We'll discuss what a consultant requires to present a professional image and the confidence of a solid, successful firm for clients in later chapters. For now, however, bear in mind that it is extremely difficult to acquire clients, extremely lucrative to maintain long-standing client relationships, and extremely difficult to lose a happy client. Since most readers are probably not CEOs of the largest consulting firms, it's useful to remember that the acquisition of clients is the bedrock of success and that such acquisition probably will originate in the areas listed earlier 90 percent of the time.

Always, however, stack the deck in your favor, and be prepared to deal with any lead (I've received scraps of paper written in haste) in an assertive, timely, and professional manner.

Here are typical examples of how I've obtained contracts:

- An ongoing pharmaceutical client of seven years' standing requested an extension of one project and the beginning of another. Originally, this client had come onboard when an internal buyer, having remembered me as a contact in a training firm I was once with, began hunting for me after I had moved out of state. The old firm passed on my new address, and I was asked if I'd be interested in what became a $14,000 project that the client believed I was suited for. I worked with

---

[6] To me, AOL as a domain for receiving professional correspondence should stand for "amateur on line."

this client for 12 consecutive years (still my personal longevity record) and obtained direct revenues of $2 million and indirect revenues (referrals, repute) of at least three times that.

> *Every interaction with a prospect should be seen as a personal moment of truth, and the consultant should always be thinking about the fourth sale, not the immediate one.*

- A buyer at one organization moved to three more and brought me in each time. This is a relationship business. Keep in touch with everyone frequently.
- A buyer at a banking client departed to become CEO of another organization. He promptly requested my assistance. The original client, for whom I had completed three projects over the past several years, was generated by a 56-cent mailing to an individual recommended by a mutual professional acquaintance. The mailing was handed down two levels and finally came to rest on the desk of someone with a particular need (itch) that my literature addressed (scratched).
- An executive with an insurance client who had used my services on a very small contract left to become CEO of another firm. I updated my mailing list and sent him a series of items. About a year later, he contacted me for a major strategy project and asked that I serve on his informal kitchen cabinet of consultants. The original client had come onboard as the result of a recommendation by the president of another consulting firm who chose not to undertake such a small project within his organization. (This client will surface again on a fishing boat in Chapter 18.)
- A midlevel manager at an aerospace client for whom I did a small amount of work was laid off. I remained in touch and provided contacts and career advice as best I could. She obtained a management position with a large health-care firm and recommended me for a succession-planning project, which led to a concurrent project for the president. She has since been promoted. My original association with her dates back to a collaboration with a training firm for which I designed and helped to implement workshops. She was not successful in implementing the workshops but was impressed by my approach and participation.

- A CEO read one of my books and asked if I could provide a workshop on the content. Once I did that, the CEO asked if I could consult with and coach her senior people. The CEO went on to purchase over 100 copies of the book she originally read.

- I had done a small amount of business with a major telecommunications firm years ago, but a job change for the original recommender resulted in my abrupt dismissal—the new man wanted his own consultants on the job. I remained in contact with his boss through periodic mailings and was asked to stop in on two occasions simply to discuss what I was doing in the field. About six months after the second such meeting, a new recommender selected me for a series of assignments.

There have been times when those contacts that have seemed most solid and well intentioned have gone absolutely nowhere despite my visits to the prospect and guarantees of my suitability. There have been many more times when a call out of the blue has resulted in a long-term, dramatic engagement. However, even those occasions weren't as random as I once believed. They were the result of my having sown the seeds for my work in the three areas mentioned earlier, and having successfully avoided shooting myself in either foot.

During the buying sequence, however, we begin with shared values, not in the spiritual sense, but in the realm of business philosophy. For example, I don't believe in downsizing as a remedy to corporate sins, so I won't take on such business.

If our values are congruent, we can establish a relationship, which means that I trust you and you trust me. We are honest with each other both in sharing information and in our candor. Only then can we establish conceptual agreement (objectives, measures, and value to the client). Buyers aren't likely to provide such information without a relationship that is comfortable.

Conceptual agreement is sufficient to provide a proposal (most consultants spend too much time on unnecessary information gathering prior to submitting a proposal when conceptual agreement with the buyer is all that's needed). An accepted proposal leads to implementation and, ultimately, results, which reinforces the relationship because you've accomplished what was agreed upon.

This is a simple yet powerful business-acquisition model. Always know where you are in the model because each step builds on the prior one.

This also demonstrates that the sales sequence is really a series of small "yeses," not one grand onslaught carried out against the buyer's defenses. From initial contact to final acceptance, the sequence might look like a series of small yeses.

You can't obtain a yes on conceptual agreement without a relationship, nor can you obtain acceptance of a project without a proposal. *It's far easier to pursue and obtain a series of small yeses than it is to achieve a contract in a single stroke.* This also enables you to understand what your next goal is and to orient your conversation and your supporting materials accordingly.

EMPHASIZING RESULTS, NOT TASKS — WHY A "DELIVERABLE" SHOULDN'T BE DELIVERED

We've already differentiated between a contractor and a consultant. The former is hired to implement specific work and to perform designated tasks. The latter is hired to provide unique abilities and talents that will improve the client's condition and constitutes a value-added component that the client doesn't already possess.

The average consultant, however, tends to categorize his involvement by describing the tasks to be performed. *Million dollar consultants, by contrast, tend to describe results.* The difference is between input and output, task and results, activity and outcome. In assessing the value added (which we'll be discussing in relation to fees in Chapter 9), which of the following is a client likely to perceive as being most valuable and unique in contribution and most worthy of a larger fee?

Task	Result
Survey all employees	Provide recommendations to improve morale
Visit field service units	Identify and resolve specific service gaps
Design training program	Improve delegation skills
Observe meetings	Enhance meeting productivity and time use
Reorganize the division	Optimize use of employee skills and talents

Interventions should be based on results and outcomes, not on activities and tasks. The more a consultant emphasizes the latter, the more she becomes a *doer* whose progress and worth are assessed in terms of how much is *done*. Moreover, the consultant's time used becomes scrutinized (How long will it take you to conduct the survey? How many meetings do you have to observe?), and the alternatives become subject to debate (Why can't we have a two-day training program instead of a three-day approach? Let us determine which field sites you should visit). The more the results are emphasized, the more the consultant is free to pick and choose alternatives and to be flexible in abandoning certain approaches and beginning more fruitful ones.

Any intervention should be based on objectives so that both consultant and client are in agreement on the end results of the engagement and the consultant is free to employ a variety of techniques and use his time to best advantage. The more the engagement is based on alternatives, the more the consultant becomes just another hired hand.

> *My approach to beginning any new project is to gain "conceptual agreement," which is agreement on the objectives to be met, measures to gauge progress, and the value of doing so for the client organization.*

There are a number of ways to view interventions, or *contracts*, as they are often called (i.e., the contract with the client regarding responsibilities, not the legal contract that one signs). However, virtually all of them take a fairly limited view. For example, the consultant may be a backstage counselor who never appears to the organization in general, but rather concentrates on helping a single individual who interacts with others. Or the consultant may be a coach who is regularly seen on the sidelines sending in advice to the players. Or the consultant may be the front person who actually takes the lead role in running the meeting or leading the project.

However, these types of categories can be self-limiting and are too often dictated more by what the consultant feels comfortable with than by what the client needs. In other words, superb consultants tailor their roles—and vary them—according to the precise client needs that have engendered the presence of the consultant. The mere act of helping the client determine the appropriate range of pragmatic interventions is the initial consulting contribution. This determination should be collaborative, explicit, comfortable, and in conformance with the end results required.

At one end of the range of potential interventions shown in Figure 1-1 are those that resolve a client's need and/or improve a client's position. In other words, the client is hungry, and the consultant must catch a fish for dinner lest the client starve. At the other end of the range are interventions that educate the client so that such needs can be met self-sufficiently in the future. In other words, the client learns how to catch a fish without help.

In some extreme and valid cases, the client has no need to master the consultant's skills and approaches, but simply requires situational, one-time expertise. This is an occasion for the "consultant as expert," in which the consultant brings the fishing gear, determines the best spot in the stream, catches the fish,

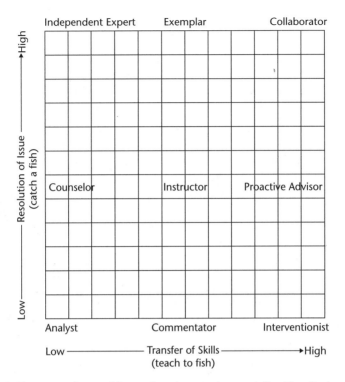

Figure 1-1 The range of potential consultant interventions as defined by client need.

cooks it, packs the tent, and departs. The client is responsible only for consumption and cleanup. The evaluation of the consultant is based on the quantity and quality of the fish caught and whether or not they have sated the client's hunger at the moment. A consultant helping with an acquisition might well serve in this capacity. I've run employee help lines for organizations in this capacity.

At the other extreme, the client needs skills transferred as the end result itself. There is no larger issue that requires reconciliation, or if there is, it is also useful as the means to help transfer the skills. The interventionist shows the client how to hold the rod, how to cast, where to stand, and so on, and demands practice and performance improvements before any fish are even caught. The client is then responsible for using the skills on an ongoing basis, although the consultant may be called on for further comment, feedback, and analysis of progress.

The evaluation of the consultant in this case is based on the client's decreasing need for outside help to sate her hunger at any given moment. A consultant helping to design and educate managers in creative problem solving might serve in this capacity. Playing this role, I've worked with managers on processes to empower subordinates.

There's nothing sacrosanct about the terms provided in Figure 1-1. The importance of this type of breakdown, however, is that it is based on the client's needs for consulting help and should be used as a template to decide collaboratively what the consultant's role should be.

Unfortunately, many consultants picture themselves as experts, instructors, or facilitators and never depart from that role. However, as Abraham Maslow observed, "When the only tool you have is a hammer, you tend to see every problem as a nail." Such categorization severely limits the value of a consultant to prospective (and current) clients.

I have a friend who is perceived as an instructor in telemarketing. He is excellent at what he does, but he finds it extraordinarily difficult to enlarge client engagements beyond telemarketing. Yet, when he works with me as an associate, he is involved in a wide variety of roles and areas. Unfortunately, he has restricted his considerable talents, not only by focusing on one content area—telemarketing—but even more so by concentrating on one type of intervention—running training programs. I pointed out that his preparation work for the training involved lengthy observation on the client's sites and evaluation of strengths and weaknesses, which constitute the core of an excellent needs analysis. That in itself is an analyst role on my chart and one that he should consider as a separate value for the client, irrespective of whether he ever runs a training program.

One Percent Solution: Unbundle what you do, don't bundle it. Your plumber doesn't offer to redesign your bathroom for free when the problem is a leaky sink. Don't try to justify your fee by throwing in more and more services. That's a sign of low self-esteem.

In other words, my friend is already using other interventions and is adept at them, but he subordinates them to his preconceived role as an instructor. When I introduce him to my clients, as an associate, his role is determined by the client's need, not his own standard one, broadening the value he brings to the situation. He has since embarked on a plan to create an identical dynamic within his own client base. (This is very difficult once the client has typecast you. The key is to avoid a predefined role with prospects so that new clients never identify you with a single type of intervention.)

Then there's what I call the *pragmatic range of interventions* because they are based on the client's need and the combination of doing for the client and helping the client to become self-sufficient—both legitimate goals. The remainder of this book will assume that the consultant is willing to embrace a variety of practical interventions. This willingness is the first major step toward exponential growth in business.

TRENDS AND LIKELIHOODS FOR THE COMING DECADE—LOOKING AROUND THE CORNER

Consulting is a growing profession, both for good reasons and for spurious ones. The good reasons include these:

- Reduced staffing results in the need for outside specialized help.
- Increasing technological complexity also results in the need for outside specialized help.
- Growing diversity in the workforce demands new approaches.
- Globalization, including opportunities and security concerns, also results in the need for outside specialized help.
- Managers who never saw bad times but are now experiencing tough economies also need specialized help.
- Increasing scrutiny by an educated public and the media also results in the need for outside specialized help.
- Other national economies need dynamic management modernization.
- Increasing emphasis on quality of life and family obligations also results in the need for outside specialized help.
- Demographic shifts radically change markets.
- Threats of terrorism and increased vulnerability demand heightened security.
- Decreasing public confidence in "big business" and government require the shoring up of both quality and perception of quality.
- Instantaneous communications have created customer-to-customer dialogues.

The spurious reasons include these:

- There continue to be no licensing or certification requirements.
- Consulting is seen as a refuge for people who have been downsized or are unhappy with corporate insecurities.
- Consulting skills can be appropriated from books, courses, and tapes, many of which are deficient.
- Fads (such as "open meetings" and "outdooring") intrigue company trainers.

- Management prefers to use outsiders rather than face unpleasant jobs.
- There is continued overemphasis on personality profiling and behavior predictions instead of focusing on true development.

Unfortunately, consulting will continue to be a profession that readily grows in quantity but not as readily in quality. The good news, of course, is that those of us who are providing professional, high-quality services will continue to grow rich. However, just as the average attorney earns far less than the members of the vaunted, headline-making defense teams (in fact, I was told by an acquaintance at the American Bar Association that the average attorney in general practice earns less than $90,000 a year), the average consultant will neither achieve great wealth nor establish a sound enough business to survive tough times.[7] Many consultants are retired people who are seeking to use their specific expertise or contacts to remain active, and many more are people holding down full-time jobs who consult on the side to earn extra income. (All too often, that work on the side is at the expense of the regular employer's expertise, time, and/or materials. I call it *white-collar moonlighting*, and it is a problem in all organizations that do not fully absorb the professional talents and interests of their managers. Ironically, the fabulously wealthy creator of the cartoon *Dilbert* began drawing it on his former employer's time.)

One Percent Solution: Economic conditions will demand that people work longer and perhaps never completely retire in the traditional manner. Consulting will be a prime alternative enabling that new dimension of work.

Overall, consulting work has tended to be reactive rather than proactive, responding to the trends, fads, and whims of the marketplace. Sometimes those who merely respond fastest are seen as innovators, but in reality, there are very few who provide new approaches proactively. For example, once *In Search*

---

[7] The late consulting guru Howard Shenson claimed in his advertisements that there are over 450,000 people engaged in the profession, of whom only 11 percent earn over $50,000 per year. He cited IRS figures as his source. A number in the "hundreds of thousands" is also supported by a prepublication reviewer of one of my manuscripts, John Young, director of the University of Colorado Executive Programs.

of Excellence[8] became a hit over a quarter century ago, there followed a plethora of consultants, trainers, and preachers who espoused "management by wandering around" and "sticking to the knitting" as though these were mantras whose very intonation would improve the operation. Today, any momentary "guru's" new book spawns a crowd of lemminglike (ratlike?) consultants. I'm weary of both clients and consultants who chant, like monks at vespers, "I want to go from good to great."

When I ask them what that would mean, they say they don't know and merely go on chanting.

In actuality, most managers I observed wandering around under such guidance only managed to get in the way and generally had no idea about what to do while they were wandering. And sometimes it doesn't matter whether the cheese is there or not. "Great" isn't always good. (Do you really need "great" accountants?) In what might be the apotheosis of consulting as a bizarre activity, there are those today who counsel organizations on how to apply for and try to win quality awards such as the Baldrige, Deming, or Nikkei prizes. Funny, I thought those awards recognized quality in products, services, and customer relations. However, sometimes the pursuit of such recognition is at the cost of tending to business.[9] Fortunately, these activities have faded severely in the face of far more pragmatic business requirements than award-winning.

Excellent consultants will explore with clients those results that actually constitute improvements in performance, service, and quality and how well business goals are being met. That is, they will help establish the objectives to be attained, not merely the *alternatives* for measuring progress.

For the foreseeable future, we will have to deal with an increasingly sophisticated consumer in an increasingly complex and volatile international economy. (This does not apply only to large organizations. Local jewelry distributors in Rhode Island, for example, purchase goods in the Philippines and Korea and then use immigrant help from Portugal to assemble and ship the merchandise, which is ultimately sold in New York to Japanese tourists.) The need for consulting help will indeed grow because the marketplace will require it.

---

[8] Thomas J. Peters and Robert H. Waterman, Jr.: *In Search of Excellence: Lessons from America's Best-Run Companies* (New York: Harper & Row, 1982).

[9] Florida Power and Light disbanded its quality teams after winning the Baldrige Award because a new CEO felt that the focus was more on compliance with the team regulations than on results for the customer. And Cadillac won the award in 1990 even though its quality was below competitors' because it had made such dramatic *improvements* in quality. In other words, if you let things slip long enough, you look good when you finally do something about it, and if you're attentive every day, you don't have room for dramatic improvement.

The good reasons for growth listed earlier are largely *market-driven*, whereas the spurious reasons are largely *consultant-driven*.

My belief is that those consultants who are able to deal with high degrees of ambiguity and who can offer a variety of the intervention roles (often shifting roles within the context of a single assignment) will best be able to provide the unique, value-added talents that meet client's needs. The tolerance for ambiguity is necessary because fewer of these needs will be cut-and-dried and simple to embrace.

One of my clients asked me to work with a newly appointed division president to enhance his ability to delegate. The parent-group president had identified this lack as a potentially severe problem because the individual would now be leading former peers. It would have been easy to have listed the various alternatives for improving delegation skills and to provide the client with options for implementing them. However, I've long since learned that few things in this business are as they first appear and that three things always jointly influence behavior: individual predispositions, the environment, and interactions with others. (Hence, my earlier aversion to consulting by personality profiling and testing.)

When I met with the president to explore whether we would work together, I didn't approach the conversation as one that would help me to understand a delegation problem. Instead, I spent the morning learning about the president's predispositions, his environment, and his interactions with others. I began to realize that the president's ability to delegate was not only a function of his personal skills, but was also related to his team's willingness to accept delegation, that there were environmental factors—turf battles, outmoded procedures, and confusion over mission—that had to be reconciled; and that there were doubts about whether all the current players were appropriate for their current positions. We spent the morning determining at what level the organization should be
performing if it were ideally successful and what role the president would be playing in that performance.

What had appeared on the surface to be a counselor's role in actuality demanded skills ranging from analyst to collaborator. This became one of my most successful client interventions ever. The client retained me for five years at $100,000 per year, with other projects bringing the total to over $600,000. I'm convinced that the key to my ability to help that client demonstrably lay in refusing to allow myself to fall into a single preconceived role based on what I'd been told. Rather, I listened, validated, and joined the client in establishing results that were to be achieved by any number of activities. By moving among a variety of roles, I was able to

- Provide facilitation sessions to top management to enhance execution.
- Work one-on-one with senior managers on *accepting* delegation.
- Visit customers to determine their perceptions of the client's services.
- Analyze the business and contribute to strategic mission statements.
- Develop the CEO's personal skills and interpersonal abilities.
- Develop, staff, and administer employee "hot lines."
- Earn more than a half-million dollars.

The best, longest-lived, and most rewarding client relationships are those that are based on conceptual agreement of what is to be accomplished. The "how" is subordinated to the "what"—the end result.

Consulting through the first quarter of this new millennium will be most profitably based on helping the client to establish need and providing the flexibility in intervention roles to meet a wide variety of needs. This is as proactive as one can reasonably expect to be and avoids the twin pitfalls of attempting to be a seer of issues over the horizon and being the knee-jerk responder to every capricious walk-over-hot-coals-while-surviving-in-the-wilderness fad that comes down the pike.

This has been a general view of the lay of the land. Let's move on to what's between the ears?

QUESTIONS AND ANSWERS

Q. *I've been continually asked by human resource people and trainers to cite costs, days, and deliverables. That is contrary to what you claim is what's desired: results. What am I doing wrong?*

A. You're dealing with the wrong people. There are virtually never true economic buyers in human resources, training, or organizational development departments. Find the real buyers who have profit-and-loss responsibility, head departments, and so forth. Never deal with gatekeepers or those who are paid to conserve preexisting budgets.

Q. *I'm told that listings on the Internet, using brokers, and optimizing my place on search engines will gain me more traction. Is this a good investment?*

A. No. Buyers do not troll the Internet looking for consultants. Focus on my "big three": buyer-to-buyer referral, commercially published books and other material, and outstanding performance that you make public.

Q. *Won't we need economies of scale in tough times and be better off joining large organizations? Isn't the solo consultant going to be being phased out?*

A. Au contraire, my friend. The agile and smart independent consultant will be able to find work by providing value on a faster, more nimble basis than those huge monstrosities (which once were the Big Eight and are now down to about three). But you can't be afraid, and you have to have faith—in yourself.

---

*Final Thought: **The good news is that anyone can become a consultant. The bad news is that you had better be able to establish a market need, develop the competency to fill it, and have the passion to do so. Two out of three aren't good enough.***

PROPULSION AND VOLITION

RUDDERLESS SHIPS ARE ONLY GOOD AT DRIFTING

HOW JOBS GET IN THE WAY OF CAREERS

In the midst of a consulting assignment at Marine Midland Bank in Buffalo (now part of HSBC), my client was attempting to explain why my help was needed in trying to align human resources strategies with the organization's business strategies.

"Throughout the bank," she reported, "there are talented people who are spinning their wheels too frequently, working hard to get things done that make sense at the moment, but aren't bona fide contributors to the bank's goals. We're no different within human resources, and we've got to be the ones to serve as an example to others in our consulting work and course offerings."

"Well," I responded (always a tremendously safe reply from a consultant), "if people are *too* focused on the details of the job at hand, what do we want them to shift their focus to? It's easy to say 'strategic goals,' but that's notoriously hard to do when you're a middle manager whose phone is ringing every three minutes."

"We all should realize that the current job is just one aspect of a full career within the organization. We need to take a longer-term view of our work. In fact," she concluded, "we criticize senior management when they focus only on short-term issues, allowing quarterly results to interfere with longer-term developmental needs. We should be equally tough on ourselves when we allow our jobs to get in the way of our careers."

And so a new concept was born—at least so far as I knew—and a fundamental goal was established for our project. *People had to stop allowing their jobs to interfere with their careers.* It was catchy, succinct, and increasingly clear as we demonstrated the difference between working hard and working smart, between aiming for short-term, temporary respite and going for long-term enduring achievement.

I've never forgotten that lesson and how well it applies to consulting work. It is very simple for a consultant to allow the daily travails of the job to become the entire raison d'etre for the practice, and once that happens—consciously or subconsciously—time becomes scarce because of the need for establishing work schedules, arranging for flights, grinding out reports, attending meetings, generating publicity, and so on. The conventional wisdom has us believe that the major impediment to exceeding a particular sales figure as a consultant (usually stated as an average of $300,000) is the impossibility of being in two places at once: if you are marketing, then you can't be delivering; if you are at client A, you can't be at client B; if you are perceived as a counselor, you can't be perceived as a collaborator.

But that particular paradigm is easily shattered once you view your work as a career that is fulfilled by generating a series of client results, not as a succession of jobs or assignments that usurp time until their completion.

One Percent Solution: It is critical that you continually reduce labor intensity if you intend to create a seven-figure practice. Do the math: you don't have the time to do four or five times what you're doing today. You have to do things differently.

Here's a specific example of such lofty notions. Bob Janson is a good friend of mine who once was the president of Roy Walters & Associates in New Jersey. His firm focused on self-directed work teams and on empowering workers throughout the organization (hence its value added was expertise, using the parameters of Chapter 1). Bob consistently referred work to my firm, and we collaborated on several projects over the years. During one such collaboration, I innocently asked him whose responsibility the final report would be. I, of course, was thinking it would be his firm or mine, and I was ardently hoping that it would be his because generating reports takes up *time*.

His response floored me.

"It's the client's responsibility, naturally. Don't tell me that you usually generate the reports!"

Oh, oh. What had I been missing. . . .

"Don't you see," he continued, "this client hasn't *asked* for any written report. He wants a system to improve communications, he needs help in implementing it, and he'll want us to keep him fully briefed on our progress and plans. However, he never asked for a report. If he wants one, then we'll give the basic information to whomever he designates, and the report can be created by his own people, in whatever style and format he prefers."

This was a very existential moment, one that I categorize as *conceptual breakthrough time* (CBT). I had always done reports because I regarded reports as a job that had to be undertaken to demonstrate tangible comletion of certain aspects of the assignment. If the client didn't request one, I made sure that I volunteered one. Bob, on the other hand, *never* did reports because he was focused on the end results that he had agreed on with the client, and a report is, with rare exception, never an end result in and of itself. If the client wanted one, Bob had no objection, so long as it was clear that generating it was the client's responsibility. Bob isn't in the business of creating reports—he is in the business of enhancing client results.

That's when I began to scrutinize my interactions with clients to determine the extent to which may job was interfering with my career. All of us can use more time, and that's understandable. What isn't understandable is the wasting of already scarce time on jobs that we make for ourselves that have no real, enduring impact on the results being sought for the client. My list of jobs that can get in the way of careers is compiled in Figure 2-1. It's amazing how much of our time can be dictated by conventional wisdom![1]

- Regularly scheduled meetings to "keep in touch"
- Periodic written reports and updates
- Physical trips to the client site when phone calls would suffice
- Needs analyses—when what's wrong is as obvious as a ham sandwich
- Presentations of interim results to various groups
- Extensive research when the issue is situational and unique
- Meals and entertaining—the world's most abused consulting habit
- Sophisticated computer applications that bring no additional value to the project
- Seeking ego strokes
- Responses to irrelevant issues and peripheral interests
- Telephone calls to "keep in touch," with no other agenda
- Paperwork and record keeping that contribute nothing to performance
- Overinvestigating without deciding: "analaysis paralysis"

Figure 2-1 Thirteen ways to let a job get in the way of a career.

---

[1]Conventional wisdom, as far as I've ever been able to determine, isn't conventional and isn't really wisdom. It is actually a description of tired clichés intended to explain away failure before it occurs.

One of my consulting colleagues once told me that he was weary of being on 12 airplanes a month just to attend meetings with a single client organization. "The meetings really are unimportant in terms of the quality of the project," he confided, "but the client has come to expect them."

Ah, but who set those expectations?

Educating the Client

One of the most important areas to master is that of educating the client. The client's expectations will be formed from your first meeting and will be calcified by the time the proposal is signed. Your conversations, materials, demeanor, resistance, and other dynamics will subliminally educate the client about the relationship.

For example, prospects often ask very early, "How long will this take?" or, "How many days will you be here each week?" I quickly disabuse them of such notions. "You might see me several days at a time or not at all for long stretches, depending on the project's needs. But you will talk to me weekly about progress and fine-tuning, that's for certain," is my standard reply.

I don't want the prospect/client to be counting the days and dividing them into my fee or to get the idea that my physical presence equals my value. We control these "learning factors," and we must manage them from the outset.

Consulting is one of the very few professions I know of in which the practitioner learns from virtually every assignment, with that learning being carried to the next assignment and the next client to enhance the value added still further. In other words, each client is paying you to learn, and while the client's check is a nonrenewable resource that you cash and spend, the learning is infinitely renewable and applicable. Imagine—a professional calling in which each client interaction makes you more valuable to prospective clients! I don't believe that a surgeon necessarily learns a great deal from each appendectomy, or that a classroom teacher learns a great deal more from the fortieth explication of the causes of the French Revolution, or that a soccer goalkeeper learns new techniques after several years on the job.

Now, don't misunderstand me; all these people can and do learn a great deal through private study, practice, talks with colleagues, and so on.

However, *very few people have the opportunity to learn continually on the job as a condition of their employment.* In fact, all too often we hear of seasoned pros in various fields whose claim to fame is that "he's seen it all before" or that "nothing surprises her." These are hardly indications of having reached the heights, however. *Usually, they're indications of the depth of the ruts in which these people are wallowing.*

The learning I'm talking about isn't merely *content learning.* It's mainly *process learning,* in terms of the what, why, and how of my craft and my clients' needs. That's why I promised in the prior chapter that you'd hear more about process vs. content. (It's true that at this point in the game, I can accurately describe a paper machine's workings, credibly discuss the role of my enzyme blockers in pharmaceutical research, and pontificate on the marketplace for online advertising in streaming banners or click-through impressions. However, I hardly consider such abilities to be of great worth in what I'm able to bring to the next client.)

Early in my career, I was across the desk from the vice president of worldwide personnel for Merck & Co., Steve Darien. It appeared that I was well on my way to nailing down a key project when Steve asked how I would go about gathering some of the data required. Thinking that I had the perfect response, I coolly intoned, "Well, there are three options for doing that." These I proceeded to describe. Then I asked, "Which do you prefer?" (You'll read later how important options are in moving both sales and implementation along.)

To my amazement, and as a fundamental contribution toward my lifelong learning curve, Steve said, "That's what you should be telling us. That's why you're here." Steve didn't need collaboration on the technique; he wanted an expert who could recommend precise courses of action and clarify exactly what would occur. To this day, whenever a client asks how something should be accomplished, I always provide options, together with the pros and cons of each, *and* my recommendation as to which makes the most sense from my perspective. I learned this from a 30-second exchange with Steve in 1986, and I've used it to excellent advantage hundreds of times since.

One Percent Solution: There may be nothing new under the sun, but there's a lot out there that you probably haven't found yet.

No successful consultant will ever have the same year of experience twice. In fact, no successful consultant will ever have the same experience twice.

The Choice of Yeses

Providing a client with a selection from which to choose—from when to have an initial meeting to how to implement the project—enhances your ability to move forward by a factor of 10. You subtly move the thought process from "Should I use Jane?" to "How should I use Jane?" and from "Should we move forward?" to "How should we move forward?" Always provide options—a choice of yeses.

The surest route to maximizing learning and enhancing your value-added potential is to focus on the results the client requires and prevent jobs and tasks from receiving undue attention and time. Every project requires a certain degree of "small picture" attention: follow-through, coordination, checks for accuracy, validation, and more. However, these are truly ancillary chores.

Similarly, your career as a consultant should not revolve around number of client engagements (in fact, sometimes quantity is the poorest measure you can apply), number of prospects contacted, or—worst of all, and more about this in later chapters—number of billable days. These are activities and tasks. You should be focusing on the broadening nature of the client work you are able to undertake, the reputation you are building, the longer-term results you are helping clients to attain, and the widening application of your expertise and experience. These are results that build your career, stimulate you as a professional, and significantly grow your business along the way. Increased numbers of jobs do not necessarily grow a business, although they can make a business more complex, complicated, and frustrating.

However, an enhanced career is synonymous with an enhanced business. This is what my friend at Marine Midland was driving at when she wanted to prevent jobs from interfering with careers. And this is what will account for financial growth as well.

WILL GROWTH CUT YOU DOWN TO SIZE?—FIRING CLIENTS

The vast majority of consultants fail to grow their businesses because they refuse to abandon business. A consulting firm is not like an automobile manufacturer, which tries to sell as many cars as possible and adjusts production to meet demand. If its business continues to grow, more assembly-line workers are hired, new plants are opened, more dealerships are established, and additional middle managers are promoted to administer the operations. Conversely, in down times, top management closes plants, furloughs blue-collar workers, fires white-collar workers, and stores unsold cars as inventory.

Consultants are vastly different. Growth depends on abandoning some lines and types of business in the pursuit and acquisition of other, more productive lines of business. (Remember, growth is not just financial. It includes broadening experiences, higher-level contacts, more sophisticated work, and an enhanced reputation. The real wealth is discretionary time.) For the consultant whose very lifeblood was sustained originally by $7,500 one-shot contracts and $3,500 speaking engagements, the attitude is usually, "*All* business is good business, and I'll never turn down a paying engagement."

There are just a few things wrong with this attitude, but they are all deadly:

1. *The paint-yourself-in-a-corner syndrome.* Reputation works in all directions. If you are known as an "inexpensive alternative," a "very reasonable speaker," or "desperate to accept any job," this is the way prospects will approach you. If word of mouth stipulates that your fee is $1,000 on a per-diem basis, a prospect will estimate that your services are required for a week and be confident that you will cost him less than $6,000. The fact that the project is worth $175,000 in productivity·enhancements to the client won't matter, nor will the fact that it would cost $25,000 for the client to accomplish the job with internal resources, even if that were possible.

2. *Quality, not quantity, is the sole measure of success.* A friend of mine, Mike Robert, has established a worldwide training firm from scratch. In fact, from less than scratch—he resigned from a former employer, struck out on his own, and never looked back. In 1988 we collaborated on a book,[2] during the writing of which he commented that approaches to direct mail were off base. "People are looking for a response of 11/2 to 2 percent to represent success," he pointed out, "which is simply an arbitrary number. If you mail out 10,000 pieces, all you need is one *very high-quality* response." Mike has based his business on this premise—find one client and do a great deal of work there rather than find 10 clients and do a little work with each. As a consultant, you are far better served doing $50,000 in business with a single client than doing $5,000 with each of 10 clients. Accepting all business as quantitatively equal, no matter what the quality, dilutes

[2]Michel Robert and Alan Weiss, *The Innovation Formula: How Organizations Turn Change into Opportunity* (New York: Harper & Row, 1988).

effort and confuses perceptions. (And $50,000 from one client is far more profitable than $10,000 from each of five clients. It's not what you make in this business; it's what you keep.)

3. *Effort applies to tasks, whereas payoff applies to results.* While managing a national field force for a training company, I discovered that it requires as much time to sell a $10,000 project as to sell a $100,000 project. The number of calls, the nature of the proposals, the types of competitive threats, and the overall time required are amazingly consistent. Thus, if each of my salespeople had x hours in a day, and both sales required the same amount of time investment, which kind did I want them pursuing? This was real rocket science, right? The only difference is in the attitude of the salesperson, and a similar attitude is necessary for the consultant. The efforts required to attract, administer, and deliver small assignments are virtually the same as those for larger assignments, so you are not making up in volume what you lose in size. By accepting any business that comes along, the consultant is doomed to poor investments of time, and she will find it increasingly difficult to break out of the box.

Every time you raise your fees and/or refuse to make concessions to gain business, you will lose the bottom 15 percent of your market. Million dollar consultants regularly abandon the bottom 15 percent of their market as a growth strategy because it frees them to expand the upper reaches of their market.

Every two years or so, you should be able to look back and identify assignments that you would not bid on or accept today. If you are accepting the same types of assignments at the same fees today as you were two years ago, you have not abandoned the bottom 15 percent of your market, and therefore you probably haven't expanded the top 5 percent of your market (which is far, far more profitable). You cannot retain all types of business and expect to grow. Continuing to take on everything means that your growth in expertise and repute aren't advancing.

Digression

I'm writing this in 2009, a record year for me, while traveling less than 15 percent of the time and working perhaps 20 hours a week. And 75 percent of my income originates with services and clients that were not in existence for me five years ago. That is the continual reinvention that is possible if you choose not to waste time and energy holding onto poor business.

I've been speaking rather harshly of abandoning business. But that's because you must not equivocate on this issue. You must stop accepting the business. However, there are alternatives to simply dumping the client, and there are ways to attend to clients who, while they may not represent your future, were certainly instrumental in paying the rent in the past.

- Establish alliances with consultants who are where you were two years ago. There is always a wealth of such talent eager to align itself with more established practitioners in order to learn, obtain business, and network. Refer your bottom-end work to talented protégés who will do an excellent job, bring credit to you for the reference, and provide continuity and support for a valued client.[3] (It is generally *not* a good idea to have such people on your own staff to perform this work because your firm will still be associated with it, which is no different from *you* being associated with it. Talent agents who handle regional theater actors are not called by major stars.)

- Explain to the client personally that you can't handle such assignments cost-effectively anymore, that you are *not* using that fact as an excuse to raise fees, and that you will refer some people to the client for consideration as a replacement. In this case, the client knows that you are helping her make the transition at no charge and that the people you are referring may not be well known by you. The responsibility for choosing someone appropriate and compatible is then clearly the client's.

- If it is a regularly scheduled series of assignments, appearances, or workshops, let the client know that the next one, next month's, or this year's will be the last you can do. Provide the client with this kind of leeway and advance notice, and continue to demonstrate that you are doing the exact same high-quality job you've always done.

- Offer to transfer the skills to the client, if appropriate. Suggest some internal alternatives, and work with the client to replace your expertise. Demonstrate the value of the catch-fish-for-yourself approach in Chapter 1. It is fair and reasonable to charge a fee for such a transition, and it's generally easy to justify it in terms of the

---

[3]Although it's not the topic of this chapter, a word on finder's fees, or commissions: whether you take a percentage of the fee for the referral is a matter of individual strategy. If you do, I feel that you have a heightened ethical responsibility for the quality of the results. Moreover, you are exacting a relatively small amount of money for yourself and a relatively large amount of money for your colleague. My preference is to create a "win/win/win" situation by expecting no consideration yourself other than your colleague's inclination to ask you to participate in projects too large for him to handle in the future.

cost savings of having the skills present internally, whenever required. Offer to support the internal person by phone and mail whenever help is needed.

• If the client is a local site of a larger organization, explain that it's time to move up to the parent. You've gone as far as you can go with the excellent support of local management, but you have assessed that the time is right to try to influence changes of policy at the corporate level. You are not abandoning your local client, but there is little more you can effectively do without intercession from higher authority. In this manner, you are moving to a higher level in your market by moving to a higher level within your client's organization. If you have a good relationship locally, management should be willing to make introductions at a higher level. If management refuses, you are in a business relationship that you should abandon anyway.

TWELVE TRIP WIRES THAT INDICATE IT'S TIME TO LEAVE

Whether you are a one-person, entrepreneurial consulting practice or the leader of a growing firm of professional and administrative people, you must consciously and consistently abandon business that is

1. Beneath your growing fee structure
2. Unchallenging ("I can do this with my eyes closed.")
3. Providing a reputation that does not fit your growth strategy ("They train secretaries.")
4. Overly specialized ("They know everything about packaging.")
5. Unable to attract the kind of talent you want in your firm (uninteresting assignments)
6. Unable to attract the kind of references you need
7. In areas and industries that are not themselves growing
8. Unpleasant and/or has rude and offensive people
9. Unethical in its actions and/or borderline illegal
10. Harsh in its demands for travel, support, and other logistics

11. Not within your strategic intent (strictly domestic when you are trying to grow internationally)
12. Detracting from your discretionary time

Finally, there is a clarion-clear call that demands that you carefully examine your markets and clients to make hard, steely decisions about leaving some of them. No matter how easy it is to accept a small assignment that comes over the phone without effort or how relieving it is to make a concession for a lower fee when business is hurting, these bottom-end pieces of business are simply not that profitable. They bring in revenue, not profit. I've seen consultants spend $4,500 of their time, materials, and overhead to deliver a $5,000 assignment.

"Oh, it's OK," they assure me, "because the business comes in at $5,000 like clockwork five or six times a year." Yeah, and they spend $4,500 like clockwork each time (or worse, $5,500).

You don't make this up on volume.

Digression

While sitting at the pool at a major professional convention, I met a woman who said that she was there merely to be able to spend time with her husband, who spent 220 days on the road each year filling 110 daily assignments.

"Why doesn't he double his fee, halve his clients, and spend twice as much time with you?" I asked, providing rare free advice.

"Oh, he could never demand that!" she laughed.

If she (and he) believe that, then he can't.

It doesn't matter at all—not at all—what your billings are or how much you make. The only thing that matters is how much you keep.

Ninety percent of all my billings go to the bottom line. That's right, I lose only 10 percent of revenues to nonreimbursed expenses and overhead. If you generate $100,000 in revenue, an overhead of 35 percent means that you will have $65,000 of pretax income, whereas an overhead of 10 percent means that you will have $90,000 in pretax income. The trick, of course, is to increase revenue while decreasing overhead, and this is exactly what million dollar consultants do.

One of the most important elements of that strategy is to abandon the bottom 15 percent of your market on a regular basis. Another is to be crystal clear about your business goals.

TRUE NORTH (THE ROAD *NOT* TRAVELED)

Every consulting business—large or small, local or international, specialized or general—has a motive force. This force is its raison d'etre, its self-concept. The problem is that while this should be a conscious force, it's often an unconscious one, created by default, by the market, by the clients, or—worst of all—by the competition.

Financial results are only one indicator of success. In fact, it's the ability to meet longer-term, predetermined goals that is the true measure of ultimate financial success. Without such nonfinancial goals, your ship is rudderless, depending on the winds and tides of the marketplace.

Strategic goals are intended to provide not just the direction but also the propulsion that enables you to navigate despite the treachery of the currents. In our marketplace, "currents" are better known as *fads*, "winds" as *perceptions*, and "tides" as *economic conditions*.

What goals do you have for your business? When I ask most consultants/principals this question, they say something like

- "We want to be the biggest firm of our kind."
- "We want to continually grow our business."
- "We want to help clients achieve the best results possible."
- "We want to be on the leading edge of developments in our field."
- "We want to reward the people in the business commensurate with their contribution."

This is hardly the stuff on which to plan your future. Oh, these are all noble enough sentiments, but they could apply to dry cleaning, driveway paving, or accounting, not to mention muffler repair and tractor maintenance.

During one stage of my life, I traveled over an hour to Boston just to have my hair cut by a woman who did a superb job. I don't have great hair, but she had great scissors. She was in constant demand. I asked her one day why she thought she was so successful. (Consultants have a way of always trying to find the common denominator. It isn't poetry, but it's good consulting.)

Her response was a revelation: she thought she was in a unique business. "Hairdressers have the consent to touch the customer," she explained. "This creates a very close bond, although it doesn't seem so. That's why I find out so much about my customers and why they share things with me that they would never share in any other business relationship."

"Isn't that a rather glorious view?" I pontificated. "After all, most people simply would say that you cut and style hair, wouldn't they?"

"Name me another professional in your life who physically touches you and moves your position around like this."

"Ahhhh . . . a doctor."

"Right! And that's who most people pick. But a doctor is threatening. You see, I'm as close to people as their doctor gets, but I'm nonthreatening. People come to me not just because I do their hair well, but also because they enjoy the relationship. So do I."

I thought about that conversation long and hard and came to realize that her success was largely based on her personal, clearly defined image of her business and her place in it. It was irrelevant whether you agreed with her or not. (After all, I finally concluded, manicurists touch you, and so do tailors, and people seem very willing to talk to strange bartenders who never touch them.) Her vision of her business and her goals was unique, clear, and tangible enough for her to act on. In other words, she encouraged people to talk (the few who didn't like to would go elsewhere), was an excellent listener, remembered details about customers from month to month, and was acutely aware of her role in the relationship. She often asked about my kids and would tell me stories of her own kids, but she didn't offer advice and was never judgmental except about what looked good on top of my head.

Here are some of the best goals I've heard from consultants—best because they are clear, unique to the profession, and tangible enough to base tactics on, day in and day out:

- "We will undertake consulting assignments that result in direct contributions to the client's profitability as measured by quarterly results."

- "We will assist in the outplacement of people in a cost-effective manner, while always respecting the dignity and needs of those leaving the organization."

- "We will design and implement workshops that result in demonstrable behavior changes on the job, as determined by customer feedback."

- "We will enter into collaborative relationships in which responsibility is shared with the client, skills are transferred to the client, and dependence on us is gradually diminished to the point of disengagement."

- "We will assist clients in enhancing the productivity of their people through needs analyses, enhanced communication, and joint decision making."
- "We will accept only short-term, value-added consulting assignments with specific result objectives and measurements that will be fee-based. We will unconditionally guarantee our work."

You don't need pages of goals. In fact, they should be brief enough for you and your colleagues to keep in mind at all times, particularly when you're in front of a prospect or during an engagement, because operating decisions should be dictated by those goals. I have found that sound goals are not hooked to any particular financial figure, do assume personal responsibility, are unequivocal (I will or we will), and include some form of outcome. They are often based on the specific kind of expertise or talent you bring to bear (outplacement), philosophy (collaboration), process skills (needs analyses, decision making), and/or timing (quarterly results, short-term assignments).

Specific goals are extraordinarily useful in explaining to prospects why they should hire you. Your goals should appear *briefly* in your literature and should serve to set your firm apart. You should be able to explain them in 60 seconds to anyone who asks. (Any consultant who can't explain precisely and specifically what he does in less than a minute needs to go sit in the corner. How many cocktail parties have you been to at which someone is asked what they do and takes the next 30 minutes rambling on without giving a clue? You can bet 5 to 2 that the person is a consultant and 10 to 1 that she is not good at it. Would it take any of your clients over a minute to tell you what kind of business *they* are in?

> **Goals provide a rudder for you to steer with and enable clients and prospects to understand what you can provide. How can a client clearly understand what you provide, and distinguish you from others, if you can't do that yourself?**

Figure 2–2 provides a basis for establishing goals. If you can't articulate what it is you stand for and what you are trying to accomplish in a client engagement, then don't even walk out your door. If you do, you're likely to accept assignments for monetary reasons alone, which means that you'll often be over your head in expertise or up to your rear in alligators. Your goals *will* be set, if not by you consciously, then by the marketplace, or the situation, or the client. And those goals *will* be impossible to live with because they will change each day. Your business won't be growing; it will be circling.

▪ Expertise and talent	▪ Types of client interaction
▪ Contribution to profit	▪ Productivity of employees
▪ Enhanced communication	▪ Employee participation
▪ Market share	▪ Customer satisfaction
▪ Quality and service	▪ Innovation and creativity
▪ Strategy formulation	▪ Problem solving
▪ Employee assistance	▪ Research and development
▪ Motivation and morale	▪ Priorities/time management
▪ Community service	▪ Safety and regulatory matters
▪ Design-to-market timing	▪ Adult learning

Figure 2-2 A basis for establishing goals. Goals can be based on personal talent, client need, or both.

One final thought: Goals can change as your business grows and matures. They should be reexamined regularly (particularly if you are successfully abandoning the bottom 15 percent of your market) for modifications. You don't want to be known to prospects as something that you used to be, and you don't want to invest in actions dictated by your own outmoded perception of who you are. A firm whose call was "to provide the best objective and rational decision-making skills" for clients may now see itself as "providing the best thinking skills, combining rational and intuitive approaches" as it has found and adopted additional technologies and disciplines.

If your consulting business is to grow, your goals have to grow and expand. The more frequently this occurs, the better you're doing.

AS IN SHOW BUSINESS, TIMING IS EVERYTHING

I recall watching Johnny Carson's *Tonight Show* one evening during his prime when his guests were Richard Pryor and Milton Berle, the former seated on the couch and the latter holding court in the guest's chair. Berle and Carson had established some nice shtick when Pryor attempted to interject something, which had the result of throwing cold water over the proceedings.

In the ensuing awkward silence, Berle leaned over to Pryor and hissed, loud enough for the mike to pick up, "I told ya, kid, pay attention to the timing. Timing is everything." He was saying this to someone who went on to be one of the most iconic comics of his generation.

There is neither a good time nor a bad time to enter the consulting profession or to attempt to enlarge an existing practice. *Good economies or bad don't really matter*. I began my practice in the mid–1980s, not a great economy, and many of us are having great years in the midst of the market catastrophes of 2008.

Many people assume that poor market and economic conditions augur well for consulting, since firms are in trouble then and need more help. Fortunately or unfortunately, this axiom has never applied to my firm, since we tend to work with excellent companies that don't use hard times as a trigger for consulting assistance.

> *One Percent Solution: Don't suddenly become a "downturn specialist" when things are tough. Stick with your core strength. Companies need value, strength, and competitive advantage in down times, as in all times.*

Similarly, good times don't automatically generate business, because during good times, few firms are enlightened enough to look beyond the short term and focus on the fundamental needs and challenges.

The timing I'm most concerned with is that of being in the right place at the right time, and this means being in front of the buyer with a back scratcher when the buyer has an itch. You don't have to be physically present, of course, but you must be present in spirit. Now, many marketers who are experts at their work will tell you that it's your responsibility to create the need (or at least to help the client to express it in such a way that you are the likely candidate to meet it).

I don't "sell," and I don't associate selling with the consulting business I like to generate—especially if selling means anything other than convincing the prospect that he has a need and that I'm the one to fill it.

You see, such marketing and selling depend on what I call the *one person, one situation* approach. That is, you must personally visit, convince, follow up, and attend to the various leaks that occur when you're trying to float a proposal. Thus, you're limited to the number of people in front of whom you can reasonably appear, and you're limited by their lack of initial agreement on the exact need you're trying to convince them exists.

I prefer a timing approach to increasing business. That timing is based on the prospective client (or current client) feeling an itch at any given moment and immediately thinking of you as having the back scratcher.

Note that this isn't dependent on your being someplace, or on your convincing the client of the need, or on carefully constructed proposals.

The client is calling you. This approach is not mutually exclusive with other approaches, but it does make life a whole lot easier.

As you read this paragraph, potential buyers of your services all over the country (and the world) are reaching decisions that they need help with. And over the ensuing day, week, month, or quarter, they will go about securing that help. Some of them will choose consultants with whom they already work; others will rely on recommendations; still others, probably the majority, will engage in some type of hunt, from the informality of making phone calls to the formality of requesting bids and proposals. I talked about the ways in which organizations choose consultants in Chapter 1, and in later chapters I'll talk about how to maintain contact with clients and prospects over the long haul.

What I want to address here is the combination of these two elements: the merging of the prospect's need (occurring at some unanticipated time) with the awareness of your potential to fill that need (from repeated contacts and visibility). This is the essence of the timing approach.

This is a state of mind that you must buy into philosophically and strategically before you can make it work tactically. That is, you must be convinced that it is far more powerful to have the buyer call you than it is for you to call the buyer.

The traditional response to growing personal service businesses has been the atavistic feet-on-the-street approach. Hire more people to make more calls to close more business. However, this is a quantitative approach to selling, not a qualitative one, and the obituaries of failed companies are filled with overly optimistic sales forecasts based on the number of people seen and the likelihood that they would buy simply because someone managed to get into their office.

When you're *invited* into someone's office, the equation changes considerably. Instead of justifying your presence and your demands on the buyer's time, you are working together to collaborate on a problem that the buyer feels comfortable addressing with you.

Thus, your marketing thrust should *not* be the number of people you see, promoting your approaches to likely buyers, or—heaven forbid—making cold sales calls. (Do *you* buy from the person who calls you at 8:30 at night offering rare Turkestan oil futures?) You should be endeavoring to make your name, firm, and talents known to as wide a variety of prospects as possible.

We'll examine specific options later, but it's important that you acknowledge and embrace this fundamental position here. During a typical week, my firm has historically received 2 requests for proposals, 4 inquiries about speaking engagements, 50 orders for books, and 12 or more inquiries for literature about our consulting activities from organizations for which we have never done any work. These are leads exclusive of current client work and extensions of current work.

Conservatively, this is about 100 leads per month, or 1,000 per year. If 10 percent of these leads result in short-term business (within 12 months) and the average contract is $50,000, that's half a million dollars generated from prospects developing a need and knowing that they should contact me.

In actuality, 10 percent is a fairly low figure, and over the longer term— 12 to 36 months—we (and you) are likely to do business with 20 percent or more of these leads.

Figure 2–3 shows how to stimulate people contacting you at any stage of your career, from neophyte to veteran. I call this *market gravity* because its intent is to draw people to you. When people approach you ("I've heard about your work and would like to see if you may be in a position to assist us"), the dynamic is substantially changed from cold calling ("Who are you, and why should I listen to you?").

Here's what to do:

- *Pro bono work.* By aiding organizations for free, your work and relationships will grow in their repute and numbers. *Suggestion*: Never do pro bono work for a profit-making entity, no matter how good the exposure. Make sure you are working with potential recommenders and buyers from prospective clients with whom you will be a peer by dint of your common pro bono work.

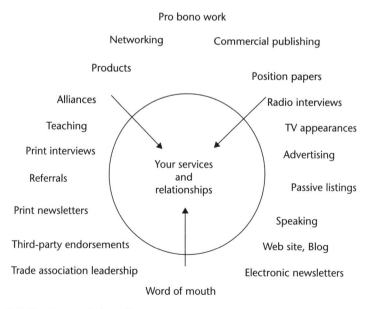

Figure 2-3 Creating market gravity.

- *Commercial publishing.* Books are golden; articles and op-ed pieces are great.
- *Position papers.* Create articles for your press kit and Web site that position you as an authority in your field. They should be nonpromotional and packed with specific techniques and high value. Establish your expertise and your position as a "go to" person.
- *Radio interviews.* These are relatively easy to obtain. Take out a listing on Expertclick.com and/or in the *Directory of the National Press Association. Suggestion:* Never pay a radio station to let you host a show. That's a scam. The talent is supposed to be the payee, not the payer.
- *TV appearances.* These are also easier than suspected through the sources mentioned previously, especially on cable and local affiliates. Again, do *not* pay money to be on a "former big name's" show. These make money only for the producers and the semicelebrities.
- *Advertising.* From the local Yellow Pages to national directories, some feasibility buyers search such listings to generate alternatives.
- *Passive listings.* These are listings in buyers' guides and various industry sources; they are akin to advertising, but are simply entries. They are also quite common on the Internet.
- *Speaking.* This is one of the best sources of generating attraction. Speak for free if you must, as long as you are in front of buyers or at least recommenders.
- *Web site.* Picture this as a much more flexible media kit than your hard-copy presentation folder. Load it with articles, techniques, and value to compel people to return (e.g., a new article every month) and to tell others. (This is also an excellent place to sell products.)
- *Blog.* This is related to a Web site. Use a blog to regularly (very important) post text, audio, and even video that promote your expertise and "go to" status. (See my blog, http://www.contrarianconsulting.com, to see how conducive these are to multimedia use.)
- *Electronic newsletters.* Send them out for free. Keep them brief and nonpromotional. Encourage people to forward them to others. One page a month should take you all of 30 minutes.
- *Word of mouth.* Do you have a clever tagline (e.g., "The Telephone Doctor"); is your business card in people's hands; do you have interesting handouts?
- *Trade association leadership.* Take the ugliest, hardest positions, such as treasurer or head of volunteers. Become president. You'll be interviewed, referred to, and highly visible in the community, profession, and/or industry.

- *Third-party endorsements.* Ask every single client, every single time, for a testimonial letter, reference, referral, or blurb for a publication. (Have you recognized the choice of yeses I just provided?)
- *Print newsletters.* Although they're more time-consuming and expensive, print newsletters are more impressive than electronic ones and tend to stay around longer. You can use a common format every month with a local printer. Use guest articles to save you work.
- *Referrals.* Ask everyone you know for leads. Don't you recommend people to your dentist and your lawyer? Why shouldn't they be referring people to you? Ask them every three months.
- *Print interviews.* Provide human interest or business angles to the local media to secure interviews for you.
- *Teaching.* Apply to be an adjunct professor at the local university, community college, or trade school one night a week. It looks great on your biographic data and will generate visibility.
- *Alliances.* Find someone who has the marketing clout that you don't, and for whom you have the competencies they lack, and create a synergy wherein $1 + 1 = 186$.
- *Products.* Create tapes, pamphlets, booklets, checklists, manuals, books, and other high-value learning tools both for income and for visibility.
- *Networking.* Provide value to people who can, in turn, provide value to you. Attend a function where this is possible at least one night a week.

How many of these things are you currently engaged in? How many are you capable of? I can guarantee that you're not doing enough.

Implement new aspects of my "gravity" every month until the attraction is overwhelming. It's cost-effective and relatively simple. If you want to make money, you have to draw people to you, not beat their doors down.

Digression

Let me bring up what some call "social media" at this point. I've researched and experimented with these alternatives ever since my blog posts questioning their efficacy in marketing brought down the wrath of the cultists.

> *I've found alternatives such as LinkedIn to be fairly effective mechanisms for keeping in touch with people and finding traditional jobs, but they're pretty hopeless as a marketing device for consultants who want to reach corporate, economic buyers.*
>
> *Limit your time on Twitter, Facebook, YouTube, and whatever else is invented between the time I write this and you read it, because this is not where true buyers hang out or look for resources. As marketing tools, these are very low priority and often painfully stupid. ("Albert is working late tonight." Now there's a piece of news that makes my time on the Internet worthwhile!)*

Up to this point, I've tried to establish what the lay of the land looks like and why it's important to clarify what's in your head. Your growth— personally, professionally, and financially—is predominantly a function of your view of the marketplace and your role within it.

If your mind focuses on making phone calls from the moment you awaken, for example, then you will take pains to ensure that you are uninterrupted in making phone calls while you are in the office. Your behaviors and actions will adjust accordingly, and you will tend to view your success in terms of your ability to make phone calls. However, if your philosophy of the business calls for a more strategic focus, then your behaviors and actions are likely to be much broader and more innovative in scope, organized to establish that reputation through a variety of means (within which the telephone will play a proper, minor role).

Only you determine how you act toward your business; the market doesn't, the prospect doesn't, and the competition shouldn't.

The opening to Part 1 of this book cites Matsuo Basho, and his philosophy is as applicable now as it was three centuries ago. Don't look around at other consultants and decide how to do what they do, only better. Look at the marketplace, evaluate what you have to offer and to which buyers, and decide how best to get those buyers to come to you while continually abandoning the bottom slice of your market to expand the top slice.

If you can maintain this state of mind, you're ready to grow.

QUESTIONS AND ANSWERS

Q. Shouldn't I wait until I'm absolutely consumed by business before I start abandoning or firing clients?

A. You will never be consumed that way, nor do you want to be. Do you want to make a million dollars by working 60 hours a week or by working 40 hours a week (or even 20 hours a week)? Besides, if you don't abandon the small stuff, you'll have no room to handle the big stuff.

Q. What is the fine line between following up with prospects and hounding them?

A. It doesn't matter; trample the line, rub it out, obscure it. This is a business. If you feel you have value for someone, you're not hounding him if you're trying to help him. Is your dentist "hounding" you by helping to prevent gum disease (which can cause heart problems)?

Q. Isn't it tough to educate clients who have been educated incorrectly by countless consultants before me?

A. Yes, but what's your point? You don't want to follow in the footsteps of fools of old.

Final Thought: Your state of mind should be that you don't have to "prove yourself" to anyone or knock people's door down. Create sufficient attraction so that people approach you interested in how you might be of help. In this dynamic, fees are academic.

BREAKAWAY SPEED

ACHIEVING ESCAPE VELOCITY

THE SUCCESS TRAP

Success may be responsible for the death of more consulting endeavors than failure is. When a strong person fails, she is likely to examine the causes of her defeat, determine what must be done to prevail in the future, and take steps to try again. Strong people learn from their setbacks and emerge all the stronger. Success, after all, is never final, and defeat is seldom fatal; it's perseverance that counts, to paraphrase Winston Churchill. (Woody Allen once said that 80 percent of success is "just showing up.")

When a proposal I've submitted is not accepted or I find that a competitor has been chosen for an assignment that wasn't offered to me, I *always* investigate the reasons. I'm relieved on those occasions when I learn that I didn't get the business because someone else had an "in" with the client or because a competitor offered to provide something that was completely beyond my capabilities or motivation or fee structure. I call this kind of situation an *uncontrollable rejection* because it's unlikely that anything I could have done would have changed the outcome.

However, when I discover that the competition provided for an intervention I just hadn't thought about, met a client's need in a more innovative way, or simply outflanked or outthought me, I strive to find out how I can prevent a recurrence. This is a *controllable rejection*, which is business lost because I failed to do something that I could have done and would have been willing to do and that might have changed the outcome in my favor.

The good thing about studying controllable rejection is that you learn a great deal about how to improve your business.

For example, I can't learn or improve much by determining that I lost a contract because the client preferred someone who happened to be located a mile from the site while I was an airplane trip away. However, I can learn a great deal by determining that the competition attended preliminary discussions using three people who, acting as a team, provided the client with a feeling of depth and competent support that I, acting alone, couldn't provide.

I once lost a survey project at *USA Today* for which I was a finalist (and was told that I had the inside track) because the ultimate winner offered in his proposal to train management in how to convey to employees both the survey results and the actions that management intended to take as a result of those findings. I had never thought to do this because every prior survey project I had obtained had involved long-distance data gathering only, with one-on-one meetings with the top executive to discuss results. However, I would have been quite willing to do this, I had the capacity to do it, and I could have done it in a cost-effective manner.

As a result of this particular controllable rejection, I now provide the option of management education in every survey proposal. Quite a few clients and prospects have complimented me on this follow-through and have been willing to pay slightly more to use it. As an extension of this tactic, I've since added six-month and one-year follow-up days to all my strategy work. The extra days cost me virtually nothing, yet they provide the client with a sense of continuation and long-term interest and enable me to remain visible on a scheduled basis.

One Percent Solution: If success is a plateau, it will erode eventually, right under your feet. But if it's a steady climb, you're always looking up.

Although I was very disciplined about finding out why I'd been rejected, I found that I had seldom asked for the reasons that led to my being selected by a client. Success will do that to you. After all, you were trying to get the business, you did a fine job in your preparation and proposal, and the client demonstrated superb judgment in selecting you. What else is there to know?

Enough of these successes, however, can lead you into a trap because you're so busy scheduling implementation and cashing checks that you aren't growing in any other dimensions. Million dollar consultants don't get that way by doing one thing well over and over. They succeed to the extent that they do because they evolve with the times and grow with increasing challenges.

Consequently, you should always try to stretch your applications and abilities until you are rejected so that you can find out why. We hear about test pilots "pushing the envelope." They don't know what a plane can do until they discover what it can't do. Then the designers can try to improve on that.

> *The only way to improve on success is to experience rejection.*
> *Successful consultants do not experience uninterrupted*
> *success. Instead, they ensure that they stretch their abilities*
> *until they are rejected so that they know what additional*
> *growth is required. Uninterrupted success leads to*
> *inevitable failure—the success trap.*

If you're not failing, then you're not trying!

A couple of years ago I received a request for a bid from the New York City Housing Authority. It was for design and implementation of comprehensive middle-management programs, something I don't normally do, particularly on the scale requested. After determining that I could provide (or acquire) the expertise and resources needed, I bid on the project, the bid alone required about 25 hours of work.

The award day came and went, and I heard nothing, so I followed up, facing that particularly perverse bureaucratic delay that public agencies have such expertise in. However, I persevered and found out three months later that the project had been awarded to Booz Allen. I also found that Booz Allen

- Had provided much more detail than I had.
- Had provided for more participant materials than I had.
- Had attended the preliminary conferences (I did not).
- Had provided more biographical information than I had.
- Had bid, successfully, over $100,000 more than I had!

My follow-up on this rejection had become quite a learning opportunity. When I am requested to bid on large public projects now, I make careful calculations about such factors, determine first *whether* to bid, and then determine *how*. Now I bid on only a tenth of such requests and am quite careful about how I do so. However, bidding on that project and finding out why I was rejected made a significant contribution to my learning curve. As a result, I have had very productive relationships with dozens of public organizations such as the Federal Bureau of Prisons, the New York Office of Business Permits and Regulatory Affairs, the Federal Reserve Bank of New York, and the City University of New York.

It was in this process that I learned that my books, experience, and intellectual property can often qualify me as a "sole source" resource, meaning that the client and I can circumvent the cumbersome competitive bidding process.

When I meet consultants who claim to have experienced unfettered success (and by the way, I *never* meet consultants who are doing poorly; it's as rare as meeting a losing politician who isn't proud that "we got our message across"), I find that such success is usually lateral. They continue to apply their expertise in a repetitive manner. While they may enjoy modest financial growth, the other measures of growth (reputation, experience, expertise, learning, self-actualization) remain stagnant.

Most important, however, their financial growth will be arithmetic and will never lead to geometric increases. These are the consultants to whom conventional wisdom does apply—they are "capped" by the logical extensions of their particular content and personal time.

Richard Foster has presented an "S-curve theory" that explains why organizations do not become more innovative than they are.[1] I've modified it somewhat to demonstrate how million dollar consultants become innovative through constant expansion of their potential clients and projects.

In Foster's S-curve, a product, process, or performance begins a steep growth pattern after its buyers accept it. This growth continues until it plateaus—usually because of competitive offerings, changes in perception, changing conditions, or buyers simply tiring of the offering. Then a new S-curve begins. I've modified this for consulting firms' growth.

The magic number for a new consulting firm is about three years. After that, the original contracts probably have been exhausted, contracts from a former employer have expired, and start-up momentum has been spent. In other words, it's time to determine whether you are a going concern or simply a person who had good contacts. *All* firms plateau periodically. For start-up operations, this is due to the factors I've just mentioned. For well-established firms, it is due to one's technology and expertise becoming dated (i.e., left brain–right brain thinking has been authoritatively debunked, the star-cow-dog strategy approach is now a yawn, and people realize that perspiration and not motivation is responsible for the ability to tread on hot coals), expanded competition entering the picture (to offer "managing total quality," "total quality management," "total management quality," etc.), and/or client and market conditions undergoing basic change (economic uncertainty doesn't favor placement firms, and economic upturns don't favor outplacement firms).

Unexamined, repetitive success in limited fields will lead to a perpetuation of the plateau, which ultimately results in the success trap. By the time the lack of growth begins to take its toll in the form of a diminished client base, declining visibility, weariness from lack of stimulation, and inability to attract talent,

---

[1] Richard N. Foster, *Innovation: The Attacker's Advantage* (New York: Summit Books, 1986).

it is often too late to try to expand the envelope. This exploration must come from a position of strength, not one of desperation.

Therefore, beware of the success trap and the false security of lateral growth. Ironically, to grow, you must fail periodically so that you are continually aware of opportunities for improvement and for expanding your envelope. This discipline will not only provide for internal stimulation, but also influence how the external world views you.

Note particularly that to move from about the midpoint of the first S-curve to the bottom of the next S-curve is relatively simple, but attempting to go from the right of the success trap to the midpoint or above of the next S-curve requires extraordinary thrust and escape velocity. This is the insidious nature of the success trap—the longer you stroll down it, the harder it is to reach the next level.

Million dollar consultants often fail. In fact, their confidence emanates from their *lack of fear of failing*. As I said, if you're not failing, you're not trying.

Digression

In the history of predation and hunting, scientists estimate that predators are successful only about 10 percent of the time. Tyrannosaurus rex required 10 hunts to feed itself and its family, as does the modern cheetah on the savannah of Africa or those pelicans you see diving while you lounge on a Caribbean beach.

Think about that. Failure is a prerequisite to success. The key is to learn from it so that your average improves to one in eight, or one in five.

THE BRAND IS YOU

If you think that people don't judge books by their covers, just take a gander at the cars around you on the freeway. People buy cars to say something about themselves, whether the object of their affection is a staid Volvo, a rakish Corvette, a middle-American Toyota, an aloof Mercedes, an exotic Aston Martin, or a master-of-the-universe Bentley.

In fact, an automobile is the most expensive lifestyle statement that most people ever make. Yet this extension of one's personality into the acquisitions one makes—a sort of anthropomorphism gone wild—embraces ballpoint pens as well as works of art, and jogging suits as well as cultural events.

Organizations make the same types of statements about the vendors with whom they choose to do business. My belief is that a consulting firm's image—or lack of one—will play a key role in influencing a buyer one way or the other as to whether that firm is right for the buyer's organization.

The consulting firm's image will be conveyed most dramatically and clearly when the buyer interacts with the firm's principals. Prior to this interaction, however, there is opportunity for the buyer to taste the consulting firm's flavor, and it is these *first* impressions that this section will address. While there are no perfect images to convey, there are some to avoid.

Name

The first corporation I ever set up was called AJW Associates. Perhaps the main reason for adopting such names is that they are easy to use in incorporation and are seldom the trademark of anyone else. The trouble, of course, is that to a buyer such names shout "one-man band" from a great distance—to the consultant! The buyer seldom cares, and a name doesn't make or break business.

The name you choose also should convey something about who you are. My firm is Summit Consulting Group, Inc. The name simply says that we are consultants and that we are an incorporated business, and this is all I want to convey in our name. The Center for Creative Leadership gives you a good idea of what they're up to, as does The Executive Edge. Names such as Sage, Quest, or Tracom leave you a bit in the dark, but this is not a cardinal sin. At least they clearly convey *company* and not *individual*. Don't agonize over the name of your practice. McKinsey & Co. has worked out just fine, after all.

Logo

This is so obvious that I have to grimace as I write it, but too many people ignore the obvious. Create a logo or look that is used consistently on your stationery, business cards, brochures, labels, and any other document that might appear in public (i.e., course materials and presentation folders). These simple pieces of paper are the first and primary conveyers of your image, and they are not the place to economize. A good graphic artist can create, design, and execute the work for you for less than $1,000, and these days all your print materials can be produced at one of the local storefront printing franchises (with the exception of multicolored, sophisticated brochures, which ought to be done at a conventional printer).

Don't use "stock" logos from the Internet or from catalogs. And don't think you can do this yourself. You don't want the client to improve teamwork on her own; you want the client to use you. Similarly, don't try to do things yourself that experts can do better.

You don't need to be fancy, but you do need to be consistent on all your print media, and you want to convey an image of professionalism and responsibility. If you don't care about the look, who's to know if you'll care about the client?

Legal Entity

My overwhelming bias is that you should use one of these three configurations: a conventional C corporation, which is how most major businesses operate; a subchapter S corporation, which flows through your individual tax return; or a limited liability company (LLC), which uses members instead of stockholders and also flows through your individual return. Check with your financial expert for what's best for you. After 20 years as a C entity, changes in the law made it advantageous for me to switch to a subchapter S, for example.

If you are not incorporated, then your legal affairs probably will appear in print as "Harvey Jones, d/b/a (doing business as) Global Consulting Group." Moreover, you will have to receive 1099s from clients who are paying you anything more than a low threshold of fees because there is no legal entity to pay taxes except for you personally. And this means that the client will require a social security number (rather than a federal ID number), and such matters can come to the attention of your buyer.

Would this make a difference? Sometimes it will, so why take the chance? (Basically, if you're not incorporated, you're an amateur.)

In the unlikely but horrible possibility of a lawsuit, it's helpful for the company to be a legal entity because, as such, *it* can be sued as a company instead of *you* being sued as an individual. A full-fledged corporation can take in partners, provide equity for them, establish credit lines, obtain insurance, maintain bank accounts, and, in general, act in a manner that the accountants like to refer to as "a going concern."

On occasion, I've had to write out a check to a client to return an overpayment, provide a discount, or reimburse the client for expenses when my wife has traveled with me to a client event. I've always felt better seeing a company check—no different from the client's own—going into the envelope. (There will be more about incorporation later.)

---

*One Percent Solution: Do **not** use an attorney or accountant who does your mortgage or who is a relative. Find someone who is expert in solo-practice professional services firms.*

> *The differences and specialties required are significant. Don't scrimp on this, either. Incorporation, depending on your state, will cost several hundred dollars. And do not heed someone's spouse who practices law who tells you that incorporation is unnecessary. Run for the hills.*

Visibility

At a minimum, you should have your business listed in the local Yellow Pages, in trade publications catering to your field, in the listings of personal professional organizations you join, and in the listings of those trade associations that apply to any specialties you offer.

At a later stage, you should consider a toll-free number for clients (they are remarkably inexpensive), regular mailings or newsletters to clients and prospects, a blog (a Web site[2] is de rigueur), advertisements (for visibility purposes only, i.e., as a supporter of a trade association's convention), and specialty mailings tailored to particular clients (a client that you know is undergoing a reduction in force receives copies of articles on helping displaced workers, whether or not you are being used in a consulting capacity). I will discuss the tactics for client contacts of this type more as we proceed.

Office Requirements

I knew I was in the posttechnological economy when an automobile dealer with whom I was discussing a purchase asked me for my e-mail address so that he could send me the newest financial data as soon as he received them. Then there was the deli that accepted fax orders for its luncheon takeout business.

If automobile dealers and deli owners were into this level of technical sophistication, then where should your consulting firm be?

These are the basic requirements for a professional office, irrespective of whether it's in an office complex, a suite that is subleased, or your home (I run a seven-figure practice from my home and have never had a separate office):

- *A dedicated business phone with at least a call-waiting feature, and preferably several lines.* The phone should have both a hold button and

[2] Here is a key area where I differ from the "conventional wisdom" you'll get elsewhere: your Web site is a credibility site, not a sales site. That is, true economic buyers don't troll the Web for consulting resources, *but they well might go to your site to check on your expertise and accomplishments once they are familiar with you.*

a conference feature. (Estimated cost: $150.[3] There are many excellent models.)

- *If you don't have full-time office help, an excellent voice-mail system.* The local phone company sometimes provides such a service, as do private services. (Mine costs $150 per month, plus a small charge when I want the professionals to record a new message.) I was once in favor of "live" answering services, but I find that the employees are often rude and always uncaring about your business. Voice mail is never rude. The key isn't who answers, but rather *how rapidly you, personally, return the call.* Most people actually expect to get voice mail today, so the distinguishing feature is the responsiveness.

- *A dedicated fax phone line, with a plain-paper fax machine that can be left on automatic at all times to receive at the sender's convenience.* The fax machine should have the capability of automatically feeding multiple sheets. (Estimated cost: under $200 for a basic but perfectly fine model.) Important: a memory feature that allows incoming messages to be saved when there is a paper jam, the cartridge is out of ink, or other nasty things occur in your absence. *Many people use their computers for fax work and don't use a separate machine, so suit yourself.*

- *A high-speed copier that can enlarge and reduce flexibly, handle various sizes of paper, and, ideally, automatically feed multiple sheets.* (Estimated cost: under $500.)

- *A first-rate computer laser printer.* There is simply no other way to create the kinds of proposals you must produce. (Estimated cost: $800 and declining steadily.) An important addition is a laptop with a minimum battery time of four hours. A color printer in addition to the laser makes sense if your budget permits. You can find excellent examples for less than $300, particularly from Hewlett-Packard. The best laptops are Macs, and the top of the line is available with a huge screen for under $3,000 as of this writing.[4]

---

[3] All costs are retail prices. You can do far better at one of the giant discount houses that handles name brands. However, the advantage of dealing with a local merchant is the proximity of service and personal attention. I find that for smaller, less complex items, such as a fax machine or a phone, discount houses are fine. But I deal locally and pay a bit more for computer hardware and copiers.

[4] Note for the excessively detail-oriented readers: neither I nor the publisher can update this book every two weeks, so cut us some slack with newer technological offerings and prices. My examples are meant as a guide using contemporary information. I can't read the future the way you read this book.

- *A postage meter and minimum 15-pound scale.* Your correspondence needs a meter for professionalism, and this combination will also save you a lot of time in the post office having your packages weighed. The meters can even include your logo or message in the indicia. (Estimated cost: a wide variety of leases and purchase plans are available. Pitney Bowes pretty much has a monopoly, although you can acquire other brands if you search. I pay a $500 quarterly lease. The scales can be set to automatically trigger the meters.)

Other equipment, such as projectors and document binders, is a matter of individual preference and frequency of need. A basic, professional office—apart from rent and utilities—such as the one described here, will probably require $5,000 to $10,000 in initial investment, depending on your tastes, computer capability, and so on. It's a small price to pay to be perceived as a professional firm. Additional equipment can include a paper shredder, television, audiocassette player, minicassette recorder, CD and DVD capability, wireless headset, label maker, and so on.

I've found that you can't go wrong by erring on the side of too much investment in your firm's image. A corporate brochure that folds three ways and fits nicely in a number 10 envelope is like a neon sign proclaiming, "We are small-time because this is what I can afford and what I am happy to have represent my firm." A multicolored brochure of 16 pages with testimonials, examples of work performed, summary of corporate philosophy, and other matters that represent your approaches might not be read cover to cover by the prospect, but the material is there if it's needed, and it certainly says, "I care about my image and how you perceive me, so a lot of thought has gone into this representation of my firm. Money was not the object." (And it's paid for with one sale.)

Note: Don't order thousands of copies of anything, no matter what the economies of scale. Even though you saved $500, 2,000 extra brochures in the closet or garage that are rapidly becoming outdated (or have an error) is much too high a price to pay for volume discounts.

I talked earlier about "all-star gaffes." No one is as knowledgeable about what you've done in the past or what your potential is for the future as you are. Others can only look about them and receive images. For better or worse, those images are the keys to the early acceptance of your participation in their enterprise. The good news is that the image is manageable and can convey exactly what you want it to. That image should represent what you can do for your clients in the future, *not* what you've accomplished in the past.

> ### Digression
>
> *In 1985, my wife convinced me not to rent an office, because I could always get one if I needed one, but why make the investment when it wasn't certain?*
>
> *My kids graduated from college in 1996 and 1997. They had gone to private schools from kindergarten through undergraduate, and their combined tuitions, paid for from cash flow throughout, came to an aggregate of $450,000.*
>
> *That is approximately what my office would have cost from 1985 to 1995 with part-time help, rent, utilities, insurance, and so on. Think about it.*

The ultimate brand is your name. There is only one you. The image you create, physically and perceptually, around your image and name will determine your ultimate brand recognition and appreciation. Tread carefully, and don't be miserly about your persona.

THE VIEW IS ALWAYS BETTER FROM THE FRONT

The moment you decide to become a consultant, you automatically have a particular approach to client interventions and relationships that has been formed and honed by your experience. If you've been a member of a large business organization, your view has been influenced by the internal and external consultants with whom you've dealt, the difficulty of pushing change through the bureaucracy, the difficulty of implementation versus the ease of relying on others' advice, and the comfort of comprehensive resources supporting you.

If you've been a member of a consulting firm, you've been influenced by the difficulties of reaching the key buyer, the discomforts of travel to undesirable sites, the pressures of meeting business quotas and demands, and the importance of retaining business.

If your background is in academia, the influences have included finding the time to pursue private interests, scarcity of resources, lack of pragmatic application to the business world, the credibility that comes with a Ph.D., and so on.

Breaking out of the experiential boxes in which we find ourselves is tough. But breaking out is important because the past is a woefully inadequate base on which to build a successful consulting firm. Its major drawback is the delimiting model you possess with which to shape client interventions. The more flexible that model (or set of models), the better you'll be at developing interventions that can meet the needs of specific buyers at specific points in time. The more you can adjust and still get the job done, the less the client has to adjust.[5]

In Chapter 1 I spoke about the pragmatic range of client interventions. Those were the roles the consultant plays in working with the client: facilitator, coach, or interventionist.

When I speak of models, I'm referring to the *processes* that the consultant uses while operating in any of those roles.

> *The one thing consultants should be certain about is that there is no one way to help a client. You should know twice as many ways to help a client this year as you did last year, and twice as many next year as you do today.*

Models are largely determined by the recent past and the route you've taken to establish your consulting firm. Although they may have worked fine for the firm you used to be with and they may work well for you at the outset, no firm grows dramatically with just one stock in trade. The best example I know of this phenomenon is the personality assessment.

There are scores of personality tests and assessment instruments on the market today, many of which are available to consultants for use in their work. They range from such commodities as Disc, which is a forced-choice, self-scoring word selection that provides astrologylike profiles, to the Meyers Briggs Type Indicator, a well-respected and fairly well-validated instrument (although it is frequently distorted to merely "label" people instead of trying to understand them), to the social styles quadrant using peer input, popularized by Wilson Learning but appearing under a wide variety of names and applications.

These instruments, and others like them, can, and often do, provide useful feedback on behavioral predispositions when they are interpreted within the context of the environments and interactions that people experience. However, rather than being a means to an end, these instruments often become an end in themselves because they constitute the only technology, or model, that

---

[5] I'm not referring to massive organizational transformation efforts here, in which near-traumatic change is exactly what the client must endure. I am referring to the vast majority of consulting assignments, in which the consultant intervenes to improve a specific client condition.

the practitioner has available. *They become a revenue source instead of a legitimate client intervention methodology.*[6]

For example, a consultant hired by the former Providence Energy to facilitate interpersonal communications came up with the idea of profiling all the managers and having their profiles printed on their coffee cups. This (so the idea went) would enable colleagues to "read" one another's salient characteristics and respond accordingly. (One can only wonder what happened when a manager borrowed a colleague's cup!) Similarly, efforts to improve communication or create a higher level of customer service often wind up in the hands of label-happy, self-limiting consultants as exercises in telling people that they're "introverts" or "INTJs" or "driver expressive" without any regard for what the client really needs (or what really helps improve performance).

When consultants overly rely on instruments and other devices that they purchase or license, they are really admitting that they don't have the smarts needed to provide value by themselves. This is a sad admission because it means that the consultant has voluntarily abandoned self-learning and taken the path of trying to capitalize on the abilities of others. This isn't worth all that much.

I once observed a consulting team trying to convince top executives to set corporate strategy based solely on a calculation of future shareholder value. Rationally, one might ask why considerations such as values, technology, future markets, and the like were not included, but I realized instantly that the firm's sole model—for doing *anything*—was its formula for calculating shareholder value under the conditions it stipulated. The apotheosis of this self-limiting dilemma occurred during a meeting in which the consultants showed their latest calculation and asked the president if that shareholder value would be acceptable in five years.

"Probably not," he said. "Investors could do better elsewhere."

"Right," replied the team leader. "So what can you do now to change the strategy that is leading you there?"

"That's an impossible question to answer," said the executive. "I'm not comfortable sitting here and speculating on alternatives that might or might not affect value five years from now. It seems as though there must be a more orderly and systematic way to generate alternatives."

He was right, of course, except that the consulting firm didn't have such an orderly and systematic way because it was a one-horse wagon even though it had four people holding the reins. These four had never taken the time to break

---

[6] For a good critique of personality testing and assessments, see Steve Salerno's *SHAM* (New York: Crown, 2005).

out of their particular box, although they *had* taken the time to dress up the box and make it as appealing as possible.

"Why was I so uncomfortable in there," the president asked me later, "when their formulas appear to be accurate, and there's no question that we'd want to improve on the value they calculate?"

"I think," I replied, "it was because you know, viscerally and intellectually, that your firm is not in business merely to enhance shareholder value. Your acquisitions, personnel policies, product development, and even financial decisions have never been made solely on that criterion. Your own annual report talks about contribution to the environment, respect for employees, customer orientation, and so forth. Investor return is obviously important, but it's never been your sole focus, and it probably won't account for your future success if you allow it to be the sole focus."

The firm did not pursue that consulting team's help in strategic planning, and I found that the consultants had invested quite a bit of money and time in the work and calculations that led up to those preliminary sessions. They were good people, with significant and valuable expertise—but all within their self-delimiting box.

As a dynamically growing consulting firm, you must continually investigate, evaluate, and decide on the applicability of additional models to use in helping clients. Some may be compatible with others; some may be mutually exclusive. In this business, however, past success is virtually never an indicator of future performance. The issues, situations, personalities, external forces, and legitimate trends change too frequently to depend on past success, no matter how substantial, as the sole basis for future interventions.

Digression

At a major banking client, I stumbled upon an internal human resources specialist asking an executive vice president questions for the Myers-Briggs-Type Indicator assessment, with the executive responding as he believed his deceased mother would have replied.

When I asked later what on earth was going on, the HR person told me that he was trying to help reconcile the poor relationship between the vice president and his mother.

This sounds bizarre, but I find it all too frequently—a complete bastardization of tools that were never meant (or validated) for the applications for which they are being used. You can't make this stuff up.

In the 1920s, Frederick Winslow Taylor introduced the application of rigorous time and measurement techniques to human performance and demonstrated significant improvements in productivity. Taylorism was the beginning of the consultant as "efficiency expert." (This was generously called "scientific management," although Taylor notoriously used a "fudge factor" to compensate for worker fatigue, which undermined virtually all of his conclusions.)

In the 1950s, the humanists appeared, and the need for more concern for people led to personnel experts and personnel departments. Theory X and Theory Y typified the poles of management (centered on task or people), and Blake and Mouton's "management grid" specified an ideal manager who considered tasks and people in beautiful harmony.

In the 1960s and 1970s, *participation* became the hot topic, *personnel* gave way to *human resources*, and we heard about T-groups, management retreats, and suggestion boxes, along with individual and corporate EST (Earhart Seminar Training, thankfully long dead, Werner Earhart actually being Jack Rosenberg).

The 1980s gave us customer-driven emphasis, just-in-time manufacturing (Taylor redux), employee involvement through quality circles, the search (and passion) for excellence, treading hot coals, and "people issues." And the 1990s presented downsizing, rightsizing, quality awards as an end in themselves, empowerment, benchmarking, and reengineering.

The new millennium has featured globilization and "flat earth" dynamics, management "scorecards," diversity focus, lean thinking, kaizen, and Six Sigma customer-driven organizations. The fads and buzzwords never end.

In business, the past is seldom an accurate indicator of the future, and those who are prone to forget history *are sometimes the least burdened.* Million dollar consulting is not about embracing the latest (or anticipated) fads, nor about predicting what will happen to a client's business. It is about growing as a consulting firm so that you can help your clients grow. If you are using the same technologies, approaches, and models next year that you are using this year, you aren't growing, and you may well be in the success trap.

You can't help an expanding number of clients in a growing number of ways if you continue to use the same old tools and knowledge. The way to grow your business is to grow your approaches, and that requires that you take some risks.

RISK AND REWARD: NO CROSS, NO CROWN

> *If you never accept an assignment that calls for your doing something you haven't done before, you will never earn significant money.*

"No cross, no crown" was an observation of William Penn.

There is a piece of conventional wisdom that admonishes the consultant to underpromise and overdeliver. The reasoning here is that the client's expectations should be kept well within your delivery capacity. Your actual delivery will then exceed those expectations, creating great joy in the heart of the client.

There are only two things wrong with this approach. First, it presumes that the client is at best too stupid to divine the manipulation and at worst an adversary who must be duped—a win/lose dynamic. Second, my observations of the most successful consultants I've known reveal that they simply don't abide by such bromides. While they never promise results they can't achieve, they are always willing to test the envelope.

Under promising and overdelivering is just another of those empty bromides that average consultants like to pontificate about. It's easy to remember, it sounds great when you're giving advice, and it imparts an aura of lofty notions and uncompromising behavior. In actuality, however, if consultants underpromised on a regular basis, clients would begin to question the degree of value-added assistance being provided. They also would critique the nature of the fee structure (the corollary for the client would be to overdemand and underpay). And finally, consultants would never grow because they would forever remain within the safe confines created by underpromising.

> *One Percent Solution: Under promising and over delivering is a victimization and poverty mentality. It presupposes that you are not really good enough to be a peer and an honest equal of the buyer, so you must "surprise" the superior buyer with your results. If you think this way, you will certainly be a victim—of your own poor self-esteem.*

In the end, all such pat advice and conventional wisdom—particularly the kind that is accompanied by finger wagging and the phrase, "When I began in this business . . ."—should be ignored. In fact, you can afford to ignore any and all advice on how to expand your business except this: there are times when the whole future direction of your career may hinge on your willingness to take a prudent risk. Should you or shouldn't you?

I spoke earlier about two aspects of consulting that are key prerequisites for growth. One was the talents and expertise you gain as you acquire and learn from a wide variety of assignments. Growth is not just a matter of increasing revenues, but equally—for the longer term—a question of expanding your expertise, talent, reputation, and experience.

I also spoke about the goals for the business—your vision of what you stand for, what you believe in, and what your image should convey to prospects and clients. My own vision and goals are clear to me and to my clients. To accomplish those goals, it is imperative that I continually broaden my talents, expertise, reputation, and experience. (This is why underpromising is anathema.)

One of the fields my firm is fairly well known in is that of surveys and market analysis. However, I began that type of work only several years after I began my practice, and I did not deliberately acquire such expertise, nor did I have experience in the field. A client for whom I had done a variety of projects wanted to discuss a sampling of management opinion on the proliferation of technology within the organization, including its impact on productivity, interpersonal communications, and personal comfort. The client didn't ask about my vast survey experience (I had exactly none), nor did we ourselves focus on the particular instruments to be used.

Instead, I discussed the results the client wanted to achieve, how the feedback was to be used, and the collaborative responsibility each of us would have in the endeavor. For example, I suggested that we create the instrument and questions, but that the client be responsible for reviewing the entire package for cultural acceptability, clarity, the accuracy of the data being requested, and its conformity with corporate legal policies. I committed to revise and refine the package until the client was completely satisfied.

We both agreed on what would constitute an acceptable rate of return (50 percent of 2,500 managers). We also agreed that the client would distribute the survey internally with a prepaid mailer addressed to my firm or a direct e-mail link. Finally, I recommended that the survey be supported by focus groups and one-on-one interviews (which I did have significant experience in), and the client concurred.

The factors I considered in undertaking survey work that I had never done before included:

- Were the client's expectations reasonable?
- Did I have, or could we develop, the expertise, talent, and capacity to implement the project?
- Did the client have significant accountability so that success would be shared jointly and problems would be resolved jointly?

My knowledge of surveys and of the organization supported the 50 percent return as reasonable. Knowing the organization and questioning techniques that I frequently employed, I believed that the creation of the survey was within my capabilities, *especially* since the client had joint responsibility in several key areas (cultural fit, legal compliance, etc.).

My firm had the capacity to administer the project; I chose two psychology professors who frequently worked with me to assist in the software programming and scoring, and they, in turn, used students on an hourly basis for computer input. Finally, my firm and the client entered into still another collaborative venture, in which the results represented a shared effort.

As always when venturing into new territory, I was careful to oversee every step of the process. The result was an 80 percent return rate, which shocked the organization's executives (and me, although I feigned lack of surprise), and a wealth of data.

Henceforth, survey work was added to that client's expectations from my firm. It added to my firm's image in the marketplace because I proceeded to offer surveys as an option in a variety of other projects, wrote some articles about procedures for high response rates, and listed the firm in several guides under "Survey: employee and customer."

When you undertake assignments as collaborative ventures with a client, you are able to expand the nature of your activities with *prudent risk*. The difference between prudent risk and imprudent risk can be stated clearly: imprudent risk would occur if you represented yourself as a survey (or outplacement or strategy) expert to a prospect, who hired you on the grounds that you were responsible for total implementation and results. You actually might have the capability to deliver such a project, but the fact that this was your first, the lack of client involvement and accountability, and the lack of a prior relationship with the client would create a high-risk situation. You might well have overpromised, and there would be a significant chance of underdelivering because the client's expectations might be very high.

Prudent risk would occur if you did not represent yourself as an expert in a field that was new to you; if there were a collaborative partnership in which you and the client were jointly accountable for design, implementation, and outcome; and if you were working with a client with whom you had a strong history.

Now you may well ask, regarding the situation involving heavy client participation: would there even be enough value-added benefits to the client to merit your outside assistance? The answer provides a fail-safe system for moving into new areas of expertise. If the client does not perceive sufficient value-added benefits ("If I'm doing all of this, why do I need you?"), then you won't be retained for the project, and you shouldn't pursue it further.

However, if the client agrees to retain you, understanding the joint accountabilities required ("We can achieve these results only by working as a team"), then the client's own decision regarding your contribution validates your approach.

Figure 3-1 provides an evaluation aid that may be useful in determining when you are taking a prudent risk in attempting to grow in new expertise and

	YES	NO
▪ You now possess or can quickly/develop the expertise required.	☐	☐
▪ You are motivated to accept the project for reasons beyond revenue.	☐	☐
▪ There is the clear potential to apply these skills to other clients/projects.	☐	☐
▪ The client is willing to participate actively and accept accountability.	☐	☐
▪ The client's expectations are reasonable and achievable.	☐	☐
▪ You possess the capacity to administer and implement the project.	☐	☐
▪ You are willing and able to be involved in each step personally.	☐	☐

Figure 3-1 How to determine prudent risks for growth assignments. All these question must be answered yes without qualification.

application. *All* the questions must be answered yes for you to undertake a new project. If you can answer all seven with a confident "absolutely," you have minimized the risk to yourself and the client and have established a strong basis for growing your expertise. If you answer no or find yourself equivocating about any of them, then you are embarking on the project for the wrong reasons (money, ego) and/or with insufficient resources, and/or with inadequate growth application for your firm.

You are reading this book, presumably, to help achieve growth. *To grow, you must accept prudent risk by entering new areas of expertise and application.* To enter new areas, you have to disregard the rubrics and bromides. It is time to begin breaking paradigms.

QUESTIONS AND ANSWERS

Q. *If you're constantly climbing and never content with the plateau, then don't you continually increase your labor intensity and work?*

A. Good point, but fortunately, as you climb, you need to constantly change your business and delivery models. Growth isn't just about amount of business; it's about *how* you conduct business.

Q. *Is it better to brand yourself or your company?*

A. If your intent is to build a business that you will sell some day, then brand your business so that the brand's worth is part of the equity of the business. But if you're following my business model, which this book is about—solo practice consulting—then you ultimately want to brand your name so that buyers say, "Get me Alan Weiss."

Q. *Don't you have to look backward to learn from your failures and successes?*

A. Yes, just as a driver glances at the rear-and side-view mirrors. But no one can drive successfully or even safely without carefully watching the road ahead for opportunity, obstacles, and options.

Final Thought: Whether you think you can do it or you think you can't do it, you're correct. Mark Twain pointed out that even if you're on the right track, if you stand still, someone will pass you by. The route to million dollar consulting is along a constant path going upward.

BREAKING PARADIGMS

WHY THE SKI INSTRUCTOR
SHOULD ALWAYS BE
IN FRONT OF YOU

TOP STRATEGIES FOR GROWTH

Let's get down to cases. The first step necessary for most of us if we are to learn how to grow a consulting business is to *unlearn*. We've all been conditioned to automatically believe certain tenets and take certain axioms on faith.

I've been calling these deceptive pieces of advice rubrics and bromides and lumping them all together as *conventional wisdom*. You may well feel that I'm simply being contrarian: trying to be different by being unconventional.

Well, you're absolutely right. If the conventional wisdom about consulting were accurate, virtually everyone could make it as a consultant, and most consultants would be wealthy. This is not what actually happens, and the reason is that the conventional beliefs about our profession are wrong.

One of the original paradigm busters, a fellow by the name of Joel Barker, attracted great interest in this pursuit. *Paradigms* are thought patterns that we take for granted and let limit us.

For example, Barker cited the discomfort of most bicycle seats, which have survived for a century in their current form. He invented a radically different seat, consisting of two separate padded supports, that is much more comfortable under one's derriere.

Barker maintains that this was hardly a conceptual breakthrough in design, but it *was* a paradigm breakthrough. You see, bicycle seats are still called saddles because they take their form and function from horse saddles. (Similarly, you've all heard the old story that current railroad gauges—the distance between the rails—originated with the old Roman chariot wheel ruts, which, in turn, were derived by the width of the rear ends of the two horses that had to pull the thing. Apparently, this is absolutely true, and we've been guided by horses' backsides.)

Barker claims that such a genesis restricts innovation in design until someone consciously breaks the paradigm, which in this case means that there's no earthly reason today to continue to pattern bike seats after horse saddles. (However, it's too late and too expensive to attempt to change the railroads.)

I call these self-limiting mental restrictions *thinking blinders*. For example, what is the reason for the logical sequence of these numbers? Anyone looking at them should be able to tell. In other words, they do not represent someone's phone number or tax code. The answer is amazingly simple.

8 5 4 9 7 6 3 2 0

I have run this particular exercise with thousands of managers over the past 20 years, and only 1 in 20 identifies the correct reason within five minutes. Most give up (including my son's eleventh-grade math teacher, who surrendered after two days because he couldn't break out of his math paradigm).[1]

> Find your unique niche, then narrowly market within it. Otherwise, the competition will eat you for breakfast. Differentiating your services is the key to success for consultants.

I received this advice before I started my firm, while I was growing it, and after I had become a major success. I'm still getting it. And this advice couldn't be more wrong.

Digression

Be careful who you listen to. Make sure you solicit the advice (unsolicited advice is meant to benefit the sender, not the recipient, and the person you're asking had better be able to demonstrate that he has been successful at what you need coaching in.

You don't want a ski instructor who sits in the chalet sipping brandy and giving you advice for the next morning. You want one who is on the slopes immediately ahead of you, successfully demonstrating what you should be doing.

The growth strategies that are available hinge on the relationships you are able to forge, nurture, and expand. Average consultants attempt to market a repeatable product, which may take the form of a training program, a canned speech or workshop, a survey instrument, or something similar. Such predefined

---

[1] The numbers are in alphabetical order; i.e., *eight* begins with *e* and *zero* begins with *z*.

products seeking their niche are nothing more than commodities, and buyers view commodities almost exclusively from a cost-sensitive position, as well they should.

> *If you learn nothing else from this book, heed only this: consulting is a relationship business. A special product may make you competitive. Differentiated services may make you distinct. But only carefully crafted relationships will create a breakthrough firm.*

A pound of nails is a pound of nails, and I'll buy them wherever they are cheapest (which includes price, cost of transportation to get there, and so on). The difficulty with such commodity consulting approaches is that the greater the consulting resources, the greater the economies of scale. Seminar factories, using mass marketing and razor-thin margins, are turning out $49-per-person one-day seminars all over the country.

Independent consultants may be successful in implementing workshops in limited locales or for clients, but high costs and low margins prohibit geometric expansion. You don't make a million dollars doing this kind of work.

Better-than-average consultants differentiate their services so that they convey some distinction to the buyer. For example, providing a needs analysis prior to the actual proposal, offering computerized comparisons against national norms with survey work, and providing free follow-ups at periodic intervals are all methods that tend to set one consultant apart from the others. These techniques provide for more of a value-added appreciation by the client, but they are still self-limiting in terms of the specific nature of the services involved. Many consultants are successful with this approach, but they are probably also the ones who say, "Three hundred thousand is the most you can generate as an individual."

> *One Percent Solution: What you believe informs how you behave. If you believe you can't make more than $300,000, then don't create a $400,000 lifestyle. But if you believe you can make a million or more . . .*

The best consultants strive to establish special relationships with clients, irrespective of their products, services, techniques, and other offerings. Relationships differ from products and services in many ways, but the most fundamental difference lies in the simple matter of payment. Clients perceive *products* (such as manuals, reports, newsletters, artwork, and job aids) as commodities for which they pay a fee. Clients also perceive *services* (such as employee hotlines, team facilitation, and audits) as commodities for which they pay a fee.

However, clients perceive *relationships* as intangibles, the value of which transcends commodity calculations. Relationships represent an incalculable, intrinsic worth that clients don't even try to put a price on.

I once used a Mercedes dealer located 45 minutes from my home. I took my business there, rather than to a dealer of the same marque five minutes away because of the relationship I had with him. My dealer's products were comparable with those of other dealers; after all, they are selling the same cars and parts. His services were comparable and standard with his manufacturer, namely, roadside assistance, a hotline for questions, state inspection on-site, and so on, but my dealer's relationship with his customers was special.

He thought nothing, for instance, of personally picking up and delivering cars to customers' homes, leaving a loaner vehicle for their use in the interim. His staff embraced the same principles of helpfulness. The salesperson who sold me my car kept in touch periodically, provided the names of new restaurants she had discovered that she thought my wife and I would enjoy, and occasionally sent my wife a flower with a note about local cultural events in her town. The dealer took me to lunch and made a point of coming over and saying hello when he knew I was at the dealership.

When the owner semiretired, that level of service disappeared, and there was absolutely no differentiation any longer. I now patronize—and have purchased two or three Mercedes from—the people five minutes away.

The strategies available for growth are legion *so long as they focus on developing unique relationships with clients*. Let's examine a method for selecting them.

MIDCOURSE CORRECTIONS

We've established that there are three basic interactions you can engage in with clients. You may sell them a product, which is a paid-for tangible. You may provide them with a service, which is a paid-for intangible. And you may establish a relationship with them, which is a free intangible.

In any of these areas you may be competitive, distinct, or perceived as special—which I like to call *breakthrough* positioning. The combination of these interactions and dimensions is expressed in Figure 4-1.

You may not sell any products at all, or they may be peripheral to your major business. For example, we provide books and MP3 downloads on a request basis, and we often design interactive and self-paced learning programs for clients, but these tangible products are not our leading edge; they are the results

	Competitive	Unique	*Breakthrough*
Product			
Service			
Relation			

Figure 4-1 A systematic way to establish strategy. [Adapted from a model first published by Alan Weiss. *Making It Work: Turning Strategy into Action throughout Your Organization* (New York: Harper & Row, 1990).]

of our relationships and services, not the primary factor in our selection by a client. As a rule, products are viewed as commodities and are very price-sensitive. You can be competitive by providing professional, high-quality materials when requested, but to be unique or breakthrough in this dimension requires a substantial investment to compete in a margin-thin business (or exceptional branding, which itself is a form of special relationship).

My advice: If you must provide products as a component of your consulting work, keep them to a minimum, keep them high quality, but *do not* use them as the distinguishing feature of your work unless they accentuate your unique brand. (There was a highly memorable "It's Miller Time" beer campaign years ago. The problem—and this is why consultants are important—is that testing found that people were saying the following, "It's Miller time—let's have a Bud[weiser]!")

All of us in this profession provide services—the paid-for intangibles— to the client. The service may be formal and contractually specified, such as a needs analysis or a series of focus groups, or it may be informal and ad hoc, such as a review of the client's sudden personnel problems or recommendations for a meeting agenda. This advice and counsel needs to be better than competitive, or else the client will see no differentiation and will select consulting help based on logistical and objective factors. ("All the consultants ask me for my watch and tell me the time, so I might as well carry the cheapest watch and ask the nearest consultant.")

However, it is difficult to be in the breakthrough category in service because there is a limit to what you can do in terms of resources and availability, especially when compared with larger firms. A high-quality personal report to the executive board with handouts, graphics, and relevant data from the competition is enough to be special. Flashing lights and dancing animals probably aren't required because consistently special service is very powerful in the eyes of the client.

Breakthrough service can be seen as cloying, self-aggrandizing, and "overkill." Thus—if you haven't already guessed—my contention is that the breakthrough category for you should be your relationship with the client.

Ideally, your strategic mix should look like the one shown in Figure 4-2. The reason for this is that your competition probably either is trying to emphasize breakthrough characteristics across the board (something that is virtually impossible and extremely expensive) or is sidetracked by a particular strength or weakness in any one of the areas on the grid. There is no need to be more than competitive in products, and you are positioned ideally—and cost-effectively—if you are deemed distinctive in service. If you can then achieve breakthrough *relationships*, you are on the way to a long-lived, growth-oriented, highly lucrative clientele.

One Percent Solution: Strong relationships and service lead clients to give you enduring loyalty and the benefit of the doubt in tough times. A breakthrough product alone seldom does that.

Products and services tend to be based on *objective* assessments of *what* you are providing and *how* you are providing it. You can be compared readily with others. However, relationships represent the *why* of your involvement; you are

	Competitive	Unique	Breakthrough
Product	High-quality Minimum amounts Support, not leading edge		
Service		Polished, professional Anticipate need Client-centered, not consultant-centered	
Relation			Anticipatory Helps in "unrelated" areas Personal bonds Visceral and trusting Based on judgment

Figure 4-2 The ideal strategic mix, emphasizing relationships, for dynamic growth.

assessed in terms of the client's comfort in dealing with you, and these are *subjective* determinations. While it can be much harder to establish these connections and it is always time-consuming to do so, they are the most important connections because they are qualitative instead of quantitative.

And herein lies the *art* of consultant selection and acceptance.

> *The ideal client relationship is one in which the client trusts the consultant to make determinations about capabilities, meaning that the client approaches the consultant with a fundamental assumption that the consultant will act responsibly to improve the client's condition.*

Ideal relationships with clients are based on total trust and candor. As opposed to the traditional client-consultant dynamic, in which the client asks the consultant to prove that the latter can meet the former's needs ("Perform for me so that I can evaluate you"), the breakthrough relationship is one in which the client asks the consultant to collaborate to meet a need ("Work with me so that we can be successful").

The client trusts that the consultant will make the assessment of whether achieving the goals is within the consultant's capabilities. In this act of trust, the critical judgment passes from client to consultant because the client knows that the consultant is the far better judge of her own capabilities and has no reason to believe that the consultant will do anything other than act in the client's best interests.

This, indeed, is breakthrough stuff.

Over the past decades (until recent scandals and the resultant proscriptions), we've seen virtually all the major accounting firms launch consulting divisions. This has happened because there is an unyielding cap on growth in the accounting business; after all, how many times can you audit the books? These firms realized that they had established, by the very nature of their confidential work, a special, trusting relationship with clients. By laterally transferring that trusting relationship to related areas (most of these firms began their consulting work by heavily basing it on financial and information systems issues), these organizations have dramatically expanded their business base with existing clients, even though their products and services were not known in any area other than financial work. (And they are still severely limited by an ingrained audit mentality, but this is a subject for another book.)

There is simply no growth mechanism in our profession as dramatic as a trusting client who wants to use your services, believing that you will provide a reason not to if you can't accommodate the request. In effect, the selection responsibility moves from the client to the consultant. This is not a responsibility to be abused or taken lightly, of course.

Taking on a project you can't handle can, in two weeks, sour a relationship that it took you two years to establish.

A final thought about fine-tuning strategy: Don't wait until you're absolutely prepared and ready. When you're about 80 percent sure/ready/comfortable, *move!* You see, the final 20 percent preparedness is dysfunctional:

1. The client usually doesn't appreciate the difference.

2. The final 20 percent will cost you more than the prior 80 percent.

3. It's an excuse not to move.

4. You can never be 100 percent prepared, nor should you be.

5. Remember Zeno's paradox: if you make 50 percent progress toward your goal every single day, you'll never reach it.

Move when you're 80 percent ready, and you can easily fine-tune the rest as you go. (And this applies to writing, speaking, networking, new products, and most of your personal life, as well. When you're 80 percent convinced that you should leave the play at intermission, do so, or you'll regret it every time.)

TEN WAYS TO DEVELOP BREAKTHROUGH RELATIONSHIPS

How do you create powerful breakthrough relationships? With patience, insight, legwork, and specific techniques like these.

1. Provide Valuable Information

You cannot overcommunicate with clients if you are providing information that enhances performance and improves the working environment. Keep a set of files on all important issues facing your clients and key prospects, irrespective of whether you are personally working on those topics or even being considered for them. My files have titles that include "Ethics," "Customer Satisfaction Measures," "Interviewing Techniques," "CEO Development," "Board Governance," and the like. I clip articles, note ideas I've heard, and collect competitive product and service literature and file it all away under appropriate headings. Once a quarter, I review the files, eliminate duplication, create a unifying theme or sequence within each topic area, and send the contents to every client and prospect listed for that category.

I have never had recipients request that they be removed from the mailing list. I scrupulously avoid any self-promotion other than the inclusion of articles I've published in the field and reviews of my relevant books.

2. Provide Essential Phone Numbers

Make the following numbers available to every client (and *client* means every key individual within the client organization): regular office number, toll-free number (if you don't have one, get one), fax number (ditto), and cell phone number. (With superb clients, I often provide my home phone number in case they need to talk on a weekend.)

About three times a year, a client will call me at home in the evening or during a weekend with a critical request or question that simply can't wait. Three at-home calls a year is a small price to pay to cement relationships. This privilege is never abused, is a sign of great trust, and goes beyond mere service. One sign that I've established the relationships I seek occurs when clients offer me *their* cell phone numbers.

Case Study

The chief executive officer of a $300 million division called me on an occasional Monday evening prior to important executive committee meetings on Tuesday mornings when he needed an outside view on a troubling issue. He always called at the same time, about 10:30 p.m. eastern time.

I finally figured out that he timed his calls to coincide with half-time on Monday Night Football. But he didn't watch football. He knew that I did!

---

3. Raise Crucial Issues

In as responsible and professional a way as possible, raise issues that demand the client's attention, even if they are not part of the project on which you are working. Make it clear—and live by the pledge—that you are not raising the issues because you want to expand your project to include them. (If the client insists that you take them on, request that the client consider other alternatives before making a decision. This sounds crazy to short-term thinkers, but nine times out of ten the client will ask you to help anyway, and fee is no issue at all. See the fee/commitment equation later in this chapter.)

While undertaking a survey of customer satisfaction for a client, I found a severe morale problem among field employees that centered on two middle managers. I informed my client in a private meeting on the principle that he ought to know and that I would not be acting professionally and in his best interests if I didn't inform him. He took independent action after consulting with his staff members and told me that the situation could have gotten out of hand if I hadn't raised it with him.

4. Recommend Other Resources

Don't hesitate to suggest other service or product suppliers. I keep lists of resources I can call on to fulfill assignments that I cannot handle because I lack the competency or the time. Some of them possess highly specialized skills, such as outplacement counseling, and some are adept at routine needs, such as workshop facilitation. When a client asks me to take on a project that I cannot handle (the client is trusting me to make that decision), I call on these resources as alternatives. The client is pleased that I can offer this help (because my recommendations carry my credibility), the person selected is appreciative of the business, and my long-term standing is enhanced.

Although I request periodic summaries of the work in progress, I seldom accept a finder's fee or commission on such referral business for two reasons. First, I don't want to convey the impression that I profit from such referrals. Second, I am then able to influence the person chosen to my best advantage (i.e., "If you learn anything about my former sales project results, let me know"; "Please provide your best rates"; "Keep me informed of anything I should convey to the buyer").

5. Go the Extra Mile

Fulfill even tangential requests with grace and timeliness. As I originally wrote this chapter, I received a call from an excellent client with a friend who needed a job. The client felt that his friend could profit greatly from spending an hour with me discussing opportunities in my field and my experience with clients. I could have simply agreed to speak with the friend by phone when I had the chance, and the client would have been happy with such service. However, I don't want to provide service, I want to build relationships, so I immediately called the client's friend and invited him to my office and to lunch as my guest at a mutually convenient time. I dropped a line to my client to close the loop and gave him a summary of our discussion when I saw him again.

6. Facilitate Client Publicity

Recommend clients for publicity opportunities that may have nothing to do with your work for the organization. Since I'm very active in the media, I am often asked for interview subjects, examples of excellent performance profiles, people to serve as judges and on panels, and so on. I not only recommend certain clients, but I also provide a synopsis of why they would be appropriate or qualified and some background on their organization.

I tell the interviewers or selectors to be sure to mention my name so that the client gives them priority in her busy schedule.

7. Make a Charitable Contribution

Each year I contribute to an inner-city charter school "in the name of our clients." Such generosity is appreciated and doesn't tread on sensitive ethical concerns about gifts. I've been doing this now for a decade.

8. Help Subordinates Unstintingly

Go out of your way to help lower-level people, whether or not they are directly involved in your project and irrespective of whether they have any direct influence on future business. They *always* have an indirect influence.

While conducting focus groups with field managers, a manager asked if I would be willing to do something similar for his representatives, even though it wasn't part of my charter and was "only" for his personal assistance in managing his people. I told him that if his boss agreed, I'd gladly do it for expenses only. We had a wonderful time, he was able to provide something special for his people, and his feedback to senior management on my help was something that only my mother could write.

On another occasion, I agreed to see a staff person after hours when she couldn't be scheduled into a focus group but wanted to make her views known. I received information from her that I hadn't heard before and that I was able to raise with future groups, enabling me to provide additional insight in my evaluation for the client.

9. Don't Be Afraid to Take a Stand

Never back away from controversy, and don't hesitate to tell the client that he is wrong. Being a sycophant is not being a consultant, and the chances are that the client has more "yes" people than any organization needs. Your worth, your integrity, and your value added to the organization will be illuminated by your stand on important matters. Jefferson said, "In matters of taste, swim with the current; in matters of principle, stand like a rock."

A few years ago I delivered the results of a survey on ethics to a division vice president and his top reports. Three minutes into the presentation, the subordinates—obviously feeling threatened—raised every conceivable objection, from the nature of the questions in the survey to the legitimacy of the responses. I told them that they could agree or disagree with the data, but that in my opinion the results were rock solid. After the meeting, I took the vice president aside so as not to embarrass anyone and told him that I thought the kind of resistance and defensiveness we had just witnessed was no doubt responsible for a great deal of the survey results from subordinates.

I also offered to cancel the remainder of the project, which called for workshops to disseminate the results, if he were the least uncomfortable, even though I had a noncancelable contract. The result was that he chose to confide in me about sensitive people issues, asked for advice in his presenting of the results to subordinates, and has enlarged the earlier scope of our work together.

10. Treat Clients as Partners

Always view the client as an equal partner. The client is not just a buyer whose decision puts bread on your table, and you are by no means the almighty experts, without whom the client cannot even open the mail. The two (or three or seven) of you are a team, each reliant on the other to provide talent and resources to meet mutually agreed-upon goals. I do nothing for you, and you do nothing for me; we do things *jointly* for a common purpose. We don't seek blame; we seek cause. We don't relish activities; we rejoice in outcomes.

After a highly successful year with a client, during which his organization beat its plan for the first time in six years, I met with his boss, the group president, to review the past year and prepare for the next. The president said, "You must be ecstatic about the results we had. You were an essential part of the process." I can think of no greater accolade.

Every year for a stretch of seven years, Merck & Co. was named "America's Most Admired Company" in *Fortune* magazine's annual poll of executives. Every year Merck sent all employees a gift, thanking them for their contribution. And every year *I* got a gift from the vice president of worldwide personnel, personally thanking *me* for my contribution to Merck's success.

This is the ne plus ultra of client relationships. We'll continue to discuss throughout the book how a succession of such relationships turns into a million dollar business.

WHY NO ONE CARES ABOUT YOUR ETHICS OR YOUR TOUGH CHILDHOOD

I've gone to some lengths to explain that the core of your firm's success is the relationships you form with clients. The yardstick of the success of those relationships will be the growth you enjoy, and I've stipulated that such growth must go beyond short-term economics and embrace your learning, reputation, expertise, and experience. The sum total of this broadening is multidimensional growth.

Such comprehensive, across-the-board growth establishes a clear, targeted position for the firm. You should not let yourself be lulled by growth in one area.

For example, an increase in your expertise alone is insufficient if your reputation in the market does not reflect it, if you are unable to apply it to new projects, and if you make no money from it. Yet many consultants continually add expertise—in the form of new people, the licensed approaches of others, and personal research—without regard for the total growth picture.

Similarly, consultants often evaluate growth in terms of numbers of new clients—a single *quantitative* measure that can ignore the *qualitative* consideration that all the new clients require the exact same treatment, providing no growth in expertise or diverse experience. Financial growth must accompany the other growth factors; it is not independent of them.

Obviously, this financial growth is essential for our businesses and our lives. My intent is not to downplay it—far from it, as the name of this book should make clear—but to dramatize the fact that real wealth in this business is a function of longer-term thinking and avoidance of complacency in shorter-term revenues. Here's a very simple equation to try to prove the point.

Establishing high-level, high-quality relationships takes more time than does a quick sale to a lower-level buyer based on such single factors as fee, deliverables, timing, and so on. In fact, it often means passing up some short-term business. However, the patience this requires is always worth it in the long run because of the fee dynamic.

> *One Percent Solution: Paradoxically, the longer you take to establish a solid, trusting relationship with a buyer, the faster you will obtain high-quality business.*

The higher the commitment of the buyer, the less resistance there is to fees. And the higher the level of the buyer, the less resistance there also is to fees. (Low-level buyers are notoriously budget-bound, and consulting services are usually not in the budget. Higher-level buyers are results-oriented and can approve budget exceptions or change existing ones.)

Quite simply, the time it takes to develop solid, high-level relationships will always be rewarded with higher fees. Of course, you still have to *ask* for them, and tactics for doing that will be covered later.

Financial growth is not the beginning of strategic planning for your business. It is the result of planning for growth in all dimensions through high-level, high-quality client relationships.

When I help other consultants to evaluate their fee structure, I never do so without evaluating the dynamic of their relationships with clients and prospects. This chapter began with a discussion of strategies for growth and ends with a discussion of fees based on relationships that are intrinsic to such growth. Your approach to your business must do the same.

If you care to evaluate your existing sales potential, you can do so with the chart in Figure 4-3.

Low buyer commitment faced with a high fee is no sale, period. However, when buyer commitment is low, a low fee isn't the answer to create the sale you need because the result is indifference. On the one hand, the buyer feels that the outcome isn't very important because not too much has been invested; on the other, you don't feel that the outcome is very important because you aren't earning the type of fee you think you deserve.

Fees should never be established at a level designed merely to acquire the business to compensate for low buyer commitment. No one will be pleased with the outcome.

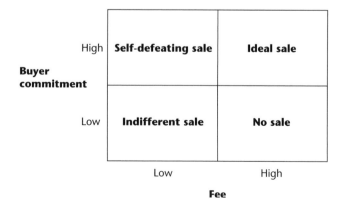

Figure 4-3 Evaluating the outcome of fee-commitment relationships.

When buyer commitment is high and the fee is low, you have placed your-self in a self-defeating position. No matter how pleased the buyer is or will be, you are working "cheap" (and perhaps losing money). Your alternative is forced: you feel you must use this sale is a springboard to a larger, more lucrative one. This can be dangerous because once you have placed yourself in the position of using a current project to justify another, you are likely to skew the results to justify further work; begin thinking of the next project at the expense of the current one; work uphill, since the client now has a mindset concerning your fee structure; and view the client relationship as one-dimensional, based on finances.

These are the very reasons why I advocate *never* undertaking a job at a reduced fee (or, run for the exits, as a "loss leader!") just to get in the door. That door can lead you straight into a relationship you'll soon need a window to escape from. The whole point of establishing relationships that result in high buyer commitment is to be able to establish a high fee structure.

The only desirable, win/win dynamic on the board is high commitment and high fees from the client. This sounds mercenary when stated boldly, but it's the logical outcome of forging the relationships I've been expounding. It's amazing how frequently consultants ignore these very simple dynamics through igno-rance of the process, undue focus on short-term goals, lack of appreciation for the relationship aspects of our business, and/or the success trap.

I've explained in this chapter the need to escape traditional thought pat-terns and eschew traditional wisdom—how to break the paradigms. If you can embrace the notion of relationship building as the core value of your consulting success, you've gone a long way toward getting ahead of the pack. Before I turn to the specific tactics of million dollar consulting, I need you to take a look at the strategies required to transform a firm into the type of consulting business I've described. It's time to turn the corner.

QUESTIONS AND ANSWERS

Q. *What if the client doesn't perceive the relationship you've established as important?*

A. The only criterion for importance is that of the client; it's in the eye of the beholder. Never judge your actions in a vacuum. What the client thinks is the only thing that matters, so you've probably misjudged what the client would see as a special relationship.

Q. *Are you saying that ethics aren't important to clients?*

A. No, I'm saying that high ethics, integrity, and appropriate behavior are givens that demand no special respect or mention. ("You have high ethics? Too bad; I wanted a consultant with low ethics.")

Q. *If I'm in a good position on your grid, can I rely on that to use my time in other pursuits?*

A. Not really, because the "gravity" on the grid is right to left. Even if you're in the position you want to be in, you have to keep innovating and improving, or you'll slide to the left as the competition gets better or customers get bored.

Final Thought: Never mindlessly accept conventional wisdom. I've seldom seen advice givers in this profession who are also exceptionally successful consultants. In this business, you've got to walk the talk. Or to put it another way, "Don't believe everything you hear, even if I tell you!" (H. L. Mencken)

CHAPTER
5

RACING THROUGH
THE TURNS

DON'T SKID, BUT DON'T STOP

SHIFTING GEARS EVER HIGHER

The most important transition period for any consulting (or entrepreneurial) business is *not* setting up shop as your own boss. It is *not* obtaining your first client. It is *not* even having a year that pays the bills and then some.

The most important transition period is escaping the thinking that confines you to small successes. Over the past 13 years, my Private Roster Mentor Program has included an attorney who has branched out into consulting areas that include the sale of small- to medium-sized businesses. After years of struggle, he finally has a staff, nice offices, and a modest practice that brings him about $300,000 a year. He came to me for formalized help because he felt "stuck."

"I'm happier making $300,000 than I was breaking even all those years," he acknowledged, "but I'm not very happy with my inability to go beyond that."

There is a consultant's "wall," it seems. Just like the distance runner, one either breaks through it or is never able to improve one's performance. The wall in this case, however, isn't caused by physiologic needs, dehydration, muscle tone, or breathing difficulties. It is caused by lack of confidence, an inability to let go of small successes, and *a sudden conservatism caused by having money in the bank for the first time.*

I've had to differentiate my offerings to the consulting and professional services communities as follows:

- *Gaining Traction*: Workshops on how to go from zero income to $300,000.
- *Six Figures to Seven*: How to escape the success trap and move into strong income.

- *The Million Dollar Club*: Seven-figure earners who convene in resort locations to discuss further growth, life balance concerns, contributions to others, and innovative ideas.

I've differentiated these offerings because there are hidden "bumps in the road" and squeamish turns that tend to cause people to slow down and keep checking the tire pressure.

Your continued growth is essential if you are to help your current and future clients in better and more sophisticated ways. It is also essential to

- Keep you vital and involved.
- Attract and retain top employees, partners, and/or alliances.
- Improve your visibility and marketing ability.
- Avoid the plateau of the "success trap."
- Maximize discretionary time, which is the real wealth.
- Prevent yourself from sitting still while other pass you.[1]

Make no mistake: if you see success as the level ground you've finally reached, it's only a matter of time before that ground erodes into a declivity. Such is the law of entropy. The only way to prosper is to continue to climb. Plateaus are meant for brief breathers, nothing more.

You must have a strategy for growth. I'm often asked if I create monetary goals each year that I strive to reach. I don't do this because such tactical goals are extremely limiting. For example, if your goal is to make $500,000 and you work hard, take some risks, and hit it, is that good? Maybe you should have made $700,000, but you were so fixated on the half-million that it became a self-fulfilling prophecy that actually *limited* your growth. (The same applies for number of new clients, additional geographies, publicity sources, and other such measures.)

I've seen this happen repeatedly in businesses of all sizes. When the sales vice president reports that "we'll be lucky to have a 5 percent increase in the Northeast," that's exactly what they have a hard time achieving.

The worst thing about having a plan is that you hit it. Don't make hard-and-fast tactical plans. You just might wind up achieving them—and little else. Focus on the strategic and the open-ended.

Figure 5-1 provides some examples of goals on the strategic level. The more focused you are on results for your clients, the more results will accrue to

[1] "Even if you're on the right track," said Mark Twain, "if you're just sitting there, someone will pass you."

Category	Strategic Results Desired
Marketing	Regular interviews on radio as a monthly norm.
	Agents obtained for book, article, and seminar deals.
	Recognized and hired by bureaus as a keynote speaker.
Relationships	All business is established on value-based project fees.
	Workshop and training business is subcontracted.
	Repeat business from existing clients grows each year over prior.
Finances	Major credit lines acquired at banks.
	Can operate without revenues during protracted dry spells.
	No receivables over 60 days' duration.
Resources	All research and interviewing performed by subcontractors.
	No projects refused because of lack of resources.
	New capabilities developed in survey work and testing.
Personal	Able to take vacations whenever they are desired.
	Net worth increases by larger percentage each succeeding year.
	Family time is increasing.

Figure 5-1 Examples of strategic goals.

your firm. And the less you create self-limiting goals with artificial "finish lines," the more you'll be able to run a long-distance race without heavy breathing.

One year I decided to raise my speaking fees. Most speakers and consultants would have chosen a fixed amount of increase, such as $2,000, or a fixed percentage, such as 10 percent. I decided to raise every fee, but situationally, depending on what was asked of me. I found, to my surprise, that I was able to dramatically raise the fees for 30-minute after-dinner speeches by much higher amounts because there aren't that many good business speakers who can tackle that tough time frame, and clients are willing to pay a premium to obtain top talent.[2] I assigned other fees based on the amount of preliminary work (participant

---

[2] After-dinner speaking is tough because it usually follows an open bar, a big meal served with unlimited wine, an awards ceremony, and droning talks by the senior managers. It is not for the timid. One night at Nissan, I followed three consecutive toasts in which everyone was asked by the visiting Japanese executives to down an entire cup of sake. Needless to say, everyone did so with gusto seldom seen in obeying orders from the top.

interviewing, on-site visits) or follow-up work (providing copies of slides, sending material for study) requested.

Over the year, these efforts produced much more than an across-the-board increase would have garnered.

To escape self-limiting behavior, you have to stop doing what you've been doing for ages. As one mentoree pointed out, "I've been doing this seminar on time management forever simply because I've always done it and can do it in my sleep—which is sometimes not far from the truth. I don't make that much, it narrows my repute, and it focuses me on clients who are too small for my growth needs."

As the doctor says, then stop doing it!

TRIAGE

There are three kinds of existing or repeat business that you will be faced with over your transition period:

1. Business that is not consistent with a growth strategy but that you want to retain because it can be developed into better business
2. Business that already represents your new, growth-oriented strategy that you want to retain
3. Business that is strictly the "old" image and should be abandoned because it cannot lead to new heights

Triage, of course, is generally applied to the medical system employed during a catastrophe, when casualties are high and resources scarce. Victims are separated into those who will survive if given immediate attention, those who will survive even without immediate attention, and those who probably won't survive in any case. Resources are allocated generally in that priority order.

Category 1 in the list deserves priority treatment. This has been sound, historically valuable business that you want to retain and further develop, but *not* in the current relationship. It may take a prolonged period, but you want to educate your buyer about the benefits of evolving the nature of your relationship. The basis for accomplishing this transition—the trust and history of results—is in place.

Category 2 is business that is already where you want it to be. It requires nurturing and the relationship building we've discussed elsewhere, but it's not as sensitive as the preceding business, which must be changed in form. Category 2 business will "survive" without extra intervention.

Category 3 business is not salvageable. It may be work that you simply don't want to do anymore or business that creates an image or association that is undesirable. This is excellent business to refer to others, a technique we've discussed in previous chapters. Retaining this business can be more damaging than not obtaining new business because it will "cement" you to wherever you are today, no matter how willing the client is to continue to send checks.

> *One Percent Solution: You cannot reach out until you let go. The first step is to release minimally profitable work that you retain simply out of inertia. Drop the baggage.*

Here are examples of each condition:

1. I increased average project fees by a multiple of 5 over a two-year period by exchanging a policy of "get the business through the lowest proposal" to one of "I want only business that results in a minimum profit margin of X." I did this by formally specifying services that I had to perform anyway (i.e., on-site observations, comparisons with industry norms) and developing relationships with buyers that helped me determine what other needs could legitimately be built into the project, although unstated by the client.

   Then I did an interesting thing: I substantially increased my project fees from what I would have charged had I not had a tangible transition plan for growth. This is not noticeable as long as you don't charge on a per-diem basis and you do demonstrate high-value-added outcomes. (See Chapter 9 for techniques.) I can still remember the very first $55,000 proposal I submitted, with my heart racing madly as the client reviewed it in front of me. When he accepted it with a simple, "Okay, it reflects everything we've agreed on, so let's do it," I knew that I had turned a corner in my career and my life.

Digression

Try to "unbundle" your services. Instead of throwing everything but the kitchen sink into your work—because you're trying to justify a fee that your self-esteem is having trouble supporting—separate out your services and provide the client with value options.

Although people talk about "scope creep" (clients asking for more work than was agreed upon), "scope seep" is worse, in that the consultant provides more work than was agreed upon at no extra fee.

2. I had "accidentally" developed a high profile as a keynote speaker in he newspaper industry. I maintained that profile through mailings and ongoing appearances at the American Press Institute and used it as a model for the types of speaking I wanted to do across industries. This was a business approach that didn't require modification, and I invested my time and energy elsewhere. I successfully developed relationships with the *New York Times, Los Angeles Times, Hartford Courant, BusinessWeek,* and others by allowing the momentum to continue unimpeded.

3. I had done individual behavioral assessments for clients by providing a written or audio description of predispositions based on an instrument I used at the time. I didn't want to be known as a "testing" firm, however, and the clients using this service tended to be small, one-site operations, a market I did not see as important to my future or my repute. Consequently, I offered this business to a woman who frequently worked on projects for me and provided her with free rights to use my instrumentation. I also provided the clients (and future inquiries) with alternative sources of such testing. Finally, I placed the entire test and its interpretation in a book[3] that was available from a major publisher (and now directly from me) so that the approach could be accessed and attributed to me.

To summarize the keys to successfully making the transition from where you are—no matter how successful—to becoming a million dollar consultant:

1. Set up a specific *strategic* plan for the major categories of your business, use the plan as a management tool to influence your decisions in running the business, and assess your success periodically.

2. Establish a triage system to protect attractive business, nurture evolutionary business, and abandon inappropriate business.

3. Assess your progress monthly using an independent sounding board as necessary to ensure that you are not blinded by temporary victories or the "resting place" of a short-term plateau.

4. Do not waver.

By engaging in this strategy, you will be developing "brands" that are essential for any successful consultant. Branding brings customers to you at a low cost of acquisition and reverses the buying dynamic. (Instead of "prove yourself to me," the prospect says, "I've heard of your work. . . .") However, brands must be

---

[3] Alan Weiss, *Managing for Peak Performance (and Pitfalls) of Personal Style* (New York: Harper & Row, 1989; Las Brisas Research Press, 1995).

specific and unique, so you must focus on your core competencies and how they appeal to market needs. [For greater detail, see my book *How to Develop a Unique Brand in the Consulting Profession* (San Francisco: Jossey-Bass/Pfeiffer, 2001).]

> *A fundamental confidence builder during times of transition is the sound client base that you already have and that you will be retaining in the future.*

FIFTEEN SECRETS OF SOUND GROWTH

In successfully making the transition from "lone wolf " to "thundering herd," you will want to safeguard key personal business and relationships.

> *There is no external force that will compel you to change the way you secure and deliver business. You must have a constant urge to examine the status quo and find out how it can be improved. This is what the best corporations in the world do—they examine their top units and then improve them. They don't shore up weak areas. You grow based on exploiting strengths, not by acclimating to weaknesses.*

These are the relationships represented by categories 1 and 2 in the list at the beginning of the previous section. No matter which of these categories the business relationship falls into, there are some techniques available to protect it while your business changes its image and the manner in which it operates. I've found that the following 15 methods apply regardless of your size, location, type of client, or consulting role.

1. Involve the Client in the Change and Seek Feedback

The worst thing you can do with an established client who has a clear image and understanding of what you've represented to the organization is to present an abrupt change in that image and understanding. Rather than present the client with a fait accompli and hope for the best, invite key people within the organization to comment on your proposed changes. Share your reasons with them; for example, you are moving away from conducting three-day seminars and toward on-site observations and one-on-one coaching because your experience indicates that such a role produces *higher-quality* and *longer-term* client results. Ask client personnel for feedback and suggestions. Keep them apprised of your progress. Ask them directly if there are aspects of your relationship with them that might be endangered or enhanced by your new strategy.

2. Present the Changes as Opportunities, Not as Threats

Determine how your new positioning will help your client, and prepare a cogent explanation of the advantages. *The client will tend to view change as a threat; you must provide the counterpoints.* Demonstrate that it has been the very nature of your relationship with this client and others that has provided for your evolving view of your work and its emphasis. Be upbeat and positive about the anticipated changes, and place them in perspective—they are natural evolutions of your growing business, which you wanted to explain to the client because of your unique and ongoing relationship. They are not watershed events that will permanently alter the relationship. (Compare them to similar changes that the client has made to evolve and change.)

3. Don't Explain the Changes and Raise Your Fees Simultaneously

Remember, these are clients in categories that are either already suited to your new strategy or capable of developing into that role. Even if you've embarked on a survey technique that the client is now obtaining elsewhere or if you are providing customer surveys at a lower fee here than you've begun charging elsewhere, don't propose or implement such changes too early. First allow the client to understand, react to, and acclimate to the changes in your business approach. Then you can introduce new services or fee structures. This could take six months to a year, depending on the original nature of your business and the client's identification with it.

4. Request Ongoing Feedback

Especially when there is a new company name, logo, materials, letterhead, and other print material, send advance copies or rough concepts to the client and request feedback. Whether or not you agree with and use the feedback, by soliciting it and listening to it, you will create "ownership" of your changes with the client. This will lessen the perceived sense of change and make the client a partner in that change rather than a perceived victim of it. Most important, since your image depends not on how you see it but on how others see it, client feedback is very useful in alerting you and your designers to whether the proposed "look" is effective in conveying the image you seek in the marketplace.

5. Introduce the Changes to Clients as a Group

Convene one or more small, informal meetings in a hotel conference room that is convenient for a group of clients, offer a continental breakfast or lunch, lay out your intent, and elicit their feedback as a group. This is an excellent investment because (a) groups are self-sanctioning and generally adopt a middle-of-the-road attitude toward change, (b) the clients will see themselves as advisors to you, which will enhance the two-way nature of the relationship, (c) the clients will have the opportunity to speak to *each other*, which can only enhance your perceived value in helping diverse organizations, and (d) better ideas emerge from a group setting, and the feedback should be quite valuable. I've concluded such sessions by presenting everyone with a bestselling business book or reference work as a token of appreciation for their participation.

6. Offer to "Grandfather" or Otherwise Safeguard the Services that Are Being Phased Out

For example, if you are no longer marketing the three-day effective-listening workshops that a particular client has requested once a quarter for three years, offer to continue those workshops for one final year. During that time, introduce a colleague or another consultant who will provide the "overlap" and continuity to continue them beyond the year. These offers are effective only if (a) you establish a definitive cutoff point, after which you will cease offering the product or service, and (b) you make an offer (whether or not it's accepted) of a qualified replacement who can smoothly continue as you bow out. Offer a sufficiently long phaseout so that the client has time to consider options and the change does not seem imminent. Do not offer these phaseouts unless you are certain that the client will consider them integral to a continued, effective relationship. They are time-consuming and deflect you from your future emphases, and they are too frequently offered because the *consultant*, not the client, doesn't want to end the service.

7. Time Your Explanation with a Client to Coincide with a Successfully Completed Assignment

After reviewing a consulting project that the client is pleased about, survey results that the client has found enlightening, workshop feedback that praises your techniques, or some similar event, use the moment to explain the changes that will be occurring within your firm. Tie in the changes to your personal development and evolution that has already been employed in the highly successful assignment just completed. Demonstrate that you are merely formalizing the effective techniques that you've been applying informally within the client's organization for some time. Hence this isn't an abrupt change, but an acknowledgment of the changes that have already been incorporated into your work and you're your approaches. Conversely, do not introduce a proposed change in the way you will conduct business in the middle of a client project or after one that has produced ambiguous or unacceptable results.

8. Reach Out Laterally to New Buyers within Existing Clients

Provide yourself with the opportunity to sell to more people within your current environment. While implementing, establish relationships with additional buyers. Ask your current buyer to introduce you. If you really believe that you have value to add, you're not "selling," but rather finding new people whom you can help in their parts of the business. If your current buyer balks at a change in your business or becomes distracted (or disappears), you will still have the "new" buyers to work with.

9. Provide Additional Value

If you really want to retain business that might be vulnerable as you change the nature of your operation, then make yourself so valuable that you can't be replaced. Provide a new electronic newsletter; offer an industry comparison; suggest that you benchmark survey results; provide some advice on a new initiative "on the house." This is simply spending money to make money, and the return on this modest investment will be substantial.

10. Focus on Growth Clients

You can grow and move most easily—retaining key clients—by focusing on the clients who are growing along with you. Identify those clients whose growth curves are increasing, and match them to your plans. This has the salutary effect of preventing a growth client from leaving you because you're no longer appropriate for its new needs!

11. Offer a Pro Bono Opportunity

I don't believe in doing pro bono work for for-profit organizations, but to help move a client over the speed bump, you may do something gratis that not only will create a positive reaction with the client, *but may also provide a glimpse of your new offerings that the client might avail himself of.*

12. Paint the Client into the Normative Picture

That's a grand way of saying that you should stress to the client that your new clients are taking advantage of new relationships with you (including products, services, access, fees, terms, and so forth), and that you would be remiss not to offer this relationship to your existing, excellent clients.

13. Create Case Studies

As you grow and expand your practice, create case studies to demonstrate the benefits of your new work. Ideally, these are related in three brief paragraphs: the *situation* you encountered, the *intervention* you provided, and the *result* that was achieved. With or without actual client names (depending on permission), these will make great cases on your Web site, in your press kit, and in your conversation about your new client paradigms.

14. Find the Early Adopters

"Partner" with those clients who tend to be innovative and early adopters to implement your new relationships. "Seed" these clients into meetings, Web site articles, blog posts, and other communications so that you create a certain critical mass and momentum.

15. Be Prepared to Move a Client Who Simply Will Not Accommodate Your Evolving Business Approach

This is easy for me to say, yet no one easily forsakes today's certain income for tomorrow's uncertain prospects, no matter how attractive those prospects may be. But here's the reality. First, *very few* clients, if any, will be this intractable if the relationship was solid to begin with. After all, you've had to accommodate client changes, and most clients do not find it unreasonable to accommodate yours, especially if your changes are presented and articulated in terms of the client's best interests. Second, if several of your clients react poorly, your proposed changes may well be too radical for a great deal of your existing business. This means that either you are making a large-scale change that is necessary if you are to achieve dramatic growth, or you are making too ambitious a change given your relationship with those clients. In either case, the feedback is essential to allow you to reevaluate your course of action.

Third, however, as we've discussed earlier and will address again, *you must abandon certain no-growth business relationships if you are to establish high-growth business relationships*. You just can't have it both ways. If you make your best efforts to retain key personal business relationships during a transition period and those efforts fail anyway, then those relationships would not have contributed to the high-growth business you are seeking to create.

Deliberately forsaking current business and current prospects seems alien to everything we're taught about marketing. Why should you lose business at all? Can't a smart marketer both retain the past *and* develop the future? In my experience, this attempt only results in your being a captive of the past and a passive viewer of the future.

EXPLOITING YOUR RESOURCES AND THOSE OF OTHERS

In a later chapter, we'll deal specifically with managing and exploiting capital once it's rolling in. However, the primary fuel you'll need for escape velocity from the lower atmosphere in the growth stages of your business consists of leveraged resources. This is not a gallimaufry of an uncle's loan, surrendered government bonds, and secondhand equipment. A fundamental reason for most new business failures is not lack of energy, poor services, or unwanted products. It is undercapitalization, and I use this term to represent more than just moola. (The greatest single problem is low self-esteem.)

Entrepreneurs can be killed more quickly by lack of resources than by any other cause. If you intend to build a legitimate, thriving, visible, growth-oriented business in professional consulting, at a minimum, you'll need access to and/or support from

- Top-flight office equipment, including a desktop computer, a laptop computer (some people use only the latter), a laser printer, a copier, a postage meter, a postage scale, a two-line phone, files, a calculator, a fax machine, and label makers. I also advise a credit card terminal and a merchant account through your bank. You can use a "virtual terminal" on your computer.
- Attractive stationery, labels, brochures, media kits, business cards, and other printed materials.
- Excellent legal help for incorporation, bylaws, contracts, and so on.
- Aggressive financial planning expertise for credit lines, taxes, retirement plans, and so on.

- A first-rate bookkeeper for monthly balance sheets, general ledgers, check reconciliation, and other such tasks.[4]
- Insurance professionals for disability, general liability, malpractice, and other needs.[5]
- A personal travel agent for airfare savings, economies of scale, maximizing travel awards, and minimizing your own scheduling time. (You can find bargains by making reservations over the Web, but the bargains are frequently illusory, and the time investment offsets the savings.)
- Audiovisual resources for slides, overheads, CDs, downloads, duplication, and so on.
- An online service provider, a Web site and administrator, and any related e-mail needs resources.
- A small but growing reference library on varied media (e.g., state-of-the-art books in your discipline, CD-ROMs with research aids, and recordings of conferences and speeches).
- Access to a graphic designer and production house for slides, materials design, and sophisticated presentations.
- A local print shop that can duplicate, create simple manuals, produce reprints, and supply other marketing needs.

These resources can't be sacrificed in tough times. In particular, *don't scrimp on the legal and financial assistance.* The attorney who closed on your house or did your will and the accountant who has done your personal taxes are unlikely to have the expertise required for your entrepreneurial challenges. Find yourself some specialists, using references, networking at association meetings, and industry listings.

Are you aware, for example, that you can build certain expense categories, such as medical reimbursements, into your corporate bylaws? Or that there are some national organizations that provide various insurance services to one-person operations at group rates? Why shop around if there are people who know the ropes? There are issues, including board meetings, travel expenses, obtaining credit, and retirement plans, that can be addressed early and comprehensively

---

[4] In all my suggestions throughout this book, I am placing a premium on *your time*. For example, while there is computer software that will calculate your taxes or reconcile your accounts, the cost to you in taking the time to use them is prohibitive because that time is not being spent on marketing, professional development, delivery, and the other vital actions your software can't do. For this same reason, you should outsource all but the most basic of audiovisual and printing needs.

[5] Disability insurance is universally overlooked, but you have a far graver risk of being incapacitated than of dying. Similarly, malpractice insurance—commonly known as "errors and omissions" (E&O)—is sometimes required by clients before you can sign a contract.

through these professionals. They also can serve as objective sounding boards when you need advice if you haven't yet formed a regular advisory body.

For example, *never* invest in anyone's offer to "guarantee" you leads or prospects, and *never* invest money to represent someone else's product or service as a franchisee. The best of these make money only for the other party, and the worst are outright scams and pyramid ploys.

Your resource plans should address three critical areas:

1. *Acquisition of the products and services noted earlier, irrespective of whether your office is at home or rented.* The former is perfectly acceptable. No one will care. The deciding factor is where you will be able to work effectively, not your ego needs. I've had only a home office for more than 23 years, right through a seven-figure practice. (In fact, the $450,000 I estimate I saved on an soffice, part-time help, insurance, utilities, and so forth over that time frame almost exactly equals the tuition of my two kids in private school from kindergarten through college. Think about that for a few minutes.)

2. *One year of your minimum personal expenses, including recurring bills (utilities and mortgage) and one-time needs (tuition and annual insurance premiums).* I recommend paring down your needs to a realistic minimum and then adding 10 percent for unexpected contingencies or miscalculations. If you're just starting out but you follow my overall approaches, you should be able to secure business within six months and be self-supporting in about twelve.

3. *Six months of nonreimbursable business expenses* (e.g., postage and phone), but not projected travel, which the client would pay for.

At any given point, a combination of cash on hand, accounts receivable, unbilled contracts, securities, and guaranteed access to credit lines should exceed the sum of these three areas. The last factor, in my opinion, should represent no more than 20 percent of your total needs.

Therefore, if your office start-up requires $10,000, a year's expenses require $75,000, and your business expenses are $15,000, you'll need at least $100,000, of which no more than $20,000 should be available from credit sources. The more working capital you amass (current assets minus current liabilities), the more latitude you have for growth, which generates still more working capital. Remember, growth is a function of growth, not of reduction. You cannot cut your way to success. Figure 5-2 provides a basic outline for figuring your working capital.

The most important factor is to *increase the top line*—revenues. The second most important factor is to *maximize the bottom line*—profits—by keeping as much of the top line as you possibly can.

Worksheet to Calculate Resource Funding

Basis Capital Requirements		Sources of Capital	
◘ One year of living expenses	$_____	◘ Cash and securities on hand	$_____
◘ Living expenses plus 10% contingency	_____	◘ Accounts receivable	_____
◘ Six months of business expenses	_____	◘ Contracts (unbilled business)	_____
◘ Start-up expenses for office	_____	◘ Credit line access	_____
Total needs	$_____	Total assets	$_____

Working capital: current assets minus current needs $_____

Figure 5-2 Working capital equation.

I keep over 90 percent.

If you are concerned about raising capital and either a home equity loan is unavailable or you do not own a home, there are two primary sources for raising money: debt sources and equity sources. Equity sources are troublesome.

1. Equity investment means that you surrender partial control of your business, however small, in return for someone else's money. Venture capitalists provide money in this way for a living. However, high-risk investors expect very high returns to justify that risk and will require that your focus be on a return on that investment in the relatively short term. They also will require that you invest virtually everything you have as a show of good faith. (Investors get fussy when they've loaned you six figures or so and your top priority is a vacation in Lower Tula Tula.)

   You will not be able to take much more than a subsistence salary for yourself. To put it bluntly, outside investors own more than your business. They own your *soul*. Is this really why you went into business for yourself—to have someone else oversee your actions and your income?

   Outside investors are like the basilisk, an ancient lizardlike monster, sitting on your doorstep. They frighten you and anyone else in the neighborhood.

2. Friends, family, and silent partners are less monsterlike in their loan potential, but not by much. First, there may be considerable personal pressure to make repayments before you actually can afford to do so. Second, the amount

of amount of money gained from this source is usually relatively small (except in the case of the really rich uncle).

3. You can invite colleagues in for a piece of your action. In fact, once you're flamingly successful, you can use the allure of equity to attract excellent people. At the outset, however, the value of such equity is highly problematic. For example, for a $25,000 investment, does a colleague receive 5 percent or 20 percent of the equity? If you've been too generous, the transaction will return to haunt you once the large contracts roll in. If you've been too parsimonious, your colleague will resent the arrangement.

Collegial equity can create highly motivated stakeholders. But this inclusion will almost always limit your personal freedom severely. Decisions to abandon business, raise fees, experiment with new approaches, and the like become committee debates rather than bold actions. I've found equity participation to be a fairly effective tool for long-term commitment and reward later on, but not for gaining resources at the beginning.

4. Some consultants have raised money by providing their products, services, and expertise to others on a licensing or fee arrangement. These "purchasers" are certainly not clients because they have unrestricted use of your proprietary intellectual capital, be it tangible or intangible. The advantage of raising some cash is more than undercut by the surrender of control and receiving only a percentage of the revenue from your contribution rather than all of it. This is a Faustian bargain. Too often you get entangled for life.

In contrast to equity funding, debt funding, however forbidding the term, leaves you in control of your destiny.[6] The best alternatives are local banks that provide credit lines but demand that only the interest be paid monthly, meaning that the capital can be repaid at a time when it is most comfortable for you. These lines are invaluable to the thriving consultant, who probably will have to take a huge year-end bonus out of the business for tax purposes. All the interest payments are legitimate business deductions, and since the company borrowed the capital, the company funds pay it back whenever feasible.

Many banks also underwrite loans from the Small Business Administration that are highly favorable, require modest fees for acquisition, and have generous repayment terms. Make sure you inquire about them.

Even when I reached the $300,000 and $400,000 marks in revenue, my business was highly uneven, and cash flow varied tremendously. (One year I made

---

[6] The ability to borrow money varies with the economic cycles, and since this book was first written in 1992, the markets have varied enormously. However, a good financial advisor can help you secure funds in virtually any economic circumstances, as long as your prospects, business plan, and personal repute are all sound.

over $75,000 in January, and in February made exactly $250 from book sales.) Some months I was scrambling for cash, and others I was investing in money-market funds to absorb the excess. My financial advisor saved the day by arranging meetings with three different banks. I chose one that offered me a credit line based on home equity for $150,000 personal use and $100,000 business use. Since then, the success of my business has enabled me to obtain an unsecured credit line of $125,000 for my business alone. If I didn't use these lines, I owed nothing, and if I borrowed, I owed only the interest, which was provided at a favorable rate.

Do you see what I mean by investing in excellent financial advice? Your advisors should be able to deliver, not just pontificate. (I have switched my primary bank because another offered me an even better deal. When you've made it in business, the banks will come to find you.)

Is there a danger in using home equity—if available—as a funding source? It depends. Are you serious about your career and your abilities? If so, there's a lot less danger in betting on you than in betting on the stock market. If you use that credit for vacations, furs, and fancy offices, you're in trouble. However, you don't need me to tell you this. The reason you're reading this book, I presume, is that you intend to be focused and resolute in your success in this field. If this is not true, then don't pursue debt financing, because the collateral is suspect.

If you can't use a home for such purposes, there are other alternatives. Consult with a good financial resource, but also make sure that you consider the following:

- *Receivables can be used as collateral.* At the nascent stage of your business, there may not be many. Banks and other lenders generally will provide about 80 percent of the value of receivables if they are contractual and payable periodically. A different version of this approach, in which the lender assumes the risk of collecting in return for a percentage of the collectible, is called *factoring.* I think that this is ill advised. Moreover, the banks may inform your clients that their receivables are the basis of a loan granted to you.

- *Inventory often can provide financing for up to 50 percent or so of its worth.* If you have a large product inventory, this could be an option. Choose a bank that understands your type of business. John Humphrey, when president of the Forum Corporation, a Boston training firm, once told me that he actually took his bankers into the vault and had them touch the master copies of his company's materials. He explained the copyrights and the revenues and helped them to make the conceptual breakthrough that this was a valuable piece of collateral. He wanted them to "handle the assets."

- *Other personal or corporate assets can be used for collateral, from vehicles to equipment to office space.* Your financial advisor can help package you in the most attractive way possible to obtain further resources to support your growth needs.

Having said all this, the less indebtedness you have, the better. However, don't be afraid of it. The only way to make money is to invest money. I've done it repeatedly to grow my business and will continue to do so no matter what level I'm at. You need to develop a mindset that reassures you that the use of debt financing is a legitimate business tool. After all, you couldn't be any more certain of the worth of the collateral.

THE 16 BASIC PRINCIPLES OF MILLION DOLLAR CONSULTING

Million dollar consulting can be embodied in these 16 premises:

1. The consultant will improve the client's condition.
2. The consultant has a trusting relationship with the buyer.
3. Client interactions will be based on competitive products, distinctive service, and breakthrough relationships.
4. Those relationships will be developed as collaborative, long-term, mutually reinforcing, and mutually rewarding ones.
5. Results are tracked by metrics that clearly indicate the consultant's contributions.
6. As a result of the relationship, the consultant can achieve conceptual agreement with the client on project outcomes (as opposed to tasks), measures of success, and value to the client of achieving those outcomes.
7. Fees are based on the value of those outcomes as perceived by the client. (The discussion should never be about fee, only about value.)
8. The client is always presented with options so that the choices are *how* to go forward, not *whether* to go forward.
9. The client trusts the consultant to make decisions as to whether the latter can achieve the former's objectives.
10. The consultant and the client share in the diagnosis, but the consultant provides the prescription.
11. The consultant must achieve multidimensional growth in repute, expertise, experience, and income if high earnings are to be a

long-lived phenomenon. (The philosophy is not "specialize or die"; it's "generalize and thrive.")

12. To establish growth at the high end of the business, the consultant must abandon the low end of the business.

13. The consultant must invest money to make money, and adequate capital is required for growth.

14. No one becomes "rich" solely as a function of the revenues she generates. It's not what you make. It's what you keep.

15. Wealth is really discretionary use of time, and money is only the fuel.

16. The consultant's self-esteem dictates the success of all the previous points.

We've discussed most of these tenets in prior chapters and have sometimes crossed the line into the tactics for achieving them, that is, retaining key personal business, obtaining financing, and so on. However, the goal so far has been to set the stage and allow you to take a strategic view. We tend to dive into tactics without an appreciation for the gestalt. The tactics that follow in Part 2, while effective and vital no matter what your business content, will create the dynamic growth we've discussed only if they are embraced within a framework that exploits their potential.

The reason the first third of this book has been dedicated to understanding and selecting strategic options is that your philosophy and your basic beliefs about your business unequivocally will determine how you actually act under the heat and light of client contact. My experience has been that most consultants are too busy trying to deliver current business, send out proposals, service key clients, market their services, network with colleagues, and occasionally spend an evening at home to afford themselves the luxury of thinking about strategy and its repercussions. Strategy isn't "long term." This is more conventional wisdom run amok. Strategy, intrinsically, is neither long term nor short term.

Strategy has to do with *who you are* and *what you want to become*, so the tactics you employ—how you get there—must be consistent with your chosen destination. If you have no intended port of call because you have no time to think about one, then no wind is a good wind. You might hustle and pant, growl and spit, and in general create a lot of whirling action, but you'll never reach the top of this profession. Goals are what excite people and generate emotion. And while logic makes people think, emotion makes them act.

Clearly, the top of this profession is worth reaching, and the million dollar moniker I use means more than merely money in the bank. At the top are client opportunities, learning, collaborative offers to *your* advantage, publishing invitations, speaking options, and rarefied travel. Together, these opportunities can enhance your personal and professional growth in a manner that few other alternatives can match.

This isn't just about getting rich, although that alone is not an unattractive aspect. It's about excellence.

> **Strategy is a framework within which you make the decisions that determine the nature and direction of your business.**[7]

When consultants tell me that they are happy with their current size and capacity or that they really don't want to grow because they couldn't handle the business or make some other excuse justifying their plateau, I shrug it off. After all, it's their life. But I do feel sorry for their clients because, ultimately, consultants who refuse to grow are shortchanging the clients who depend on them no less than an automobile company that refuses to use the latest safety technology undermines its customers or a bookkeeper who resists the newest computer technology creates more expense for clients.

Clients cannot survive, let alone thrive and dominate their markets, by sitting on a plateau, no matter how lofty. The consultants they seek and deserve should be just as committed to the dynamics of strategy, tactics, growth, and achievement.

Million dollar consulting uses a belief system and strategy that prevent mere jobs from getting in the way of important careers. This is difficult in that it requires the worst kind of hard work—focused self-discipline. However, this is nothing less than you'd require of your clients. It is this long-term and strategic approach that ensures that the light at the end of the tunnel is new territory, not an onrushing train.

Let's turn now to the ways to thrive in this new territory.

QUESTIONS AND ANSWERS

Q. How do you keep the client from thinking that your changes are about extracting more revenue?

A. First, you need that trusting relationship I talked about. Second, you need to offer more value, for example, greater access, proactive help, monthly briefings, a common chat room for peers, and so on. Create the perception of much more value as well as the reality.

---

[7] From Benjamin B. Tregoe and John W. Zimmerman, *Top Management Strategy: What It Is and How It Works* (New York: Simon & Schuster, 1980).

Q. *How frequently should I review the growth criteria? Can I become obsessed with this?*

A. Twice a year makes sense to me, especially if your income is not matching your aspirations and desired lifestyle.

Q. *What if I can't get to the buyer to form that trusting relationship?*

A. See the sections on getting through and past the gatekeepers. Intermediaries, HR people, trainers, and assorted blockers will kill you. Never content yourself with anyone who can't sign a check.

Final Thought: *Your philosophy or view of your business may seem like an abstraction, but it's the rudder that keeps you on course. Don't get carried away by a particular sale or success. I've seen too many consultants become trainers or facilitators or something else they had no intention of becoming merely because they followed the path of easiest money and/or least resistance. Follow your own path, no matter what the competing allure.*

TACTICS:
IMPLEMENTING
MILLION DOLLAR
CONSULTING

IF YOU DON'T BLOW YOUR OWN HORN, THERE IS NO MUSIC

SQUIDLIKE MARKETING

NETWORKING IS NOT WORKING A ROOM

No matter how you begin in this profession—as a neophyte or as one blessed with a backlog of business—you will need tentacles that reach into areas of prospective business. Call it the "octopus condition," which may sound like a Robert Ludlum novel, but it's a real need nonetheless. (In fact, a squid might be a better analogy because squids have 10 arms and you're going to need all the arms you can get.)

I can trace about 90 percent of my current business to just *four* sources, and even they are interrelated. One is a consulting firm I worked with for many years (Kepner-Tregoe, in Princeton, New Jersey), where I gained wonderful contacts throughout the business community. A second is one of those contacts (a great guy named Art Strohmer, now retired) in one of the most prestigious companies in the world, Merck, who provided some of my first independent consulting work. A third is the transience of top executives at that company, who were actively sought by other firms and who later asked me to work with them. A fourth is the repute of my books, which has gained me entry into firms such as Hewlett-Packard (a woman by the name of Marilyn Martiny read the original *Million Dollar Consulting* in 1992 and began a wonderful decade-long relationship for me—I had also worked for Hewlett-Packard in the 1970s while working with Kepner-Tregoe, so you can see how these things all interrelate).

When you work with those kinds of firms, word travels. (I know an excellent speaker, Glenna Salsbury, who simply states that *all* her business has resulted from a single marketing event a decade or so ago.) The "tentacles" are about quality, not quantity.

In 1986 I joined the National Speakers Association (NSA). I've since served as the president of my local chapter. I speak several times a year at chapters around the country or at national events for that organization.

Three or four times a year, I learn something that can help me immediately. Is this too small a return on too great an investment? You be the judge. You don't have to learn something every time.

In fact, I've created an entire approach around this pursuit of gradual learning. I call it "The 1% Solution: Tools for Change." I've learned that if my client improves by just 1 percent per day, in 70 days the client is twice as good. The same applies to you and me. The secret of improvement is not inventing the new atomic-powered cell phone or some other great fell swoop. It is having the discipline—and the tentacles—to improve by 1 percent per day consistently. This is how you become a million dollar consultant on the fast track.

At one meeting I heard one of NSA's "name" speakers who I thought was dreadful and who would quickly sour a relationship if I ever introduced him to a client as a resource. However, halfway through a condescending presentation, he mentioned that he always provided a client with the option of paying the full speaking fee in advance in return for a discount.

I immediately came to life. In this business, control of receivables and management of cash flow are essential. I'd gladly provide a discount if I received payment at booking rather than after the delivery of a speech. (I require a deposit to hold the date anyway, so the client has to send a check for some amount.) I knew I had my 1 percent.

I began offering a 10 percent savings to clients for speaking dates, and to my amazement, *80 percent* of all such clients took advantage of it. Then I came upon the next 1 percent. If this option was so attractive to speaking clients investing $10,000 to $25,000 for an appearance, wouldn't it also be attractive to consulting clients, who were investing 10 or 20 times as much? Absolutely, to the degree that today, 75 percent of my consulting proposals are accepted on the basis of full fee in advance for a discount of 10 percent.

In fact, when the economy gets shaky, clients prefer this option. (Several of my best clients, making excellent profits and at the top of their industries, operate internally as if they're *losing* money. When a buyer sends an invoice to purchasing that stipulates a dramatic savings if payment is made immediately, the check arrives in my office with the ink barely dry.[1]

And what do you think the impact is on my bankers when they see that I collect a high proportion of my fees in advance, and the money is on deposit?

---

[1] No, I do not inflate my fees so that the discount is a "phantom" reduction. My discounts are legitimate and come out of my margin. The worth to me of money in hand, with no receivables or periodic billing, and the client's "full attention" to someone who has already been paid is monumental.

Digression

Some clients have policies that make it mandatory for them to accept any terms that provide a reduction in fees. That's right—mandatory. You never know.

Payment in advance is in the best interests of the buyer. The project can't be cancelled as a result of changed conditions or shifting priorities. There is less administrative work.

You will not receive payment in advance unless you ask for it. When you do ask, you may obtain it 50 percent of the time. Therefore, ask!

They can't do enough for me. I'll expound on how to use such techniques to manage your bankers in Chapter 14. It's not unusual for me to sell out a workshop at $5,000 per participant six months in advance, because people are drawn to it and because my policy is full payment. I never refund money, although I will grant credits.

When I asked a buyer at Merck who was spending about $250,000 per year with my firm why he always paid me in advance, he told me that it wasn't the discount, although that helped to justify his actions. "If I pay you in advance," he said, "no one can cancel my project!" There is an advantage to the buyer in paying you in full at the outset. It's up to you to make this manifest. I learned another 1 percent that day.

Thus, from an otherwise horrible meeting and an unpleasant speaker, I learned of a technique that would dramatically improve my cash flow and financial options. In all candor, I don't think I would have come up with this myself because I thought that asking for 50 percent on commencement of a project was "state of the art." In any case, I wouldn't have implemented the technique as soon as I did, even if I had eventually had the brainstorm.

I've also learned at association meetings how to order my own books through discounters at larger savings than through my own publishers, how to obtain radio interviews on a regular basis, and how to appear to be effective on the Internet with a minimum of technological investment .

I always seek to identify what I call "keepers" at association and networking events. These are small, one-sentence ideas that can have that 1 percent exponential impact on your business. Here are some examples:

- Courier express all proposals and confirmations; don't mail them.
- Contact every client and prospect once a quarter with *something*.
- Provide your own written introduction when making a speech.

- Create a blue-chip reference list to automatically include for prospects.
- "Seed" meetings with prospects with current clients who sing your praises.
- Don't provide written reports unless the client has a need for them.
- Create and continually update a standard press kit; don't rely solely on a Web site.
- Create a business *and* personal e-mail location.
- Always have your own e-mail domain; don't use services such as AOL ("amateur on line").
- Call the event planner when you arrive on site.
- Know the prospect's stock price before you enter the meeting.
- Shop the customer's business before visiting the buyer.
- Create products that both provide revenue and market you well.
- Keep the buyer talking as much as possible.
- Don't worry about answers; have the right questions.

These and similar techniques are discussed throughout this book. All of them were generated by networking and through memberships, and all of them are "keepers": they are single sentences that one can remember and, at least in my case, immediately and continually apply to improve business.

This is not the place to attempt to provide a comprehensive listing of organizations, periodicals, and networking activities. You must be selective; because there are so many options, you can invest all your time pursuing the full range, leaving no time for your own business. Some will apply more than others, depending on your specialties, preferences, stage of growth, and so forth. Instead, I'll "prime the pump" by suggesting specific activities of varying types for your consideration. If you were to adhere to this list, I suspect you'd be in excellent company, and your list of "keepers" would grow considerably.[2]

1. Join at least three organizations that offer regular meetings and the opportunity to interact with your peers in the industry.[3] The American Management Association is decent, though not as good as it used to be, because it

---

[2] Annotations and locations of various resources are in the Annotated Resources at the back of this book.

[3] Run like crazy from outfits that grant you "initials" representing such things as "Certified Management Consulting Professional" or the like for a $250 "membership fee." These are bogus, and everyone knows it. Similarly, don't pay for "services" that will "provide 50 leads a month" or "provide all the materials you need to set up a consulting operation." You're better off investing your money at the tables in Vegas.

provides seminars and workshops, breakfast meetings with influential authorities, books, videos, cassettes, and a fine reference library that you can access online. The dues are reasonable (about $300 a year for regular membership at this writing), and the benefits are genuine for a newer consultant.

Other organizations for consideration include the National Speakers Association, if speaking is a large part of your practice; the American Society for Training and Development, which is oriented toward a broad variety of workplace issues and has heavy training and human resources representation; the Society of Human Resource Management if your practice is primarily in the human resource area; the primary consultant's association, the Institute of Management Consultants, and the Society for Advancement of Consulting®[4] and trade associations that represent your present or targeted client base, such as the American Bankers Association. Three of these may be all you can handle, and you may choose to change memberships until you find the combination that provides the best networking and the most "keepers."

As a rule, if you're contributing but not learning, then you're engaged in pro bono work, which is laudable, but don't confuse it with networking. If you're not taking notes that you later use and you're not making contacts whom you later call, you're not benefiting. If you find that memberships are a "chore" that falls to the bottom of your priority list, either you haven't understood the marketing value of this investment or you've joined the wrong organizations.

If you're not getting the 1 percent a day, then either the organization isn't offering anything, or you're not working hard enough to find it.

2. Create a reference library that includes marketing resources such as *National Trade and Professional Associations of the United States*[5] I subscribe to the *Official Airline Guide* pocket edition because I'm often forced to make changes in my schedule en route. I also keep a wide variety of atlases and travel planners near the phone, though these days you can keep them *on* your phone if you're using the iPhone or similar technology.

There are myriad sources on the Internet that are covered in later chapters and in the Annotated Resources at the back of this book. Several of them will create maps that will—literally—lead you right to the prospect's door.

---

[4] IMC is the Institute of Management Consultants, which offers membership for individuals. It is the only body that credibly certifies consultants, demanding evidence of client work, passage of an examination on professional ethics, etc. The trouble is, it has been totally unsuccessful inbranding the designation, so buyers don't know of it. SAC® is the organization I founded, Society for Advancement of Consulting® which is for successful consultants and offers "board approvals" in specialties when the consultants' clients so testify.

[5] Published by Columbia Books, 1350 New York Avenue, N.W., Suite 207, Washington, D.C., or online at Columbiabooks.com.

> *Joining organizations and taking the time to network is an investment, no different from buying office equipment or creating a marketing piece. You are negligent if you don't focus on achieving the maximum return from that investment.*

3. Establish a circle of informal advisors, and make it a point to contact them once a month. Put them on your mailing list, and treat them as you would a prospect. That is, send them items that may be of help in their pursuits, offer assistance whenever needed, and keep them abreast of your plans. Then seek their feedback and counsel. Are your mailings effective? What image are you conveying? Does your firm stand out from the crowd? How can you improve your approaches?

Your "inner circle" should include other consultants, clients, vendors (e.g., your printer or graphic artist), professionals (your financial advisor, but probably not your attorney because attorneys are usually terrible businesspeople), and others whose judgment you respect, including friends, business associates, and community leaders.

You can't get too much feedback because you can always ignore irrelevancies, but you can be in a position to get too little, which is an occupational hazard of our profession (and a menacing shadow for "lone wolves"). Networking doesn't mean "selling"; it means establishing quid pro quo relationships with others that result in their improving your condition and you improving theirs. You're serving as consultants to each other. This reciprocity is important.

4. Establish collaborations with other consultants. Early in my career, I often was asked to subcontract in a project by another firm, and I've often asked others to perform in that role for me. This is a high-margin approach to business because no direct marketing is required, only a relationship with a kindred firm that contacts you at the right moment. Some firms called me every two years, but they called, at the "cost" to me of a quarterly contact or offer of help.

I invited the principal of another consulting firm to bid on a project at Merck at one point. A division of Merck required a training program that I didn't provide, and designing one for the client was inappropriate because excellent packages were available on the market. I asked for no fee or commission, and the client evaluated my recommendation along with several others. When the firm I recommended was chosen, the client decided that the program was to be placed in a configuration (competency-based, self-paced learning) in which it had never before existed. As a consequence, the buyer and the consulting firm both approached me with the request to adapt the material because my firm was ideal for that type of design work, and no such configuration currently existed.

Merck got exactly what it needed, my counterpart obtained a key business relationship with a superb organization, and I profited with another project. This win/win/win affiliation is an enduring and highly profitable way to conduct business. Note how much more substantive this approach is than the empty "alliances" that result from merely exchanging business cards.

People are forever giving me a business card and suggesting that should I ever need a specialist in economic development consulting (or whatever), I should give them a call. On what basis would I ever invite them into a client or even a prospect? Because they had a card and spoke to me for 30 minutes? That isn't networking. It's wasting business cards. Memberships, networking, and affiliations are aggressive, proactive marketing tools if you use them in that capacity.

One Percent Solution: A business card is a medium for enabling contact information to be retained. It shouldn't be used as a billboard of services, be clever and cute, or have your photo. When was the last time one of your buyers gave you a card with an advertisement on the back, a photo on the front, and a fold-out portion?

Assuming a leadership position in an association not only enhances your ability to market yourself, but also creates excellent visibility for your firm and enhances your repute, a key growth element. Prospects believe what they see and hear, and the more people there are talking about you and representing you, formally and informally, the more your phone will ring.

In the 1990s, a decade into my career, as mentioned earlier, I served as president of the New England Speakers Association, a highly visible and active organization. I was prepared to invest the required time and tacitly accepted that my business might suffer slightly from the diversion, which was perfectly acceptable to me. In fact, I can trace $250,000 of business that resulted *directly* from that position while I was in it. In this business, few good deeds go unrewarded.

ALLURING MUSIC

Figure 6-1 provides a checklist for publicizing your firm and its work.[6] How do you rate at the moment as your chief publicist?

Publicity and Promotional Alternatives			
	Pursued		
Options	Always	Some-times	Never
▫ Mailings to clients with items of interest	☐	☐	☐
▫ Mailings to prospects with items of interest	☐	☐	☐
▫ Published articles in relevant periodicals	☐	☐	☐
▫ Pro bono work for community, government, and nonprofits	☐	☐	☐
▫ Speeches at trade associations and conferences	☐	☐	☐
▫ Presence on the Internet	☐	☐	☐
▫ Exhibiting at trade shows	☐	☐	☐
▫ Requests from satisfied clients for referrals	☐	☐	☐
▫ Interviews in newspapers and magazines	☐	☐	☐
▫ Book publishing	☐	☐	☐
▫ Listings in directories and trade publications	☐	☐	☐
▫ Advertising for visibility and/or leads	☐	☐	☐
▫ Business listing in phone book yellow pages	☐	☐	☐
▫ Audio series or recordings of speeches	☐	☐	☐
▫ Networking with other consulting firms	☐	☐	☐
▫ Membership in client industry trade associations	☐	☐	☐
▫ Professional publicists and agents	☐	☐	☐

Figure 6-1 Options for publicity and promotion

[6] I'm working on the assumption that you've heeded the admonitions from Chapter 3 about brochures and letterhead and that your mailings would include these "standard" items.

There's no need to pursue *all* the areas. In fact, it would be dysfunctional for you to do so. At any given moment, you should be actively involved in at least a third of them, however, and those should change as your firm and its clients evolve. Here is a brief rundown on each of the options and my assessment of their value. These are specific tactics as applied to the "market gravity" strategy we discussed in Chapter 2.

Mailings to Clients with Items of Interest[7]

This one is a must. Some of my colleagues in direct mail and marketing tell me that you can't contact clients too often. My own bias is that once a quarter is sufficient for current clients[8] because you're interacting with them on an assignment anyway, but that nonactive clients could probably be communicated with monthly via an electronic newsletter, mailed "briefings," or some other kind of consistent device. I've already discussed the clippings files and similar techniques to gather relevant and/or provocative information, distill it, and send it to appropriate clients. I send out an occasional audio or print download. E-mail is also a highly useful option.

Mailings to Prospects with Items of Interest

This, too, is mandatory because it is a cost-effective way to keep your name in front of potential clients. If your resources and time permit, a quarterly or monthly mailing is appropriate. You also will learn from these mailings when key people leave their positions because of a promotion, reassignment, or departure for a new firm. This allows you to update your mailing list. I mail situationally during the year based on the information I've distilled and its application to those on my lists.

Published Articles in Relevant Periodicals

It is easier to be published than you might believe, and once you've been published the first time, it gets easier and easier thereafter. I once submitted an article to a training industry monthly publication for no fee. Once it was printed, I suggested a column, again for no fee. Once the column was running, I used it to (1) send to my mailing list and (2) gain credibility with larger publications to write for them. Eventually, the publication began paying for my columns, and, more important, I generated more than 70 articles, with reprint

---

[7] Periodic client/prospect communications, publishing, speaking, and pro bono work will all be discussed in detail later because they are the most dramatic marketing vehicles available for growth, and some readers may desire step-by-step techniques.

[8] By *current client* I mean an organization for which you have conducted assignments within the past 12 months. The term *client* without that qualification refers to any organization for which you've done work, irrespective of the time frame.

rights, on topics that were extremely productive for my business before I moved on to other marketing pursuits. If you have no writing experience, begin modestly by offering free submissions to publications that need pieces—local newspapers, industry newsletters, and trade magazines, for example.

Use these to gain credibility at the next level, and be patient. My first article was for no fee for *Supervisory Management* in 1969. By 1975, I was in *Management Review*, and by 1979, I was in the *New York Times*. As of 2009, I've since published more than 600 articles and 30 books in 9 languages. Publishing of virtually any type provides tremendous credibility, and this effort should be an ongoing one. I've never stopped pursuing it.

Pro Bono Work for Community, Government, and Nonprofits

Is your town establishing a search committee to choose a new police chief? Does your school board need help with its human resources planning? Are the Girl Scouts looking for local board members? Does the chamber of commerce need consultants to work with small businesses? This work provides the opportunity for you to gain visibility, meet potential contacts, and demonstrate how you can successfully apply your craft.

Chapter 11 will address pro bono work as a professional ethic, but for now I'll simply recommend it as a pragmatic method for gaining publicity and contacts. You will be interacting with other community leaders, many of whom are executives in local and national businesses. There are usually minimal expenses attendant to this work, and your time is well invested.

Speeches at Trade Associations and Conferences

Even if speaking is not an income source for your firm, it should be a publicity technique. There are bewildering assortments of local, state, regional, and national conventions for nearly every industry you can think of. I've spoken in front of the Eastern Region Nurserymen's Association, the Pharmaceutical Manufacturers of Canada, the Inland Press Association, the Executive Round Table of Jacksonville, the Central Illinois Employer's Association, the International Association of Professional Women, the National Fisheries Institute, and more than 500 other groups.

As in publishing, you can begin for no fee, addressing local groups (Rotary chapters are always seeking business speakers for weekly meetings) and then move on to larger groups. My current (domestic) fee is $15,000 and up for a keynote speech, during which I have the opportunity to address several hundred to several thousand people and after which I'm besieged with requests for more information.[9] Usually, you receive bookings for more speeches from people in

---

[9] Don't be bashful about charging for your speaking with the same aggressiveness you should use in your consulting fees. Psychologically, buyers believe they get what they pay for.

the audience. (This is when it pays to have reprints of articles and a first-class brochure available for distribution.) Every time I think of the opportunity to address hundreds of potential clients at one time, with the credibility provided by being a featured speaker, I wonder if I've died and gone to heaven.

Presence on the Internet

A home page is a wonderful passive marketing effort (people can come to you at their convenience). Your Internet site (more about this later) should feature user-friendliness, meaning a minimum of boring text about how good you are, graphics that are relevant and helpful (they take forever to download under some conditions), easy linking and, most of all, an interactive nature (see Chapter 13). Provide a free "article of the month" for downloading, an order form for your books, a request option for more information about a timely topic, or an e-mail link to contact you. The biggest drawback of most Web sites is that they are little more than static ads. Create a dynamic presence that impels visitors to return on a regular basis.[10]

One Percent Solution: Your Web site is not a sales vehicle; it is a credibility vehicle. Corporate buyers don't troll the Web looking for consultants, but they will go to your site once they've met you or heard of you. Hence, emphasize expertise, testimonials, and how your clients are better off (not credentials, methodology, or company history—no one cares).

Exhibiting at Trade Shows

This is an option that many of my colleagues pursue, although I generally don't. Virtually all trade shows have exhibitors' areas within which participants can learn about your services, pick up free literature, and ask questions. For my money, this is too much of a commodity undertaking—most firms that are successful at it are selling products of some type, be they course materials, books, or equipment. Exhibiting costs are fairly high. The space rental, display creation or rental, and local drayage costs can easily reach $5,000 or more. It is difficult to interest people in abstract services in such an environment, and the leads you do get are apt to be from all over the country, making it very expensive to engage in any type of personal follow-up.

---

[10] Visit my Web site (http://www.summitconsulting.com) and you can download hundreds of free articles, audio, and video; request a catalog; or order hundreds of books and CDs. You'll find similar opportunity at my blog: http://www.contrarianconsulting.com.

The one exception I've found is this: if you're a featured speaker at the conference, you may do well at attracting people to your booth. Of course, you're still faced with the problem of qualification and follow-up, and you'll need help to staff it. It's often a good idea to collaborate with a few other speakers/consultants to create more "critical mass" in exhibits.

Requests from Satisfied Clients for Referrals

I once had an insurance agent whose name I still remember more than 30 years later, Hap Mapes, who saw me twice a year, every year, whether I needed additional insurance or not. And he ended every meeting the same way: "Alan, give me two or three names you think might be able to use my help with their insurance needs." He was relentless, and I know he did this every day with every client he saw. If you don't request such information, you might never receive it. And if you've established the types of client relationships I've been discussing, it's easy to ask the question.

"John, you know a great many people in this industry and in the business community in general. Given the kinds of results we've achieved together here, do you know of anyone in need of similar assistance whom I should call on?" When you get those names, whether or not the people will see you immediately, they should go directly onto your prospect mailing list. By doing this, with discipline, you should be able to increase that list by at least 100 names a year, which represents, with a quarterly mailing, 400 contacts annually. [If Hap Mapes saw 200 clients twice a year, obtained 3 referrals at each meeting (1,200 leads), and closed only 5 percent of those leads (60 pieces of new business) for an average commission of $5,000, that's $300,000 of first-year business just based on referrals, not counting further business and further referrals from that group. Are you asking for referrals every time?]

Interviews in Newspapers and Magazines

"Human interest" stories often are written about a local consultant who assists major organizations, has written a book, or has designed a technique to aid in performance improvement. Keep local and national editors on your mailing list. I've been interviewed by a local newspaper twice for my consulting and writing, and then by national media such as *USA Today*, and the *New York Times* for my views on behavior in light of Wall Street venality. I've lost track of the number of times I've been cited in major media outlets.

Editors are always looking for a new slant or a sidebar on an existing debate. They will never know you're a source if you don't keep your material and ideas in front of them. This is particularly true of in-house organs. Client publications are always looking for articles and interviews. You can reprint these with impact equal to an article appearing in the trade press. Despite my 30 books and continuing mention in national media, one of my most influential reprints is a full-color, four-page interview run in an internal Merck magazine on the subject of ethics and values. In return for the interview, the client provided me with 2,500 copies and the right to reprint. Consumers Power, a utility client, provided a splendid layout—with illustrations—for an article on risk assessment that has turned out to be one of my most popular publicity pieces. You never know.

Book Publishing

This is simply an extension of article publishing, with one or two distinctions. First, an agent helps, and you can get one if you put together a professional presentation of your articles, your consulting clients and results, your credentials, and a couple of sample book chapters. Video tapes and recordings of any speeches you've done will help because they will indicate marketing potential and the fact that you're a professional. My first three books, however, were published without an agent, working directly with several major publishers before reaching agreement with HarperCollins.

Second, don't publish a book merely for publicity. You must have something worthwhile to say to your audience, or you will be wasting your time and money. This is where a literary agent earns her keep. The agent will tell you whether you have a marketable book, and if not, why not. The chances are that if you can sell an agent on representing you, the agent can sell a publisher on publishing you. *Do not self-publish or vanity-publish*, at least not to help your promotion as a consultant. These efforts are completely transparent, and executives (just like reviewers) are not impressed. However, a book from a major publisher is worth tens of thousands of dollars in promotional "punch."[11] I completed over $300,000 in project work for a Times Mirror division that contacted me because one of its senior people suggested one of my books to the president. More than $400,000 in project work at Hewlett-Packard is all attributable to one book ordered by one person, who then gave me a call. This is exactly how it's supposed to work.

Listings in Directories and Trade Publications

You can be listed for free in many publications and for a fee in others. An example of the former is the annual listing of consultants published by *Consultants*

---

[11] I'm advocating here the effectiveness of using book publishing as a promotional alternative. The "how-to" technique for writing a book is a subject for a book in and of itself. The interested reader is referred to the monthly magazine *Writer's Digest* and the annual reference book *Writer's Market*, both published by Writer's Digest Books, 1507 Dana Ave., Cincinnati, OH 45207 (800/888–6880) for specific ideas, sources, and publishers. In addition, there is an ocean of tapes, seminars, and guidebooks on book publishing offered through these sources, which is why membership in such groups was advocated in a prior section of this chapter. See Chapters 11 for more on publishing options.

News;[12] I receive frequent inquiries from the listings, but their use by firms sending out bids in certain subject areas is even more valuable.

With a minimum of legwork and a modest investment, you can easily be listed in a dozen directories each year. (*Recommendation*: Eschew the "Who's Who" listings of various types, which require people to pay to receive the book. These are nothing more than vanity listings, and everyone knows that they have no significance other than the fact that the checks of the firms included cleared the bank.) Every month I receive interview requests from my listing in Expertclick.com.[13] The American Institute of Architects became a $156,000 client after finding my name in the ASTD *Buyer's Guide*. It's the only business I've ever traced to that source, but that's more than enough to justify it forever.

Advertising for Visibility and/or Leads

These are really two separate objectives. I rarely advertise for visibility and never for leads. My experience has been that people are not influenced by ads when choosing consultants. However, they may be somewhat more sympathetic to a consultant whose name and/or firm is familiar. Generally, I've found that placing ads for the purpose of generating leads is not a fruitful pursuit, and my colleagues in the industry bear this out. *Exception*: a highly targeted ad in a special issue or theme publication when you also have an article appearing in that issue can attract responses. If you do advertise, be as specific as possible: cite client names, specific types of projects, and any results that you have permission to publicize. Offer a free article, tape, or book to dramatically improve your response rates, and place a code in your return address so that you can track which ads produce the best results. Some consultants do advocate an ad in the local Yellow Pages when local work is available and desirable, so I've added that next.

Business Listing in Phone Book Yellow Pages

You get such as ad for free if you have a business phone line, and for a modest amount you can use bold print and some descriptive lines or, for a bit more money, run a display ad. This is money well spent if your prospects and business expansion are local. It is not money well spent if you simply live near an airport and your business is primarily out of state. However, make sure that you always have a business listing. Many organizations have called directory assistance to locate my company after reading an article or hearing about me and being told

---

[12] Published by Kennedy Publications, Templeton Road, Fitzwilliam, NH 03447.

[13] Broadcast Interview Source, 2233 Wisconsin Ave., NW, Washington, DC, 20007 (202/333-4904). Visit the Web site at http://www.expertclick.com. A listing in the book also gets you a listing on the Internet site.

only the city in which I'm located. As stated elsewhere, I strongly recommend an 800 line so that you are as user-friendly as possible. Someone tried to solicit me recently for his promotional services and left a long-distance number to return his call. I told him that if that was an example of his promotional prowess, I'd pass.

Audio Series or Downloads of Speeches

Whenever I make a speech, I provide in the contract that the client may record the session on audio- or videocassette with no additional fee due me and may distribute those tapes to participants. However, *the client must provide me with two master copies of any such recordings for my own use.* These are "free" marketing tools that I've used to great advantage. Many speakers charge for such recordings, insist on royalties, or want to sell their own tapes. I simply want to make copies, which I send to prospects. It costs about a dollar or two each to duplicate an audiotape in volume, including a label and a box. (Videos are more effective as "audition" tapes to acquire more speaking assignments, but audio is wonderful for prospects to listen to in their cars to understand what your approaches are about. And such tapes are far more credible when they are recorded in front of a "live" audience, even if there are flubs or minor problems.)

I've taken several such tapes and had them packaged as a "series" on various topics, which lends the same kind of credibility that publishing does because the production company's name, not mine, is on the material. My major albums, such as "Winning the Race to the Market," are composed of three major presentations and a fourth interview, with supporting workbooks.

Networking with Other Consulting Firms

This was mentioned in the preceding section. It is an effective marketing tool in that it is free and unlimited. Put other consultants on your mailing list, keep them apprised of what you're doing, and develop those relationships. If you look at other consultants solely as competitors and "threats," you will never benefit from them. However, if you see them as colleagues and the sources of opportunities, sooner or later one of them will pass your name along for a project that he cannot handle. This is long-term marketing, and it's a niche that shouldn't be ignored. I was recently booked to speak in Barcelona at the worldwide conference of one of the largest search firms in the world. I had maintained a twice-a-year communication with one of the principals, and he decided that I'd be a perfect resource to address his colleagues. (In the deciding communication, I had included an interview recorded on cassette tape—see the preceding category—demonstrating how these alternatives can be readily combined.)

Digression

The five keys to networking, as told to you by an introvert (me):

1. *Distance power.* Network with those who don't know you so that there are no perceptions to "undo" or overcome.
2. *Unique multiplier.* Try to find the one person who has many contacts with different buyers, for example, a board member.
3. *Nexus person.* Who is the one person who can immediately connect you to a buyer? ("You must meet my boss"; "You must meet my cousin.")
4. *Adhesion principle.* You have to give to get. What are you offering that will create a reciprocity and obligation? (To a search executive: "May I give your name to a client seeking to obtain new talent?")
5. *Contextual connection:* You are both there for a given cause (awards, politics, charity, etc.), so make the best of it.

Remember: networking is a process, not an event!

Memberships in Client Industry Trade Associations

If permitted, join the trade associations that the preponderance of your clients and prospects belong to. You probably couldn't get into the American Dental Association (unless you're already in the field, of course), but I'm not sure that there are prohibitions against becoming a member of the National Retail Merchants Association or the International Association of Tourism. Sometimes associate memberships are available. These affiliations will keep you abreast of what's happening in industries that are important to your business, afford you the opportunity to meet key people in the industry regularly, and provide you with the inside track on speaking at conferences or publishing in industry newsletters and house organs.

A key accelerator for these memberships: try to accept a leadership or other high-visibility position.

Professional Publicists and Agents

There is a plethora of agencies that will publicize you. I pursued several to see if they would undertake a "pay for performance" option—that is, they would get a commission on business generated through their efforts. As you might expect, there were no takers. Most such firms will charge a monthly retainer to "guarantee" that you will get articles in print, be interviewed by print and broadcast media, and in general receive a heightened image. With the exception of a good literary agent, I'm skeptical. However, the option exists, and you just might find the right chemistry with someone.

Be aware, though, that this is probably the most expensive option on this list and that most of these firms don't really understand a solo consulting practice (or consulting at all).

One Percent Solution: If you agree with me at all that this is a relationship business, then why would you put a third party in the middle of the relationship?

THERE IS NO OBJECTION YOU HAVEN'T HEARD

As you proceed with your music, some people—who represent potential paying customers—may object to the tunes. Don't be too hasty in throwing out the score.

To step down from my metaphor: there are no new objections. That's right, every one has been heard—and heard kazillions of times. If we hear something new, either we haven't been listening previously or we haven't done our homework.

Although most objections will sound like

- I don't know if we're ready to do this.
- I'd like to look at some other people and get back to you.
- We've tried that, and it hasn't worked.
- I need more details and references.
- We'll have to have guarantees.
- We have other priorities at the moment.

The real objections come in only four flavors:

1. I don't trust you.
2. I don't need what you have.
3. I don't have the time to do this.
4. I don't have the money to do this.

If you can master a reply to the major areas, you can deal with the multiple variations with which they are expressed. So here is one rule and four responses.

The Rule

You must be talking to an economic buyer. That is, you must be dealing with the person who can write the check and make the ultimate decision. If you're not, then all bets are off. Don't bother rebutting "gatekeepers'" objections, but instead spend your time on trying to work through or around the gatekeeper to find the true buyer. Most of the consultants I work with who have problems acquiring business are seldom talking to an economic buyer.

Response 1: No Money

There is actually never any money, in the sense of allocated funds. No one awakes in the morning and says, "Let me budget $125,000 in case a consultant comes into my office with a bright idea I didn't anticipate." Oh, some projects come with their own allocations, but most of the time the money has to be found. Economic buyers can find money easily.

The "no money" response scares away most consultants. The key here is never to focus on price, but rather to focus solely on value. Don't quote a fee until you have conceptual agreement about value. (See Chapter 10 on writing proposals.) If you're discussing fees early in the discussions, you've lost control of the discussions.

The rebuttal here is: "Let's not even worry about budget for the moment. Let's focus on what you need and how much an improved condition might mean to you and the organization."

> *One Percent Solution: Money and budget are never resource issues with economic buyers. They are priority issues. The money is available and the buyer can get it, but does the buyer want to give it to you?*

Response 2: No Urgency

Many buyers legitimately will feel that the timing may be better later and/or that the issue isn't important enough to invest in now or suffer disruption for now. Inertia is always a factor: objects at rest tend to stay at rest.

Therefore, you have to create urgency.

Ask the buyer, "What happens if you do nothing?" Point out that the condition isn't stable but worsening, that a brief window of opportunity will be lost, or that a competitive leap will be impossible. When someone tells you that the timing isn't right, this means that he doesn't feel a sufficient sense of value from your proposition to overcome his inertia.

The rebuttal here is: "You can't afford not to act quickly, and I want to show you exactly what this means to you and the organization."

One Percent Solution: Time, like money, is not a resource issue; it's a priority issue. There is time, but will the buyer provide it for you?

Response 3: No Need

The buyer here simply doesn't see the applicability or the return on investment for your solution or initiative. There may well be issues, but the prospect doesn't sense them. There is a lack of awareness ("We have a highly diverse organization, and we receive virtually no complaints about unfair treatment").

The essence of marketing is to create need, not merely respond to it (or else why would anyone have ever purchased a Walkman audio system years ago or an iPhone today?). Every buyer knows what she wants, but few know what they need, and the difference between what they think they want and what they actually need is your value added.

The rebuttal here is: "Let me provide you with some evidence of where you're falling behind the competition because you're looking through a microscope instead of a telescope. It's not about increasing sales, it's about reaching brand new markets."

One Percent Solution: There are three kinds of need: (1) a preexisting need (strategy, teamwork), (2) a created need (e-commerce), and (3) an anticipated need (managing virtual teams that are globally dispersed and speak different languages). If you can't produce need from those three dimensions, you're in the wrong business.

Response 4: No Trust

This is the most serious and basic of the objection areas because the prior three are often specious and are ruses used to camouflage the fact that the buyer doesn't trust you. This doesn't mean that you may steal the silverware, but it does mean that your credentials, experience, demeanor, collateral materials, explanations, or any of a host of other dynamics is suspect.

The best way to overcome no trust is to build a solid relationship prior to trying to make a sale. Provide honest and candid feedback. Don't become a "yes man." Find out what the buyer's hot buttons are. Never attempt to sell a prepackaged solution or to "solve" the prospect's problem during your initial 20-minute meeting. Relationship building may take an hour or a year. Ironically, the more patient you are in making a sale, the faster you make it.

The rebuttal here is: "I'd like to know something about your issues and explain my background so that we can make a mutual decision as to whether we should go to the next step together. My projects are partnerships and collaborations, so it's important that we share our thinking with each other." Remember that you must appear as a peer of the economic buyer—a potential partner—not as a salesperson or a sycophant.

> *One Percent Solution: Trust is based on the honest belief that the other party has your best interests in mind. If that's demonstrated and manifest, even negative feedback will be greatly appreciated.*

PRODUCTS BUILD BRANDS

One of my (many) early mistakes was to advise people not to produce products too early. (I'm constantly amazed by how stupid I was two weeks ago.) I have since come to change my mind, radically.

Products are a great way to brand. In fact, they

- Create early revenue streams.
- Create "buzz" about you.
- Create marketing materials.
- Force you to create intellectual property and the equity therein.
- Form the bases for new services.
- Are a cheap way to gain international recognition.

- Are eminently suited to the Internet.
- Can be readily updated and kept current (or abandoned and replaced).

The key to a product is to have something to say. That is, what's in it for the consumers or customers? What value are they receiving? If this is satisfied, price is no object. (One of my most popular books is a little over 100 pages and sells for $149, but its title is *How to Write a Proposal That's Accepted Every Time*.)

Here are some simple ways to begin formulating and selling products:

Booklets. Create a 50-page work, including any illustrations, charts, and graphs, on a core competency of your practice. Get someone to write the foreword, and interview some of your peers. Provide checklists and guides. This booklet could be on recruiting, selling, service, focus groups, expert witness positions, technology use—virtually anything. Plan to have four or five of these, optimally related to a common theme.

CDs and downloads. Record your speeches, and use an additional mike for the audience. Have the recording professionally edited. Keep the intention in mind so that you don't use dated examples or mention the client's name (which can cause legal obstacles). Make sure that you include specific techniques and practical approaches. Don't be reliant on visual aids that the listeners can't see.

Albums. Combine textual material with the audio. Now the listener does have the visual aids and job aids. Incorporate a workbook or manual. These are best in combinations of two to four cassettes and one or two workbooks.

Manuals. Document your approach to call center service, interviewing, performance evaluation, establishing intranets, and so on. These should be "how to" manuals with indexes and step-by-step instructions. You can turn these out in both beginner and advanced versions.

Newsletters. Hard-copy and electronic newsletters are attractive if they are well done and consistent. Use outside contributors who are happy to get the publicity. Charge for both one- and two-year subscriptions, with a discount for the latter. These newsletters can appear monthly, bimonthly, or quarterly, but no less frequently than that. You'll need professional help on design and printing and perhaps distribution. (You can use a source such as databack.com for convenient and automated subscriptions, publishing, and so on for very little money per issue.)

I'm not advocating bumper stickers and coffee mugs. But the preceding product categories are relatively inexpensive to get into and can create superb word-of-mouth marketing, aside from the cash flow.

Note that I haven't mentioned self-published books because with rare exceptions these are vanity efforts that consume the author, aren't popularly received, and don't have credibility. I know you can cite me an exception, but I'm citing you the rule.

You can use the Internet and your Web site to market these products and, of course, take orders for them. This is why you should consider a secure Web site and a credit card terminal for your office (Https indicates a secure site, by the way).

The length of time you have been consulting has no bearing on product quality or pricing. The key factor is the value in the eye of the consumer. Think product early.

INTEGRITY AND ETHICS

I've reprinted a business card that was given to me by a fellow consultant whom I will call Marty Scott. The card is illustrated in Figure 6-2. If you think the information looks crowded on this page, you can imagine how it looks on a business card. And when was the last time you saw *both* "Dr." and "Ph.D." surrounding one person's name like a pair of bookends? Then we must have the professor title and the university, of course.

I find this kind of ego trip to be poor form, not just in terms of professionalism, but also in terms of endangering any chemistry that one is seeking to build with the prospect. A card should state your name, position, and firm. It's a reference piece for the client, not an advertisement. Even sillier than Marty's card are those that say "Mary Jones, M.A." I'm not familiar with a protocol that

---

Dr. Martin Scott, Ph.D.
Professor of Management
and
Human Resources

Global Human Resources	Dumpster Hall
Strategies, Inc. (GHRS)	School of Management
100 East West Drive	Famous University
Arrogance, RM 10101	Big City, SS 01010
(555) 123–4567	(010) 111–0000
Car phone: (555) 765–4321	e-mail: bigshot@wired.com

Figure 6-2. A business card "billboard."

shows graduate degrees listed after one's name. (I first thought these people were all from Massachusetts.)

What's next—"Alan Weiss, B.A., licensed driver, registered voter"?

I happen to have a Ph.D., but as one of my college professors explained, I choose to use my "maiden name" in most instances, particularly in business documents. (And "I'm not the kind of doctor who helps people.") I will use the honorific when such credibility is needed or requested by clients or prospects, but not simply as window dressing. (It's most helpful in getting restaurant reservations.)

Using any other initials at all, whether graduate degrees, certification of courses completed, or professional recognition, is unnecessary at best and amateurish at worst. Many organizations hand out self-congratulatory honorifics every hour. The point, of course, is that such designations help to establish a pecking order within the association but mean next to nothing outside it. I've never met a buyer who made decisions based on such "insider" recognition.[14] (I can actually claim the "right" to put after my name Ph.D., CMC, CSP, CPAE. That's 14 letters, of which only three are recognizable, and even that designation has no special marketing credibility. In fact, you can be at a distinct disadvantage by being pinned as an academic.)

Your personal conduct is your primary marketing device. It's the fundamental "look" of the business and what prospects put most credence in. Consequently, the way you comport yourself will determine not just *whether* you obtain the client, but also *on what grounds* you obtain the client.

This is often the essential element in the type of relationship that ensues. The key relationship aspect of our business is often established prior to the actual "sale," influenced by the buyer's comfort in dealing with you.

Personal conduct is not "dress for success," whatever that means. It is, rather, about the integrity of your positions and the candor with which you express them.

Whether you have an ongoing relationship with the chief executive officer or are relegated to lower-level managers is often determined before the initial meeting is even 10 minutes old. First impressions will influence whether an executive feels that the relationship should exist at her level or at a lower one.

---

[14] I recently called the president of a speaker's association chapter. Her answering machine produced this unbelievable message: "You have reached Sarah Smith, author, speaker, consultant, and president of Global Beliefs. . . ." I assume that she consults, writes, and speaks on modesty. The larger your operation, the less you have to hype it. No answering machine, to my knowledge, has ever made a sale.

I once fired a salesperson who had simultaneously sold two pieces of business in the casino industry. His sales were based on using each organization as a reference for the other, even though, at the time, he was simply meeting with each and had made *no* sales. Although he got lucky and neither buyer contacted the "reference" prior to signing a contract, I knew that we would be compromised if the two clients eventually compared notes and that such practices were a recipe for long-term disaster.

Before I could even approach the clients, they *did* find out about the subterfuge, and though they honored the existing contracts, they neither sought nor accepted any additional proposals from me. You will often be in a position in which the prospect requests an industry reference, examples of work performed, resumes of other professionals in your firm, and similar information that you literally may not have. The answer is not to dazzle the prospect with footwork or to scramble for the exits.

PRESSURE YOU CAN FEEL AND BREATHE

The answer is to treat the request as an opportunity, not a threat. You see, you are the best possible person to anticipate requests that you will have difficulty fulfilling. For example, if you are a "lone wolf" and your firm is called "Multitudes of Pros, Inc.," you know that you might be asked for background on the multitudes. If you're meeting with a prospect in the airline industry and you've never done business in the transportation field before, you probably know that industry references may be a sticking point.

Or if you're being considered for an employee survey and you've never conducted one (you're "testing the envelope"), then you can reasonably expect to be asked about it.

By anticipating such awkward questions and requests, you can prepare for them. And by preparing for them, you can steer the discussion in the direction of how you can improve the client's condition without being flustered by the question, without trying to come up with lame examples, and without having to sit there like a lump dropped from the skies. The keys are candor, clear preparation for the question, and crisp examples of what you can do for the client.

One Percent Solution: Anticipate the likely tough questions ("Isn't it dangerous for us to rely on someone with no colleagues or staff?") and prepare six to ten conversational responses ("You will always be talking to the principal").

Let's examine some common dilemmas that anyone trying to grow his business might face.

Dilemma 1: You've Never Worked in the Industry

This is one of the most common challenges for consultants who are seeking to expand. There has to be a first time in every industry. My advice is to develop examples from similar industries and demonstrate the relationship. If you are facing an airline executive, explain your work with rental car firms, highlighting the similarities in scheduling, catering to both business and recreational travelers, administering frequent-driver awards, and the like. If you're approaching health-care organizations for the first time, emphasize your work with pharmaceutical companies and their interactions with doctors, pharmacists, regulatory agencies, consumer action groups, and so on.

You also can describe work you've done for vendors and peripheral suppliers. Perhaps you've never worked for an automobile company, but you have worked with General Electric sites that provide electrical components to automobile makers.

Finally, demonstrate that you've studied this industry, regardless of all else. If you can identify the key issues facing the industry, indicate how your work relates to them, and let the prospect know what the outcome of their resolution might be for the organization, you will help to overcome the "never worked in the industry" dilemma.[15]

Most of all, however, remember this: the last thing that Mercedes-Benz needs is another automobile expert. Presumably, the company has those people falling from the rafters. What the company *does* need are people who are adept at conflict resolution, performance evaluation, coaching and counseling skills, and similar process expertise. A health maintenance organization president said to me once, "You've never worked in health care, so how do I know you can be of any help to us?" I replied, "Yes, and I never worked with automobile manufacturers before Mercedes, nor with pharmaceutical companies before Merck, and it didn't seem to bother them. What's your point?" (It's one of those situations in which the prospect either hires you or throws you out, but it does cut to the chase. In this case, I got the job.)

---

[15] These tactics are remarkably effective if you do your homework. For example, while trying to convince a computer manufacturer to do business with me, I found that General Motors was the country's leading manufacturer of computers because so many of them go into every car produced. I had worked with GM, and I used this as support for my familiarity with computer manufacturing.

Dilemma 2: The Client Wants a Cast of Thousands

Early in the process of embarking on growth, identify at least six people whom you would be proud to use in implementing projects. (For many of you, this may be old hat, or you might have full-time staffs. But bear with me for a moment.) These people often come from the ranks of

- Freelance consultants
- Retired professionals
- School faculty with available time
- Self-employed professionals who can invest the time
- Graduate students with specialized skills
- Full-time professional people with situational time available
- Unemployed professionals seeking temporary assignments

As you can see, this is a diverse group. You can best locate good people by networking in the manner described earlier in this chapter. My financial advisor is a source of people who are seeking to enter the consulting field or have been abruptly terminated from their positions. A colleague who serves on a bank board with me has helped with professors. Several other consultants provide me with freelancers whom they use. The beauty of such references is that the people involved tend to be highly qualified. (This is why it's always a good idea to be kind to people who approach you when they need help, even if you can't provide anything at the time. You never know when you may need them.)

The next step is to have the individuals provide a detailed résumé of their work experience in return for being considered for future assignments with you. These résumés are the documents you will provide to prospects on your letterhead—along with other salient company information and brochures—when you're asked for a description of your staff member and their qualifications. Tell prospects the truth if they ask—these aren't all full-time staffers but are people used situationally, which allows you to cover a wide range of assignments with the least overhead, which is of tremendous value to your clients.

Finally, have a business card created for every such person whom you actually may employ. You can get a couple of hundred cards for less than $25 at any local storefront printer. Put your logo, business address, and number on the cards (and alert your office staff, if you have one, to take messages for these individuals). Provide each contract person with your letterhead and literature as required, but try to have all communications go through your office. For example, put your firm's central e-mail site on all the cards.

Over the years, My staff has included college professors who specialize in psychometric testing and surveys, a woman who specializes in testing and assessment, a man who is expert in telemarketing and sales techniques, a woman who is an excellent researcher, a woman who does the legwork for strategy data gathering, several local housewives who are available while their children are in school, and a dozen others who have provided value-added services for me and my clients while receiving significant fees and their own multidimensional growth in return.

Dilemma 3: You've Never Worked on This Particular Type of Assignment

This is a fairly easy one as long as you don't get drawn into a ridiculous exercise in trying to "force-fit" projects you have worked on into the prospect's category. ("No, I've never worked on succession planning, but we did design a retirement program that is remarkably similar.") Once again, stress the opportunity.

Provide the prospect with a clear plan and proposal for improving his condition. You might mention that the very fact that you haven't worked on an identical project motivated you to study it carefully, research the background, and create the existing options. Provide several options for undertaking the project, with the pros and cons of each and your preference.

The focus on the various alternatives available for tackling the project, coupled with the evidence of the careful thought that went into them, will deflect and subordinate the issue of whether you've done the exact same work before. You also want to emphasize that you are adept at the *process* of improving the client's condition, not the *content* of the client's organization or of this particular issue.[16]

Always, always, always provide the prospect with a choice of yeses, not the single choice of "do it or don't do it." Once the prospect is trying to select which option seems best, the eventual contract is just a formality.

Dilemma 4: The Prospect Has Never Heard of You

This will mean more to some prospects than to others, but it's the easiest dilemma to deal with. Have a list of references in your briefcase at all times. Make sure that they are current and that they specify exact titles, addresses, and phone numbers. Explain that your firm is in the category of "best-kept secret"

---

[16] Which is why the role of "content expert" as described in Chapter 1 is not the most lucrative or promising in terms of growing your business.

(I refer to mine as a "boutique consulting firm" with such strong word-of-mouth references that we do not need to advertise), provide your "blue chip" client list, provide the publications you've written for or been interviewed by (see the earlier section on promotion), and explain that your strategy is to succeed through dramatic client results, not competitive advertising.

The key here, too, is being prepared for the question or challenge. Acknowledging that you've heard the issue raised before and that you're accustomed to the question helps relax the atmosphere and adds to your stature. I've often turned the tables and asked, "How do you succeed when your competitors have better-known profiles?" I'm almost always told, "Because we work harder," or, "Our service is better," or, "We establish excellent client relationships."

"Really?" I respond. "Then it looks like we have a great deal in common."

I'm not going to insult you by telling you to shine your shoes, comb your hair, and dress well. However, I am going to tell you that "presence" is more than just physical appearance. It is the manner in which you handle yourself, which I believe must always be with confidence, honesty, and integrity. You needn't compromise these traits because you have no reason to.

You are trying to help the prospect understand how you can help improve her condition in a client relationship. If you anticipate the dilemmas and prepare to deal with them, they are not dilemmas at all, but opportunities to show the prospect how well you conduct yourself and how able you are to meet client needs.

The look of the business is your look. Clients will believe only what they see in you and hear from you. However, the people working for you also represent you, and it is important that they embrace your ideals and convey your image as effectively as you do.

QUESTIONS AND ANSWERS

Q. How do I know with whom I should network? Don't I have to "work the room" to find that out?

A. Try to get a guest list in advance. Ask the organizers whom they are expecting. Watch who tends to draw and attract others. Look for people who are smartly attired and well groomed.

Q. How many brands can I have?

A. The ultimate brand is your name. But you can have a multiplicity of brands if that suits your business. I use Million Dollar Consulting, Balancing Act, and Architect of Professional Communities among others, and so on. But I want people to say in the end, "Get me Alan Weiss."

Q. *How do I really withstand the pressure of needing business and being in a powerful person's office and presence? Don't I have to please him?*

A. Here are some points to consider:

1. You're evaluating whether you want to do business with him, as well.

2. He needs your value in order to improve.

3. You are not trying to "sell" anything, but to start a partnership.

4. Never be afraid of failure. If you're not failing, you're not trying.

Final Thought: You're not in the consulting business, you're in the marketing business. I know this sounds harsh, but here's an even more frightening thought: your consulting skills may be good enough right now to implement the business you acquire, but I'll almost guarantee that your marketing skills aren't good enough to continually acquire business. Need I say more about where you ought to focus your ongoing 1 percent improvement?

CHAPTER 7

EXPANDING RESOURCES

GROWTH FOR PROFIT'S, NOT GROWTH'S, SAKE

OPTIONS AND FORMULAS

If your firm is to grow dramatically, you occasionally will need people to assist you. These people may be in the form of employees, partners, or subcontractors, or they may come through alliances with other firms and/or other innovative arrangements. None of these relationships is mutually exclusive. There is one consistent thread, however.

No matter what the relationship, you want people who

- Are highly competent and represent your firm well.
- Bring their own value-added to your needs.
- Adhere, strategically and tactically, to your objectives.
- Are ethical, honest, and law-abiding.
- Understand and accept their role.
- Ideally, can be used on a long-term basis.
- Are economical to protect your own margins.
- Are themselves successful, and parting will not be difficult.

Hold onto your chairs: The *worst* option for attracting and using people who meet these criteria is to hire them as full-time employees. There are four basic reasons for this:

1. *Full-time people are full-time overhead.* They must be fed and housed irrespective of business conditions, the government expects certain tax and record-keeping protocols, and the employees expect certain benefit and perquisite arrangements. This detracts directly from the bottom line—your *personal* bottom line.

2. *Managing employees is a tremendous drain on your time.* You will have to conduct and sit through meetings, deal with personnel problems, complete performance evaluations, and attend to the various and sundry needs of others. There is a growth-inhibiting tendency to focus more on internal matters than on client matters.

3. *Your personal actions will be subject to the dynamic of an employee-employer relationship.* For example, it is difficult for many people to purchase that new Mercedes in a year in which you have frozen salaries or reduced bonuses. Despite what others do or do not contribute, *your* personal decisions will be judged in light of *their* conditions.

4. *You will be forced by law to share certain benefits and perquisites that should normally accrue only to you and your family.* In many respects, you are creating an entire "second family" when you hire employees. (And, unfortunately, these family members sometimes sue.)

Hiring people is too often a matter of ego rather than business. I've acknowledged that it is important to provide prospects with a feeling of depth and to provide clients with an assortment of talents, but these objectives can be met in a variety of innovative ways. In any business, people are the most expensive asset. Consequently, we need to use some imagination in obtaining and using such assets. The only people I recommend hiring as full-time employees *if absolutely necessary* are those who provide secretarial or administrative support or who have highly specialized skills that are required daily (for example, a researcher or programmer who can be kept busy full time through the bulk of your contractual work when outside contracting is cost-ineffective).

> *I have been asked to come to the aid of too many entrepreneurial consultants who set up a "corporate welfare state" and mistakenly saw their obligation as helping their employees rather than helping clients (and therefore, themselves). The roadside is littered with failed practices that crumbled under the weight of full-time staff.*

Part-time hires can include

- Specialists needed for a particular long-term project that will use them on a constant basis for the duration of the assignment
- Office support staff to handle exceptionally busy periods of a known duration

- College interns and temporary help who are doing legwork while learning the business for a summer or project

There are three options that are far superior to any others for obtaining the talent necessary to help develop your business.

1. Acquiring Partners

It is generally better to own 50 percent of a million dollar business (or one-fifth of a $3 million business, for that matter) than it is to own 100 percent of a $100,000 business. If you can find people who share your vision and discipline, you may have a legitimate partnership.[1] They also must bring in complementary new talents, not a duplication of your talents.

I have never liked partnerships in which the investment or stake of the partners has been unequal, as in "I'll put up the talent; you put up the money." Partners should be just that, sharing risk and reward equally. (It's fine to allow a person to buy into the partnership over time as long as the time is specified and full equality is the result.) Partner candidates should possess the characteristics shown in Figure 7–1. These characteristics may seem self-evident, but they must *all* be met.

> *One Percent Solution: There are two ego indicators of "success" that can actually undermine success: the insistence on acquiring staff and the belief that you need a formal office to house them.*

- They provide a business base or financial investments equal to your own.
- They share your ideals, goals, and vision about the business.
- They have a track record of success.
- They are genuinely likable; the chemistry is positive and rewarding.
- They share your risk-taking quotient.
- They make the whole greater than the sum of its parts.
- They helps you to stretch and grow.

Figure 7-1 Essential qualifications for prospective partners.

[1] I mean this in the figurative sense of an equal partner, not in the legal sense of the form of the business. The firm can remain a corporation and needn't be a legal partnership. Doctors, attorneys, and accountants increasingly have abandoned partnerships for incorporation.

Simply bringing in a needed talent, providing access to a new client base, or being "a helluva person" is insufficient for a partnership, which is really tougher than any marriage (which is why many marriages have fallen apart when the individuals decide to work as partners in a business venture). In fact, it's deadly.

For example, there's no criterion in Figure 7-1 about being geographically proximate. It may make sense for partners to be geographically dispersed or to live next door. In either event, the partnership equation demands great trust, and trust is based on common goals and beliefs, not on revenue division or on being next door.

Diverse talents are required because you don't want to get better at things you're already quite good at. Instead, you want to stretch. You'll have to like each other because each of you is going to make some errors that will affect the other. At times you may be bringing in disproportional amounts of business. Also, you'll disagree on some approaches. These are legitimate business conflicts. They shouldn't be aggravated by personal conflicts.

Partnership is not about equal opportunity employment. It is about a soul mate.

The result of joining forces must be to create a whole that is larger than the parts creating it. If you and your partner each have a $250,000 business and two years after joining you are 50 percent owners of a $500,000 business, you've wasted your efforts. The nonfinancial gains you might have derived (for example, exchange of ideas, mutual critique, or companionship) could have been accomplished through networking and alliances. Partnerships should increase business geometrically, or they're not worth it.

A partnership should create a combined business base that is at least 25 percent larger than the sum of the two firms. The collaboration of two $300,000 firms should result in combined annual billings of $750,000, for example. Metaphorically, I call this "1 + 1 must equal 64."

One final caveat on partners: I have seen partnerships that were made in heaven descend into hell in the blink of an eye. Partnerships are extraordinarily difficult to escape from and frequently result in the demise of the entire firm. A good friend of mine finds himself in the position of being the controlling partner of his firm and the predominant business generator. His "minor" partners will be seeking to retire by selling their equity to him, which means that he will have to work harder than ever to provide funds for people who haven't been pulling their weight for quite some time. How does he raise the money to buy them out—by remaining on airplanes for the next five years, selling a portion of his ownership to investors, or some other odious solution?

Make sure of two things before you embark on a partnership. First, diligently ensure that the partnership will provide payback far in excess of the sum of the parts. Second, create a "prenuptial agreement" so that you can disengage with a minimum of chaos if the arrangement deteriorates.

> ## Digression
>
> *Charles had an $800,000 firm in which he was the sole rainmaker. He supported six delivery people, full-time employees who never ceased to remind him that delivery was the heart of the firm's success (it wasn't, of course; new client acquisition is the heart of any firm's growth and success).*
>
> *He denied himself and his family to support these employees in good times and bad, never taking a full bonus for himself, never firing anyone, never demanding that they bring in any additional business themselves.*
>
> *Charles, overweight and a chain smoker, died of cardiac arrest at 44, alone in a hotel room far from home.*

2. Forming Alliances

Alliance is one of the most bandied-about words in consulting (at least, as of this morning), but it's really an old method with continual practical application.[2] Through networking, memberships, and other contacts, you can establish strategic alliances with other firms. This is a reciprocally beneficial relationship in which the smaller firm obtains access to larger markets and organizations and the larger firm obtains specialized expertise and/or situational help in a cost-effective manner.

The membership organizations cited in Chapter 6 are excellent sources for meeting principals of other firms, often on a social and informal basis. I've noted that a major source of business for me is referrals and requests from other consulting firms. These alliances may result in occasional or frequent collaboration. If they are effective, they are highly lucrative because the marketing has been done for you. Moreover, your visibility in delivery becomes an important marketing tool. And generally, since your fee structure is known to your allied partner, your inclusion is not fee-sensitive.

I encourage all consultants to pursue alliances at every opportunity. This is an excellent technique for leveraging your marketing impact and visibility and for engaging in multidimensional growth as you observe your allied partners applying their techniques and talents. Alliances involve no confining contractual obligations, can be initiated and ended with relative ease, and often lead to still

---

[2] Many sources include subcontractors as a form of alliance. I've separated them here because I believe that they differ fundamentally in aspects of control, leverage, and access.

more alliances. However, they don't simply happen—they must be pursued through networking and memberships.

Remember, placing other consulting principals on your mailing list is not giving away the family jewels—it's inviting in the appraisers.

Alliances and the related subcontracting that follows are superior to partnerships in most cases because, with these options, you retain absolute control while achieving leverage for multidimensional growth.

Case Study

Some years ago I made the acquaintance of Wayne Cooper, chief executive officer (CEO) of Kennedy Information at the time. (I had known Jim Kennedy, one of the great forces in this profession, who sold his company to Wayne and his brother.) We decided that we had complementary resources to bring to the table.

Kennedy Information has widespread newsletter distribution, marketing reach, and a reputation in research and large-firm analysis. I was a known "brand" in consulting, was published widely, had created some consulting workshops, and had a strong reputation with solo practitioners via my mentorsing program.

Kennedy and I created a new newsletter, "What's Working in Consulting," replacing my homegrown one ("The Consultant's Craft"). We organized a series of high-end seminars called "Rainmaking" that Kennedy promoted and I delivered. And I've published three of my books under the Kennedy imprimatur.

We had some disagreements, but we trusted each other, and we both profited handsomely from the alliance. These synergistic relationships are the catalysts that propel your business forward exponentially.

Although the Coopers later sold the business and the newsletter ceased publication, I continue to publish and market three books through the current owners of Kennedy Information.

3. Subcontracting

Many of my colleagues hate this term. I guess it sounds too much like the general contractor calling in an electrical expert. If it pleases you, you may think of these relationships as "short-term contractual," "situationally dictated," or "nonemployee subordinates." To me, however, it's subcontracting, and you won't have power if you refuse to use good electricians.

In subcontracting, you obtain the services of other consultants for a specified fee arrangement or other participation under your direction. (If the other consultant is on an equal basis with you in terms of decision making and initiative during the engagement, then you haven't subcontracted for specific help; you're in an alliance or a partnership.) Subcontract work entails specialized skills and/or specific tasks as directed by you. These may include interviews, workshop facilitation, creation of a questionnaire, establishing customer focus groups, designing electronic and Web-based interventions, researching an industry, and so on.

The client may or may not know that the extra help is not actually a part of your firm. However, the client does know that the tasks are to be performed under your auspices and that you, personally, will not be performing them, although you are accountable for their quality.

When I obtain a project that requires subcontract help, I estimate the amount of assistance I'll need and build those fees into the project fee. Subcontractors are paid based on their contribution and the work they perform, not on the size of the project I've obtained. I also will pay different fees to different subcontractors if they bring a specialized expertise or are simply better at what they do. Each is a separate negotiation, and I am free to pay based on value, just as they are free to refuse work. I never hire based on the lowest fee; I always hire based on the most value—the degree to which my condition is improved by using their help. (Ongoing inside joke: I tell them never to read my work on value-based fees.)

My main reasons for using subcontractors, even if my margin is decreased, include the following:

1. I need the "legs" to deal with the volume of work.

2. I need specialized expertise that I don't possess.

3. I need a break—I just don't want to do the work.

4. I have better uses for my time.

Subcontractors are relatively easy to find in the networking and membership process. I receive a résumé a week from someone who wants this type of work. I also ask my colleagues in the business to recommend people, as I will for them, thus creating a win/win/win situation for all concerned.

If I am ever uncertain whether I need subcontracting help, I err on the side of not using it. I can always change my mind later, but I don't want to start a project with an obligation or with a large cost load. True, I may take a large hit on my profit margin, but this is huge anyway, so the damage is minimal.

(For those of you who have identified subcontractors as having established a strategic alliance with you, I have no quibble, just as you might consider yourself a subcontractor to your larger, strategic partner. The categories are worth separating, however, because you may be often in one and virtually never in the other, depending on the nature of your business and your contacts.)

> *It is always better to grow and retain control than to grow and surrender even partial control, unless the latter provides extraordinary growth.*

Of all the options for growth involving other people, I've found partnerships, alliances, and subcontracting to be the most effective in developing the business while protecting my interests. The latter two are the safest. I recommend partnerships only when the synergy of the partners creates a substantially larger business than the mere addition of those being partnered. *Most consulting partnerships eventually fail*, often with grave repercussions for each individual's future business.

No matter what options you choose, there is a need to recognize good people when you trip over them. After all, you are no doubt preaching this to clients. But how do you practice it yourself?

Digression

If you agree that wealth is discretionary time, then reducing labor intensity is as important as building business. After all, you can build business to the point where earning more dollars actually decreases your wealth. We've all seen the "workaholics."

You can always make another dollar, but you can't create an additional minute.

Here are some quick techniques to reduce labor intensity:

1. Shift all the work you can to the client. This is valuable to the client, because you are transferring skills, enabling the client to perpetuate change without you, and developing the client's people. Utilize the local talent.

2. Critically review mindless activities you perform for yourself that have no bearing on the client. Don't produce reports that simply sit in dusty binders on remote shelves. *Never base your value on such deliverables.* That's what amateurs do.

3. Use subcontractors for anything that:

   a. Bores you.

   b. Requires bodies but not great expertise.

   c. Requires specialized expertise that it's not worthwhile for you to acquire.

4. Never accept tasks from the client (number of days you must be present, meetings you must attend, presentations you must make). You're the consultant, and you know what methodology and approaches are appropriate. Your value isn't in your physical presence.

5. Charge a fortune if you must do everything. That enables you to take on less work elsewhere. ("Fortune" can never be less than six figures, by the way.)

HOW TO HIRE THE BEST AND AVOID THE REST

Invariably, the least expensive people you can find to assist on a project are not the best qualified. However, the most expensive are seldom the best qualified.

The first step in finding excellent people (whether for subcontracting, alliances, partners, referrals, or whatever) is to understand what kind of people you're seeking. Are you in need of people with specific talents, for example, people to run workshops, create learning materials, conduct interviews, design test instruments, or counsel employees? Or are you in need of conceptual and strategic thinkers who can work in ambiguous situations with a client and identify patterns or suggest procedures? Do you require experts, exemplars, or collaborators?[3] Are you searching for a subcontractor, a sounding board, or a potential alliance? One critical mistake that consultants make, one that makes the cobbler's children seem well shod by comparison, is choosing people on the basis of "chemistry" alone.

Interpersonal relationships are certainly essential. After all, you must trust those with whom you are working. However, warm and cuddly feelings by themselves are insufficient. The individual must be suited for the type of work or relationship you have in mind. I've seen people hire researchers who couldn't

---

[3] See Chapter 1 for the pragmatic range of interventions.

understand computer databases. All too frequently I see content experts used in workshop situations, although they don't know a thing about adult learning and have no facilitation skills. No matter how well you like and respect a person, if he is ill suited for interviewing because of poor listening skills, then that person is a square peg in that particular round hole.

> *Ergo, rule number 1: Identify the traits, performance objectives, and skills required.*

Next, use your networking, memberships, and affiliations to meet people. Don't simply try to find people when you discover that you have a need. This inevitably will create undue pressure to turn up a "warm body" and diminish the quality of your selection decision. You should have an established pipeline of people that you can tap into whenever necessary.

I've often found that certain bid requests will demand a profile of the consultants who might work on the project. If experience in the health-care industry is an evaluation criterion, I will include people from my pool with the requisite skills who have that background. If experienced sales trainers are considered important, I'll select several of those.

I met an independent consultant at an industry conference who was a specialist in sales training. We became friendly and decided to share an occasional working breakfast to compare notes. I discovered that he had skills that were applicable far beyond his chosen niche and soon invited him to participate as a field interviewer on several projects. As he has learned my system, he has become even more valuable in a wider range of projects and is now one of my prime subcontractors.

> *Selecting people who can provide value added to your business is as important as identifying potential clients.*

I maintain a special file for my pool of resources that is constantly being modified and expanded. It's as important as my prospect list, in that these are the people who enable me to leverage my business.

> *Thus, rule number 2: Aggressively identify and establish relationships with good people as a continuing pursuit.*

Finally, once you've recognized your needs and identified potential candidates, how do you know which ones are the right ones for a particular assignment, The client shouldn't be the guinea pig. The answer here is that you must spend time with the people you've identified, no matter what potential role you envision their playing. Here are my recommendations:

- *Alliance relationships.* Visit their offices and get to know their staff. Sit in on an internal meeting, if possible. Learn how they interact with clients, and ask about other alliances they maintain so that you can talk to those firms. Offer them the same courtesies. Determine whether there is a philosophical fit and a true complementary connection rather than a duplicative one.

- *Task subcontracting.* Ask for samples of their work. Sit in on a workshop they are conducting. Ask for references from their clients.[4] Give them a sample situation, and ask for their resolution (that is, to provide some questions they would ask in interviewing under these conditions).

- *Conceptual subcontracting.* Ask for client references. Give them a situation and ask them how they would react (for example, a client's employee approaches the consultant and discloses confidential financial information). Describe the model you intend to use, and ask them to support it *and* attack it. Ask what their favored models are to see if there are conflicts (for example, the candidate believes that right-brain thinkers can't be organized in their work habits, a position that you find abhorrent).

- *Potential partners.* Spend an extended period of time together, professionally and socially. Collaborate on several projects. (I believe this is as important as a test drive prior to purchasing an expensive car.) Share detailed financial statements with each other and with appropriate financial advisors. Check client and professional references extensively. Bring in a third party to play devil's advocate to the venture. Convince yourself that the combined business will grow by at least 25 percent in the first year. Clearly delineate responsibilities and duties. Meet the other staffs and subcontractors.

---

[4] Here is an interesting and important dynamic: as useless as references are in standard hiring conditions, client references on consulting work are almost always highly useful. There are no legal problems attendant, and clients will be quite candid if you ask the right questions; for example, "Why is Joan better than other people you've hired for the same type of work?" If a candidate can't give you client references, she either has no experience or has not performed well.

Note that these are detailed, time-consuming activities. A lunch is not good enough for selecting a once-a-year survey designer, much less a future partner in your business. If you're not willing to invest this kind of time and energy, then you will never develop your business effectively.

If you fail to do this, you're leaving your own future to the trial-and-error method of random people selection. Incredibly, most consultants I meet spend more time choosing their electrician or their dentist than they do choosing the people who can have a profound effect on their future. (And they preach quite a different sermon to their clients!) By the way, this type of careful scrutiny allows for candidate self-selection.

The candidate is often the one who says, "You know, I'm beginning to realize that I'm not quite right for what you have in mind. But I think I know someone who is."

> *Hence, rule number 3: Invest all the time it takes for you to be absolutely comfortable that the person is right for the job.*

A final word about fees before moving on to the next section about rewarding people: I *never* offer a fee or a per-diem rate to subcontractors. In the first place, I want to wait until I'm convinced that the individual is appropriate for my needs. (This is the "conceptual sale" I talked about earlier as pertaining to clients.) In the second place, I want the subcontractor to cite a fee for *me*. I often find that such fees are extremely reasonable because the other consultant has not pursued a comprehensive fee strategy (they have not read Chapter 9), and I might have begun at too high a level. On the infrequent occasions when their fee is too high, in my opinion, but the candidate is excellent, I am in a position to negotiate. In any case, if I've made the investment cited earlier to determine what my needs are, established a candidate pool, and gotten to know each potential candidate, I'm on extremely solid ground about relative value added and commensurately appropriate fees.

> *Remember, never pay subcontractors based on the size of your project or provide them with a "piece of the action." Only partners get a piece of your action—because they are bringing you a piece of their action.*

COLLABORATION: POTENTIAL HIGHS AND DEEP, DEEP LOWS

Your business will grow substantially once your presence is no longer necessary to establish contact with a prospect. There are two conditions that create this salutary situation: (1) prospective clients call you (my "gravity" concept), and (2) others bring prospective clients to you. In the first instance, there is no reward or remuneration due anyone. In the second instance, however, there are these possibilities:

- You've received a referral from a client or other consultant with no reward due.
- You've received a referral from another consultant with whom you have a finder's-fee arrangement.
- You've received an assignment within an alliance relationship, and no reward is due because the other consultant has included your fee within the overall fee structure.
- You're contacted by another consultant who needs your collaborative help in securing, designing, or delivering the business.

Let's discuss the two situations in which you'll need clear guidelines for rewarding the people who deserve reward and are not otherwise covered: finder's fees and collaboration.

Finder's Fees

I said earlier that I don't usually demand finder's fees when I refer work to others, being content with the ability to influence the implementation and gain information from my colleague. However, there will be others who may request finder's fees from you when referring business (and you may wish to request such fees of others at times, which is quite proper and ethical).

I'm going to define a finder's-fee situation in this manner: finder's fees are paid on business that is referred and that would not otherwise reasonably have been obtained. Thus it is appropriate to pay a finder's fee for business that would not otherwise have come your way.

My position on the amount of the fee is

1. Fifteen to 20 percent for business that the other party has closed and that requires only your introduction to and acceptance by the client, and all you have to do is be sure not to insult anyone present

2. Ten to 15 percent for business for which your introduction has been arranged but your skills are required to close the sale

3. Five percent for a name of a buyer, where you have to create your own entry

4. A thank you and a small gift for cold leads that require your skills to obtain entry and close the sale and that eventually result in business

I don't pay, nor do I expect to be paid, for cold leads, which are names and background information that may constitute a marketing opportunity. These are simply professional courtesies that result from active networking and similar favors done for others. If a meeting with the buyer is arranged for you through the auspices of the referring consultant, then financial consideration is due if business results because the marketing process has been considerably shortened (velocity has been accelerated—see below).

Because your skills, repute, and decisions are instrumental in obtaining the business, 10 percent is adequate recompense.

However, if the business is conceptually closed by the referring consultant and that consultant's repute, skills, and decisions also have been responsible for convincing the client to consider your participation, the marketing process has been virtually completed. All you need to do is not spill coffee on the carpet or insult the buyer's spouse.[5] In such cases, a finder's fee of up to 20 percent is appropriate.

In both cases, I'm assuming that the referring consultant is not involved in the actual design or delivery of the project. Naturally, these fees are always negotiable, but I find these percentages to be equitable and commonly accepted. You also must stipulate the *duration* of the finder's-fee arrangement.

My position is that the arrangement is for the current assignment only unless it is a pilot, in which case there is justification for including the subsequent project if the pilot is successful. In some cases, when I am introduced to a key executive in a large organization, I will include a time period of up to a year for any business that results. While nothing is cast in stone, my rule of thumb is to ensure that the referring parties feel fairly treated so that they will refer additional business to me . One referral is merely a business event.

---

[5] Do not take this lightly. I was once concluding such a "done deal" when the buyer asked me if I'd like a cold drink. After cavalierly asking for a diet soda—which required a search—I took a gulp that went down my windpipe, and I spewed soda all over his desk. My last recollection of him is wiping soda off his leather-covered calendar and the graduation picture of his daughter. I no longer accept refreshments from anyone whose check has not yet cleared my bank.

Digression

For those of you who are professional speakers and pay 25 percent to a speaker's bureau for business, you need to reach an agreement on consulting business that flows from a speaking engagement. I'm unwilling to pay 25 percent of a six-figure consulting fee to a bureau, although 10 percent is reasonable. However, you must establish this before the fact. [See my book Money Talks: How to Make a Million as a Speaker *(New York: McGraw-Hill, 1999).] Some bureaus now ask for more than 25 percent and ask you to fund their marketing or buy the bureau's services, which is absurd.*

Continuing referrals are a consulting career, period. Providing only 10 percent of a $100,000 contract may be a short-term device to maximize your cash flow, but granting 20 percent or more for a $1 million contract is a long-term investment that will develop your business dramatically.

Collaborations

I've been in some sticky situations involving revenue splitting when two or more consultants collaborate. Otherwise amicable cooperation can be undermined when a colleague feels shabbily treated or when you feel you have been taken advantage of. Thus I've devised a formula, reflected in Figure 7-2, for rewarding collaborations that I communicate to anyone even approaching me with an idea. I want it clear from the outset. I've found that my colleagues are grateful for the concept, and I've never had difficulty with a collaborator who has accepted it.

In this system, an assignment is separated into three component elements: closing the sale, providing the technology, and implementing the project (you can choose a fourth or fifth if you like). Closing the sale involves getting the buyer's

	Sale ($\frac{1}{3}$)	Technology ($\frac{1}{3}$)	Delivery ($\frac{1}{3}$)	
Consultant A:	X%	+X%	+X%	= share
Consultant B:	Y%	+Y%	+Y%	= share
Combined:	$\frac{1}{3}$ project	+$\frac{1}{3}$ project	+$\frac{1}{3}$ project	=full project

Figure 7-2 A formula for sharing revenue equitably.

name on the contract, which may include onsite presentations, personal meetings, providing materials and references, convincing the recommenders, and so on.

The technology involved may be formal and tangible, such as test instruments, classroom materials, computer programs, and proprietary intellectual material. But technology also can be informal and intangible, such as skills in running focus groups, observations of operations, assessment of communication techniques, backstage counseling, and so forth. Technology encompasses the wherewithal—the talents, materials, approaches, skills, and judgments—that is necessary to improve the client's condition.

Finally, delivery is the actual implementation[6] of the technology. Tangible technology may be implemented by persons other than the owner or creator. Intangible technology is usually reliant on the personal skills of the possessor. I can equip someone else to use my model for establishing strategy, but I can't equip someone else with the skills and traits I use to develop the relationship that allows me to "shadow" and provide candid feedback to CEOs. Each consultant provides a portion of each of these three components, from 0 to 100 percent. Here's an example:

A colleague approaches me with a request to use my technology in establishing succession-planning systems for a client of hers. She is about to submit a proposal for $126,000.[7] She wants me to help her with the model I use and to spend some time overseeing her initial on-site implementation.

Using the model, we arrive at the formula shown in Figure 7-3.

I've reflected 100 percent credit to her for closing the business, 100 percent credit to me for providing the technology, and shared credit for implementation, reflecting her doing the preponderance of the work but my presence for oversight. She receives 58 percent of the total fee, and I receive 42 percent. I would not have had the business without her, and my implementation responsibilities are important but limited. She could not have closed the project

	Sale ($\frac{1}{3}$ = **$42,000**)	Technology ($\frac{1}{3}$ = **$42,000**)	Delivery ($\frac{1}{3}$ = **$42,000**)	
Her:	(100%) 42,000	+(0%)0	+(75%) 31,500	=$73,500
Me:	(0%)0	+(100%) 42,000	+(25%) 10,500	=$52,500
Us:	$42,000	+$42,000	+$42,000	=$126,000

Figure 7-3. Equitable revenue sharing: Example 1.

[6] Implementation, in my system, includes follow-up activities.

[7] Where did this number come from? See the fee structures in Chapter 9.

without my approaches, and she has the main implementation responsibility. I found this fair. So did she.

Let's look at another case: I approach you with a request for help in convincing a prospect to proceed on a strategy-formulation project. He requires a "show of force," and your name is recognizable in the field.

Your presence could be the deciding factor in the client's choosing our collaboration over that of the competition. We will both need to be present for implementation because the client will expect to see both of us regularly.

However, the technology is all mine, and you've used it in the past and are comfortable with it. The ultimate proposal is worth $240,000.

In Figure 7-4 we see that I'm receiving 70 percent of the total fee, and you are receiving 30 percent. The sale was set up primarily by me, but your presence was required to help close the business. The technology is mine, and we share equal implementation responsibilities. Is $72,000 fair compensation for you to lend your name to the proceedings and share equally in the implementation using my technology? Is your involvement worth $72,000 to me?

As you have probably observed, the serious discussions occur around the contribution of the collaborators in each of the three areas.

One Percent Solution: Sales acquisition is more difficult, by far, than developing methodology or delivering and should be rewarded accordingly.

Should you have received more than 40 percent credit for participating in the close of the business? Can we shift the implementation responsibility one way or the other, creating leeway in that area? These questions should be answered prior to the agreement on collaboration; they also can be used to reconcile inequities if

	Sale (⅓ = $80,000)	Technology (⅓ = $80,000)	Delivery (⅓ = $80,000)	
You:	(40%) 32,000	+(0%)0	+(50%) 40,000	=$ 72,000
Me:	(60%) 48,000	+(100%) 80,000	+(50%) 40,000	=$168,000
Us:	$80,000	+$80,000	+$80,000	=$240,000

Figure 7-4 Equitable revenue sharing: Example 2.

conditions change during the collaboration. (I've been involved in projects in which a colleague's technology was required more than anticipated, or in which the client requested one of us to play a more substantial role in implementation than the other.) Unlike finder's fees, this system *is* based on a "piece of the action" because the relative contributions of the collaborators are responsible for the action occurring. And what if one party feels that $72,000 isn't sufficient compensation for the time investment required for his half of the implementation? The answer is, either increase the project fee or don't enter into the collaboration.

However, don't be lulled into sacrificing the other party's share to make a colleague happy. This creates resentment, inequity, and, ultimately, unsuccessful collaborations. You cannot base collaborative fees on anything other than the total project fee and the appropriate contributions of each party. Individual fee structures or rates are beside the point.

(Note that you also can change the percentages; there is no reason that each contribution must be worth a third. Acquisition can be 50 percent and each of the other contributions 25 percent if you so choose. *I recommend 50 percent for acquisition, 30 percent for methodology, and 20 percent for delivery.*

Maximizing short-term cash flow is the act of a "lone wolf." Creating enduring relationships that provide referral business and collaborations is the mark of an established professional firm.

My credo is: "Always help the other person get rich." This applies no matter what relationship or fee system you prefer. I don't just want the *project* to be successful; I want the *relationship with my colleague* to be enduring, whether it's small referral business, situational alliances, reliable subcontracting, or large-scale collaborations. This is why you can use a reward system for others to help your business grow dramatically.

However, the accent must be on using others to develop your business, not using others to abandon your business.

LEVERAGE: DON'T GIVE UP THE SHIP

As you leverage your growth by working with and through other people, you will find yourself in various stages of disengagement from project details. This is difficult for those who feel that "I'm the only one who can do this correctly" and easy for those who feel that "I'm the dealmaker."

Too many consultants fall in love with their own methodology. Success in this business comes from marketing, not from the depth of consulting expertise. I know that this is heresy to many of you, but all the nonrainmaking consulting gurus are working for somebody else and merely earning a paycheck.

Someone else can do the legwork. The truth of the matter is that you are the key link in the relationship with your clients. While such a relationship should evolve to include others who work for you and your firm's image in general, it nonetheless ultimately depends on you. If your relationship remains sound, the client will always give you the benefit of the doubt. A poorly conducted briefing session by one of your people or a misdirected document from your office will not be the match that lights the fuse that blows the relationship apart.

Instead, the client will call you with the attitude that the two of you have a mutual problem or have both been the victim of a performance error.

No matter how many people you employ or subcontract with, focus on sustaining and evolving the personal relationship you've established with key buyers in each client. In some cases, this may mean that a significant portion of the project is delivered by you. For example, you may make the executive presentations and personally counsel the top officers. In other instance, you may simply have to visit the key people once a month or once a quarter to discuss the results that your team is producing. There often will be ongoing clients that require only a monthly phone call and a yearly visit.

The balance and perspective that you must constantly adjust apply to what I call the *velocity* of the sales process. The velocity is the rate of change in motion or position relative to time. The elapsed time of a sale in the consulting business is usually lengthy. In obtaining a new client of any magnitude, it's not unusual for six months to a year to elapse between the first meeting and the signing of a major contract. Anything that can be done to increase the velocity—the movement toward agreement on a project in as short a time as possible—is highly advantageous, whereas impediments to velocity can be deadly. There are few things as profitable as a project that closes within 30 days of your first meeting the buyer.

However, the elapsed time to secure *repeat* business is often quite brief. In many cases the client will ask you to undertake a project as a follow-up to one you are completing or to investigate issues raised that were tangential to the current assignment. Or the client will call you because "itch" has developed, and your prospect-based timing approach (see Chapter 2) makes you the right person at the right time, meaning that you make a sale instantaneously. There-fore, where is your investment better made, out on the street spending all your time trying to sell new business, or working with existing clients trying to max-imize repeat business? Where is the greatest potential to accelerate the veloc-ity of the sale?

> *Employing others is not a tactic that frees you from a client account. It is a strategy that allows you to further develop your relationship with that client.*

There are many more forces aligned against sales velocity within prospects than there are within clients. In fact, many of the forces working in opposition to velocity within prospective clients—for example, various internal agendas—can be turned into forces enhancing velocity in client accounts (when you're familiar with the internal agendas, you can strive to help meet them). Million dollar consulting means obtaining 80 percent of your business from existing clients, which both increases revenue and decreases marketing expenses. Not only is it more cost-effective to sell to existing clients and not only is it easier to make that sale, but it is also a higher-velocity sale.

> *One Percent Solution: Resources are a tool allowing you to move toward seven figures, not an anchor entangling you in five figures.*

Consequently, don't make the error of using other people (whether alliances, subcontractors, or employees) to free you up to pursue new business. While new business should receive attention, your top priority should *always* be to nurture and evolve existing client relationships. This is the pursuit that other people free you up to accomplish.

The fact that you bring a crew onboard doesn't mean that you give up the ship. It means that you have the leverage and the time to understand the work-ings of the ship that much better. When you use additional resources, you have the opportunity to do the following:

1. Arrange periodic meetings with the key buyer(s) to review the team's progress and discuss ongoing modifications to the project.

2. Use the team's observations and insight to develop a list of critical issues that should be presented to top management, separating those that are within the purview of the existing project from those outside it.

3. While the team is fulfilling assignments, spend nonstructured time with the client to observe and understand the essential aspects of the client's communications, operations, and interpersonal relationships.[8]

4. Invest time in getting to better know and establish relationships with other key members of management who were not a party to the decision to hire you. (This is one of the few occasions when a lunch meeting may be an ideal alternative.)

Case Study

One of the most effective client retention/expansion techniques I've ever seen was executed by the consultants (field engineers) of the Calgon Water Treatment Company when it was owned by Merck in the early 1990s. The field consultants would actually become part of internal client task forces, teams, and meetings. They were integral to the success of those bodies.

The clients would no more have considered replacing them (or looking for competitors when new projects arose) than they would have considered cutting their own residual talent. The former CEO at Merck/Medco, Per Lofberg, once cited me to his staff as that "insidious kind of consultant who becomes a germ we cannot get out of our system." I was quite proud.

5. Investigate practices within the client's competitors and/or industry practices in general to provide more insight into the client's condition and the kind of improvement possible.

6. As opportunities emerge, begin to formulate plans for addressing other issues through further projects. (Don't present these in a transparent sales effort. Simply have them ready so that when the

[8] Only a fee structure that is not based on per-diem rates will afford you this opportunity, which is why I find fees based on time so restrictive and why fee structure influences so much more than merely the amount of money you are paid. See Chapter 9 for a detailed discussion of fee structures.

client feels the "itch," you are ready to respond, thereby enhancing the velocity of the sale.)

7. Try to establish your team members as members of internal client task forces and committees. This is one of the most effective techniques I've ever observed in creating synergistic relationships, and one that can't be effective if you are a "lone wolf " trying to do everything. This is a prime example of using others to build your relationship.

Using other people within a client relationship is a technique to help you gain, not relinquish, control. Once you're onboard the vessel, you want to get to the bridge. And once you're on the bridge, you never want to give up the ship.

We're about to enter the middle of this section on tactics, and it's appropriate that we do so by discussing a central part of your business: fee structure. Thus far, we've covered your personal conduct and promotion, the affiliations that are possible with others, and the leveraging effect of using additional resources with clients. Let's move now to how that adds up to a million dollars.

QUESTIONS AND ANSWERS

Q. *How do I protect myself when I have to hire people I don't really know and can't afford to investigate thoroughly?*

A. Use them on a brief assignment in a low-key manner. Never ever throw untested, unvetted people into your major accounts. You're better off in that case working much harder yourself.

Q. *What if I simply can't find anyone good on short notice?*

A. Always investigate having the client's personnel take on a large part of the work, with the benefit of transferring skills to them. This is one of my key techniques for reducing labor intensity.

Q. *Some delivery people insist on a commission for any repeat business they generate. Is that a good deal?*

A. It's a good deal if you are sure it's not business that would have automatically resulted from the quality and effectiveness of the work. Don't forget, delivery people are very, very common and easy to obtain. Sorry, but that's the fact. Reward only sales that could not be expected.

Q. *What about collaborating with friends on a handshake or "gentlemen's agreement," or just the honor system?*

A. Don't. Ever.

Q. *How much money can I reasonably expect to generate working solely by myself out of my home?*

A. It depends on how smart you are, how non-labor-intensive your offerings are, and how much clients trust you. There is no limit. But there is probably a limit to how much money you actually need to gain discretionary time, the true wealth.

Final Thought: You are working mightily to build a business, taking prudent risk and sacrificing cherished moments. Do not become a slave to the demands of others who owe you their success. It may be excusable to accept demands from a terrific client, but it's never acceptable to bow to the demands of employees or subcontractors. It's your ship. Run it.

MAKING MONEY WHEN THEY HAVE "NONE"

HOW TO MAKE MONEY WHERE MOST PEOPLE CAN'T

NONTRADITIONAL MARKETS

There are entire segments of the economy that are outside the traditional corporate markets, but that need help in strategy and tactics as much as anybody else. At first blush, consultants tend to ignore them, with the exception of specialists in those areas, because they are too difficult to access, have little apparent money, or require an excess of attention.

The people who do specialize in the markets I'll be discussing in this chapter often suffer from limited opportunities, excessive turbulence from minor economic disruptions, and tight budgets. (I've worked with people who do outstanding work, yet starve—for example, in the educational market.) The answer, I believe, is to be willing to enter these markets when sufficient opportunity presents itself, but *not* to specialize in them. In fact, I've found that one of the most effective marketing approaches you can take in these areas is that you're bringing in a wider frame of reference, solutions, and experiences from much larger and diverse organizations targeted on the specific concerns of the specialized organization. In other words, it's an advantage that you're not a specialist.

Case Study

A medium-sized hospital not far from my home asked me to meet with the executive committee to discuss a reorganization project. The CEO explained that the committee had heard of me and read my books and had decided to talk to me, even though the members "realized that a hospital expert" was probably needed.

> *My allotted 45 minutes turned into 90. We got along famously. I could see that I had shaken their belief in the hospital expert requirement. Nevertheless, a month later, I was politely informed that the committee had chosen a hospital consulting firm from Massachusetts. The committee felt that the firm was "totally educated" in the field.*
>
> *Six months and several hundred thousand dollars later, the hospital was teetering on insolvency, the CEO had been fired, and the consulting firm was gone. An executive committee member whom I ran into at a play during intermission told me, "We should have had the guts to choose you. We would have avoided the incestuous advice and obtained a truly fresh approach."*

One Percent Solution: If it pays for you to network with people who do not know you, it also pays for firms to hire consultants they do not know, with the goal being to inject fresh air into stagnant rooms.

Trust me, you can't overemphasize the need for a breath of fresh air.

TWELVE CRITERIA FOR CONSIDERING NONTRADITIONAL PROSPECTS

Here are the criteria I would use in considering entrance into any of the following nontraditional markets:

1. The prospect comes to you requesting help.

2. The prospect is close to home and represents terrific economies for you (and for him or her) because of this proximity.

3. You have a superb lead to a buyer whom you can meet expeditiously.

4. You have worked with key prospect people in a pro bono cause, civically, in service clubs, or in a similar way.

5. You have, from experience or happenstance, learned a great deal about the operation (for example, a good friend worked there, or you once worked in such an operation).

6. You have a diversity of business, and this project won't consume your time and energy.

7. The project will add to your credibility and/or provide excellent referrals and testimonials.

8. The client clearly has a budget (for example, the organization is spending on marketing, travel, staff, and so on).

9. Your competencies (not necessarily your content knowledge) are a good match for the prospect's needs.

10. You have a passion for the cause or the goals.

11. You've worked successfully for the prospect's customers or suppliers.

12. You've spoken at one of the prospect's major trade associations.

If these criteria largely apply (that is, 7 of the 12), then you're probably wise to at least consider the business.

FAMILY-OWNED BUSINESSES

Family-owned businesses can be huge. Cargill and the Carlson Companies, for example, are multibillion dollar operations. They should be treated like any large corporate client that is publicly traded. I've done strategy work for a billion dollar construction firm that was privately held and paid taxes as a Subchapter S!

I'm talking here about the approximately $200 million and below operation that is closely held. These companies range from franchise operations to small manufacturers and from independent insurance companies to Internet experts.

The buyer here is almost always the owner. Assorted executives have very little buying power and are, in any case, loath to make major recommendations on expenditures. You must meet with the owner. Then bear these distinctions in mind:

- This is a highly emotional sale, *even more so than in the corporate world.* The owner generally considers herself an expert in everything because the company has been built successfully on her energy.

- You are competing with mortgage payments, kids' braces, tuition, and vacation funds. This is not an abstract "corporate purchase," but a direct competition with personal lifestyle and dedicated funds in many cases. You won't find that with the vice president of manufacturing for Toyota.

- If there are other family members in the business, there can be hidden veto powers. A trusted brother or aunt who is in charge of sales or finance can exert tremendous influence.

- Money will almost always be cited as an issue, but if you look around, you'll see that it's being amply spent on other things. True, there will be no budget for consultants, but the key to this sale is to focus on *value* and *advantage to the owner* so that a personal benefit is clearly defined. For example, there may be long-term goals of expanding, making an acquisition, taking more money out of the business, reducing travel, gaining wider recognition, and so forth that you can use as your leverage in the sale.

- There are new opportunities to promote. For example, spending for travel for a consultant will not be very acceptable, and your being local will be a significant advantage. Also, you can use local (and more easily gained) references—such as a lawyer or an accountant—that would be irrelevant for a large corporate entity.

If you see some advantages in this market (for example, the opportunity to travel far less in dealing with local people and the ability to gain referrals in a closely knit community), here are some marketing and sales techniques that work well:

1. Join local service groups, such as Rotary, Kiwanis, and chambers of commerce, and seek visible positions. These small business sales are often based on friendships within the general community.

2. Speak and conduct workshops at local business meetings. You can find these in the local paper at least once a week.

3. Write for the local business publications or business sections of newspapers.

4. Ask your lawyer, dentist, doctor, accountant, graphic designer, and other professional contacts for referrals. (You refer people as a courtesy to them, but they don't refer people to you because they seldom have an accurate idea of what on earth you do.)

5. Network among your neighbors and at social events.

Small business owners operate on two fundamental "buying signals." First, they absolutely must trust you because they are literally giving you money out of their own pocket. (I've had business owners literally take out a checkbook and handwrite a deposit check for me.) Second, they love to have local referrals, and references assure them that you're high quality.

When you actually obtain business (or are in the process of obtaining the business), here are some fail-safe techniques:

- *Always get at least a 50 percent deposit, and try to get paid entirely in advance by offering a discount.* Discounts are attractive in this market. However, the market is so sensitive to a myriad of personal and professional factors that a project can be canceled abruptly and a handshake rescinded. *Always get at least 50 percent of your fee on commencement.*

- *Include or ignore expenses.* The business is probably local, so don't "nickel and dime" by charging for mileage or duplication. Absorb all small expenses. Send a minimum number of invoices.

- *Document carefully.* There will tend to be misinterpreted conversations. (Owners are notorious for selective listening.) Summarize meetings in writing, and send hard-copy support. Create reports for this type of business. Make sure that you get a signed proposal or contract, no matter how firm the handshake. Explain that it is required by your attorney and your financial advisor.

- *Do get testimonials and referrals as the project evolves successfully.* Don't wait until the end. This community is rife for networking on referrals and endorsements.

- *If this is agreeable to the owner, consider local newspaper coverage for mutual publicity.* You also may want to play to ego and cowrite an article based on the project's success.

- *Never take sides in family disputes.* Don't allow yourself to become the "excuse" as to why one family member's ideas are better than another's.

- *Refrain from too much high tech.* You don't need PowerPoint presentations and intranets. Make these assignments as personal as possible (even if the client is a dot-com).

- *Don't accept bartered work, trades, "exposure," or referrals as your principal mode of payment.*

- *Don't befriend your client.* It will compromise your effectiveness and also lessen your ability to demand payment, support, and other resources.

One Percent Solution: Small businesses represent over 75 percent of all employment in the United States. Remember, you're providing value to a similar entity—you are also a small business!

- *At the first sign of trouble, stop.* If you're not paid on schedule, stop work until things are reconciled. If there is no access where access was supposed to be provided, stop until you find out what has changed. Remember, this is a turbulent and often unpredictable environment.

The family-owned business can be lucrative when the preceding conditions and techniques are considered and applied. I wouldn't want to make a living exclusively in this area, but you may be far smarter—or tougher—than I am!

THE PROFITABLE WORLD OF NONPROFITS

Peter Drucker, not exactly chopped liver on management standards, wrote that the Girl Scouts may be the best-run organization in America. Nonprofit has never been a synonym for noneffective.

Nonprofit organizations range from the United Way and the Red Cross, which are huge organizations, to the local Little League and shelters for battered women. They are ubiquitous across the land, and they represent huge infusions of time and energy. Just like their for-profit cousins, they are expected to meet budgets, retain talent, create positive public relations, provide for employee safety, and so on.

Nonprofit organizations have money. Management may regard it scrupulously and penuriously, but the money is there. The key is to convince the buyer that an investment in your value will further the goals of the nonprofit within budgetary constraints. Return on investment is the same in both worlds in terms of being a compelling force to determine success.

Case Study

I was serving on the board of a woman's shelter alongside the chief of police of the town in which it was located. During the second year of my term, the chief said to me, "We have to earn accreditation from the state, and part of that process is having a strategy for the department. I've been impressed by your contribution here and think that you can help us. Would you be willing?"

"Well, Chief," I stammered, "my pro bono dance card is rather full."

"Oh, we have a grant to pay for the help."

> *"Sit down," I yelled at the armed man "Let's talk ..."*
> *I wound up doing a strategy retreat for the top-ranking*
> *police brass (try doing that yourself when every participant is*
> *packing heat), and later, after my board term expired, I was*
> *invited back for pay by the shelter to do something similar*
> *for it.*
> *I'm constantly surprised at how stupid I was two*
> *weeks ago. There are a lot of ways to make money in the*
> *consulting profession.*

The nonprofit buyer is almost always going to be the executive director, unless you're dealing with one of the giants. The executive director is usually a full-time, decently paid professional who runs a staff composed of both employees and volunteers. However, there is usually also a board of directors to consider.

Board members of nonprofits are usually chosen for the wrong reasons—that is, they are "rewarded" for their fund-raising and/or their financial contributions with a seat on the board. In reality, board members should be skilled in governance, but they seldom are. I mention this because your proposal will often go to the board, which frequently must approve any major expenditure. At the board level, you must *not* provide a "dog and pony show." Instead, find out from the executive director who will be present at the board meeting, and create your presentation around them.

Show the attorney, for example, the legal safeguards or minimum risk. Show the accountant the great return on the investment. Show the state representative the terrific public relations effect. Treat each of these people as your customer, and demonstrate a benefit face to face.

One of the best ways to do business with nonprofits is through that very board. The chances are that right now you know people serving on the boards who aren't aware that you might have the answer to some of their challenges at the nonprofit. Network among your friends and professional colleagues. Attend fund-raisers and special events hosted by the prospect.

Some of these boards actually comprise more than 30 people! It's hard *not* to know at least a half-dozen of them if the nonprofit is local!

> *One Percent Solution: Nonprofits have a success motive*
> *that's equal to a profit motive. Show the key players how you*
> *will help them meet and surpass it.*

Here are the distinguishing characteristics of local nonprofits that may be helpful in marketing to them:

- *They almost always demand a discount or a deal.* You should be prepared to point out that you do not have a separate nonprofit fee schedule or discount because you treat them with the same responsiveness and energy as any private-sector client. (Believe me, their bank, their cleaning service, and their legal representatives are not providing discounts.)
- *Much of the staff will be dedicated but essentially uncontrollable volunteers.*
- *The executive director will need the board's support for any new initiatives.*
- *Publicity, fund-raising, additional volunteers, and enhanced constituency services are the major "hot buttons."*
- *Convoluted models and plans aren't well accepted.* The more straightforward and simple your proposed intervention, the better.
- *Decision making is slow.* Plan to make frequent contacts.
- *State grants and other funding sources are often used.* You may have to qualify under the grant procedures or provide additional documentation.
- *It is often possible to arrange external sponsorship for your work.* For example, a huge local bank may be willing to subsidize your complete fee in return for the public image of supporting a fine cause. Explore this—and suggest it to both the nonprofit (there might be a precedent) and a local potential benefactor (there also might be a precedent).

Use the board both ways. You can enter the nonprofit through the board member contact, but you can also enter the board member's organization via the outstanding work you perform for the nonprofit. This is a wonderful revolving door that's right in your own backyard. You also may be able to parlay this into publicity with the local media, both print and broadcast.

Some consultants make their livings entirely in the not-for-profit world, helping with grant writing, government regulations, volunteerism, solicitations, governance, and so forth. This may seem like a tough way to market, but if you add up the nonprofits that exist within a gas tank of your home base, you'll find that it's an exceptionally rich market in which not many consultants are actively soliciting business.

Once again, if you can pick and choose and add this area to your repertoire, it may make a wonderful augmentation to your income stream.

Digression

If you choose to do pro bono work (provide services for free, which you should never do for a for-profit), I suggest these criteria:

- *You believe passionately in the cause.*
- *You establish clear parameters, no different from those for a paying client.*
- *You expect and demand full participation from the nonprofit staff.*
- *In return, you request a platinum-plated testimonial.*
- *You have access to the board, so that it can choose to avail itself of your services.*
- *You receive appropriate publicity for your work in the media.[1]*

B2B AND A TO Z

The so-called business-to-business (B2B) dynamics have been emphasized over the past few years, but I find this marketplace to be unpromising. I haven't changed my mind about this since the last edition of this book.

Essentially, I'm talking about businesses that simply cater to other businesses, such as an Internet firm doing Web design for other small businesses or a graphic designer who creates brochures for professional firms.

There has been an even further narrowing of this category to electronic B2B (the market which has never met the hype surrounding it, created by people who want to sell you ideas for mining it).

One Percent Solution: If the deal sounds too good to be true, it's probably illegal or unethical. Do you really seriously consider the oil futures that are peddled over the phone to you at 8 p.m.?

I believe that the key here is to treat these companies as if they were any other small business (and they are almost always privately held). The B2B aspect is immaterial. After all, they need to

---

[1] Note that donated services are *not* tax-deductible.

- Find and attract new customers.
- Expand their product and service offerings.
- Gain competitive market share.
- Grow intelligently (most tend to overexpand early).
- Gain public awareness and repute among prospects.
- Lower their costs dramatically.
- Lessen the costs of acquisition.
- Create annuity business (customer retention, notoriously weak).

Do *not* get involved with the following:

- Taking on a project for a "piece of the action."
- Becoming a franchisee yourself.
- Agreeing in the project to personally solicit business.
- What is now called "multilevel marketing," in which money is derived almost solely through membership fees paid by new members. This was once called "network marketing" and even earlier a Ponzi scheme.

Treat this as a typical client engagement, with normal understandings and safeguards. These firms are almost always short of cash, so tread carefully. Frankly, of all the markets I discuss here, this is the one with the least potential and the greatest downsides.

Case Study

A member of my mentor program became passionate beyond belief about B2B to the extent that he became a franchisee, invested money, and allowed his own $250,000 consulting business to take a backseat.

A year later, he had lost his investment, was spending an inordinate amount of time trying to extricate himself, and had a $75,000 consulting practice left.

This is not the road to million dollar consulting.

Unless you have an exceptional relationship and a wonderful (cash) deal, eschew B2B work. You'll be romanced and courted, but this segment can waste tremendous amounts of your time and energy.

STILL OTHER PEOPLE WITH MONEY

Where else can you work? More places than you think. Here are sources of consulting that I leaped on when I needed to put bread on the table and/or that I continue to entertain when they come my way at no risk and with interest for me:

- *Professional firms.* There are dental, medical, accounting, design, contracting, and other firms that need help with an acquisition, a sale, acquiring talent, and so on. They are usually run by people who are highly skilled in their craft (dentistry), but in little else because they've had a specialized education and a highly focused business experience. They require situational help. Speak for free at their awards ceremonies or other events.

  I've helped consultants become specialists in the sale of medical practices. (One was an attorney who quintupled his income, moving from a lawyer's hourly billing to a consultant's value-based fees.) *Caveat:* Be careful with legal firms. I've found that it's nearly impossible to move them off their own ridiculous hourly billing practices in terms of how they should pay consultants, and they are notorious nitpickers. This has not changed since this book was first published in 1992. The only legal association or firm that has hired me to help it radically rethink its business was an Australian legal association in 2008!

- *Start-up companies.* Regardless of the state of the economy, there are always enterprises being born. The founders are usually adept at their technology and methodology, but not much else. They need help with marketing, public relations, cost control, and so forth. A great way to make inroads inexpensively: establish relationships with venture capitalists (who fund such start-ups), and convince them that their huge investment in the company can profit from an "insurance policy" in the form of your work with management, ensuring intelligent operational decisions.

  These start-ups are commonly associated with dot-coms, but every day there are new dry cleaners, coffee shops, contractors, small manufacturers, retailers, and so forth.

Digression

The personal coach or "life coach" has become an acquisition with great cachet of late. All good consultants have had to coach. You don't need a specialized certificate from some boot camp on coaching. (Who certifies the certifiers?)

> *Entrepreneurs, executives, business owners, athletes, entertainers, and myriad others whom you might not traditionally reach are often in the market for a personal coach.*
> *If you have the skills and passion, pursue the opportunity by adjusting your Web site, press kit, publishing, and other marketing efforts accordingly.*

- *Entrepreneurial coaching.* Associated with these start-ups are the entrepreneurs who make them happen (either by founding or by funding them). Many are thrust into positions that are new to them: facing the media, managing staff, and working with banks. They need a personalized and often private coach.

  I've seen successful coaching done with political candidates, local media personalities, recently promoted small business people, new firm owners, and a host of others who are smart enough to realize that their past skills and behaviors may not be adequate for their new accountabilities. This is also a great market for referrals, meaning that a few good backstage coaching assignments will turn you into a local "celebrity": "You really need to get Jane Thomas to help you in your new position."

- *Franchises.* The franchise marketplace is growing (especially as people become disenchanted with corporate work), from auto body repair to donuts. You can help here on either end. The franchiser will want local outlets to hit the ground running, and beyond the corporate training program (sometimes great, sometimes nonexistent), there is a good case to be made for help "on the ground" as the new enterprise ramps up.

  At the local level, the new franchisee may see the need to ensure success with the temporary help of a nearby and accessible consultant. In either case, it's a great market for a process consultant who can help with business acquisition, staff practices, and advertising without regard to the nature of the business. (Remember, no content expertise is needed.)

One Percent Solution: Look around as you go through your day. With whom are you doing business locally? What firms do they represent? What nontraditional sources can benefit from your expertise?

- *Local outsourcing*. I've worked with several consultants who specialize in human resources expertise for small firms that can't afford their own in-house capability (and probably shouldn't). They come in as needed and help with hiring interviews, terminations, training, conflict resolution, reward systems, and so on.

  You can do the same thing with safety (a member of my mentor program does nothing but Occupational Safety and Health Administration compliance and audit preparation and makes a great living at it, and another who focuses on compliance with the integrity and safety requirements for personal information stored in corporate electronic records), purchasing, accounting, information technology, and so on. Outsourcing is huge in major businesses, so there is no reason why you can't do it on a micro basis and make a fortune without ever leaving town.

Case Study

I've been approached periodically in my career to help with what are euphemistically called "multilevel marketing" efforts. My value system does not embrace this market, which essentially makes its money from recruiting new members and distributors, not from selling products or services. At some point, of course, the potential new recruit pool dries up, and the last people in the programs—in other words, most people—make virtually no money.

These recruitment efforts based on paying original members with newer members' fees began life as Ponzi schemes (named after the original perpetrator). They evolved with political correctness to pyramid marketing, then to network marketing, and now to multilevel marketing. I don't buy it, despite the absurd claim that they give everyone a chance to succeed.

Legitimate businesses must contribute value to the environment in the form of products or services for customers. I've proved in other books that by the time you reach the sixth or tenth round of these schemes, you'd need a population the size of Cincinnati to provide a profit for people who are just joining as distributors.

Thus you won't read about this market in this book. Million dollar consulting is about win/win, not win/lose.

- *Local trade associations and professional groups.* These are ideal not only for income, but also for marketing. They may be local chapters of national organizations or associations that are specifically focused on local conditions. I've spoken, for example, at an awards ceremony for independent insurance agents and run a strategy retreat for the Rhode Island Junior League. I charged each far less than my normal rates, but I made good money for brief work within 20 minutes of my home.

  In addition to the paid gig, you'll be in front of scores (and sometimes hundreds) of people who fall into several of the preceding categories, either as buyers or as recommenders. It's relatively easy to find the local executive director or program director and discuss your participation.

- *Serendipity.* You never know when someone might be appropriate for your assistance. Keep your ears open at social and civic events. Read the local newspapers assiduously. (I know a woman who says that she never reads the local newspaper because the *New York Times* provides everything she could possibly need. Sure, everything except local business leads.)

  I was referred to a one-week (actually, three-day), $18,000 local project at a $20 million company because the owner was referred to me by the president of the university where I once taught one evening course a semester. I taught that course because I volunteered to do pro bono work for the president when I read that he had been appointed and moved from out of town to take the position. He and the small business owner met at an awards ceremony.

  On another occasion, my wife, a member of the League of Women Voters, arranged for me to moderate the debate between candidates for attorney general on the local public television station. That led to business at a small business awards ceremony, which in turn produced business with a dozen small businesses that I never would have approached (and that never would have approached me). All of this occurred without a penny being spent on marketing or business acquisition. The total business exceeded $50,000. Keep your radar in action, and keep watching the screen.

There is a plethora of diverse markets outside your door. I've added this focus as a separate chapter in this edition of this book because it is more important than ever for consultants to fully recognize and exploit all the potential that's in front of them. Turbulent economies and uncertain world events make this a prudent course of action.

Don't worry about this type of business detracting from your "brand" or your repute. I've successfully worked with the largest companies on the planet as well as with local entrepreneurs. Being competent at one doesn't disqualify you from working with the other as long as you manage your business and your image effectively. You don't want to lead with small and obscure markets in your corporate marketing literature, for example, although the local market may be impressed if you use national references and examples to demonstrate the "bargain" that the local firm is getting just by dint of your being resident in the same neighborhood.

QUESTIONS AND ANSWERS

Q. *What about the start-up entrepreneur who wants to give me a piece of the action instead of a fee?*

A. Over 95 percent of the time, these "ownership" options are worthless. Accept the deal *only if* you also collect cash up front; you don't need the money for your cash flow or bills, and the amount you are offered is significantly higher than your fee would have been. These are almost always bad deals.

Q. *Small business owners often want to pay for "performance." Is this reasonable?*

A. No, because you don't run the company, they do. You can't possibly control all the variables involved (What if two key people leave or a competitor develops a new technology?), so it's unfair for them to expect you to be reliant on anything other than the quality of your own work.

Q. *How do I approach a board of 15 people that the executive director claims will debate and make the final decision on my being hired?*

A. Start with the chair and establish a relationship. Take the position that you are evaluating the board as a potential client, just as it is seeking to evaluate you, so you'd appreciate a chance to meet the chair and establish a relationship.

Q. *I've been approached by firms that claim they will provide me with consulting research, leads, and tools, such as personality profiles, to use for a set fee. Isn't this a good example of business-to-business connections?*

A. No, but it is a great example of your giving your money away. Find out how many people in the firm were top, high-earning consultants themselves. You'll find that they were not, and that they are making their living by selling to consultants, having never sold to clients!

Q. Nonprofits are always crying poverty, and it does seem as though they are impoverished. Can't I cut them a break?

A. You can cut them whatever you like, so long as they cut you a check. Not long ago, the CEO of the United Way was making in excess of $400,000 per year (he was later dismissed amidst a scandal). The managing directors and executive directors of local arts groups with budgets of several million are generally making six figures. You have to pay for talent, and that includes consulting talent.

Final Thought: You may want to consider a second set of marketing and collateral materials—and even a separate Web site—for these smaller markets to keep them segregated from your larger marketplaces. This eliminates any worry about confusion over your focus or your brand and simultaneously provides the image of concentration on each market.

STOP THINKING THAT TIME IS MONEY

IF YOU'RE CHARGING A PER DIEM, YOU'RE STILL JUST PRACTICING

DON'T BE AS DUMB AS THE LAWYERS

For those of you who have turned directly to this chapter, welcome to the book, but let me apprise you that there is some material in the preceding chapters that has a bearing on fee structure. By way of review, here are some instances and conditions that might justifiably cause you to cite fees at levels *below* your usual level.

- To gain access to an industry or client with large long-term potential
- As a subcontractor who is experiencing no marketing expense
- As a referral who is experiencing no marketing expense
- For a long-term client with major potential still ahead who is asking you for special consideration
- For pro bono work or work for nonprofits and public agencies
- To gain other benefits, such as instructions, referrals, testimonials, travel, and so on

Note that none of these reasons includes "tough times" or "business is slow." Whatever your fee structure is—and we'll examine several alternatives in a moment—you must adhere to it. If you do, you'll find your business growing steadily over the long haul. If you don't, then your approach is "whatever the market will bear," and your short-term income will be at the expense of your long-term wealth.

Fees are part and parcel of your overall strategic approach to your market. They should never constitute your single driving force, nor should they be dictated by the client or the competition.[1] Moreover, there is nothing unprofessional about saying, "I can answer that when I learn some more and have time to consider how we might help you," in response to, "How much?" However, once you say, "We charge $1,500 a day plus expenses," you've had it. From this point on, your fee can only decline and your margins erode. (And you are shortchanging your own value. Think about this: failing to get an additional 20 percent that you deserve over two or three years can easily add up to seven figures of lost *profit*.)

What I call the *formulaic method* of establishing fees is one that I don't favor but that requires explanation because it is so often advocated by individual consultants and principals of small firms. It's actually a strictly arithmetic approach that begins with your determining what level of income you require to support your desired lifestyle. (Note how delimiting this is from the outset. By establishing what you'll "need," you are already capping your potential.) For our purposes, let's say that Charles Consutant determines that $200,000 in after-tax money will support his lifestyle, pay tuition, provide for a vacation, and afford some savings after the pretax (company) money pays for medical and retirement plans and assorted fringe benefits. Thus Charles calculates that a gross income from consulting of $280,000 will provide for company expenses, personal expenses, and personal taxes.[2]

Now sharpen your pencils. Charles calculates that there are 220 working days available to him during the year once he subtracts weekends, holidays, and vacation time. Of these, he estimates that he will be booked 70 percent of the time, meaning that he will allocate the remaining 30 percent to marketing, promotion, and other non-revenue-generating activities. (If you have employees, these nonrevenue days multiply like libidinous rabbits, which is why Chapter 7 discourages full-time employees.) This leaves 154 days available to generate revenue. If we divide Charles's $280,000 revenue needs by 154 billable days, we arrive at $1,818 per day.

---

[1] In my strategic consulting work with a wide array of organizations, I've found that very few are driven by profit. Almost all businesses are driven by their products, services, markets, technology, or related strategic areas, with profit a derivative of success in that pursuit. Consulting firms are no different. For an excellent discussion of these driving forces, see Benjamin B. Tregoe and John W. Zimmerman, *Top Management Strategy: What It Is and How to Make It Work* (New York: Simon & Schuster, 1980).

[2] If you have a chapter C firm, it should always break even at year's end or show a *small* profit or loss. The preponderance of the profit should be taken out as salary; otherwise, you will pay a corporate tax on earnings and then an individual tax when you ultimately take these earnings out. Any large loans to you will be interpreted as dividends, which also will subject you to double taxation. Incorporated personal service firms of this type should not show large profits. Your banker will be sufficiently happy to see the sales figure that translates into personal income. However, Subchapter S and LLC firms allow income to flow through your personal tax return, so no such machinations are necessary, another advantage of the latter two forms.

Thus, using this formula, Charles should establish a per-diem fee of $1,800 per day. Therefore, when he formulates a proposal for a project, he knows that his time must be accounted for at the rate of $1,800 per day. Or if a client asks, "What will it cost for you to spend two days with us?" Charles knows that $3,600 will cover it.

Candidly, this backward calculation of a daily rate is amateurish and, worse, severely self-limiting. However, so many consultants inappropriately cite daily rates that I want to take the time to explain why they are such a bad idea before moving on to more fertile ground. For the newer people, avoid this miasma. For the veterans, get out of your rut.

What happens if your lifestyle needs are $450,000 a year? Is this so ridiculous? It's not even "half of million dollar" consulting. A couple of kids going to good schools, a decent vacation or two, the luxury of a wonderful house to return to after time on the road, intelligent retirement planning, elderly parents who need support, philanthropic work—these are not uncommon events or desires. Moreover, if you are undertaking the major risks of being on your own, you should at least be in a position to enjoy commensurate rewards. It is silly to take major risks when your return is less than it would have been staying in traditional organizational life.[3]

At $450,000, Charles's per diem would have to be about $3,000 a day. This is not all that uncommon for big names in the business, but it's stretching it for most people, no matter how talented and how endorsed they may be. And what of a desire for $1 million? Well, that comes to $6,500 a day, or $4,500 if you worked every one of those 220 days and did nothing else. Daily rates are limited because they are based on a finite resource: time.

There are substantial risks in this profession—and substantial rewards. It is ridiculous to assume the former without capitalizing on the latter.

Why on earth would you want to work every potentially billable day? Wouldn't it make sense to spend more time on the other elements of growth I've discussed, including personal expertise and repute? And why not take four

---

[3] Ben Tregoe, an early mentor and member of *Training* magazine's "Hall of Fame," once told his staff during a heated discussion of company benefits, "We're all refugees from large organizations—that's why we love this profession." I'm continually astounded by people who seem willing to take significant risk but are reticent about seizing proper reward. I once advised a strategy client that if his goal was only a 5 percent return on the business he owned, he ought to liquidate the business, invest the equity in government securities, and sleep better at night.

vacations a year or spend time watching your kids play soccer to make up for the nights you weren't there to help with their homework? Billable days place emphasis on activity, not on result. The measure of your success at year-end isn't the number of days you've worked but the amount of money you're able to keep. Period. Banks won't give you credit lines based on billable days worked, and no one will be impressed by the amount of time you spend on airplanes. A focus on per-diem rates established by determining financial needs will focus you on the wrong activities and waste your precious time and energy.

You want to encourage a collaborative relationship with the client within which the client feels free to call you at any time. This includes people *other* than the buyer who signs the checks, so a multitude of people can call you without incurring an expense, thereby making you more valuable to more people. When clients are on a daily rate system, they hesitate to call you for help when they may really need you because they are forced to constantly evaluate their request in terms of real-time, current expense. They must make an investment decision every time they may need you! Consciously or unconsciously, they are calculating, "Is this problem worth $2,500 to have Charles come over? What if we find that he'll need three days—it's not worth $7,500, is it? Even if it is, we'll be better able to afford it next quarter." These conversations occur all the time in these circumstances.

Let's face it, if days of your time are your fundamental device for making money, you are going to try to maximize the days of your time that you use. This is human nature and is often basically survival. Consequently, when you create a proposal or respond to a request for help on a particular problem, your tendency will be to maximize your involvement, although the consultant's *real* value added is in improving the client's condition with minimum involvement. It is extremely difficult to establish the types of relationships I've been discussing when you are citing a daily rate to a client and then describing the number of days you will be needed. It's that much more difficult for the client to commit to the keystone of the relationship—allowing the consultant to determine whether he can improve the client's condition—when the qualitative benefit is viewed within the context of the quantitative measure of days required and costs per day.

> *One Percent Solution: Fees are based on value, not on your time, which has no intrinsic value to the client. You can always make another dollar, but you can't make another minute.*

If you are perceived as selling days, you will not be perceived as an equal partner in the relationship. And the converse of the client's hesitancy to call you is your hesitancy to suggest legitimate additional investigations because such pursuits, no matter how justified by the project, mean that you're suggesting more self-aggrandizing days.

Finally, your scheduling and energies will be hampered by the need to minimize time use. It's grueling, for example, to conduct employee interviews or customer focus groups. I limit myself to a half day of interviewing or two focus groups a day, for example. However, if the client sees two half days of interviewing, there will be a normal question about why the interviewing couldn't have been combined into one day, saving the client one day's per diem.[4]

Sometimes you can best schedule client work or combinations of client work and your own marketing activities in portions of days. As long as the client results are met within the deadlines agreed upon, the particular activities and timing you use shouldn't be the focus. But they inevitably will be if the client perceives that the way you spend your time is directly proportional to your fees.

> *If you want to make a million dollars or more in this profession, charging by time units isn't the route for getting there. Not only are the amounts self-limiting, but the opportunity for multidimensional growth also can't be exploited if maximizing days at the client is the driving force of your business.*

When prospects request a day of my time for which they'll pay a fee if our discussions *don't* lead to a project, I usually request that only my expenses be paid. This pleases the prospect, gives me an opening edge in building the relationship, and makes me very objective about the discussions that day. Personally, it's an essential component in my strategy to "think of the fourth sale first," not the immediate one. You have to invest money to make money. Have prospects demanded that I cite a per diem rate? Of course. And I've always declined, stating that I work on a project basis only and that our collaborative responsibility for results dictates that the client's people should never be hesitant to call me and that I don't ever want to be hesitant about spending additional time on site whenever I feel it's necessary to achieve our goals. If the prospect can't work that way, then I'm never going to establish the relationship I need, and I'm not interested

---

[4] Don't even think about charging by the half day or by the hour. Assuming that you're traveling, you can't use the other half day for anything else, and your financial calculations for the year are based on a full per-diem rate for a day with a client. Besides, can you picture a top executive saying, "We need consulting help. Get me someone who has a reasonable hourly rate"? Technology consultants in particular fall into the "hourly trap."

in short-term income. (Remember, we've heard every objection under the sun, and it's simply negligent not to be utterly prepared for them.)

A final word on formulas that result in daily rates: yes, I know that attorneys and kindred professionals scrupulously assess hourly fees. Most attorneys, however, don't do as well as Charles Consultant's $280,000, much less $1 million. And attorneys don't establish relationships; as a rule, they provide a technical commodity—legal advice and representation.

How many individuals or corporations view attorneys as collaborative partners, and how many view them as necessary evils? The attorneys who make the most money are those who take contingency fees. If you win, they win. If you lose, they lose. This is as close to collaboration as the legal profession gets.

Dick Butcher, a character in *Henry VI*, says, "The first thing we do, let's kill all the lawyers." I'm not certain, but I believe he was reacting to their billing system. Besides, doesn't it bother you that attorneys only "practice" law?

In the United States, lawyers bill in 15-minute intervals, which is completely crazy until you consider the fact that Australian attorneys customarily bill *in 6-minute increments*! How can they attend to their business? At this writing, the average solo practice attorney in the United States. makes less than $100,000 per year.

I ask you again: who wants to be as dumb as a lawyer?

> *Since the original edition of this book in 1992, the premise that has become most popular and that has most become identified with me in the consulting profession is value-based pricing. During that period, consulting firms of all sizes around the globe have asked me to help them convert to this approach. A decade later, this should tell you something. So have architectural, design, and accounting firms. But not one law firm.*

DEMAND AND SUPPLY ARE NEITHER

One of the easiest methods to use in establishing fees is simply to emulate the competition. If you are networking effectively and talking to clients regularly, it's relatively easy to discover what the average rates are. Then you can make a determination as to where you want to position yourself within that range. For

Activity	Range
Consulting day, on-site	$750 to $2,500*
Consulting day, off-site (in office, research, etc.)	$500 to $2,500
Keynote or other brief speech	$500 to $5,000
Half-day workshop	$1000 to $3,500†
Full-day seminar	$2500 to $10,000
Executive retreat, per day	$2500 to $7,500
Systems (i.e., succession planning) implementation	$10,000 to $50,000
Employee or customer surveys	$15,000 to $100,000+
Strategy formulation	$50,000 to $150,000
Organization or department diagnosis	$50,000 to $200,000
Organization redesign and restructuring	$100,000 to $500,000

* Many consultants will assess fees by the half day or even by the hour. I've found hourly fees from as low as $35!

† These are sometimes billed "per participant," ranging from 100 to 500 per person, especially when the consultant is providing formal, proprietary participant materials. Hence, a class of 25 people might result in a total fee of $2,500 to $12,500, depending on the perceived value of the takeaway materials.

Figure 9-1 Fee ranges for various activities. Market demand requires that a consultant take a position within a range.

example, Figure 9-1 shows the average ranges I've found for the activities listed.[5] These rates vary with experience, geography, and even the client's urgency, but the ranges encompass the predominant fees assessed at this writing.

If you determine that your client and prospect base is accustomed to paying $2,000 to $4,000 for a day's consulting help and you have embarked on a strategy of assessing per-diem rates, then you must decide where in that range you wish to be positioned. Do you want to be seen as the most economical alternative? Will such a position help get you in the door and enable you to obtain more lucrative contracts as a result of the quality of your work? Or do you prefer to establish at the outset that the client gets what the client pays for and that your value-added help more than justifies your position at the higher end of the

[5] Since I've already discussed the weaknesses of being activity-oriented, it should come as no surprise that I don't favor the market-demand approach to fee structure. However, these comparisons should prove to be of help in comparing your current billing practices.

fee range? Do you intend to use the entire range as a negotiating technique and attempt to get whatever the market will bear?

If you are going to use a market-demand system for establishing fees, I think it should follow the sequence displayed in Figure 9-2 so that the underlying, consistent basis for your fee decisions also reflects your longer-term strategy.

In the figure, the sequence calls for isolating the various activities you will be undertaking for which you are assessing fees. You then evaluate the prevailing market ranges for each activity. Now comes a step that most consultants completely ignore: you should apply your strategy to the individual ranges. For example, if your strategy is to enter new clients as an economical alternative with the intention of building long-term relationships and increasing revenues as a result of a multitude of assignments, you will tend to position yourself toward the lower end of the ranges. The exception will occur in those activities for which you may need outside expertise, licensed approaches, subcontracting help, and so on. (This is why the activities should be evaluated separately; some will be more cost-effective than others.) Having applied this strategy and considered your resources, you can assess a fee for each activity, the sum of which adds up to your overall project fee.

> *One Percent Solution: You have a "supply" of 365 days. But wealth is discretionary time. Hence, you could easily increase your income while decreasing your wealth.*

The lack of a systematic method to arrive at fees in the market-demand approach can result in one bad situation and one catastrophic one. The bad situation occurs when you lose business because your fees are too high when

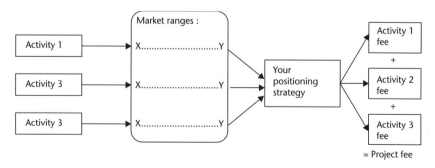

Figure 9-2 Establishing market-demand fees. Strategic planning takes precedence over "what the market will bear."

compared with the perceived value added. The catastrophe occurs when you obtain business for which you've cited much too low a fee when compared with the perceived value added.

The fee may reflect 1 activity or 20 activities. The total fee may be substantially different from someone else's fee because of the strategic positioning factor. By using this method, however, at least you are able to arrive at market-demand fees that *also* reflect your image to the client and your longer-term market plans. It is the absence of this systematic determination that creates a trial-and-error method for the consultant and tremendous confusion for the client. Despite the improvement in using a system to arrive at market-demand fees, the entire approach suffers from some severe shortcomings that must be considered carefully when establishing a fee structure:

1. There is a tendency to be constrained by the ranges, never approaching the higher end and settling comfortably in the middle as a safe, noncontroversial position. This will never lead to dramatic growth.

2. You are helping the prospect to make comparisons based on the activity and opening the door to comparative shopping based on fee rather than focusing on conceptual agreement on objectives and consideration of value added.

3. There is a tendency to charge whatever the market will bear irrespective of value added and longer-term strategy. When fees are based solely on the client's ability and willingness to pay, the basic collaborative relationship (we will work together to improve your condition) cannot be established because a win/lose relationship (the more you can pay, the more I can make) preempts it.

4. It is very easy to be "positioned" by the market. That is, clients and prospects frequently compare notes (particularly if you are intelligently building referral and repute business). It is difficult to charge one client a higher rate than another for what the client perceives as an identical assignment, regardless of legitimate differences in preparation, tailoring, resource use, and other elements that may apply to one and not to the other. "She implements a performance-evaluation program for $25,000" is a far inferior statement to "She is the best at implementing performance-evaluation programs tailored to your particular needs and situation."

5. A key long-term growth strategy calls for providing current clients (who should be constituting about 80 percent of your yearly business) with more favorable fee arrangements than new clients. After all, current customers shouldn't be subsidizing new ones.

A market-demand fee system inhibits this strategy because it's difficult to decrease your position in the range continually without creating excessive pressure on your own margins. Also, your current clients will be citing your current—not your original—fees when they refer you to prospects. This is a difficult box from which to escape.[6]

6. You are locking yourself in to rates, and a client will *never* say, "Those were your rates when we began, but I think they should be higher now." With value-based fees, on the other hand, it's easy to raise fees by demonstrating more value and a higher ROI.

Market-demand approaches to fee structuring are somewhat superior to formulaic methods based on income needs. However, I hope you'll appreciate that they are rather short term in their strategic orientation and can be highly superficial and transparent to clients and prospects alike.

I've been advocating the improvement of the client's condition and the consultant's value-added contribution to that improvement as the litmus test for effectiveness in this business. Let's see how this ethical starting point can also form the basis for establishing fees based on perceived value. This, I've come to realize, is one of the core elements of growth in our profession.

THE VALUE FORMULA

The quickest way to become wealthy in this profession is to do superb work and to be paid high fees. I've tried to establish a foundation for the position that fees will always be artificially depressed as long as they are correlated with arbitrary, objective measures, such as days, hours, projects, numbers of people, and the like. The secrets of receiving high fees are

- Create a great perception of value.
- Base fees on the client's perceived value of your assistance.
- Ask for them.

Here are two examples of the role that value plays in establishing fees. In the first instance, one of my clients approached me with a request to design a training program that his company would market through his offices around the

---

[6] One of the surest signs of a consultant simply charging what the market will bear is that of new clients actually paying lower fees than existing ones. When existing clients learn of these inequities, relationships that took years to build can be destroyed in an instant. This is another reason why market-demand fees can be antithetical to long-term relationships.

world. However, he wanted me to accept a smaller fee in return for a percentage of the sales. I usually turn down contingency fees and was ready for a healthy negotiation, but he hit me from behind. He opened with, "Alan, this has nothing to do, and everything to do, with your value. I couldn't begin to pay you fairly with a fee based on value. It's strictly a matter of my ability to pay. Oh, I could pay you $40,000 or $50,000, but your work here would be worth well into six figures. That's why I want to offer a royalty with no time limit."

Well, he had me. I wasn't prepared for that attack, with him conceding the value issue and turning it into *his* argument! It was one of the few instances in which I've done work for "a piece of the action."

I used this same reasoning with my financial advisors not long ago. I felt that their bill was too high because of incorrect billing allocations. (They bill by the hour and fraction, which is cumbersome and, I'm convinced, severely limiting.) Their hours should be declining, even though their value to me is increasing. However, they bill on the former, not the latter!

"David," I explained to one of the partners, "don't misunderstand, your value to me is substantial, and I have no complaints about the quality of the work. But over the past several years, as I've adhered to your reporting and detail requirements, the hours needed to plow through my books should be steadily decreasing. I think your people are applying incorrect measures."

My financial advisors are limited. They can audit my books and calculate my taxes only so many times, and they can't raise their hourly rates beyond certain competitive points. Further, my mundane work—the bulk of my financial reporting—increasingly requires junior, lower-billed partners. You see, it wasn't a matter of value, just one of numbers of hours—their loss, my gain. They reduced my fee, to their credit (and to the bizarre nature of their utterly senseless billing system).

One Percent Solution: Tasks are repetitive when they are repeated, and repetitive tasks, should cost less because of economies of scale. Outcomes, however, are more and more valuable as they are repeated and annualized.

Establishing fees based on value requires adherence to these conditions:

1. You never cite a fee before you're prepared to do so, no matter how much pressure the client exerts. "Just give me a ballpark estimate," is a request that will always land you in the bleachers, not the box seats. Ballparks are surrounded by concrete walls and iron fences.

2. You must be willing to live with ambiguity. You have no responsibility to provide the client with numbers of hours worked,

numbers of reports prepared, your payments to subcontractors, or any expense other than travel documentation. In fact, if a client focuses on these issues, you haven't made a conceptual sale. You must be willing to cite project fees that fairly represent your value to the client plus your expenses in fulfilling the assignment.

3. You must spend time building the relationship to the point that the sale is made conceptually and *all* important decision makers are onboard. At this point, even if your value-based fee isn't accepted automatically, it will meet much less resistance, and any negotiations can be handled much more easily.

4. If the client does want to negotiate the fee downward, do so by explaining the kinds of value that will be lost with each decrement of the fee. Never take a position in which you lower the fee but do not remove services and value. The client has the choice as to how much value justifies what investment, but should never have the choice of benefiting through your sacrificing your margins. This is not collaborative. This is a transfer of wealth from you to the client (value provided for no investment).

5. Be prepared to walk away from business. Once you are perceived as someone who will negotiate fees downward, you will always have pressure on you to do so. I once worked for a training firm that was so poorly managed that it always lowered its fees in the fourth quarter in·order to meet its plan. New fourth-quarter clients benefited, often at the expense of longtime clients who had ordered earlier in the year. Consequently, everyone began to wait for what our clients called "the fire sale," and 65 percent of the company's business occurred during December! You must be perceived as someone who does superb work, requires a high investment, and will not lower fees without the client commensurately sacrificing value.[7]

One of the most fundamental distinctions of million dollar consultants compared with the rest of the field is their willingness to turn down business. The vast majority of consultants accept any assignment on the grounds that something is better than nothing. They ultimately relegate their professional lives to such trade-offs.

---

[7] For over 70 ways to increase fees, see my book *Value Based Fees*, 2nd ed., (San Francisco: Jossey-Bass/Pfeiffer, 2008).

Once I had to find a subcontractor to produce a video to accompany a project I had designed for a client. I knew that more such collaborations would be necessary, so I needed a firm that I'd be comfortable with for the long term. I searched in Providence, Boston, New York, and Chicago. Video production firms provide estimates based on commodities: editing time, number of crew members, number of actors, background music, visual effects, and so on. The estimates for my video work—the exact same specifications were provided for all of the 12 firms I'd selected—ranged from $10,500 to $47,000! All the bells and whistles were the same. However, the firm that established the best relationship with me (collaborated in choosing actors, invited me to lunch, showed an interest in longer-term work, and actively listened to my editing ideas) cited a fee of $11,400.

There are several lessons here, not all of them obvious. First, there is that terrible box constructed by citing fees based on activities and tangible deliverables. The comparisons were odious at the high end. Second, it helps to shop around with such firms, and your prospects will shop around just as I did if they can make such clear comparisons. Third, if you are at the high end in such commodity offerings, you'd better be able to differentiate your services. ("Why are you charging $40,000?" I asked a New York firm's account representative. "Because that's what we all charge," he replied vaguely.)

Fourth, however, is the fact that the company I chose could easily have charged me three or four times as much, and I would have accepted the fee in light of its excellent relationship building, had I not been placed in a limiting fee structure of its own making! That firm could easily have cited a fee of $30,000 without breaking it down by number of crew members or actors' pay and by emphasizing the way in which its team would work with me, the team's willingness to hold unlimited meetings and involve me in the editing.[8] These are valuable opportunities that I can't easily put an individual price tag on. In fact, I ultimately invited my client to the shooting, with the blessing of the production company, and he was very impressed at the effort on his behalf. This was worth a lot to me, and my value was enhanced in his eyes. (The production firm has since gone out of business, which is a great regret but hardly a great surprise.)

Believe it or not, a great deal of my advice to other consultants—as well as to contractors who work on my house, local businesspeople, and entrepreneurs—is that they are charging too little. But guess what? Except for a tiny fraction, they are all afraid to raise their fees because they are unable to embrace the preceding five conditions.

[8] "Unlimited meetings," like "an open-door policy," is an offer that is virtually never abused. I've never experienced a client requesting unnecessary meetings because the client's time is as valuable as mine. Hence, this is always a good offer to make, and I always make it in writing.

Basically, the value formula you should be using resembles this:

- Quantitative benefits times duration, plus
- Qualitative benefits times emotional impact, plus
- Peripheral benefits times perception

$$\frac{\text{Peripheral benefits times perception}}{\text{Fee}} = \text{Value}$$

THE VALUE DISTANCE

When you boil it all down, how do you know how much to charge? Figure 9-3 contains the questions I ask. Now remember, these questions are asked in view of the five conditions cited earlier being met. Many of them I ask the client, and

---

1. What is the outcome of this project worth to the client?
   a. If quantitative, what is the amount?
   b. If qualitative, what are the effects?
   c. How does the client describe a successful outcome?
   d. To what degree is the client's condition improved?
2. What is your direct contribution to that outcome?
   a. Are you accelerating what would have occurred anyway?
   b. Is the outcome dependent on your unique talents?
   c. Are you facilitating or also delivering?
   d. Are you observing, diagnosing, or prescribing?
3. What is your current relationship with the client?
   a. Is this a longtime client?
   b. Does this assignment provide for professional growth?
   c. Does the assignment present stressful conditions?
   d. Are there difficult deadlines?
4. What are your costs to complete the assignment?
   a. Was there marketing cost or other costs of acquisition?
   b. To what degree ate subcontractors required?
   c. Are there extensive travel requirements?
   d. Are there materials or other deliverables required?

Figure 9-3 Establishing the value of the client's investment. These questions help to determine value-based fees.

some of them I ask of myself. Note that none of them refers to the client's budget. If this turns out to be a constraint in terms of the fee you arrive at, you can then negotiate down by sacrificing value.

In addition, the client must view the fee as an investment, no different from an investment in education or new equipment or better security. The focus then turns to the *return* on that investment, and the return is a far superior point of negotiation than is your fee.

Practicum 1

Let's say that you've been asked to design and implement a new performance-appraisal system for a client. You've done these before, and you have a model that has been very effective. You've done a succession of projects for this client, and you know the operation well. You estimate that you'll need about 20 days of your time and two subcontractors for 10 days each. There will be some administrative work and a few reports, plus the new forms you'll design. You estimate the following project fee:

Personal time	
15 days onsite @ $1,500	$22,500
5 days offsite @ $1,000	$ 5,000
Subcontract time	
20 days @ $750	$15,000
Administrative time	
40 hours @ $25	$ 1,000
Materials and deliverables	
Printing, collating, artwork	$ 1,000
Total project fee	$44,500

Assuming that the client pays all expenses, your gross margin is 62 percent, out of which you're paying for lights, rent, phone, and so on.

Practicum 2

Let's apply the questions in Figure 9-3 to this scenario.

1. The client estimates that the performance-appraisal process requires about $400,000 a year in management time, and feedback indicates that about a quarter of all the time spent is redundant—correcting errors on feedback sheets caused by poor directions; misunderstandings of the process, necessitating retraining; and ratings overruled by superiors who don't agree with subordinate assessments because of earlier inability to reach agreed-upon performance goals. A successful outcome also would vastly improve morale because the

current evaluation system is widely viewed as a paper-pushing exercise, not as a legitimate assessment of contribution.

2. The client knows that the system must be changed and is particularly impressed by your approach, which uses employee focus groups to create "ownership" of the new system, and by the fact that you've implemented it successfully in organizations that provide glowing references. You are prescribing the solution and designing the system, working with the client's human resources group to implement and assume responsibility.

3. This is a long-standing client who has been a pleasure to work with. It will be a relatively easy project because you know the client and possess the model. It should allow you to be considered for increasingly sophisticated organizationwide assignments.

4. There was no marketing whatsoever on your part. Time demands on you personally are reasonable. Other costs equal $17,000. The client will pay all travel expenses.

Based on these considerations, the value to the client, and your contribution, the client's investment will be $86,000. This is a gross margin of 80 percent.

One Percent Solution: Fee setting is both an art and a science. The science is easy, because you have to accept some ambiguity to assist in the art.

The worth to this client is a minimum of $100,000 in salary annually, plus the morale factor. The conceptual sale is tight. On the other hand, this is a long-term client with significant potential, and the model is already in existence.[9] You know that you have fixed costs of about $17,000, and you should allow for inevitable contingencies bringing this to $20,000. Thus the range for this project is probably from about $50,000 to $100,000. Given your positioning strategy, you decide that $86,000 represents an equitable investment given the return. (The client agreed in real life.)

Could you have charged a fee of $79,500 or $91,750? Probably. Just as you could have charged the $44,500. Now don't go screaming down the hall. I said that there would be ambiguity. You have to determine a comfortable fee—an

---

[9] This is strictly a pragmatic consideration. You have every right to charge for proprietary intellectual material and approaches every time you apply them, just as a royalty is paid on a song every time it is played commercially or a book every time it is sold.

acceptable client investment, in light of the value that is the client's return on this investment. *This is your responsibility.* Excellent restaurants charge not merely by the cost of the meal ingredients, but also by the ambiance and service—the entire dining experience. First-class airfare is not based on the size of the seats and certainly not on the caliber of the food alone.

> *The ultimate test of a value-based fee system is the client's acceptance of the investment in terms of the value perceived.*

How much is a kidney transplant worth? How about a cast for a broken leg? Almost any doctor can do a good job with a cast, but very few can transplant a kidney. And do most people choose their doctors based on their fee, their bedside (well, office) manner, or their quality? (When was the last time you heard the demand: "Get me the cheapest brain surgeon you can find!"?)

Value-based fees are not a technique for the faint-hearted, in the sense that you have to make some bold decisions (albeit with input and cooperation from the client) about the improvement in the client's condition and the justifiable investment in achieving it. This is why the conceptual sale is so important and why value-based fees are utterly dependent on it.

Once the client agrees on the value, the investment becomes quite reasonable. No one gets something for nothing. And this brings me to the second point raised at the beginning of this section. Once you've understood your own worth and value to the client, you can establish fees that equitably reflect that contribution. Then you have to ask for them.

What I call the *value distance* (see Figure 9-4) is the perceptual movement created by proceeding from what the client believes she wants (a training program)

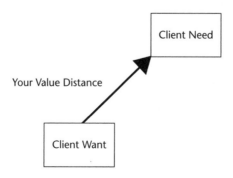

Figure 9-4 The value distance.

to what is really needed (a new relationship with clients that creates less attrition and more repeat business). That's the movement that takes you from a $15,000 "event" to a $115,000 consulting project based on highly valuable outcomes.

HOW TO RAISE FEES AT ANY TIME, WITHOUT RAISING CAIN

No matter what system you're using to set fees, you should periodically evaluate whether they should be raised. If you're using formulas, then your basic needs and aspirations may have increased. If you're responding to market demand and competition, you may find yourself inadvertently lagging. And especially if you're using a value basis, you have to determine the current value for the client and your current worth to the client.[10]

> *The absolute indicator of when to raise fees is when your value increases in your client's view.*

You should review the appropriateness of your fee philosophy every year because, with proposals in the pipeline and negotiations ongoing, it's likely that an increase won't hit your books for 12 to 18 months. For this reason, proposals should always have effective dates specified; for example, "The terms and conditions of this proposal are effective through August 31 of this year. Acceptance after that date may necessitate increased fees or altered conditions." It's not all that unusual for a client to pull out an undated proposal a year after the fact and announce, "Surprise! I just got the budget approval, and I sold the project to the committee." If that work now involves subcontractors because of your own changed circumstances, your margins could suffer seriously.

Other Reasons for Raising Fees

You Are Not Perceived as a High-Powered Organization because You Are So Inexpensive

Don't laugh. Raising fees can increase business by forcing your proposals to be approved by higher-level management, which has higher budgetary limits. This

---

[10] As a rule, distinctions that are locked into products or strict discipline tend to diminish in worth because conditions change, competitors move in, and approaches become passé. Distinctions linked to talent and relationships tend to increase in worth because talent can adjust to changing conditions and relationships are intrinsically valuable.

is a very effective strategy for the bold at heart. I decided to do it after becoming disgusted with a General Motors training manager who told me he wanted "the cheapest proposal possible" in order to save as much of his budget as possible.[11] Who needs this guy? (And I don't hesitate to point out that I've done much better than General Motors over these ensuing years. Accident? I think not.)

You Are Asked to Do Important Work
That Is Personally Unattractive

Higher fees really do offset unpleasant assignments. My wife tells me this every time I miss a social event for an assignment that sends us on another vacation, and I tell myself every time I'm in a town where the restaurants all close at 9 p.m.

You Want to Distance Yourself from the Pack

If you find that you are bidding on proposals with other firms among which there is little differentiation, you already know that several of them will attempt to bid low. Very few of them, if any, will deliberately bid high. By doing so, you will force the buyer to examine the value-added dimension you bring to the table. It's your job to ensure that it is distinct from the others.

You Want to Test the Waters

I spoke in earlier chapters about expanding the envelope. Remember the second rule of the preceding section: you have to ask for the business. How do you know what you're worth if you don't use the market to try to find out? If clients have been accepting proposals for two years at $75,000, instead of finding new ways to pat yourself on the back, maybe you should be investigating why you haven't been charging $125,000. It's not worth it? Says who? Only the client can determine worth, and if you don't give the client a chance, you'll never really know.

To summarize, develop a strategy for fee increases no matter what system you are using, and particularly if you are basing fees on perceived value.

One Percent Solution: You must abandon existing, low-margin clients if you are to have the energy and capacity to reach out to new, high-margin clients. You're doing those clients a favor even more than you're doing yourself one.

---

[11] Some years ago, I delivered an afternoon speech to Atlantic Electric for $7,500 and the exact same speech that evening for free as a pro bono gesture to the Rhode Island Personnel Association. The utility executives thought it was the greatest thing since cold beer; the personnel association sat there like stumps. Go figure. I'm more convinced than ever that not only do people get what they pay for, but they *perceive* that they get what they pay for.

When you do raise your fees, one thing almost always happens: you lose the bottom 15 percent of your market, both current and potential. However, this is okay. I talked in earlier chapters about growing at the top of your market by abandoning the bottom end, and nothing will do this faster than a fee increase. It is difficult at first to turn down business. "Gee," the client will say, "we really want to use you, but we can't possibly afford that amount." There is obviously no conceptual sale here based on value, and there may never be. Some clients aren't interested in value; they are interested only in activity and budget. These are the clients who will fall by the wayside as a result of fee increases, and this is all well and good.

FORTY WAYS TO RAISE FEES

Let's end this chapter with 40 pragmatic ways to increase your fees. You may want to copy these and hang them on your office wall (or the ceiling of your bedroom):

1. Offer options of increasing value with commensurate increasing investment.
2. Never discuss fee, only value. Allow the buyer to see the actual fees only in the proposal itself.
3. Gain conceptual agreement on objectives, measures, and value to the client and buyer prior to creating a proposal.
4. Link the buyer's personal objectives with the goals of the project.
5. Respond to pressure to lower fees with the offer to remove value.
6. Never ever quote a time-based or time-and-materials fee.
7. Make comparisons with other client's investments (for example, equipment maintenance, errors, failure work, travel) that show the project investment to be extremely reasonable in comparison.
8. Provide a discount for full fee paid in advance.
9. If you're local, emphasize that expenses are included. If you're not local, consider calculating them and including them in the fee.
10. Talk about both the immediate annual return *and* the longer-term annualized return.
11. Consider the nonquantitative benefits, such as alleviated stress, better repute, enhanced communication, and so on.
12. Cite the fee as an investment and focus on return on investment rather than on costs.

13. When confronted with how "others" or "the last consultant" did it, explain that your method is better for the client.

14. Point out the ethical conflicts in time-based billing.

15. Bear in mind that when you're dealing with six-figure fees, a swing of $10,000 one way or the other doesn't matter at all (and with five figure fees, a few thousand dollars doesn't matter).

16. Provide so much value in the initial meetings that the buyer will ask, "What would I get if I actually hired this person?"

17. Create very clear project objectives so as to avoid scope creep and margin erosion.

18. Pay subcontractors by the time unit or other means, but not by a percentage of the project.

19. Stick like glue to the economic buyer. Refuse—*refuse*—to deal with purchasing managers, lawyers, or human resources directors for the negotiations.

20. Abandon the bottom 15 percent of your business at least every two years to allow yourself the capacity to accept higher-fee business on a regular basis.

21. Practice stating high fees in the mirror without falling down giggling. This destroys the effect in front of a CEO. (Yes, I'm serious about this.)

22. Charge a premium if you do all the work yourself (without subcontractors) to create a "single filter" or to maximize confidentiality.

23. Charge a premium for overseas work (for example, I add 50 percent for Europe and Latin America and 100 percent for Asia and the Pacific Rim, since I live on the eastern seaboard of the United States).

24. Accelerate your payment schedule and follow up ruthlessly on receivables over 30 days old.

25. Turn down bad business. It will cost you more than you'll ever make from it.

26. Collaborate with those who can secure large accounts and for whom you can increase value.

27. Make sure anyone you hire as an employee can bring in significant new, value-based business.

28. Seek out economic buyers laterally during your implementation work.

29. Respond to scope creep requests by sending a new, amended, larger proposal.

30. Don't allow the dreaded scope seep, wherein you volunteer to do more work.

31. Raise fees to create perceptions of higher value. Play to the buyer's ego.

32. Introduce new value to existing clients to raise fees for current clients.

33. At year-end, emphasize early payment, since many organizations have to use up any leftover budget money.

34. Practice saying, "We can do that together." Don't hesitate. Jump at the opportunity.

35. If payments are late, pursue the buyer, never the accounts payable people or intermediaries.

36. Have the client absorb all expenses, bill monthly, make your terms "due on receipt of invoice," and follow up in 30 days if you're not paid.

37. Quote in U.S. dollars drawn on U.S. banks, which is a huge benefit when you're doing business outside U.S. borders, even in Canada.

38. Build strong brands and nurture them, because people will come to you asking how you can work together, meaning that fees are no longer even an issue.

39. Never allow taxes to be deducted from your fees. It is never warranted. Check with your attorney.

40. Keep "boilerplate" wording out of your proposals, or they will wind up in the legal department. See the previous section about "who wants to be as dumb as a lawyer?"

RETAINERS

Retainers represent access to your smarts. They are not projects—nothing that you implement, nothing that you execute. They are methods of compensation for the client's being able to call upon you for advice and counsel.

There are three conditions to assess in a retainer relationship:

1. *Who?* How many people will have access to you? Only the buyer, his team, or others?

2. *Duration.* Will this be for a month, a quarter, or a year?

3. *Scope.* Is this during eastern business hours if you live in New York, or western business hours because the client is in San Francisco?

Would you make appearances on site, or only via e-mail and phone? What about weekends?

Having assessed these criteria, create a retainer fee per month. My suggestion is that no retainer be for less than a quarter, and that it be payable at the beginning of the period, so a $7,500 monthly retainer would be payable on the first of the first month of the three-month period, with $22,500 due. If the client opted for six months, then reduce the fee somewhat, e.g., to $40,000.

Allow both the client and yourself to make a decision about renewing early in the last month of the period.

Beware: never allow a retainer to cover unrestricted client work in the form of a succession of projects, or you will kill yourself. Retainers are strictly for access to your advice (which is usually easily done remotely and even time-shifted), though occasional appearances may make sense. They would then be "plus expenses."

I'm using *retainer* differently from the way lawyers use it, as they are only asking for a deposit against their hourly billing. I'm using it to refer to an amount paid to guarantee access to you over some finite period. Go back to the "art and science" aspect: never worry about "how much access," because clients never abuse it. I've had clients call me once a month and feel it was well worth the money, because the timing and urgency were critical to them.

As you become a more seasoned consultant, more and more of your business should become retainer business, which not only dramatically increases income on a non-labor-intensive basis, but also adds to your real wealth: discretionary time.

QUESTIONS AND ANSWERS

Q. What if my fee could have been lower after I get into the project?

A. So what? If the client is getting value and feels that there is a strong ROI, that's all that matters. You're not a Realtor, who is allowed by convention to make only 6 percent, before expenses, on a house sale!

Q. What about performance fees and contingent fees?

A. If you're going to accept a piece of the action, make sure you receive some cash up front, and make sure you don't need the money for your living expenses. My experience is that for every secretary who says she got rich with Google stock, there are a million people who took a piece of the action and wound up with pure air.

Q. *What if the client asks me the basis for my fee structure?*

A. Anticipate that question, and say something like this: "My fee is based on my contribution to the value you derive from this project, providing a dramatic ROI for you and equitable compensation for me."

Q. *What happens if other consultants are charging by the day and seem much less expensive than I am?*

A. You have to demonstrate (1) that you are far more valuable, and (2) that it is actually more cost-effective to pay a fee based on value (e.g., with no meter running).

Q. *If I'm not getting any business, isn't that an indicator that my fees are too high?*

A. No, it's an indicator that you're not establishing a trusting relationship with the buyer, who would otherwise say, "We'd love to use you, but can you do something about the fees?" (At which point you demonstrate the ROI on your value, and offer options.)

Final Thought: You can never go back and recoup lost fees. The earlier and more aggressively you establish high fees, the richer you will become. Period.

MID-BOOK INTERLUDE

FOR BOOMERS, SECOND CAREERS, RETIREES, AND MATURE NEWCOMERS: HOW TO TURBOCHARGE YOUR START

WHAT'S THE SCORE?

It's appropriate, here in the middle of the book, to talk directly to those of you who are in midlife, personally and/or professionally. And the lessons reflected herein will apply to those of you who may be younger and just starting a practice, as well as to those veterans who may be seeking a "fresh start."

Test yourself on the following traits and strengths if you're seeking to start or reestablish a solo consulting practice, and score yourself on a scale of 10 (I have this to the nth degree) to 0 (I don't have a clue and would have to acquire this).

1. Business experience in any sector to the point where I can readily discuss business issues, understand balance sheets, and generally display business acumen in conversations. (Score): _____

2. A plethora of contacts from my prior and current business, social circles, old school ties, civic activities, professional trade groups, and extended family. _____

3. Some knowledge of counseling or coaching or consulting, gained from participation, collaboration, observation, or some other means. _____

4. Discretionary time that I can apply to creating the logistical support and promotion needed to launch my new endeavor. _____

5. A support system of family, significant others, friends, and/or colleagues who will provide solicited feedback and encouragement. _____

6. Sufficient funds to maintain a conservative lifestyle for a minimum of six months without any new business or funds emerging. _____

7. The resilience to accept rejection and learn from it, to bounce back from disappointment, and to abandon ego so that I can continually learn._____

8. Business or community connections in areas such as graphic design, computer help, printing, and technology that can be accessed readily and with confidence. _____

9. Technological and Internet familiarity to the extent that I can easily research, find contacts, move files, create spreadsheets, and so forth._____

10. Distinctive skill sets in processes, such as problem solving, conflict resolution, strategy, financial analysis, decision making, risk assessment, and so on._____

Tally ho. Here's the analysis:

- 80–100: You are safe making a major commitment and investing whatever you can to charge ahead.

- 60–79: You need to shore up some areas, which you can do concurrently with your start-up, but make specific plans to acquire what you're lacking.

- 40–59: Make a plan to acquire what you're lacking in both contacts, skills, and behaviors before you make your full-time consulting investment. Plan to take six months or more to do so.

- Below 40: You're not ready, and the deck isn't just stacked against you, it's missing the face cards. Spend at least a year preparing, and then reassess.

Keys: You really need to score yourself at least a "7" in numbers 1, 2, 4, 5, and 6. That's 35 points right there.

WHAT'S THE ROUTE?

If you want to ramp up rapidly for million dollar consulting—say, hit $300,000 very quickly and grow from there—here is the best route.

Establish the Fundamentals

Set up an office, at home or elsewhere. The key is privacy and insulation from kids, deliveries, and random interruptions. Home offices are fine provided that anyone else living there knows the rules; for example, when the door is closed, consider it locked; never use the business line, even if it's accessible on other phones in the house.

Establish Your Conceptual Base

What is your value proposition (how will the client be better off once you leave)? This should be expressed in a single sentence as a business outcome for the client so that it informs both your behavior and the prospect's questions.[1]

Who, by title, are the probable economic buyers who can authorize a check for that value?

Create the Collateral

Begin with a physical press kit (media kit, presentation kit), which minimally includes

- Typical client results (typical, not historical, so be creative).
- Array of your services.
- Biographical sketch.
- Client list (if you have one, or "organizations we've worked with" if you did so under other auspices).
- Testimonials (if you have them).
- White papers (position papers) of two to five pages each, nonpromotional, providing insights and pragmatic help around your value proposition. (Have about six of these in there, with your copyright and contact information, fold-overs, not stapled, on good paper.)

Now, find an outstanding Web designer and duplicate this electronically. Remember, this is for credibility, not for sales, so adjust the message accordingly. You want to come across as an expert, not a slickster.[2]

Create letterhead, business cards, and labels of high quality with professional design. Use four colors, not two. If you can't afford a designer, hire a student in the art program at a local college; the result will suit you quite well until you can afford to make a change down the road.

---

[1] This is not the dreaded and ineffably stupid "elevator speech." If you live in New York and start talking to people on elevators, you're very likely to find yourself thrown off on a floor you hadn't intended visiting.

[2] The best guy in the country for this is Chad Barr at chadbarrgroup.com.

Begin Marketing

The question here is how to reach your buyers (from above) and how to enable them to reach you.

To reach the buyer, immediately do two things:

1. Call everyone you know. Contact everyone who is part of your plethora of contacts (see question 2 in the self-test) and ask these two questions once you've explained your value proposition:

   a. Could this be of use to you?

   b. Whom do you know who could use this, and would you be willing to introduce me?

   If you do this religiously with your 75, or 180, or 325 contacts, you will receive leads. However, you must be comfortable and shameless (see question 7 on the self-test).

2. Target 12 people. Choose a dozen (or 8 or 13) organizations within a two-hour drive of your home that meet most of these criteria:

   a. They are doing well (so they have money to invest).

   b. They have a history of using external help (read the press, talk to employees).

   c. They appear to have a need for your kind of value (do some research online or with people who know the company).

   d. You have some premise or excuse for making contact (they were featured in a local news article, you heard the president speak at a meeting, you met a key manager at a social event).

   Send the probable buyer a simple letter expressing your value, enclose your press kit, and indicate that you will call to follow up at 10 a.m. on Friday (or whenever).[3] When you call on Friday, tell the assistant or secretary that you're "calling as promised." (If you can't find someone's phone number or e-mail address, call the switchboard and say you'd like to send the individual a letter of compliments about something.)

Create Market Gravity

If you draw people to you, there is a reversal of the usual dynamic ("Prove how good you are") because of your brand or your repute ("I've heard you're good; how can we work together?"). The gravity chart is shown in Figure 2-3.

---

[3] Key marketing mistake: suggesting that people get back to you or that you'll follow up at some vague future time.

However, I'd suggest you begin with the big four of gravity:

1. Speak wherever you can where buyers and/or recommenders gather. Do it for free if you must, but leverage it by recording it, getting names, providing handouts, and mingling before and after.

2. Network like crazy. Networking is not "working a room" or spending wasted hours on LinkedUp or Facebook. It means attending events where you can meet critical buyers. Here are Alan's five networking secrets:

   a. *Distance power.* People who know nothing about you have no preconceptions or misconceptions to shed. You're actually better off networking with strangers!

   b. *The unique multiplier.* Find people who, though they are not buyers themselves, know a great many buyers because they are a supplier, customer, mutual club member, advisor of some kind. That one contact can lead to many solid introductions.

   c. *The nexus person.* Find the person who can provide an immediate introduction to an important buyer. This may be an assistant ("My boss should meet you"), a relative ("My cousin needs this"), even an ex-employee ("My boss at my last company is looking for someone like you").

   d. *The adhesion principle.* Why should this person remember you? You have to "give to get." Always provide value immediately (an idea or reference) and future value ("May I send you something?"), and then follow up to see if it's been of help.

   e. *The contextual connection.* Remember that you're usually together for a common purpose—an awards ceremony, fund-raiser, political event, community activity, and so forth—so make the most of your common interest to create an immediate relationship.

3. Publish wherever you can, whether in newsletters, magazines, online, on others' blogs, or somewhere else. Get your message out. Sometimes small, specialty publications will reach your potential buyers far better than mass media. If possible, write a regular column.

4. Use the Internet. Add value to your Web site weekly. Start a highly focused newsletter. (The reason there are so many electronic newsletters is that people are reading them.) Begin a blog if you have the time and energy and content (see questions 1 and 4 in the self-test). Find reporters' queries and try to be interviewed (see the Annotated Resources for some logical approaches and resources).

Act as If You Mean It

Once your marketing is being introduced, don't act as if you're entering the business; act as if you're an expert in the business.

- Dress well. Have a couple of great suits and appropriate accessories to make a highly professional first appearance.[4]
- Join the appropriate trade and professional groups and seek a visible, leadership position.
- Write letters to the editor that are relevant to your value proposition whenever and wherever you can.
- Send out press releases at least twice a month to announce new ideas, speeches, client work, and so forth (see Associated Resources).
- Seek alliances with other solo practitioners or larger firms if there is specific business that can draw you together and make the whole greater than the parts. ("Conceptual" alliances are a waste of time.)
- Engage in continual self-development. Seek to raise every score to a 10. But be careful to whom you listen. Your avatars should have a proven track record of success in areas that are important to you. Ignore arbitrary "certifications" and diplomas. The key is: are you learning from the best of the best?
- Blow your own horn, or there is no music. Let people know of any and all successes.

What are you going to be doing to be perceived as a top consultant in your field?

> **One Percent Solution: We are here not to survive, but to thrive.**

WHAT'S THE POINT?

You and I are not in this business to make money. We are in this business to add value to clients, which will earn us equitable compensation (if we assess our fees correctly).

---

[4] Some things that do not cut it: men with dyed, chestnut brown hair—go grey or bald, it's okay; women with plastic shoes—buy good leather and wear hosiery; a cheap pen to take notes—use a Cartier or Mont Blanc; looking like a pack animal—take notes during a meeting, don't move in with your own office equipment.

You and I are not in this life to run a business. We live to fall in love, to help others, to contribute to the environment in which we find ourselves, and to apply our talents in as many ways as possible.

Hence, we don't have "professional lives" and "private lives." We have lives. You have a life. The question is how to best enjoy and share it.

Here are some best practices and best learning that are exclusively presented here. Having just conducted the eleventh Million Dollar Consulting® College, and always learning more than anyone else, I'll share some insights:

- If you don't understand something, do two things. First, question it immediately, because otherwise the ensuing structure will have a weak foundation. Second, try to apply it in your circumstances to integrate the learning.

- People learn in different ways, so notes, recordings, mind maps, and holographic telepathy are all fine with me. But if you don't have three things (or less) to move forward on at the end of the day, you may have quantity but not quality.

- "The One Percent Solution: Tools for Change" says that if you improve by 1 percent a day, in 70 days, you'll be twice as good. But if you don't learn carefully and instead become confused, the opposite can actually occur. People can get dumber.

- When creating pragmatic representations of conceptual images, whether brands or graphics or process visuals, it is always better to work with a small team that you trust for quicker and higher-quality results.

- Failing, and learning as a result, among peers is better than mindlessly succeeding among inferiors.

- Emotion is as important as intellect in integrating learning.

- The female advantage in learning: less ego investment and more openness. The male advantage: less tendency to take disagreement personally and more tendency to focus on the issue, not the person.

- Groups don't bond through dumb icebreaking exercises. They bond through sharing challenges, contributions, disagreements, and socializing.

- All groups claim that they want to stay in touch and reconnect. The ones that do so most successfully always have an organizer or organizers who take on that responsibility.

- If the facilitator isn't learning constantly, she should go into another line of work. Simply doing something well and receiving plaudits for it is like watching people applaud a movie you made years ago.

I'm asked why I left organizational consulting after such success, and my reply is that I got bored, because there are primarily 11 things that are going on, and to say to a CEO, "It's numbers 3, 7, and 10; that will be $245,000," was not going to fly. Here are my observations so that you can avoid getting bored:

1. Leadership is inept in that key people are not serving as avatars of the behavior they are seeking in others.
2. Team building is sought when, in actuality, the organization has committees and needs committees, not teams.
3. There are silos headed by powerful people who are defending their turf.
4. Problem solving is prized over innovation, and "black belt nine delta" nonsense takes over people's minds like a bad science fiction movie from the 1950s.
5. There is excessive staff interference instead of support, typically from HR, finance, IT, and/or legal.
6. There are too many meetings that take too long and are overwhelmingly focused on sharing information—the worst possible reason to have a meeting. The organization's talent and energy are being squandered internally instead of being applied externally.
7. The customer's perceptions of the organization's products, services, and relationships are different from the organization's perceptions.
8. The reward and feedback systems are not aligned with strategy and are not encouraging the appropriate behaviors and discouraging the inappropriate.
9. Strategy and planning are mistaken for each other.
10. Career development and succession planning are not wedded.
11. The organization is bureaucratic, in that it focuses on means and not ends.

I'm sending you to the second half of the book now. After the first half, you're ready to understand my interlude. In the second half, plan to put this philosophy to work.

CHAPTER 10

BULLETPROOF PROPOSALS

DON'T TRIP AS YOU'RE ABOUT TO CROSS THE FINISH LINE

PREPARING THE BUYER

The most important aspect of creating proposals that are signed by buyers is the preparation before you even type a word. Proposals are won or lost by what happens in the events leading up to them.

Let's be clear about what a proposal *is*; it is

- A summation of the conceptual agreement between you and the buyer
- A template that will govern the boundaries of the proposed project
- A formal contract (when signed) that protects both you and the client
- The reference point for details as the project unfolds (for example, it can be shared with other key people in the project)

Let's be clear about what a proposal *is not*; it is not

- An exploration of client interest
- A negotiating document
- Unilateral protection for either party
- A rough draft or changeable outline

A proposal is a summation, not an exploration. It confirms the conceptual agreement between consultant and buyer and demonstrates options, with attendant return on investment.

Most proposals fail because the groundwork hasn't been completed. Rather than working hard to establish conceptual agreement with the buyer, the consultant takes the easy way out and provides a proposal. This is the equivalent of trying to teach a graduate course by mailing in notes for the students to read. No one will think very much of the experience, and pretty soon, people will simply stop showing up.

Prior to submitting a proposal, here are the musts to maximize your chances for its acceptance (I hit 80 percent of my proposals, although I submit far fewer than most people).

The 10 Key Steps

1. *Find the economic buyer.* If you're not dealing with the buyer, then nothing else you do matters. Proposals to gatekeepers may as well be thrown in the trash. Don't waste printer ink. Determine who can write a check for your particular value, even if this takes an extended period of time.

2. *Establish a trusting relationship with the buyer.* Proceed to the point at which you see evidence that you are candid with each other, you can push back, and the buyer is willing to share his ideas and experiences. Listen far more than you talk. These relationships can be instant, but they usually require time to reach fruition. Ironically, the more patient you are, the faster you can develop a superb proposal.

3. *Establish objectives for the proposed project.* These should be business outcomes (not deliverables, tasks, or your methodology) determined by asking such questions as

   - What would you like the end result to be?
   - How would things be different from now at the conclusion of the project?
   - Ideally, what three things must be accomplished?
   - How would you like to be known as a result of this project?
   - What must be changed, fixed, or improved the most?

One Percent Solution: A proposal is a summation of a previously established conceptual agreement with an economic buyer. If you understand that reality, then you will take much more time and apply much more discipline before creating one.

---

4. *Establish measures of success for the project.* These are the metrics that will govern agreement on progress and your role in that progress. Ask these types of questions:

- How will you know that these outcomes have been achieved?

- What indexes will you use to tell you that we're on the right track?

- What is the range of improvement you'd like to see, what is minimally acceptable, and what represents overwhelming success?

- What current measures are you using that we can apply?

- What measures that are unique to this project should be created?

5. *Establish the value to the client organization (and/or the buyer personally).* This is a critical nuance in focusing on value and not on fees and in demonstrating later the tremendous ROI that you are providing. Sample questions might be

- What will the outcomes mean to you and the organization?

- How much improvement, conservatively, do you expect from a successful project?

- What is this worth on an annualized basis and a longer-term basis?

- What does this mean quantitatively (sales, market share, profit, retention, etc.)?

- What does this mean qualitatively (repute, health, comfort, convenience, ego, etc.)?

6. *Explain the options available.* By indicating that your proposal will contain alternative ways to approach the project, you are establishing the fact that there are differing value packages available at differing investment levels. Most important, however, you are subtly moving the client from "Should I use Alan?" to "How should I use Alan?" This is a powerful tool that I call the choice of yeses.

The choice of yeses psychologically moves the buyer from the binary question of "should I?" to the pluralistic question of "how should I?" This nuance, when used adroitly, will increase the likelihood of your proposal's being accepted—and at higher fees—by at least 50 percent.

7. *Do not focus on methodology or deliverables.* The client is the expert in automobile manufacture or pharmaceuticals. You wouldn't presume to tell the buyer how to install fuel injection systems or create enzyme blockers. You are the expert in consulting. The client should not presume to lecture you on focus groups, audits, reorganizations, or evaluations. You may touch on it ("We will use focus groups, interviews, and surveys"), but don't go into detail ("We'll use 12 focus groups, survey administrative employees, and interview 10 percent of your customers).

8. *Never mention fees.* Tell the curious client, if you're asked, that all details, including investments and options, will be in the proposal and that you can have that on the buyer's desk in 24 hours. No one needs to know fees the same afternoon. Moreover, you want to focus on value in discussions and in the proposal so that the fees emerge at the proper time. Premature discussion will only lead to false objections and blockages, such as, "We've never budgeted that much," or "This may have to wait until the next fiscal year."

9. *Establish that the proposal will be there by courier within your quickest time frame.* This must be an integrated process. I promise the proposal overnight. If you are more comfortable with more time, then use 48 hours. Remember, however, that the more time that elapses, the more things can go wrong. No buyer I've ever met has decided to increase my fee by stalling for time.

10. *Establish a clear follow-up date.* The conversational question is this: "If I have this on your desk tomorrow, I'll plan to follow up by phone two days later. Or do you prefer that I follow up that same day? I also can stop by if that makes more sense." (Note the choice of yeses.) Never allow yourself to be in a position of ambiguity, where the buyer can inadvertently miss you or deliberately avoid you because she wasn't expecting your call.

Case Study

I was asked to work with a London-based consulting firm that was having problems acquiring new business. The firm's proposals were lengthy and rambling, but even worse, the firm measured the effectiveness of its people based on how many proposals each of them created and mailed.

> *Consequently, a chance meeting in a pastry shop would
> generate a proposal. When I looked at rates of success,
> I found that the rate was under 15 percent, yet the
> proposals were soaking up valuable professional and
> administrative time.*
> *I changed the measure to accepted proposals and
> introduced the preceding 10 steps. Expenses were reduced
> immediately, and the hit rate eventually climbed to over
> 50 percent, all with no capital investment.*
> *Proposals are won or lost in the planning.*

CREATING THE PROPOSAL IN 2.5 PAGES

I've found that there are nine steps to an effective proposal. You may have six or twelve, and this is fine. However, my nine steps have worked for me and my mentoring participants wonderfully well. They result in about 2½ pages, no matter how large the project. Most consultants turn their proposals into tomes that could rival Proust's *Remembrance of Things Past* and that bore the reader just as readily.

Whether you are new to the business and can use an expeditious format for creating proposals or are a veteran who realizes the need to unlearn bad habits, I'm absolutely confident that these nine steps will work for you. [How confident? Well, I've written an entire book on the subject, *How to Write a Proposal That's Accepted Every Time* (Fitzwilliam, NH: Kennedy Information, 2002). I can't keep it on the shelves, and it's used by the "Big Five" as well as by solo practitioners and everyone in between.]

THE NINE COMPONENTS OF A DYNAMITE PROPOSAL

1. Situation Appraisal

This is two or three paragraphs on the client's current condition and why the proposal has been sought. It should reflect what you and the buyer have already discussed and be focused on the problem or improvement and not on mere restatement of the obvious.

Poor Example

FedEx is a highly innovative express delivery service headquarterd in Memphis, Tennessee, that has become to a global carrier, offering differentiated services and acquiring related businesses. (You see, the company already knows this, so it fails the "so what" test.)

Good Example

FedEx has had labor problems, and lawsuits have been brought by so-called independent contractors who are proving, legally, that they are and should be treated as employees. The brand is no longer powerful enough to create an unending flow of top talent, competition is tougher than ever, and operating expenses are expected to continue to climb as a result of fuel uncertainty and aging aircraft. (FedEx may know this viscerally, but you've just make it explicit and powerful.)

The situation appraisal begins the positive nodding in agreement as the buyer reads your proposal.

2. Objectives

These should be bullet-point objectives emanating directly from the conceptual agreement reached in the preliminary work. Typical examples might be:
"Our objectives for this project include

- Creating revenue in over 50 percent of new accounts through cross-product selling
- A radical decline in the time invested by the chief executive officer (CEO) in playing referee among competing units
- A reduction to zero of clients complaining about too many visits by differing people who have not coordinated their efforts
- And so on"

3. Measures of Success

These, too, originate in the earlier conceptual agreement.
"Our metrics will include

- Monthly reports of new business by product type
- A personal journal of time allocation for the CEO
- A quarterly report by the client service vice president on key customer complaints
- And so on"

4. Value to the Organization

This completes the reiteration of the conceptual agreement. "The value to State Street Bank will include

- A reduction in selling costs
- Larger average new business acquisition
- More positive customers willing to be proactive in inquiring about additional services
- A freeing up of 25 percent of the CEO's time
- And so on"

To emphasize, the conceptual agreement becomes points 2, 3, and 4 in the proposal. Bullet points are fine for both brevity and power.

5. Methodology and Options

This is the place where you *briefly* discuss the options (choice of yeses) available to the client. You want to give the buyer a sufficient taste of the differing value— the least of the options will more than satisfy the objectives, but additional options will deliver still more value.

Example

Option 1:   We will interview key personnel in the three business units, observe operations, and monitor customer responses. We will recommend the best and quickest means to eliminate duplication and avoid contradiction. We will train key participants in the coordination necessary and create and install measures and monitoring devices so that management can quickly audit daily performance.

Option 2:   This includes Option 1, but we also will interview key clients prior to the internal changes to use their inputs for the most targeted possible corrections. We will interview those same clients three months after the changes to create further fine-tuning and also to emphasize to them how the organization has heeded their suggestions.

Option 3:   And so on.

Note that options are not just "more of the same" (for example, we'll interview 100 people rather than just 50), but are legitimately and clearly differing value packages. I favor three or four (two is too few, and five becomes confusing and harder to differentiate) in an *ascending order* of value (there is no mention of investment yet). Buyers tend to percolate upward when given choices.

> *Every buyer loves to reduce price, but none wants to reduce value. When you give buyers options of increasing value, they tend to migrate up the value chain (and therefore the investment chain). I call this rapid ascent "The Mercedes Bends."*

6. Timing

State clearly when the project can begin and the likely range of its duration. Use calendar dates, not relative dates. Don't commit to a firm ending date. Educate the buyer at this point that there's a reasonable range, based on access, cooperation, unforeseen events, and so on.

7. Joint Accountabilities

This is another section that is overlooked by most consultants. Let the client know that this is not something that "you do for the client," but rather something that you and the client collaborate on as peers.

Examples
My accountability includes

- Adherence to agreed-upon deadlines
- All administrative and office costs
- Monthly progress reports in person
- And so on

Your accountability includes

- Access to key individuals on mutually convenient dates
- Provision of all information having a bearing on the project
- Payment in conformance with the terms below
- And so on

Our joint accountabilities include the following:

- We will alert each other of anything we learn that may materially affect the success of the project (for example, mergers, key people leaving, etc.).
- We will respect each other's confidentiality and proprietary materials and approaches.
- We will achieve reasonable accommodation for conflicts, unforeseen events, and other priorities.
- And so on."

8. Terms and Conditions

My favorite part: this should be the first time the buyer sees the fees. The buyer has been affirmatively nodding through all the foregoing, and now, through sheer momentum, he should continue the positive reaction right through the fees.

Terms and conditions should state

- The fees, as in
  - The fee for Option 1 is $45,000.
  - The fee for Option 2 is $72,000.
  - And so on.

- Payment terms, as in
  - A 50 percent deposit is required to commence work, with the balance due in 45 days. (See Chapter 14 on payments for guidance here.)
- Discounts or special features, as in
  - A 10 percent discount can be obtained with a single full-fee payment at commencement.
- Expense reimbursement terms, as in
  - Expenses will be billed monthly as actually accrued and are due on presentation of our invoice. Expenses will include air, train, rental car, taxi, lodging, food, and related expenses; they will not include fax, copying, phone, courier, office support, and related expenses.
- Statements of any special features, as in

- We are fully covered by errors and omissions insurance and liability insurance. Please make all checks payable to Summit Consulting Group, Inc.
- Your deposit, in the absence of your signature below, also will indicate acceptance of this project and the terms and conditions as stated herein.

> *One Percent Solution: Some people can issue checks but not sign legal documents. That's better than vice versa! Enable them to do what they do best: sign the check!*

Someone asked me once if I did all my own administrative work. I said, yes, most of it, because I can type 60 words a minute and try to keep it to a minimum.

"But, surely," she said, "you don't bother with your own invoicing."

"Are you kidding!" I yelled. "I live to invoice. To paraphrase Descartes, 'I bill, therefore I am.' I get that thing perfectly formatted on the screen, hit the print button, then have a cigarette!" (I smoke only an occasional cigar, but you get the idea. It's a very Cartesian philosophy.)

9. Acceptance

I like the client to sign right there on that piece of paper while continuing to nod positively. Thus, the last part of my proposal is the space for acceptance, which I've already executed. I send two copies, one to keep and one to return (always by courier). Always send hard copy. Faxes look terrible, and electronic stuff looks worse and can easily be seen by the wrong people. Overnight, high-quality hard copy is the key.

Example

Your signature below indicates acceptance of the terms of this proposal indicated by the option you have checked.

___Option 1   ___Option 2   ___Option 3

We accept the proposal above and the option selected.

For Summit Consulting Group, Inc.:	For Acme Company, Inc.:
Alan Weiss, Ph.D.	Joan Martin
President	Executive Vice President
Date:_____	Date:_____

Case Study

I had sent a $250,000 proposal to what was then GRE Insurance in New York to help the company with merging cultures after a merger. The executive vice president was the buyer and clearly was positively disposed.

A week after I sent the proposal, I received a check for $125,000 and began work. I did not receive the signed proposal, but I figured it was in the mail. Sixty days later, as scheduled, I received the second installment and had a quarter of a million dollars in the bank for what would be a six-month project.

I never did get the signed proposal! After successful completion of the project, I figured out what had happened—the buyer could readily approve two $125,000 payments, but he could not easily get the proposal past his legal department without a great deal of wrangling, obfuscation, and delay. Thus he opted simply to pay the bill!

This is why I now state in terms and conditions that, in effect, your check is as good as your signature. Have I mentioned that I'm constantly amazed at how stupid I was two weeks ago?

HOW TO FOLLOW UP AND CLOSE 88.79 PERCENT OF THE TIME

The client may well call you immediately or return the proposal immediately and give you the go-ahead. Barring this:

1. Call the buyer as promised on the assigned date and time, established by you prior to submitting the proposal. (I find that there is no advantage to presenting a proposal in person because the buyer will still ask for time to consider it, as she should. Similarly, there is no need to follow up in person if all seems well.)

2. Don't push, commit, or even talk. Just say that you're calling as promised, and let the buyer state his position.

3. If positive, establish a start date.

4. If clarification is needed and the buyer isn't ready to commit, establish a very quick follow-up date.

5. If the buyer has reservations, deal with them honestly. Accentuate value. Do not lower fees (see below).

6. If the buyer says no, find out why. If the objection is rebuttable, do so. If not, learn your lesson. Never beg or rend your garments.

If the buyer says that Option 3 is desired at a lower price, point out that this is why you have Option 1 and Option 2. If the buyer says that even Option 1 is slightly too expensive, offer to lower it by also removing value ("We won't do the international aspect," or, "We won't provide individual management feedback"). Remember, buyers love to reduce price but hate to reduce value.

If you reduce price without reducing value, the buyer will merely keep pushing, wondering how low you can go. And you deserve it because you don't believe in your own value. If the discussion is about price and not value, you've lost control of the discussion.

Some proposals won't be accepted no matter how scrupulously you've followed the process. If this weren't the case, I'd be charging $1 million just for this book. Most will, however, *if you have the patience and discipline to follow this process.*

I want to reinforce my "The 1% Solution: Tools for Change." You may not find this entire book worthwhile, but that's not the point. The key is to extract your 1 percent per day. I've found that this approach to proposal writing is one of the most significant changes even veteran consultants and well-known firms can make. For the new consultant, it can accelerate your growth exponentially.

So remember: it's preparation, conceptual agreement, a nine-step proposal, and systematic follow-up. You don't need your résumé, or pages of credibility statements, or details (heaven forfend) about your methodology. Your relationship with the buyer should have taken care of your credibility, and the buyer doesn't really care about your methodology—only about results.

Maybe you can't write a proposal that's accepted every time. But you can write one that's accepted 80 percent of the time.

And that's not bad if you want to be a million dollar consultant.

QUESTIONS AND ANSWERS

Q. *What if the buyer insists on a price range, at least, before discussing details with you and allowing you to create a proposal?*

A. Remember that no client needs an immediate number except to disqualify you, that clients hate to lose value, and that they act in their own self-interest. Simply say, "It would be irresponsible for me to cite you a fee without knowing exactly what's needed. But if I can ask you a few questions, I can have a proposal complete with fee in your hands by tomorrow."

Q. *What happens when the client volunteers that there is $50,000 (or whatever) in the budget for the project?*

A. Go through the same steps. Then determine whether you can provide value for that amount of money. If so, provide options, If not, tell the buyer why not. *(Hint*: If you can, always provide one option above the budgeted amount. If the client likes your value and can find $50,000, then he can probably find $65,000 just as easily.)

Q. *If you'll be using other people, shouldn't you include their bios and details in the proposal?*

A. No. Why would you? If the client has a relationship with you, she won't be swayed further by arbitrary names and credentials. If you don't have a relationship, this information still won't help!

Q. *How long should you wait before following up?*

A. Make the follow-up date with the buyer before you submit: "I'll get this to you by FedEx on Wednesday and plan to call you on Friday at 10 to see how you would like to proceed. Can we schedule that call right now?"

Q. *What option will buyers choose most often?*

A. My experience is that they choose Option 2 about 50 percent of the time, and Option 3 about 35 percent of the time. Option 1 comes in last at 15 percent, which is pretty much what you want.

Final Thought: When you send your proposal, put it in your presentation folder (two copies) and include a brief cover letter confirming that you're sending the proposal as promised. Offer to start on a "telephone handshake" if the client is ready to begin immediately. Once you show up, you've poured cement on the agreement.

CHAPTER 11

OMNIPRESENCE

ABSENCE DOESN'T MAKE THE HEART GROW FONDER; IT MAKES PEOPLE FORGET

COMMUNICATE CONSTANTLY

There is an apocryphal story in the sales business about a salesman who outsold his colleagues by 200 percent every year. Yet, according to all the tests administered to the sales force, he scored the lowest in sales aptitude and selling skills.

His own district manager had thought that the salesman was just lucky and recorded on his evaluation that his potential was limited. After the third year of record-breaking sales, however, the home office decided that it had better discover the secret behind this guy's success, so a corporate psychologist was dispatched.

"Show me exactly what you do in front of a client," instructed the psychologist.

"I place the product manual between us," said the salesman.

"Yes, yes, and then what?"

"Well, I ask the client if he would like to buy the product on page one," said the salesman, as if speaking to an innocent child.

"And what if the client says no to you?"

"I turn to the second page, and ask if he would like to buy that product."

"And if he again says no?"

"I turn to the third page . . . "

"All right," yelled the Ph.D., "I get the idea. But what if you go through all 147 pages of products and the client has said no to every single one?"

"I turn the book over," said the salesman, clearly explaining the obvious, "open it again to page one, and ask the client if he would like to buy that product."

It's amazing what can happen if you just keep talking to the client and asking for the business.

I am now going to share one of the most elemental secrets underlying growth and wealth in this business. It is inexpensive, simple, and both tactically and strategically effective, and yet most consultants ignore it completely.

In fact, by my estimation, at least half the readers of this book will say, "Of course!" and then proceed to ignore it completely.

Do I have your attention?

You don't get business that you don't ask for. You don't even get remembered if you don't do things that are memorable. If we agree that 80 percent of your business should come from existing clients and that the long-term relationships you are seeking—within which the client trusts the consultant to make key decisions about accepting projects—are dependent on ongoing communications, then you must devise a strategy to remain effectively within your clients' field of vision. This is the essence of the timing strategy I discussed in Chapter 2.

> *It is actually difficult to contact clients too much. It is easy to fail to contact them frequently enough. If there is anyone anywhere who has ever sent you a check for your services and with whom you haven't communicated in the past six months, then you will never reach your growth potential. The secret is simple: establish an ongoing dialogue with clients. In the worst case, a monologue will do.*

There are several options available for continuous client communications:

1. Print
   - Letters
   - Brochures
   - Newsletters
   - Article reprints
   - Job aids and checklists
   - Posters and sayings
   - Cartoons
   - Testimonials and examples of assignments completed
   - Published articles
   - Interview transcripts
   - Survey results and reports
2. Phone
   - Calls to "stay in touch"
   - An 800 number and hotline help to encourage use
   - Information relayed on meetings or events of interest

- Reminders of long-term follow-up responsibilities and dates
- Introductions to third parties, that is, customers for your client
- Messages reminding of follow-up activities the client should undertake

3. Events

- Interviews with the client for industry journals
- Attendance at industry and professional meetings that the client attends
- Hosting periodic conferences on topics of interest
- Acting as intermediary with other clients for mutual learning
- Hosting breakfasts or lunches with a small group of peers
- Pro bono activities

4. Internet

- Web page updates and additions
- "Password" Web site reserved for clients
- Regular e-mail contact
- Branding in your e-mail signature file
- E-mail with ideas and suggestions
- References and/or hyperlinks to relevant sites
- A chat room on your Web site
- Interaction on your blog
- Involvement in various "social media" channels
- Teleconferences and Webinars

5. Personal

- Visits to the client without any particular agenda
- Entertaining key buyers
- Sending holiday cards or gifts (as permitted)
- Participating in mutual charity events and fund-raisers[1]
- Seeking out common community and social events
- Sending "I'll be in the neighborhood" cards
- If practical, involvement in the client's products and services

6. Other

- Coauthoring articles with the client
- Sending fax messages and information
- Advertising in industry publications that the client reads

---

[1] See the final section in this chapter, on pro bono work.

- Exhibiting at trade shows that key clients will attend
- Asking the client to help *you* as a critiquer, advisor, editor, or some other role.
- Inviting the client to be on your advisory board
- Breakfast or lunch meetings that you sponsor on relevant topics for the industry
- Seeking a quote or a case study for a book you're writing

Some of these might be better suited to your client base than others, but all of them could be applicable. Are you reviewing a list like this and devising a strategy for ongoing communications objectives for each individual client? Once you've done this, you can work on the tactics. Here are some examples from each category.

Every so often I'll send along a cartoon with my name on it. A lighter touch is important in communications. As a result of this, one of my clients sent me a cartoon about consultants that I then shared with everyone else on my list, with credit to the sender. This creates a community of clients who feel that they belong to a common interest, represented by your firm.

A phone call is entirely justified by your intent to inform a client that an event of interest is approaching. This might be a guest speaker, sponsored by a management association at a breakfast meeting (which is why these memberships can pay such dividends for you). You may choose simply to inform your client that a subject that you know is of interest to the client is being discussed, or you may choose to invite the client to be your guest.

Using what I call events, you might bring two or more noncompetitive clients together to discuss the problems inherent in managing a diverse workforce, discuss the rewards of going global, compare succession-planning approaches, or investigate the efficacy of part-time workers. As the intermediary, you may or may not actively participate in the meeting. However, the simple act of creating the opportunity is significant.

One Percent Solution: There is an inverse proportion between the distance you travel and the resistance to seeing you. The greater the distance, the less resistance.

Whenever I'm going to be traveling, I review my lists so that I can send cards or make phone calls letting clients (and prospects) know that "I'll be in the neighborhood." It's very common for these people to invite you to see them because they know that your expenses are paid and that it's a no-obligation opportunity to get together. Generally, the farther you're traveling, the easier it is to set up the meetings. I'm based in Rhode Island, so when I travel to nearby

New York, the "in the neighborhood" approach isn't very powerful because I'm there often, and it's only an hour's trip if a client needed a special visit.

However, when I'm in Chicago, people will usually see me, and when I'm in California, I can always get an appointment if people are in town. When I go to London or Hong Kong, people will usually change their schedules to accommodate mine.

Finally, the "other" category includes asking clients to help you. This may take the form of an unpublished article you'd like them to critique before you submit it for publication. Or you may request feedback on a new brochure you're developing. Many firms establish client advisory panels that convene regularly to discuss trends in business and finance.[2]

These are some of the tactics that apply within the communications strategies. They're really not much different from the salesman who opened the product manual to page one and asked, "Would you like to buy this?" Since this is a *relationship* business, we have to keep turning the pages to alternative communication methods to maintain and develop the relationship, but just like the salesman, we have to be persistent in continuing.

Some clients will never respond. However, *no one* will respond if you don't initiate and maintain these avenues of contact. When the client feels the itch to do something, you want your firm to be in that client's mind. If the client needs something, you want the client to be dependent on you to provide it. When the client thinks of unsolicited support and valuable information, you want your name to be associated with the solution.

Ongoing communications are a modest investment. More than anything else, periodic client contacts require the volition to want to engage in them and the innovation required to make them unique and targeted to the client's needs. This volition (to create the strategy and allocate the time) and this innovation (to develop personalized tactics) constitute one of the elemental secrets underlying million dollar consulting.

PUBLISHING COMMERCIALLY

The greatest single solo marketing device I've encountered is publishing.[3] Putting your ideas and approaches into print immediately does three things:

1. Your own thinking is solidified and your approaches are systematized as you work to communicate them. You discover elements of your work that weren't as obvious before you wrote about them.

---

[2] This is an ideal way to obtain testimonials from your clients to be used on the dust jackets of your books; it is also an opportunity to cite their assistance in the acknowledgments.

[3] Publishing is the gold standard. But the platinum standard is a buyer-to-buyer direct referral.

2. The value of your ideas is validated, in that "selling" an editor requires that you present original and worthwhile ideas for the editor's readers. Editors are besieged with material, so working through that obstacle course can be accomplished only with valuable material.

3. Your credibility skyrockets. I conduct workshops on how to get published for people who have never written for publication before. The best method is a sequential one that I call the *staircase approach*, beginning with local publications and working up to broader impact and, if you are so inclined, a book. The idea behind publishing is not to be blatantly self-aggrandizing but to let the value of your work speak for you.

As I discussed earlier, my progression included writing articles for no fee for publications (some of them no longer with us) such as *Supervisory Management, Manage, Training News*, and a dozen others like them. I moved on to do a column (for a modest fee) for *Training News*, wrote for the *New York Times*, and was interviewed by such publications as *USA Today* and *Success* magazine.

I then began writing for *Success, HR Magazine, Training* magazine, and others, and contributed chapters to two business books. When I approached publishers with my first book, I received three offers and accepted one from Harper & Row (now HarperCollins), which published my next two books after informal discussions, the third with an advance.

The book you are reading, from the preeminent business publisher in the world, I was asked to write, and this is the fourth edition, spanning more than 16 years. And I've now graduated to a regular business column and op-ed pieces.

I published my first article in 1969. I entered the consulting business in 1972, founded my own firm in 1985, and published my first book in 1988.

The period from 1969 to 1988 is irrelevant; the period from 1985 to 1988 is the important one because only after beginning my own firm did I experience the growth necessary to provide something that was worthwhile saying in a book! Thus, in three years I was able to gather the material and experiences that allowed me to approach 18 publishers and garner three offers, and I've since published books in 1989, 1990, 1992, 1995, 1997, 1998, 1999, 2000, 2001, 2002, 2003, 2007, 2008, and 2009—30 in all, with three more under contract, appearing in nine languages.

The experiences that make for interesting books—when you are oriented toward multidimensional growth—never stop. Throughout this period, I've continued writing articles and columns, doing interviews, and contributing to a wide variety of publications. This is why my phone rings. And although, for expediency, I now have an agent, you don't need one.[4]

---

[4] I recommend the book by Jeff Herman titled *The Insider's Guide to Book Editors and Literary Agents*, 2009 (www.jeffherman.com/guide), which comes out every year. Disclaimer: Jeff is my agent, but I have no financial interest in this work.

Vanity publishing (where you pay someone to print your book) and self-publishing (where you print it yourself, often with publicity and distribution assistance) are terrible ideas if market credibility is your objective. These attempts to "have a book" are as obvious as a ham sandwich. Reviewers throw them out, bookstores won't carry them, and executives are smart enough to know the difference.

Remember, if you can't convince an editor to publish you, you probably haven't yet developed anything worthwhile to say. (Self-publishing is fine if you want to create Web site and "back of the room" sales, but it is better done after you've achieved some kind of commercial success.)

If you write a book for publicity, it will go nowhere but to your head. If you write a book intending to help your readers, it will generate tremendous publicity. Write a book when you have something important to say, not before.

Digression

At professional speakers' conferences and some consulting groups, you will hear about some author who self-published and sold 200,000 copies of **What I Learned While Recovering from a Cold.** *These are almost always exaggerations, and the one in one-hundred-thousand self-published books that actually succeeds doesn't make it viable for everyone else.*

Here is my brief formula for getting an article into print. This applies to any of the early steps in the staircase. You may be able to jump two or more of the steps at one leap, or you may find yourself on several at once. I continue to write monthly columns at no fee while writing books for considerable advances. These are not mutually exclusive activities. However, you have to start somewhere, and if you want to start from scratch and still stand an excellent chance of getting published, here's how to do it.

How to Get an Article into Print

1. Determine what subject you want to write about.
   a. Why are you the person to comment on the topic?
   b. How will this subject enhance your business, repute, or standing?
   c. Why is the subject relevant at this time (and for the next several months)?

    d. What "angle" or "slant" do you have to make it compelling? *Don't be afraid to be contrarian.* The world doesn't need another piece on reengineering.[5]

2. Determine where you want to publish the article.

    a. Who is your audience, and what do they read?

    b. Don't be afraid to ask your audience.[6]

    c. Where is it most reasonable for you to be successful?

    d. Research publications and study their style.

    e. Sometimes very small but highly targeted publications (e.g., industry newsletters) can be most effective for you. I was never published in the *Times* until I sent them an article that I realized was just what they needed!

3. Prepare a professional inquiry.

    a. Send it to a specific editor's attention.[7]

    b. Specify what, why, examples, uniqueness, length, and delivery date.

    c. Request specifications.

    d. Always enclose a SASE[8] if you send hard copy; include your full signature file in electronic submission.

    e. Cite credentials—yours and the article's.

    f. You may send multiple queries for the same article to various publications. Don't bother following up, editors respond only if they like something.

        This step must be more carefully executed than the actual article!

4. Write it like a pro.

    a. Use specific examples, names, and places.

    b. Write it yourself, but solicit critique.

    c. Write it to the specifications.

    d. Make sure that you include your own biographical data at the end.

    e. Request free reprints or reprint permission or discounted reprints.

    f. Don't self-promote; let the substance do it for you.

---

[5] See "Contrarian Consulting" in Chapter 12.

[6] This is the opportunity to involve your clients, as suggested in the section opening this chapter.

[7] The Herman book and *Writer's Market*, both cited earlier, are excellent sources.

[8] A common abbreviation in the trade, standing for "self-addressed stamped envelope."

g. If rejected: resubmit, resubmit, resubmit.

h. Don't overwrite; write what's on your mind without worrying about the "great American novel." (When you edit, you'll find that the piece is amazingly good.)

i. Attribute things you borrow, but don't try to dazzle with superfluous references.

j. Be critical and analytical; readers respond best to provocation and the opportunity to look at things in a new way.

k. When in doubt, start a new paragraph.

l. Use graphics when appropriate, and try to load in the metaphors and similes.

m. Use modern formatting and style (e.g., skip only one space between sentences, not two, and put commas and periods inside quotation marks, not outside), or you'll look like an amateur. Use prior articles as credentials to write newer ones.

Here's my route for getting a book published once you've ascended the staircase. Book publishing is slightly easier when you have a long track record of articles and columns to support it, but these are not prerequisites.

The most important aspect is convincing a publisher that your book will sell, and the way to achieve that is to do your own homework, because the editor hasn't the time or the inclination to do it for you. It is difficult to get your first book published, but with a targeted, systematic approach, it's much easier than most people think.

How to Get a Book Published

1. Determine what it is you have to say.

   a. Your particular expertise from education, experience, training, or circumstances.

   b. Your ability to pull together disparate things that others haven't.

   c. Your ideas, concepts, theories, and innovations. If you've nothing constructive to contribute, don't write a word.

2. Determine which publishers are most likely to agree with you.

   a. Examine their current books in print.

   b. Request their specifications.

   c. Ask people in the business.

      If business credibility (and not pure ego) is your objective, do not vanity publish or self-publish—it's a waste of time, and no one is impressed.

3. Prepare a treatment (proposal) for the publisher's review.

   a. Why you?

   b. Why this topic?

   c. Why is this topic handled in this manner?

   d. What competitive works exist, and why is yours needed?

   e. Who is the audience?

   f. When would it be ready?

   g. What are the special features (that is, endorsements, self-tests, etc.)?

   h. Provide *at least* the introduction and one chapter, a table of contents, and summaries of the other chapters.

   If you can't sell it to the publisher, you'll never sell it to the reader.

4. Write it like a pro.

   a. Invite clients and/or respected authorities to contribute.

   b. Use a sophisticated computer and software.

   c. Don't use a ghostwriter. If someone else writes your book, why does anyone need you?

   d. Always take the reader's viewpoint.

   e. Schedule your writing sessions just as you would your other responsibilities.

   f. Use trusted others to review, critique, and suggest.

   g. *Always* attribute anything that's not yours.

   h. Keep it "future-current." Remember, it will be published eight months to a year from your submission.

   What is published represents your values: Are you proud of what you've written?

> ***One Percent Solution:** No one writes "a book." People write chapters, composed of pages, composed of words. Start with the words, and it's a lot easier.*

---

5. Market it like a pro.

   a. Don't waste undue amounts of time looking for an agent because most of them tend to listen only to previously published authors. But do see if you can get an introduction to one from another author.

b. Don't get discouraged. Keep submitting, and find out why you've been rejected.

c. Read contracts carefully because they will specify author's discount, planned promotion, expenses you may incur, and so on. Run it by your attorney.

Remember, a successful business book sells about 7,500 copies. Don't expect to be on Oprah or Imus the following Monday.

How to Exploit Your Published Book

1. Send it out to every reviewer you can find.

2. Establish an account with a wholesaler, such as Ingram, so that you can buy the book at a steep discount and earn royalties when the wholesaler buys it from the publisher. This is almost always better than a publisher's direct discount to an author.

3. Have extra copies made of the jacket cover and include it in your press kit. You can print promotional information on the reverse.

4. Post it in color on your Web site with descriptive and ordering information.

5. Have colleagues write glowing reviews for you on Amazon.com.

6. When you speak, occasionally hold it up and cite some research you did in writing it.

7. Send free copies to your best clients.

8. Include it in your press kit for high-potential prospects.

9. Use excerpts as position papers.

10. Send it to all local broadcast media outlets and suggest an interview that would be relevant to their viewers and listeners.

11. Extend the event. For several months you are the author of the "soon to be released," then the "just released," then the "recently released." That can extend your publicity and promotion over a year!

Publishing will, at first, require a substantial investment of time. However, you can usually find that time on airplanes and in distant hotel rooms. Once you've broken into the field, you'll find it easier and easier to publish, both because your skills are developing and because your credibility is growing. The staircase method is useful to ensure that you also grow as an author and avoid the "success trap" of publishing repeatedly for a limited audience.

When executives read your books, they may not immediately ask you to consult. However, they often will ask you to speak.[9]

PUBLISHING YOURSELF

Having reached this point, let's place self-publishing in some context. Creating your own books, booklets, tapes, manuals, and so on makes sense under certain conditions.

Ten Good Reasons to Self-Publish

1. *You are already established in commercial publications.* If you've published with a known publisher, then your self-published works gain credibility through association. At the moment, about 20 percent of my product line is self-published.

2. *You've claimed reversion of rights.* When a commercial book goes out of print, the author usually has the option to claim further printing rights (rights "revert" to the author). You can publish a virtually identical book, but with your imprimatur instead of the original publisher's. Usually, the publisher is obligated to sell you the films and other printing materials at a reasonable cost.

3. *You want to create "back of the room" sales.* If you speak frequently, people will buy an average of 10 times as many products if they are physically available than if they are available only by catalog or single sample. Once people have heard a good speaker, they are highly inclined to purchase products.

4. *Your market is highly specialized.* If you are consulting in the merger and acquisition of small, privately owned physical therapy practices, for example, there may not be sufficient audience to attract a publisher, but your audience may well welcome a book directed at its needs, however it's published.

5. *You have a client who will underwrite it.* A major client may agree to pay for the publication of your book and 1,000 copies for every one of its salespeople. The book may be tailored to the firm's specifications, but in underwriting the cost, the client enables you to produce a book.

---

[9] See my book *Money Talks* New York: (McGraw-Hill, 1998) for a view of the speaking profession analogous to this book's analysis of the consulting profession.

6. *You are combining disparate elements.* Albums of printed material, audiocassettes, CDs, and/or videocassettes are often popular with buyers and not amenable to publishers' standard formats. The uniqueness of the diverse content may make the product popular.

7. *You're providing electronic access.* Publishing on the Internet is regarded in widely different perspectives. Major novelists as well as business authors have placed their work on the Web, either for free download or for download on the honor system (usually with dreadful results—many have ceased doing it).

8. *You're guaranteed distribution.* Amazon.com and others have programs for self-published authors (Amazon Advantage Program).

9. *You're so confident of sales that you know a distributor will be impressed.* A wide variety of books, from *The Celestine Prophecy* to *Chicken Soup for the Soul*, were originally self-published and, when a cult following boosted sales, were quickly picked up by major distributors and, eventually, publishers. It's not common, but it happens.

10. *Your ego demands that you have "a book."* This is the worst reason of all, but if you're staying up nights over it, get it out of your system.

Be aware that the great preponderance of self-published books are simply dreadful. However, I wanted to give you a balanced view because there may be occasions that justify your creating your own products in this manner.

Case Study

I had claimed reversion of rights to my book on strategy, **Making It Work.** *I had republished it as* **Best Laid Plans.** *A midlevel manager at the Times Mirror Company ordered it from my Web site. She was in the training group, and she noticed that I had a chapter about strategy specifically for training firms.*

She passed it on to her group vice president, who asked me to visit her in San Jose. The ultimate result was a $350,000 contract over three years. I'm not sure anyone in the entire place ever read the complete book.

I'm not offended.

SPEAKING OUT

The perfect synergy for a consultant works something like this:

- An executive reads your book or article and asks you to speak to his management staff.
- As a result of the speech, you're asked to consult on pertinent issues.

and/or

- As a result of a speech you deliver, executives in the audience ask for more information, and you send them articles and/or books.
- After reading the material, they ask you to consider several consulting projects.
- During a consulting project, you provide copies of articles and/or books to key client managers.
- Having read your material and worked with you on your project, they request you to address one of the trade or professional association conferences.

These sequences can occur all the time if you are in a position to exploit them. If you have written nothing, or if you don't "do" speeches, then such potential synergy is academic. In such a case, your marketing will also be anemic and academic.

Making speeches before in-house management conferences (that is, the *New York Times* Regional Newspaper Group), industry trade associations (the American Bankers Association), business associations (American Management Association conferences), professional specialty groups (annual conference of the American Society for Training and Development), personal development groups (the Business Roundtable), and university management extensions (Case Western Reserve University's Weatherhead School of Management) provides high-impact marketing.

The visibility is excellent, the opportunity to promote your approaches is ideal, and you earn immediate credibility merely by dint of having been invited to speak.

Here's some valuable information: the Credit Union National Association has 52 state credit union leagues as members and an annual budget in excess of $5 million, and it publishes seven different periodicals and holds meetings once a year.[10]

---

[10] All citations in this section about associations are from *National Trade and Professional Associations of the United States* (Washington, D.C.: Columbia Books, annual). You can also access it on the Internet.

The American Chemical Society has 150,000 members, also a $5 million budget, costs $99 a year to join, publishes 27 periodicals, and holds two meetings a year.

I could tell you similar things about the Broadcast Promotion and Marketing Executives, the National Association of Jai Alai Frontons, or the Shoe Service Industry Council. I can do this because the appropriate source books are available each year for about $300, and they also contain the names of the executive directors, addresses, phone numbers, and information about the history of the association.

Once you break into these groups, you have the opportunity to capitalize on word-of-mouth publicity. The best strategy is to begin with modest regional groups for little or no fee and then work your way to their national parents. Another sound approach is to gain entry from your clients. A banking client can introduce you to contacts in the American Bankers Association and even recommend you for a speaking slot (members frequently are asked to nominate speakers).

How valuable are speeches? In 1996 I spoke 50 times, ranging from 45 minutes to 3 hours. *Every one* was a result of a request to me based on prior speeches, consulting work, or my books and articles. The groups have ranged from Mercedes-Benz dealers to the American Press Institute and the Pharmaceutical Manufacturers Association of Canada. It's not uncommon for me to be booked to speak in, say, Barcelona, for one hour for a four-figure fee (during which time I literally bumped into Princess Caroline of Monaco in a tiny elevator).

As a result of a deliberate strategy to speak less and travel less, I spoke only 25 times in 2008. But I made four or five times the money doing it that I had in 1996, despite the economy. That's because my brand is so much stronger. It's not unusual for me to get $25,000 to $45,000 for a single day on site, and don't forget that I made my living and my brand primarily as a consultant, not as a speaker.

An attorney friend of mine recently made the transition into full-time consulting, specializing in dental practice buyouts, mergers, and partner financing. After several harried weeks trying to decide on advertising, direct mail, and other options to reach his potential audience, he came to me for advice. I suggested that he approach every state and regional dental association with a proposal to speak on his topic. After his first few efforts were accepted, he is now in great demand and will be appearing before national groups with considerable fanfare (and considerable fees—people will pay you handsomely to market your services on the speaking circuit).

If this strategy works so well for an attorney pursuing business from dental practices, how well might it work for consultants with a broader-based constituency and, consequently, more options?

Case Study

I had worked as a consultant for Cologne Life Reinsurance for three years. One day the CEO asked if I knew any good speakers. I thought he was putting me on.

However, he explained that he had that year's program chair for the American Council of Life Insurance and needed a keynoter for the council's meeting of 250 CEOs! He simply never knew that I was a professional speaker, and I had never bothered to inform him!

Let your consulting clients know the full gamut of your abilities and competencies, and do so periodically.

There are plenty of courses, books, and seminars on how to speak. The venerable Toastmasters International is still superb, as are membership organizations such as the National Speakers Association. Private firms also provide development in the area. It's not my goal here to teach you how to speak, but it is my hope to convey to you how to get speaking assignments. This is as good a place as any to explain what should be in your press kit, which has a variety of uses but is particularly helpful in pursuing speaking opportunities. [And if you're at all interested, please see my book *Money Talks: How to Make a Million as a Speaker* (New York: McGraw-Hill, 1998).]

One Percent Solution: You don't have to be a professional speaker, but you had better be a good enough speaker to command a room or a meeting if you want to influence others in this business.

Figure 11-1 shows the contents of a professional press kit oriented toward obtaining speaking assignments. (Such kits should be preassembled but tailored each time for the particular client and use, so the articles included, testimonials, and personal experience may differ in each case, just as they would for various consulting prospects.) The kit should be in the form of a professional presentation folder, with pockets for material, room for books or CDs, and a place for a business card. (DVDs are also quite popular now.)

▪ Corporate brochure	▪ Third-party articles validating
▪ Black-and-white glossy photo	your work
▪ Personal experience in the	▪ Personal biographical sketch
subject area	▪ Testimonials from clients
▪ Interviews conducted with you	▪ Articles you've written
▪ Audio- or videocassettes of	▪ Book reviews or similar notices
prior speeches	▪ Fee schedule for speaking
▪ List of clients	▪ List of references
▪ Examples of specific work in	▪ Professional affiliations
the industry	▪ Honors or awards you've won

Figure 11-1 The contents of a press kit. A professional press kit denotes a professional speaker.

Circulate your press kit to the association executives in the fields that are relevant to your work. Send it to independent meeting planners.[11] Provide it to clients who are in a position to pass it on to their professional affiliations. Make it a habit to send out three press kits a week in targeted mailings. (This is something a secretary can do even while you're traveling. It's the essence of marketing productivity.) Follow up with phone calls. And mail repeatedly. If people are deemed worthwhile to receive the press kit, place them on your mailing list for your regular client mailings, and send a new press kit to them once or twice a year.

There are speakers' bureaus that book speakers for a commission based on the fee. Speakers' bureaus often help only when you don't need them; that is, they disdain speakers without a national reputation and embrace those who are already well known. They are often demanding and unreasonable in their working relationships, and some of the most unethical stories I've heard in our profession emanate from relationships with speakers' bureaus.

There are, however, many excellent ones, and it's worth your time to find them and develop relationships with the principals. (Beware of any bureau that charges you to "evaluate" your materials, wants to charge you to appear in "showcases," or charges you for inclusion in its catalog. That is what the commission

---

[11] In all cases, send it only to a specific person by name, with a personalized letter; for example, "I've been told that you are arranging the Miami conference with an emphasis on productivity. . ." While it takes some work to find names and specific items of reference, this investment is paid back handsomely by the fact that the odds of the recipient's reading the material are enormously improved. Blind mailings are never worth the effort because meeting planners and association executives are flooded with them.

is supposed to cover. If you're already paying the bureau, why should it place you?!)

> *Million dollar consultants are passionate about what they do and how they do it. There is no more natural forum than a speaker's platform to disseminate those views and share that passion. This is known as painless marketing.*

I have not yet met a top consultant who does not take to the lectern as opportunities develop. And make no mistake, a consultant with practical experience in improving clients' condition is a valuable speaker and in great demand. A professional speaker who is not really a consultant (remember the definitions in Chapter 1) but who talks on "inspirational" topics or repeats a standard performance on the podium is not as much in demand these days by major corporations.

Buyers—and audiences—are requiring practical, results-oriented business advice more than ever before. There is a wonderful opportunity awaiting any consultant who takes the time and invests the energy to learn to speak well, organize experiences and approaches, and seeks out the people who can arrange the audiences that will lead to increased business.

PRO BONO WORK

Pro bono work is work that is done for free. Chapter 18 will deal with such no-fee work in the context of contributions to the environment and ethical issues. Here I want to deal with it as an investment in your future success because pro bono work can rebound into lucrative fee-paying opportunities.

And let's be clear on another thing: pro bono work is work done without fee at your initiative or as a result of someone else's request and your unhindered decision to comply. It is not work done for free because the client has refused to pay your fee but you still want to complete the project (to keep it from a competitor, to be in position for a legitimate project, or for some other such reason). That situation isn't pro bono; it is desperation! There are no chapters in this book on desperation because you must always deal from a position of strength if you are to be successful and to grow in this business.

As a rule, never do pro bono work for a profit-making organization. Don't let companies fool you with the "e" word—exposure.

There are obvious candidates for pro bono work: the local Boy Scout troop, your children's school (public or private, at any level), business associations (for example, the chamber of commerce), hospitals, religious institutions, and so on, depending on your areas of expertise and local need. I've found that by helping a school fund-raising drive to set its strategy, by offering organizational diagnosis to an arts council, by critiquing the decision-making processes of a charitable board, or even by discussing leadership skills with volunteer association officers, my name and talents become known. These organizations are often excellent laboratories to apply your skills and are equally often valuable learning opportunities because nonprofits sometimes perform *more effectively* than the for-profits.[12]

As your talents and contributions become known—and they should, because your contribution is a rare one to these organizations—you will find that your colleague volunteers often hold key positions in attractive, potential client organizations. They'll often solicit your advice about *their* organization's problems while working with you in the volunteer activity. This places you in the appealing position of (1) giving them some advice and encouraging them to contact you for more, (2) sending them some of your materials that address the issues they've raised, and (3) putting them on your mailing list for periodic communications. Sooner or later the timing approach will work, and they will feel an itch that prompts them to think of you. (It's hard to turn down the luncheon request of a fellow board member.)

Ironically and shockingly, the greatest impediment to pro bono work of this sort is that many organizations will opt not to use the help! I've been turned down by school boards, business recovery councils, and volunteer groups of many types despite my credentials and references and despite their clear need (and often appeals) for help. The reasons vary, but they are usually twofold. First, an outside consultant can create fear among those who know that they have been performing poorly but have been able to conceal the fact because of a lack of scrutiny. These people often want to control the consultant's intervention, and this is ethically unacceptable to me.

Second, there is sometimes a bureaucratic requirement of one type or another that is unattractive or impossible to meet (volunteers must contribute financially to the cause; 40 hours of background instruction is required; you must reside within a certain geographic area).[13]

---

[12] See "Do Good and Good Will Follow," pages 183–196, from my aforementioned book, *Best Laid Plans: Turning Strategy into Action Throughout Your Organization* (New York: Harper & Row, 1990; East Greenwich, RI: Las Brisas Research Press, 1995). Consultants can learn a great deal from nonprofit structures and operations and can impart this wisdom to conventional private-sector clients.

[13] A joint Providence Chamber of Commerce and Council of the Arts endeavor aimed at securing management consulting help for art institutions is my favorite boondoggle. After advertising for business executives to serve as consultants—whom they would "train" in consulting techniques—they turned down my offer to help because I wouldn't commit to their rudimentary and tedious "training" process. In other words, I wasn't a consultant until they told me I was! Bureaucracy, of course, is the triumph of means over ends.

Thus, it's important that you volunteer frequently and diversely until you establish a win/win relationship with groups of your choice. Don't be discouraged by being brushed off. It's an occupational reality for volunteering consultants.

> *One Percent Solution: Focus on pro bono work that puts you in regular contact with people you want to meet, either as buyers or as recommenders. Don't take on positions where you staff the phone by yourself or merely operate out of your home.*

In volunteering your services, underpromise and overdeliver. Unlike the normal client relationship, it's important here to be regarded for what you do *and* for what you say.

Here are the guidelines I've found useful for considering whether or not to undertake a pro bono job:

- Do I believe unequivocally in the cause?
- Can I commit the total time required by my promise and by the expectations of the organization? Just because I'm volunteering doesn't mean that I don't have to live up to my commitment. If I can't appear at every meeting and perform every task, I won't accept.
- Is the group organized in such a way that I'll be able to make the contribution I'm capable of? If a politically oriented officer holds veto power, for example, the group probably can't make the best use of my talents.
- Is the group involved in a public good? The legions of lemminglike volunteers for the defunct est organization were certainly doing something for nothing, but it was to enrich the coffers of an individual and his organization.[14]
- Is there an impact or outcome to be made, and can my contribution be recognized as supporting it? Any local school fund-raiser, charitable event, or chamber of commerce undertaking would seem to fill this bill. The California commission investigating self-esteem, once parodied so well in the comic strip *Doonesbury*, did not.

---

[14] est stands for Earhard Seminar Training, one of the first and, in my opinion, most dubious of the self-awareness guru-school movements. It was a questionable ethical undertaking rivaled in squeamishness, for me, by today's "multilevel marketing."

- Are there other people involved, directly or indirectly, with whom I would want to establish a relationship? Will I work side by side twice a month with the presidents of two state banks? Will I present the report to the governor at the quarterly progress meetings? What kind of networking will I be able to establish? "What's in it for me?" is not the primary reason for wanting to do good works, of course. However, when you consider pro bono projects within the framework I've defined in this section, it's quite reasonable to analyze what benefits might emerge for you.

- Will the nature of the particular pro bono opportunity appeal to a client or prospect who may be involved with that cause? Health-care prospects will look more favorably on a firm that, although it has no current health-care clients, has done volunteer work in setting strategy or evaluating personnel for community health-care projects. If one of your client CEOs is a chairperson for the Red Cross, for example, and you're considering volunteer work anyway, the Red Cross certainly has a built-in attraction.[15]

- Is there a clear path to disengagement if desired (e.g., term limits, tenured commitments, moving on to other responsibilities)?

Volunteer consulting work should never be done if it conflicts with your client responsibilities, nor should it be done as a substitute for an orthodox client relationship. However, I believe that it should be a normal and ongoing part of your investment in your own success—a low-key marketing approach that will do good for you as you do good for others. It's often overlooked.

I find that I'm almost always the sole consultant involved in volunteer efforts, amidst bankers, retailers, educators, insurance professionals, and utility executives. It's more than slightly ironic that one productive path to million dollar consulting pays no immediate fees, which may be why so few venture into it.

I completed a pro bono strategy session for a women's shelter and was immediately hired to do the same for the local police department, business that I ordinarily would never receive. The chief of police was on the shelter's board. He hired me on the spot.

Despite the best investments in success and the greatest diligence in trying to develop your business and your personal capabilities, uncontrollable events can intervene. Let's see how even bad times can become good times if you'll let them.

---

[15] This fits in with the communications tactics under "special events" discussed earlier.

THE ESSENCE OF MARKET GRAVITY

Over a decade ago I developed a concept called "market gravity," which is the larger universe from which these various elements in this chapter arise. You can see it in Figure 2-3 and 13-4.

As you revolve around the sphere you can see the diverse elements available to you (more so now than ever, in an electronic age) that are both passive (Web site) and proactive (press releases or interviews). For a solo practitioner seeking to create a seven-figure practice, the gravity wheel is critical to ensure that you have ongoing marketing efforts in place. This belies the old rubric about being unable to market and deliver at the same time, or needing staff to perform marketing tasks.

Decide which of these best fit in your comfort zone. Put those in place. Then choose those that are slightly out of your comfort zone and pursue them. Finally, as you get more comfortable and successful, pursue those you thought you'd never get to.

I use them all, even at this stage of my career. You'll read about virtually all of them at various points in this book. You must create your own gravitational pull. Once you do, clients will come rushing up to you.

QUESTIONS AND ANSWERS

Q. *What about publishing a chapter in a book with "name" authors who allow me to do so for a fee?*

A. What about one of the nuttiest scams going? Those "name" authors don't need you or the book; they do this to produce revenue for themselves from people like you, and no one buys the book. Spend your time and money on legitimate efforts, not worthless shortcuts.

Q. *How much should a speakers' bureau receive if I obtain repeat business from a speaking engagement?*

A. Usually speakers' bureaus demand their normal commission of 25 percent (or worse) for "spin-off" business, meaning more speeches obtained at that client. However, my rule is that if I obtain consulting business, I will provide only a 10 percent commission on the first project. The bureau doesn't deserve 25 percent of a six-figure deal, even though it introduced me.

Q. *How much can I deduct for pro bono work on my taxes?*

A. Only the mileage, and even that at a lower rate than business mileage. You cannot deduct services provided under any circumstances.

Q. If I do self-publish in conjunction with commercial publishing, what would make it most closely resemble commercial publishing?

A. Put an ISBN number on your work (available from J. D. Bowker through the Internet), place it on Internet sites such as Amazon, use a professional graphic artist; use four colors on the jacket or cover, have it printed, not run off your computer, and generally follow the formatting you see in major books.

Q. How much of your "marketing gravity" constitutes a critical mass for success?

A. I do all of it. I'd suggest you should be engaged in a minimum of six of the techniques at any one time, more if you can. If none is comfortable or makes sense, then you're in the wrong business.

Final Thought: You must place your name and repute in front of prospects at every opportunity. There are scores of ways to do this, all described in the foregoing pages. If you don't blow your own horn, there is no music.

HOW TO MAKE BIG MONEY IN BAD TIMES

KNOWING WHEN TO HOLD 'EM AND WHEN TO FOLD 'EM

EARLY WARNING SIGNS OF BUSINESS DECLINE

This section is concerned with your business, not the general economy, which will be covered in the next section. I'm not suggesting that you should be an economic prognosticator, which is a rough equivalent to the astrologers I mentioned in the preface. However, I will suggest that you be prudent in assessing your own cards and realistic in deciding how to play them. A lot of people have lost the farm pulling for an inside straight.

There is a tendency in our business to look no further than the latest client check. Those with great foresight sometimes look all the way to the longest-term signed contract. However, you have to look past all the guaranteed stuff and into the realm of the uncertain. You have to know what's at the other end of your pipeline.

The pipeline approach to sales forecasting and early warning of business decline is illustrated in Figure 12-1. At the near end of the pipeline are your current implementation assignments, and within the pipeline are your contracts waiting to be implemented, moving up to their turn in the flow. At the opposite end of the pipeline are the prospects and targets that you would like to induce into the flow. Along the way are the repeat business deals with current clients and the short-term proposals that are accepted (these are wonderful but rare, like the inside straight).

As I write this in late 2008, I'm receiving scores of e-mails from colleagues requesting entry into my mentor program. They typically had $225,000 to $800,000 in business last year, and they now expect to perhaps squeeze out only $75,000 to $200,000 this year. Three months ago they had dozens of tentative contracts lined up, and today they have only a few certain and several possible. How many of us can live on a quarter of last year's income or expectations, especially with growing families and increasing obligations?

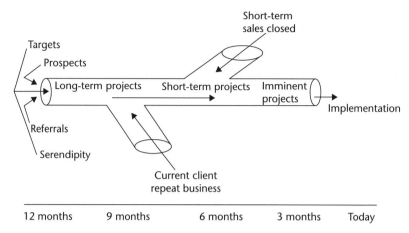

Figure 12-1. The business "pipeline."

Some of these people are over 50 years old, which is late in life to keep fill-ing pipelines. (Two problems, quickly revealed: they bill out at an hourly rate, meaning that they must bill 50 to 80 hours a week to make a quarter of a mil-lion, and they don't gain conceptual agreement prior to proposals, which is why so many tentative yes responses become final no responses when the prospect gets cold feet.)

Long-term contracts are those that are due to conclude in about 12 months. (Many organizations cannot, according to their own policies, make multi-fiscal-year agreements.) This means that they are assignments requiring a long time period for completion, or they are projects that you won't begin until several months hence because of either the client's schedule or yours. In either case, you know that you'll be working and receiving income "out there," which, for my purposes, is about 12 months. As the due dates approach, these become short-term projects, with implementation responsibilities about 6 months or so away. Finally, they become *imminent*, meaning that you'll be starting the implementa-tion at any time.

> *One Percent Solution: Pipelines come in all sizes and capacities. The dimensions are all created by you.*

Now here is the snag that trips up most consultants who try to forecast their business and, consequently, their cash flow. *Everything in my pipeline is signed and sealed.* In almost all other cases, however, consultants use prospects and potential business as the flow in their pipeline. (As with the individuals just discussed.) This "potential pipeline" creates several instant hazards:

1. The pipeline will not be a predictor of guaranteed business. It is a predictor of *potential* business. In actuality, if none of the potential materializes, the pipeline could be totally empty at any given moment. It's not a pipeline so much as a sieve.

2. If the potential is realized, it is often imminent business. That is, the consultant calculates that a potential deal will require 12 months to close. If that's accurate, when it does close, it's now due to be delivered. What of the shorter-term business, repeat business, and other imminent business? How does one coordinate all this? Is it really feast or famine?

3. Marketing activity should be aimed at the other end of the pipeline to create contracts within the pipeline. If the pipeline is filled with potential business, where is the marketing effort to be focused? Wouldn't you have to market *within* the pipeline as well, since this business is pending and could go either way?

4. There is a false sense of security in having a great deal of potential business lined up. One tends to ease up on marketing at the source of the pipeline to concentrate on the "sure things" within it. If these things fall through, there is little entering the system.

5. Consultants are dysfunctionally overoptimistic in projecting potential business. ("He returned my call and said he liked my approach, so this will probably be $35,000 in a couple of months." In reality, this isn't even a real economic buyer, just a lonely training manager desperately seeking companionship!)

The area I designate for prospects considering proposals is outside the entrance to the pipeline. I focus my marketing efforts there (mailings, speeches, articles, interviews, blog, books, and so on) and place referrals there as well. Only after an agreement is signed does the firm enter my system. This means that any adverse effects—prospects rejecting a proposal, the competition beating me out for an assignment, a verbal approval being overturned, and the like—are outside my pipeline.

Thus, I can look about a year out (often with my bankers at my shoulder) and get a realistic view of cash flow and profit.[1] And I know that I must continually

---

[1] Even if clients avail themselves of discounts for payment on signing, I still allocate the revenue stream according to the implementation dates. In this way, I know that a $125,000 project is to be implemented in three months, regardless of whether the client has already paid the invoice.

corral and cajole business into those pipeline openings. This is much easier to do at the long-term end than at the imminent end because I have time to work on the prospect, and I don't feel a desperation in trying to close the business.

When the pipeline is dry, the pressure builds to create business that is virtually ready to be delivered, and this is usually poor business at poor fees.

Digression

The most frustrating question that I'm often asked in coaching consultants is: "What are the best ways to raise short-term cash?" The answer is: "There aren't any."

You can and should call everyone you know, go back to past clients and offer new value, and so forth. But, in reality, this is not a "quick cash" business, because even referrals and leads and business from those sources will take quite a while for ultimate approval and a check to clear your bank.

The preventive actions I'm describing are far better than the contingent actions, which are all that remain if you fail at the preventive.

Fourteen Pipeline Red Flags

These are the red flags that will indicate that you may be looking at some business economic problems in terms of flow, velocity, and volume:

1. The pipeline is filled with potential, not signed business.
2. The business in the pipeline is not evenly distributed but is clumped together at one period.
3. You have no idea who the prospects and targets are that constitute potential entries into the pipeline.
4. Every organization in or around the pipeline is an existing client—there are no new prospects represented.
5. Repeat business from current clients is absent from the pipeline.
6. No referrals appear or make it into the pipeline.
7. All business enters the pipeline at the same entrance, for example, two weeks out or three months from now.
8. Pipeline business disappears without warning.

9. There are clumps and gaps instead of a smooth flow.

10. Some pipeline business is contractual, and some is simply probable.

11. Projects that do come to fruition are invariably at lower fees than expected.

12. The inputs to the pipeline are reduced to just one or two conduits.

13. You don't physically view your pipeline weekly because you don't expect any changes.

14. You're getting business that was never in your pipeline (meaning that you aren't controlling potential very well).

If these or similar conditions occur, you can bet that your cash flow and stability will suffer in the months ahead. While it's always possible to deal with these conditions on a contingency basis—borrow money, go after short-term business, scramble for subcontracting work—it's far better to prevent these desperation measures by examining your flow for the red-flag conditions and taking appropriate preventive measures.

This is a paper exercise that can be done on a plane or while waiting for an appointment. There's really no excuse to be surprised by assignments drying up. Yet so many of us, caught up in the euphoria of current business and its delivery, blandly assume that there's more where this came from. The only real measure of whether there is more is in scrutinizing the pipeline for real business and lining up enough prospects to clog the entrances to the pipe. *I don't want to see the light at the end of this tunnel. I want so many prospects lined up that all I see are bodies clambering to get in.*

THE FIVE "UP-TIME" RULES

There is an old apocryphal story about a speaker pitching his cassette series, which I'll call, "How to Think Positively and Grow Very Rich." He had explained all its benefits, cited the cost as an unbelievably low $495, and told the audience that it could buy the series right then and there and receive a 10 percent discount off the unbelievably low price. He wound up his spiel by asking, "Can anyone cite a reason *not* to buy this invaluable set of tapes?"

After handling some routine questions, the speaker acknowledged a man in the middle of the audience with his hand raised. "I think your approaches are wonderful," said the man, "but I have a perfect reason not to buy. I can't afford it."

There was an unmistakable agreeing murmur from the crowd, which was cut off by the speaker with an extraordinary retort.

"That's exactly why you should buy it!" he yelled. The crowd was confused. "Tell me," continued the speaker, "how old are you, sir?"

"Thirty-one."

"Did you graduate from high school?"

"Yes."

"Did you graduate from college?"

"I have an associate's degree from a junior college."

"Have you been continuously employed since graduation?"

"Yes. I've worked for three firms."

"What's your current position?"

"I'm a payroll supervisor for the local hospital."

"So," summarized the speaker, moving toward the man, "you have an associate's degree, have never been unemployed, and at the age of 31, after over a decade of continuous employment, you can't even afford to purchase a set of tapes for $495 that you think are wonderful! That's why you need them—because you haven't been thinking positively, and you *certainly* haven't grown rich!"

After the meeting, the crowd surged around the product booth, frantically waving money and credit cards. So the story goes.

One Percent Solution: You are what you believe. You behave in the manner in which you talk about yourself. That can be either frightening or invigorating. That's for you to determine.

If you believe that times are bad for you, they will be, because your actions will be predicated on dealing with bad times. If you believe that all times can be good for you, they will be, because your actions will be consistently supporting your growth despite conditions around you.

In the aftermath of the September 11, 2001, tragedy, consultants worried if there would be work for them in the near future. Yet there has been active business amidst cataclysms: in the Depression, during both world wars, during the Vietnam War, after recent hurricanes, during gas crises, during unpopular wars, and during economic chaos.

If there is business being transacted, there is a need for consulting. My business has been consistently strong irrespective of the economy, consumer confidence, the stock market, and myriad other traditionally worrisome factors. My finest year to date has been 2008, with over 2 million in revenue (which is 90 percent profit), and I'm not alone: I began the Million Dollar Club this year for a dozen of us who were enjoying great prosperity. The initial offering filled immediately.

If you think you can do it or you think you can't do it, you're right in either case.

Rule 1: Use Down Times as a Spur for Taking Action

Often, the very objections that people raise also hold the reasoning to convince them that they should proceed. In down times, consultants often hunker down and assume the worst. Sometimes they actually put themselves out of business (see the advice about not selling the conference table near the end of this chapter). However, there are some clear actions that enable you not merely to avoid down times, but also to continue your growth despite them.

I've established that the conceptual sale is the key to selling new business. This is more important than ever in down times.

If a client says, "I couldn't agree more that we ought to undertake this project, but we just can't afford to," you are in the position of the preceding speaker to reply, "That's *exactly* why you have to begin now. The longer you wait, the more you'll fall behind, and the more expensive it will be to catch up. The sooner you make the investment, the more money you'll save. If money is the only thing stopping you, let's work out a payment schedule that alleviates that pain as much as possible, and let's start generating the payback immediately."

If prospects persist in stating that money is the hang-up after stating that they need what you're suggesting, you haven't really made the conceptual sale. Once the conceptual sale is made, the prospect will see the cost in terms of an investment on a future return, and the mechanics of a payment schedule can be worked out easily.

Rule 2: Diversify Geographically

During the early 1990s, while most of the country experienced some degree of recession, New England was actually in a depression. Many of my colleagues in the consulting and speaking professions had been severely affected, often to the point of pursuing traditional jobs in sales or administration, hoping to go back to consulting when things improved. (Of course, this meant that they weren't really consultants, but rather people whose hobby was consulting. Can you picture an attorney or an architect going into insurance sales because business is poor?)

I continued to grow during those tough times. Revenues increased by 45 percent from 1989 to 1990 alone. You see, I had only five clients in all of New England. The rest of my business was all over the country, with some in other countries.[2] You cannot allow your business to be overly concentrated geographically, not

[2] See Chapter 18 for obtaining international clients. Also see my book (with Omar Kahn) *The Global Consultant* (Hoboken, N.J.: Wiley, 2008).

just because of regional economic conditions,[3] but also because a strong regional competitor can sometimes overwhelm you.

In the latter part of the 1990s and into the new millennium, my consulting revenues were 35 percent in the Northeast, 45 percent in the remainder of the United States, and 20 percent overseas. My product sales and other streams of income are about 35 percent international. Business ultimately should be as diversified as a good investment portfolio.

Many of us have had great years despite the 2008 economic meltdown because we are able to do business all over the world, physically and/or economically.

Rule 3: Don't Be Vulnerable to the Same Economic Conditions Threatening Your Clients

The economy is like a hydraulic system. When something goes down, something else goes up. Even in the worst of times, *someone* is doing well.

I've found that some industries do well regardless of the economy as long as they're well managed. The pharmaceutical industry is one example. There are others that do well in bad times—self-help, for example, because people are more likely to make repairs or build something themselves rather than buying new. And then there are the industries that thrive when the economy rebounds, such as air travel, hotels, and recreation. The pet care and pet health industry is almost always strong.

If you're a content specialist, it's somewhat more difficult to diversify industrially. However, my advice to all is to diversify by industry and sector to the maximum extent possible. Try to obtain clients who do well consistently, clients who thrive during downturns, and clients who thrive during upturns.

The outplacement business thrives during economic downturns; executive search thrives during economic upturns. A true consulting business thrives during both. Diversify your client and prospect portfolio.

Rule 4: Increase Your Personal Productivity

Every week you have approximately 40 hours (if you intend to live a balanced life) to invest in your growth. In the worst times, you won't be using any of those hours to deliver client projects, deposit checks in the bank, or close business. Therefore, during these worst of weeks, what is the opportunity for you?

---

[3] Periodically, states such as Florida and California have attempted to pass sales taxes on service firms, which would make consulting services more expensive for the client (or decrease the consultant's margin if absorbed). These tax liabilities pose a significant threat to growth.

Activity	Hours per week
Call two "old" clients a day to maintain communication	5
Call two prospects a day to follow up on proposals	2.5
Send letter/package/press kit to five targets a day	5
Network by phone with colleagues once a day	2.5
Research or write an article for magazine publication	5
Research speaking possibilities in associations	2.5
Volunteer or perform pro bono work locally	3
Read professional literature for personal growth	3
Attend an association meeting or conference	3
Create/upgrade your press kit and examine others' kits	2
Plan a client conference or select advisory board members	2
Plan "in the neighborhood" mailings for future trips	1
Call subcontractors to review current or planned work	2
Spend time with or develop an alliance partner	2.5
Plan the next mass mailing to your list	2
Take your banker to lunch or pay a courtesy call	2
Surf the Internet to find prospects	1
Examine and upgrade your professional listings	1

Figure 12-2. Eighteen actions to take during a "down week."

Figure 12-2 shows a suggested 40-hour "down week" schedule that is consistent with pursuing multidimensional growth despite conditions around you.

The more astute among you will have noticed that there are more than 40 hours represented. This is so because some items may not apply to you (although if you're following my advice, they should), some of you will invest more than 40 hours, and some of you may be able to move more quickly than the time I've allocated. No matter. The point is that there is *plenty* to do even when there's no client work to be done.

Rule 5: Watch the Company You Keep

Finally, I've always tried to work solely with companies with which I'm proud to do business. I don't accept assignments that require drastic cost cutting through the ranks in order to fund lucrative executive bonuses; I won't lie to or deceive client employees; I won't assist a company that is treating its customers badly or selling obviously inferior products or fraudulent services; and I won't work with executives whose orientation is bigoted or crude.

Quite simply, clients who treat their employees and customers shabbily will treat their consultants shabbily. In poor times, they will refuse to pay the bill or honor their commitments. They will make unreasonable demands, take credit for your contributions, and blame you for any shortcomings. Companies and managers who act poorly in good times will act horribly in bad times.

My rule of thumb for evaluating the acceptability of a client is very simple: Would I purchase stock in this firm? Would I invest my own money and future in the quality of this firm's management, strategy, products, services, and employees? If I'm not certain—or if I'm certain I wouldn't—why on earth would I want that company as a client?

CONTRARIAN CONSULTING: ESCAPING THE RIP TIDE

Changing times are often interpreted as bad times. Changes can threaten consultants because their precious matrices, formulas, and models may no longer be applicable or embraced. Is anyone out there still enamored of transactional analysis as a management tool[4] or applying Maslow's hierarchy of needs as a pragmatic method for motivating people? Left-brain/right-brain thinking has been debunked, thank goodness, and any current fad will also give way to its successor in good time.

People are no longer singing the praises of reengineering, and total quality management is no longer a fight song.

Million dollar consultants welcome change because it represents *opportunity*, not threat. Change provides the possibility of demonstrating new talents, helping clients in new ways, and embarking on entirely new approaches. Change is essential for dramatic growth to be possible. And one excellent way to exploit change—indeed, to *create* change—is what I call contrarian consulting.

The speaker mentioned earlier who took an objection and turned it inside out by using it as a validation was being contrarian. "I can't do it" is followed by "that's why you should do it." I open many executive conferences by asking, "How many of you truly believe in training?" Every hand always shoots up. After looking around the room, I tell the audience that I don't believe in training. "You train animals," I explain, "but you must *educate* people." (I heard the poet Maya Angelou comment on that once and never forgot it.)

This comparison and the immediate challenge to traditional clichés rivet attention and create quite a stir. I am instantly different from other consultants

---

[4] It's still used in therapeutic approaches, as it should be and was always meant to be.

these people have worked with or considered.[5] The first article I ever wrote for a publication (which eventually paid me to write a column for three years) was titled, "The Myth of QC [Quality Control] Circles," and it was written at the peak of the popularity of those employee-participation programs. (My point was that management often used the program as a substitute for its own responsibility for quality and didn't follow through on participants' suggestions, making the situation actually worse than it was before the program's implementation. This turned out to be the rule rather than the exception.)

My advice to clients is often to reduce training and invest more in education. Learning should be as close as possible to the application of what's learned, and seminars are notorious for sterile learning that is quickly forgotten because it can't be readily applied. Now how many consultants do you think have been telling their clients and prospects that there's too much training going on?

Many organizations believe that quality is what they think it is, which usually means "zero defects." I tell them that what they think is irrelevant. It's the customer who will determine what quality is, and what I can help the organization learn and apply is just what criteria the customers are using! Quality, I patiently explain, is not the absence of something in managements' eyes (that is, defects), but the presence of something in the consumers' eyes (that is, value).

> *One Percent Solution: Contrarian doesn't mean "wrong"; it means "against the prevailing conventional wisdom." Scarily, it seems to me that common sense these days is actually contrarian.*

If you don't think that this gets attention, then you just haven't tried to stray from the beaten track. Most quality approaches I've seen—with six- and seven-figure investments—are all backward, in that they focus inward and not outward.

> *A unique approach is required if a small consulting firm is to win the same types of major lucrative contracts won by larger firms. You don't become unique by trying to do what the larger firms already do. You become unique by beating a new track—a contrarian track.*

---

[5] This is consistent with the strategy outlined in Chapter 4 of distinct service and breakthrough relationships. Contrarian positions are wonderful tools for implementing that strategy.

I've found that in bad times and in times of uncertainty and change (which is most of the time these days), executives are not falling back on the tried and true. They are receptive to new approaches and are willing to swim upstream if there is someone credible to guide them. I have no intention of trying to develop a strategy matrix to compete with that of the Boston Consulting Group. However, I'm happy as a clam to offer clients a strategic approach that places strong emphasis on values at two different levels in the organization (strategic and tactical), which most of them have never even thought about. I don't want to compete with Accenture to design outplacement programs in times of staff reductions. Instead, I gain entry and attention by explaining how to *add* superb talent during down times that otherwise would be out of reach. And I won't touch merger and acquisition work for firms that are in excellent shape and are seeking to expand. However, I will implement a program for them to reduce their workforce over time, since smart management always should seek to stay as lean as possible, and the best time to ensure this is when the firm is in a position of strength and can treat people well, not during the desperation of economic problems and indiscriminate layoffs.

Digression

The way to escape a riptide, which mercilessly drags swimmers and even waders out to sea to drown, is not by trying to swim against the strong current. Instead, counterintuitively and contrary to what you'd imagine, you swim a few yards parallel to the beach and perpendicular to the riptide. This takes you out of its current to where the water is once more quite calm.

Your normal reaction would probably kill you in a riptide. You have to think and act differently.

Are you getting the picture? If you take nothing else out of this book, understand that a central element in achieving wealth is to acquire the same large contracts that major consulting firms do with a small firm's smaller overhead and better economies of operation. However, it's virtually impossible to do this by trying to outperform the big firms at what they do so well to have grown so large.

You must seek out different paths that aren't always in the mainstream, but that you can justify and substantiate as being of tremendous value added in improving the client's condition. This is what I call *contrarian consulting*. It will get you speaking engagements, it will get you published, it will get you noticed, and it will get you rich once you become good at it.

> *Sign on the office wall of one of my clients: "If you're not the lead dog, the scenery never changes."*

I'll conclude this section by offering a few of my choices for those organizational issues that justify trying to swim against the current (see Figure 12-3). Remember, however, that these are my observations based on today's conditions. They may all be mainstream by the time you read this!

We've now examined what to look for in terms of your personal business down times, what to do to be productive in general economic down times, and how to swim against the current (and escape the riptide by ignoring the current) to create opportunity in down times or up times. But what happens when things get really bad? What do you do when you look up and see deep-sea creatures swimming in the waters above you? Don't panic—I'm here to tell you that we've all been there—and that you should do what you've been doing all along.

THE MYTH OF CUTTING EXPENSES (DON'T SELL THE CONFERENCE TABLE)

One of my friends runs an international training firm. When he gathers together his partners from around the world, he often hears lamentations of woe from areas where the economy has gone sour or a large client has defected. Invariably,

Issue	Contrarian View
Managing employee diversity	Assimilating employees
Day care for employees' children	Aged parents (at home) day care
Problem solving	Innovation
Succession planning	Boosting high-potential people
Merit pay for individual performance	Merit pay for team/organization performance
Handling complaints	Preempting complaints
Formulating strategy	*Implementing* strategy
Managing tasks	Managing outcomes
The employees serving customers	The employees *as* customers
Conflict resolution	Encouraging conflict

Figure 12-3 A contrarian view of contemporary business issues. Too many consultants simply try to follow the pack.

his partners recommend cutting expenses, cutting staff, and adopting a lower profile. After the cutback alternatives are exhausted, my friend gives what I call his "last-dollar speech."

"If you had only a dollar left," he asks, "would you try to stretch it out for as long as possible to feed your family increasingly meager meals each day, or would you invest the whole amount in a marketing plan that might create enough business to feed your family in proper style for a year or more?"

One Percent Solution: You cannot "cut back to growth." You must invest for growth. You can't harvest if you haven't planted. Go out and buy the seeds.

I'm always impressed by his logic whenever my prospects are dimmer than I'd prefer—after all, the dollar eventually will be gone, but the marketing effort can perpetuate itself.

There is a centrifugal force in our profession that pulls people toward conservatism when times seem bad. Risk is one thing when there's a hundred grand in the bank and clients knocking at the door, but it's quite another thing when your banker is a stranger and no one is knocking at the door. Yet the last thing to do in bad times is to pull in your horns and try to eke out an existence by reducing expenses "until things get better." In most cases, things don't get better unless you do something to make them get better, and you don't make things happen by doing less—you must do more.

Can you picture a professional sports team that has finished a mediocre season of .500 ball announcing at a press conference: "In view of our uninspired past season, we've decided to cut back on the coaching staff, reduce practice time, eliminate recruiting efforts, and halve the size of the conditioning area. We think that this will substantially improve our position for next year." The press would have a field day, season ticket holders would forsake the team, and the general public would lose interest after having a good laugh.

Now substitute publicity for press, clients for season ticket holders, and prospects for the general public, and you'll begin to see why even tacit plans to cut back your operation will create loss of repute and relationships.

When the Competition Seems to Be Retreating . . .

- Contact their existing clients, especially the ones that chose them over you.
- Take out a larger ad or listing in key market publications.

- Forge alliances with organizations cutting back on the kinds of competencies you can provide situationally.
- Speak at trade conferences, for free if you must, to accelerate your name recognition in a weakened field.
- Take very strong stands on issues in writing; don't be middle of the road or equivocal.
- Talk confidently, act confidently, and assure people that you can help them despite the times.
- Increase your testimonials and references so that people are assured.
- Pursue referrals vigorously and on every possible occasion.
- Consider taking a leading, highly visible position in a trade association or professional group.
- Offer contrarian articles to newspapers, magazines, and Internet publications.

In Chapter 14 I'll discuss credit lines and banking relationships in some detail. The point for now is, do not panic when things look tough. If you reduce your expenses by eliminating client mailings, attending fewer meetings and net-working events, putting in an answering machine to replace office staff, and the like, you are panicking. No matter how much you save, the "dollar" eventually will run out.

How do tough times become good ones? For starters, remember that the times are tough for others as well, and they are probably cutting back. This means that the same, continuing investment on your part for marketing and pub-licity *will carry even a better return because there is less perceived competition.*

Also, clients are impressed by consultants (and any outside professional or vendor) who act consistently in good times and bad and whose service and qual-ity performance do not vary. Third, no one knows anything about your personal successes and failures except what you choose to reveal. A cutback in your mar-ket profile and uncharacteristic behavior (that is, refusing to extend credit, demanding expense reimbursement for trivial items, and arbitrary fees) will tell clients and prospects exactly what you don't want them to know.

You are never alone in tough times, but you can be alone in exploiting them for opportunity. Your attitude must be: "Everyone else has it tough. How can I exploit my position?"

One group of partners I know had periodic meetings about the hard times that had beset their firm. Two of the three continually sought increased visibility and better marketing avenues and a generally more aggressive role in client support. The third, Carl, repeatedly argued for drastic cost reductions, which the other two sometimes acquiesced to for "consensus" reasons. Finally, when things were at their nadir, Carl once again asked for cost cutbacks. When asked what was left to cut back, he suggested selling the large maple conference table in the firm's lone meeting area.

"It's worth about 500 bucks," he explained, "and that will pay the rent next month."

"And our clients and prospects," responded one of the others, "will sit on the floor or remain standing!?"

The conference table wasn't sold, the partners stopped trying to reduce expenses, and Carl eventually became a subcontractor for them. He wasn't cut out for taking risks, and he never again earned significant reward.

It is a terrific temptation in tough times to stop spending and treat each dollar as if it were a vanishing resource that would never be seen again. There are a host of things wrong with this philosophy.

Digression

The impresario Mike Todd (one of Elizabeth Taylor's husbands) was once pushed by his financial people to reduce spending because he was 13 million in debt.

"What?" he yelled. "Do you want me to buy cheaper cigars?!"

In other words, some cutbacks just don't matter in the overall scheme of things.

If You Don't Invest during Tough Times . . .

1. You will cut back on your marketing just when it can deliver the biggest return because the competition is cutting back.

2. Clients will immediately detect any reduction in service commitments, jeopardizing relationships that required years to build.

3. Prospects are not impressed by firms that stint in the acquisition process; they are impressed by firms that send several people to initial conferences and don't attempt to charge back expenses for exploratory meetings.

4. Your bankers are not nearly as concerned about expense control as they are about income. In fact, bankers lend money against some reasonable payoff. A marketing campaign, a new product, or a publicity trip can provide payoff. A reduction in expenses does not provide incentive to an investor.

5. You will effectively blunt your multidimensional growth. Networking, memberships, pro bono work, and related activities all take a hard hit when expenses are reduced.

6. You will not be attractive to recruits, subcontractors, or alliance partners. No one is comfortable with someone who is attempting to work on a shoestring or someone who pays her bills late or doesn't invest the proper resources to get a job done in a high-quality manner. These sources of income and assistance to your firm will evaporate.

7. You will become totally reactive because your ability to invest in proactive measures will disappear. Consequently, you will be too late, too often, with too little. It is virtually impossible to practice contrarian consulting, for example, in a low-profile reactive mode.

8. You lose the momentum gained from prior growth by reducing to a standstill. You can broad jump much farther by racing down the approach than you can by standing at the edge of the pit.

9. You get one chance with prospects, and if they detect an inferior operation, they will quickly depart. This applies to the quality of your letterhead, the shine on your shoes, your response time, and any number of small things that indicate whether an operation is strong or struggling.

10. Finally, you are taking the risks of an entrepreneur. Be bold, and bite off large chunks. You're not in this to stick your toe in the water. You're in this to make waves.

One Percent Solution: "No cross, no crown" (William Penn). If you don't take risks, you will never reap the rewards available to an entrepreneur.

I talked in Chapter 3 about the success trap. Here I am talking about the *failure trap*. You can fail in this business only if you allow yourself to fail, and one of the surest ways to do that is by adopting a failure mentality when times are tough. Cutbacks and cost reductions are symptoms of failure and self-defeat, and represent a poverty mentality. Consistent relationships and activities, during all times, are signs of a success mentality. You establish the image that you convey to the client, and your image is notoriously transparent.

I've never met a consultant who wasn't doing "fabulous" business. Everyone I meet in the business tells me how great he is doing. And that's funny, because I meet a great many consultants who double-bill clients for expenses,[6] are dressed poorly, don't have any current literature, never attend industry or trade conferences, and haven't tried anything new or adventurous in years.

They are as obvious as a ham sandwich, and if they think that their clients and prospects can't see what the rest of us can, they are about as intelligent as a ham sandwich.

Bad times can be especially good times if you allow them to be—if you step away from the pack and the panicky responses. What would you advise a client in a highly competitive industry when economic conditions seem bleak? If you would advise that client to do anything *other* than to exploit the opportunities that others are unprepared or unwilling to address, not only are you lacking the stomach for this business, but you are also lacking the mind for it.

QUESTIONS AND ANSWERS

Q. *Isn't a pipeline just a rolling forecast that is bound to change?*

A. Not if you leave the assumptions and potential outside the pipeline intake conduits and include only contracts. In that case, very little will ever change except your bank account.

Q. *You really don't advise at least prudent cuts when business slows up?*

A. What's prudent to you and prudent to me? My advice is to conduct business as usual all the time: aggressively seeking buyers and gaining agreement on proposals.

Q. *How useful are a good banking relationship and credit lines during tough times?*

A. It's good to have them there, but they can be poison to use. Banks tend to increase interest rates, your credit rating will be lowered if you borrow substantially, and creating debt is never, ever good. It shouldn't be an early fallback position.

---

[6] This is the practice of visiting two or more clients during a single trip, but billing each one for the total expense rather than a pro rata share. Not only is this unethical, it is stupid.

Q. How do I discipline myself to do the right things during "up times"?

A. Use your calendar. Write in the steps and tasks for every week and treat them as serious appointments, not flexible, minor events. The best leverage you'll ever have is when you're strong and times are good.

Q. What about my partners, who believe that we should retrench, pull in our horns, and ride out the storm in the basement?

A. Quite a mixed metaphor, but a very simple reaction: leave them in the basement and go out on your own (or find new partners). Don't allow their weight to sink you.

Final Thought: The great successes in life have been those who didn't merely ride the wave of good times but were able to swim through the roiling waters of bad times. As an entrepreneur, you should have only one forward gear—full throttle.

CHAPTER 13

TECHNOLOGY IS A TOOL, NOT A FOOL

HOW TO USE TECHNOLOGY AND STILL HAVE A LIFE

SIGNS OF OUR TIMES

Over the past several years, I've probably attended 20 sessions on the impact of high technology on our lives and businesses. Each of the presentations was notable for at least one technological glitch. Such is modern life.

However, I am no Luddite, lurking in the shadows and fearing the Mithraic language of downloads, cyberspace, e-anything, social networking, twittering (does that make you a twit?), and firewalls. I'm with the in-crowd, with my own very dynamic Web site, four different e-mail drops, Alan's Blog on contrarian-consulting.com, Alan's Forums (a global destination for consultants interacting round-the-clock), registration with search engines, and enough computer para-phernalia to require that I visit the gym regularly to stay in shape merely to carry the proper connecting wires and rechargers when I travel. This entire chapter was inconceivable at the time I wrote the original manuscript for this book in 1991. It's de rigueur now.

I began to appreciate the power of technology and the political require-ments for it when Merck started consistently asking for fax access in the late 1980s and Hewlett-Packard integrated me into its voice-mail systems in the mid–1990s. Primitive, true, but nonetheless it represented the wind change prior to the tsunami. Some of my clients communicate exclusively by e-mail, maga-zines want articles submitted electronically, my Apple computers disdain to even accept anything that isn't wireless or telephathic, and computer-generated graph-ics are noticeable only if they are absent in any contemporary presentation using visual aids.

This is not a matter of deciding to use technological prowess any more than it's a discretionary decision to use the phone, a calculator, or a copy machine. You are no longer (as I learned while chatting with Walter Mossberg, the superb *Wall Street Journal* technology columnist) "on the Web" any more than you are "on the grid" when you plug in your toaster or your Stairmaster. It's an omnipresent condition.

Today, the urban legend has it, a casual reader of the weekday edition of the *New York Times* is processing more information than an inhabitant of the sixteenth century processed *in an entire lifetime*. The sixteenth century was not exactly chopped liver—it was the time of Luther and Erasmus, of the Renaissance, of exploration and discovery. Nonetheless, we are asked to assimilate (or at least consider) enormous amounts of data today. In the consulting profession, how does one remain current conversant with, and connected to the events not only in our discipline, but also in the domain of our clients? The only answer is to use technology as the catalyst, *but not as the constant companion sucking out all our energy.*

Case Study

A woman I didn't know called to request my resource list (a list of people willing to subcontract) so that she could select some help for a law firm for which she was consulting. I returned the call and asked for her e-mail address. The list is strictly electronic and would be 40 pages if printed.

"Oh, I don't have e-mail," she said, "so just print it out and fax it to me."

"I don't think so," I told her.

"Are you so superior you won't do that for me?"

"No, I just don't work with amateurs."

She turned out to be a part-time dabbler who picked up what money she could by promising the world but was able to deliver nothing. If you don't want to use e-mail, then you might as well also rip out your phone.

When I began my consulting career in 1972, I was (as low person in the pecking order) often crawling around what was known as the wet end of paper machines in southern mills. These huge plants employed hundreds of low-skill workers who maintained the monster machines with the manufacturer's manual in their back pockets and years of practical know-how and intuition in their heads. They often used brute force and could devise jerry-rigged solutions on the spot.

Today, the new generations of those machines require a handful of people covering all three shifts. They sit in control rooms and observation booths, monitoring computer information and changing the programming as needed. Brute force is applied only to the soda machine when it fails to cough up a Coke during the graveyard shift. It's a brave new world out there, and we'd better get accustomed to it.[1] Oh, and then there's the fact that paper (along with steel, rubber, and textiles) is not the major industry in the United States that it was when I was younger.

One Percent Solution: Invest in great technology, but don't worry about having the newest and the best versions of everything. The only test is: does it work for you?

My Internet connections can draw a detailed map with directions for virtually any business address in America. And that's just my iPhone. Rental cars now contain global positioning systems using satellites that take you—complete with back-seat-driver audible warnings—through every turn, exit, and adjustment along the route.

We simply can't afford to watch this parade wend its way by us. The Internet and its accoutrements haven't changed the face of consulting, as many gurus would have us believe, but they have offered marvelous ways to improve our effectiveness and efficiency.

CYBER MARKETING

I'm convinced that aggressive marketing over the Internet is akin to cold calling in real life—not many people are going to purchase consulting services from someone they've never heard of who approaches them out of the blue, be it by phone or by e-mail. However, passive marketing and visibility are effective on the Internet, no less than articles, interviews, ads, and listings can be effective in other media.

One Percent Solution: A consultant's Web site is not a sales tool; rather, it is a credibility tool. Economic buyers go there after they have heard of you, not before. That dictates how the site should look and feel.

---

[1] I heard noted leadership authority Warren Bennis state once that at some time in the near future, a factory would have only two workers, a man and a dog. The dog would be there to ensure that the man didn't touch anything. The man would be there to feed the dog.

Here are 10 quick techniques for Internet marketing success. Choose those that are best for you. No two of them are mutually exclusive, and I know people who do all of them.

1. *Contact prospects and clients by e-mail.* I do not mean that you should make solicitations. I mean that you should provide a periodic contact that is of some worth. You might use e-mail in place of a regular mailing (although you shouldn't abandon regular mailings altogether because they provide the opportunity for substantive enclosures). Randomly e-mail key people with items of interest and/or opportunity. One of my e-mail "partners" continually provides me with interview sources, and I appear about a dozen times a year in publications that came from his mailings to me.

2. *Establish an interesting Web site.* Note the operative word: *interesting.* The Internet is crammed with meaningless sites and vacuous poster boards. Create a site that compels people to visit repeatedly. Find a designer/marketer with the demiurgic talents required. For example:

   - Post an article every month that can be downloaded.
   - Archive past articles for access and downloading.
   - Conduct a raffle or giveaway for people who register each month.
   - Provide a free newsletter copy for those requesting it.
   - Provide a link to your e-mail so that people can correspond.
   - Use graphics and sound that change periodically.
   - Offer products for sale.
     Visitors to my Web site have a choice of pursuing special topic areas (such as books or workshops) or accessing hot tips. In addition, a wide variety of services is offered, including licensing and "schedule on demand."

3. *Use bookmarks to establish direct links with reference sources.* These online citations save you the trouble of continually looking for sources. You can access reference works, consulting associations, airline schedules, meteorological conditions, biographies, company locations, and a host of other invaluable information.

4. *Host a chat session.* I regularly conduct "chats" and online interviews with interactive displays, often including slides and graphics. You can direct people to more of your work, and the credibility is no different from having been interviewed on the radio or in the print media.

5. *Join information-exchange groups.* There are groups that meet formally at certain times or informally on a drop-in basis to discuss consulting, speaking, entrepreneurialism, finances, and just about any related topic imaginable. You can learn a great deal, contribute, build relationships, and enjoy significant growth by allocating as little as an hour a week. I host Alan's Forums (http://www.alansforums.com), which is home to over 40,000 posts and constant, global discussions on ethics, fees, politics, and dozens of other topics.

6. *Research your clients and prospects.* There is a wealth of information on major companies available through the major search engines that will help you prepare for your approach, meeting, proposal, or phone call. You also can send out e-mail notes to your networks asking for information from anyone who can help. People are remarkably responsive on the Internet. I once left a message in one place in a limited group asking if anyone knew a broker who could sponsor speeches in Australia, and I received three different leads within 48 hours. When I asked for help in creating a certain type of electronic file, 17 people responded within 20 minutes![2]

7. *Build your own newsletter.* I began "Balancing Act" seven years ago with 40 names of people who I thought would not be upset by my sending an unsolicited newsletter. I now have nearly 8,000 subscribers with virtually no promotion. The newsletter can be obtained— and is archived—on my Web site. One of my mentorees has successfully launched a weekly newsletter on sales tips that gains him business all over the country because it is passed around far beyond the subscriber list. This is highly effective and virtually free marketing.

8. *Subscribe to an interview service.* There are services that provide daily updates on reporters working under deadline and the topics they require more information about. You might find someone from the *San Francisco Examiner* working on a story exposing the futility of downsizing or a reporter for *BusinessWeek* pursuing information on why the glass ceiling hasn't broken. If it's up your alley, you can respond by e-mail and possibly arrange an interview. With any discipline at all, this can get you mentioned somewhere in the country on a weekly basis. You also can accomplish this by joining

---

[2] Be careful, though. I find platforms such as Linkedin to be nearly totally worthless. They claim to "connect" you to hundreds of thousands of people, but 99.9 percent of the communication is inane ("I'm working late tonight") and is usually concerned with finding a job or connecting with old friends (or old jobs). This stuff can absorb hours of your time if you allow it to, with very little return.

Expertclick.com or PRleads.com. Sometimes I'll find six of my mentorees cited in a single column in the Sunday *New York Times*.

9. *Link your Web site to others.* Many organizations will welcome a reciprocal arrangement, wherein your Web site is linked to theirs and theirs to yours. This increases the exposure and potential hits exponentially as long as you ensure that the connection makes sense. For example, it's logical for you to be interactive with a business school, but not so logical for you to be listed with an auto parts dealer (or with a competitor).

10. *Use your signature file intelligently.* You're sending thousands of e-mails a year. Include your contact information, a testimonial, information about a book or workshop, and so on. You never know who's going to read it and respond. It's free space with a huge potential return.

> *The Internet can be as boring as any other medium. It's up to you to attract people and entice them to want to know more about you. Technological novelty has been replaced by technological ennui.*

If you use some ingenuity and dedicate some otherwise down time to surfing the Net, you'll turn up all sorts of opportunities that are unique to you. For example, I found out that Amazon.com will also include my self-published books, so I've included them, and now I receive monthly orders from Amazon.com and, more important, monthly checks. (This is the Amazon Advantage Program.)

You also have to be prepared for success. Colleagues who run a "humor institute" fortunately were picked as one of the month's hot Web sites, but unfortunately were not prepared for such largesse. They had nothing to offer for sale, no way to track visitors (there were over 20,000 hits in a few days; such is the power of the medium), and couldn't keep up with the requests that were made. If you're going to do anything, assume that you'll be successful and prepare for the best, not the worst.

SOCIAL MEDIA AND OTHER FALLACIES

The problematic term *social media* has been applied to platforms such as YouTube, FaceBook, LinkedIn, Twitter, and scores of others. Hear me now: corporate buyers are not finding consultants on these platforms *because they are not looking on these platforms.* The folks with vested interests in them (or no life) who are shoulder deep in them of course take umbrage at my position.

Social media are fine (if you can excuse the inanity and often obscenity that you'll find in places such as YouTube). If you go to TED, for example (http://www.ted.com/), you'll find some outstanding thinkers presenting provocative ideas in under 20 minutes. That's great stuff. I don't consider it social media, just another example of powerful communications. But let's not split semantic hairs.

You don't market on LinkedIn, though you may find an old college classmate who cheated off you during finals. You don't achieve corporate fame on Twitter, though you may attract some unemployed people who are honestly curious about how you wash your hair or start your car.

> ***One Percent Solution: Use social media to socialize. Use marketing media to market.***

Whatever you purchase in technological terms will be obsolete before you can unwrap it. Who cares? Make sure that you buy something that you can use intelligently for the next several years, not something that will make you the envy of the gadgetry-challenged. You should be concerned about utility, not about being leading-edge.

Ask yourself these questions when considering any kind of equipment, from computers to cell phones to fax machines:

- *What is the end result you expect from this equipment?* This will help you determine how many bells and whistles you need. For example, a plain-paper fax machine that allows you to retain copies and keep transmissions in memory may make sense in terms of your basic communications needs. A fax machine with the capacity to store 100 numbers in memory or one that doubles as a copier may not. And if you're using computer software that can utilize your computer as a fax, why are you even hosting a fax machine in your office?
- *With whom will you be communicating?* If it's a large number of people all with the same message, some kind of networking arrangement or listserv may make sense. If it's to be single individuals, each with unique communications, high quality will be a necessity.
- *What are the volume requirements?* I have found that it's wise to plan at least three years down the road. A couple of years ago, I said to my

computer supplier that I wanted the capacity to deal with the volume I foresaw five years hence. He suggested a Mac Quadra 840av, with scanner, laser printer, color printer, and high-speed modem, along with an Iomega backup disk drive. It lasted for nearly five years, before being replaced by a G3 desktop. Then I acquired the Titanium G4 laptop. My plan for these purchases was to obtain three to five years of outstanding service. (I know many of you are surprised, but I find Macs to be idiot-proof, intuitive, and quite easy to use. With today's software, I can easily communicate with my clients' personal computers without any difficulty, so there are no compatibility problems.) I now have Intel-based Mac desktops and laptops, 30-inch cinema screens, a wireless home via Airport Express, and so on. I tell you all this because, by the time you read it, both you and I will be on still more modern gizmos.

- *What trends do you expect to capitalize on?* If you're going to be using a computer on the road, don't just buy a laptop, buy one that is compatible with your office equipment (they can access each other remotely and transfer files by infrared devices) to maximize efficiency and minimize duplication of effort. For example, can they synchronize with Palm Pilot (or your PDA) technology? I use a flash drive to keep all my files right in my briefcase to plug in wherever needed.

Case Study

I use an iPhone for expense reporting and my contact list, with phone numbers. However, I don't use it for my calendar, notes, or files.

One client had to frantically reschedule my meeting—which involved a five-hour flight —when his secretary pointed out that he was scheduling using the calendar for the year 2012. I've watched consultants desperately try to use the primitive stylus to take complex notes at a client conference.

Use what makes sense as a tool, but don't confuse means and ends. It's better to use 20 percent of a technology's potential effectively than it is to be utterly flummoxed by trying to use the other 80 percent that is inappropriate, inadequate, or indecipherable.

My service standard is to return all calls within 90 minutes during business hours. This is much easier than it appears, although clients and prospects invariably are knocked out by the responsiveness. I never have a tough time returning calls because of a lack of equipment or accessibility.

Are the calls expensive? Less and less. We'll soon be able to use cell phones on airplanes and I can send and receive e-mail on some. Are they worth it? Unquestionably. My monthly phone bills used to be about $2,400. An entire year's worth—just under $30,000—were paid for by one modest contract or a couple of speeches. Today, my office phone, three car phones, and my wife's and my personal cell phones cost about $450 per month.[3]

Another form of personal assistant is a contact manager. These software packages enable you to track clients, prospects, visibility outlets, and many others; provide the option to trigger contacts at set intervals; and keep track of prior discussions and agreements. They also come with autodial features, boilerplate letters, and other time-saving options.[4]

BLOGS AND BRANDS

There are, according to some best guesses, about 200 million blogs extant in the world. You read that correctly. (There are only 30 million Canadians alive, and about 28 million Australians, so consider that.) And most of the blogs are pure crap and imbecilic, because

- The author has no expertise, credibility, or experience.
- You can't identify who is writing it.
- It is written sophomorically.
- It is poorly formatted and presented.
- It is irrelevant.
- It is driven by ego.

Generally, if someone has a brand, he will have a successful blog:

- Personal businesses: David Meister
- Sales: Jeff Gitomer

---

[3] And, of course, my iPhone provides e-mail contact, photos, a camera, Web browsing, location GPS, music, and so on. It replaces at least four other gadgets.

[4] I'm all in favor of time saving, but not at the cost of individuality. Most boilerplate stuff, be it proposals, confirmations, or other documents, looks exactly like that: generic pap. It's always a good idea to customize anything you put in writing.

- Innovation: Seth Godin
- Coaching: Marshall Goldsmith
- Solo consulting: Moi

Note that the brand draws people. Now, there are those (including the esteemed, aforementioned Seth Godin) who would claim that blogs create brands. Yes, one time in 100,000, like the first-time novelist who gets the million dollar advance. Don't bet on it.

My blog (http://www.contrarianconsulting.com) has text, podcasts, video, commentary, and all kinds of features that accrue each week. My brand gets people there, and the quality keeps them coming back for more. If you want an effective blog, develop a powerful brand.

Technology can expedite your business, or it can homogenize you to the point of nonrecognition. The choice is yours.

Just as there are letterheads and stationery available from supply houses that give consultants that professional look without the expense of a designer and a personalized touch, there are technologies that can provide a mass approach for the lone wolf who has to rely on the kindness of strangers. (Many blogs look alike, being similar in their horrible design and terrible presentation.) However, those stock letterheads can be an obvious giveaway that you're operating on a shoestring if the prospect recognizes the design (and there are finite options here), and that prospect can feel an impersonal touch if your move to efficiency overcomes your need for singularity.

For example, most e-mail systems will allow a file attachment that creates an automatic "signature" appended to your letter to identify you beyond your screen name. It's the equivalent of a letterhead. This is an appropriate—in fact, necessary—addition to your e-mail because the correspondent may want to send you something in the regular mail, fax you, or phone you. It's silly to have to exchange further missives to obtain this information, so it's only logical to include it in all correspondence on the Web. (*Note*: Many consultants do not include signature files, and their image screams "unprofessional.")

Mine looks like this:

Alan Weiss, Ph.D.
President
Summit Consulting Group, Inc.
Box 1009
East Greenwich, RI 02818
401/884–2778 Fax: 401/884–5068
http://www.summitconsulting.com
Alan@summitconsulting.com

Member:
Professional Speaking Hall of Fame®
Recipient:
American Press Institute Lifetime Achievement Award
Recipient:
New England Institute of Management Consultants
Lifetime Contribution Award
"One of the most highly respected independent consultants in the country."—*The New York Post*
"One of the top motivational speakers in the country."—
The *Providence Journal*
Visit Alan's Blog: http://www.ContrarianConsulting.com

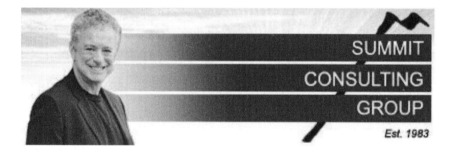

I choose to include a brief credential and a plug for my newsletter, along with my contact information.

It's easy to set this up with a wide variety of personal handwriting fonts available today for any computer. Even if you print your name conventionally, it still improves on the formal letterhead information that follows. Clients have told me that it makes a big difference, and every little bit counts.

> *Use technological assistance to increase your personalization, not to decrease it. Just as your materials shouldn't look like everyone else's, neither should your technological presence.*

Another drawback of the electronic letter is its propensity to go on forever. After all, you merely have to hit "reply" to send a quick response, no matter how inane. The trouble is that we're also taking up someone's precious time in doing so. Refrain from corresponding simply because it's easy. If someone sends you a light response, absorb it like a sponge, don't react to it like a spring.

Don't make cold calls on the Web. Just as legitimate buyers aren't going to purchase consulting services over the phone or by direct mail, they aren't going to respond to blanket Web mailings, especially since the junk mail on the Web has the flavor of those classified ads at the back end of *Popular Mechanics* ("You too can make a zillion dollars at home by watching paint dry!").

Don't get more bells and whistles than you need. The latest computer isn't necessarily the best computer for your purposes. Chances are that you need something for mail, word processing, spreadsheet work, file management, perhaps project management, and some light graphics work (unless you're an instructional designer who creates your own programs). Most midrange equipment can handle this. I found that I used my scanner about once a quarter, so I got rid of it when I upgraded my system. My color printer gets rare use, but it was a bargain and will stand me in good stead for many years.

You'll probably use less than 35 percent of your equipment's total capability in terms of technological prowess. So go for large-scale memory, large storage, and best price. I don't even upgrade to the latest operating systems on my Macs unless they provide significant improvements and minimum problems.

THE CLIENT AND TECHNOLOGY

There are some marked advantages to exploit in developing and nurturing the client relationship using technology. While nothing replaces the credibility of personal meetings, intellectual breadth, empathic listening, and insightful responses, there are augmentations available using technology as a resource.

Here, then, is a sample list of options depending on your proclivities, expertise, and innovation:

- Suggest that you become part of the client's voice-mail system so that internal people can access you readily in a fashion that's familiar to them. Conversely, you can leave messages in a manner that's consistent with the company's preferred format. I did this with Hewlett-Packard for years. It made me a part of the team and a natural to include in the next project that came along.

- Encourage people to contact you by e-mail, and make sure that every contact knows your e-mail address. This enables you to send and retrieve messages at any hour. Another benefit is a subtle psychological fact: people who are uncomfortable or won't disclose much on the phone tend to be far more accessible and sharing via e-mail. If you don't believe it, try leaving simultaneous and duplicative voice and e-mail messages and see which people provide the best response to using each option. People respond more quickly and sincerely to e-mail than to voice mail.

- Provide key clients with a pager/beeper access number. I suggest that you limit this to your best clients and most important contacts. It can help to give them a sense of your accessibility for them. (*Devil's advocate position:* I don't own a pager and never will. I call in frequently enough to get my messages, and I equate pagers with lower-level people. No chief executive officer I've ever known wore a pager, and I'm not about to do so either. But that's me.) This may work best when you're actually on a large client site.

- Change your fonts and styles to match the client's so that you can provide camera-ready master copies that will fit immediately into the client's manuals and literature.

- Scan your clients' logos and/or graphics into your system so that you can incorporate them into client work, making for a highly customized and dedicated piece. (Don't forget that there are legal requirements that have to be met when using others' logos, trademarks, and other such material, so get the proper permission.)

- Create direct-dial features on your phone and fax, and have key contacts within the buyer include yours on their equipment so that assistants and secretaries can rapidly make connections in their absence.

Finally, think about creating value right from the outset using technology as an aid. Here's a typical scenario:

You're finally in front of the buyer after some hard work, prolonged trying, or plain serendipity. No matter. This is your chance. Are you so nervous—or so intent on proving how good you are—that you're apt to blow the meeting within the first five minutes?

What most of us don't realize is that there are three possible outcomes to this meeting, and two of them are good. One is that the buyer buys— end of story; send an invoice. A second is that the buyer wants to continue the relationship, ranging from the high end of "send me a proposal" to the low end of "you should deal with some of my people on this." Even the latter relegation to subordinates carries the potential of moving back to the buyer. After all, she sent you to them, so there is some clout in this position. Only the third, "Never darken my doorstep again" (read: "Thanks for your time, we'll get back to you"), is fatal. The odds are actually in your favor, unless you don't place the right bets.

Therefore, what do you do to improve the odds of one of the first two responses taking place (remember, you must be with the economic buyer, or all this is academic)? My advice is to provide immediate value. For free. On the spot. You want the buyer to be thinking, "If I'm getting this much out of an exploratory meeting, what would I get if I actually hired this person?" Technology can come to the rescue.

THE VALUE OF VISUALS

One of the best devices to provide dramatic value is the use of a visual aid. I call these "process visuals."[5] The criteria for such an aid during an exploratory meeting are captured in my *SIGN theory*:

- *S*imple: The other person can relate to it immediately.
- *I*nteractive: The buyer is interested in seeing where he fits.
- *G*eneric: It applies to any business.
- *N*atural: It blends nicely with your style, and you "own" it.

The benefit of such a visual is that it focuses the buyer on a common point that the two of you are sharing, implies value, and forces the buyer to think about your point conceptually rather than considering how much your fee will be, if there's a budget available, what time the next appointment is, and so on. In other words, you want the buyer's agenda to match your agenda. This alignment creates marvelous focus.

Visual aids are perfect for today's technology. You can create a professional single sheet, an overhead, a small card—a wide variety of aids that you can keep in your briefcase. (They can also be drawn on the spot on an easel or even a pad. I know that this sounds casual and risks a sloppy appearance, but the ability to produce a visual to fit with a buyer's condition at a certain moment carries tremendous power.) If you can provide a concrete example of an abstract problem— a process known as *instantiation*—the buyer will immediately react positively to your ability to illustrate her condition. Thus, it's important that the visuals revolve around processes rather than content. This means that you don't want to create an image of someone selling computers but of the sales process itself, irrespective of the product or service. Figure 13-1 provides an example of such a visual aid.

[5] See my two books: *The Great Big Book of Process Visuals, or Give Me a Double Axis Chart and I Can Rule the World* and *Son of Process Visuals.* Both from Las Brisas Research Press, 2005 and 2007, each with a CD for transfer of the images to your own work.

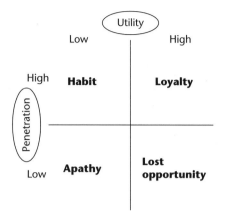

Another Way of Viewing Penetration and Value

Figure 13-1 A two axis visual aid.

I use this aid to demonstrate to buyers who have concerns about sales productivity that there are four basic conditions that reflect their relatioship with customers. If the utility (the value) of what they provide is considered high and the penetration into the customer account is high, they are in a "loyalty" condition that probably won't be affected by economic downturns or competitive action. If the utility is high but the penetration is low, they are losing a valuable opportunity, not only financially, but also in terms of longevity. If penetration is high but value is perceived as low, then the customer is simply buying out of habit. And if neither is high, the account is apathetic.

One Percent Solution: A process visual enables you to involve the prospective buyer in the diagnostic, which is a very powerful sales mechanism.

Note that this aid can be changed readily on a computer to use different terminology, include the client's organization, or use color. It can be customized for every client meeting if you so choose, even within the same organization.

As you've probably assumed, I now ask the buyer to identify where most of his best accounts are, what the sales force is being educated to provide, how people are rewarded, and other such information. This simple double-axis chart fascinates the buyer because he or she probably hasn't looked at things in quite this way before. The buying sign in this example is the question, "So how do we move our customers to the upper right quadrant?" Bingo.

I have a hundred of these devices that I can create at a moment's notice that will involve the buyer and accelerate my perceived value in the buyer's eyes. It doesn't matter whether this is drawn on a pad or displayed as a four-color card that the two of you gaze at. I've even asked the buyer to write percentages in each box reflecting the ratio of customers in each condition. Now the buyer is actively using my model.

It's important for consultants to be diagnostic in the sales process and prescriptive in the implementation process. It's amazing how often they just screw that up.

People who don't understand consulting very well often ask me, "What model do you use?" Consulting isn't a model—it's a process. This process uses models according to client needs and conditions. If you only have one model, you're a one-trick pony, and you ought to go out to pasture.

Scott Adams produced a *Dilbert* cartoon showing "Ratbert the Consultant" drawing matrices that he couldn't explain very well but that he promised to change into concentric circles with labels and arrows. The buyer is seen thinking, "I'm under the consultant's spell." Like most great humor, it's rooted in reality, although my approach is neither arcane nor devious. You do have to get the buyer "under your spell," meaning that the lure of your value and the pragmatism of your approach must outweigh the traditional inertia against buying.

Figure 13-2 is another example of a visual aid to gain credibility and involvement. This one is even simpler than the first one.

In this visual aid, I explain that the buyer has access to 100 percent of the organization's talents. People have only 100 percent of their energy and ability to give. ("Give me 110 percent" is a nice aphorism, but it means absolutely nothing.) I ask the buyer how much of that talent and energy is being applied *externally* toward the product, service, customer, and relationship and how much is

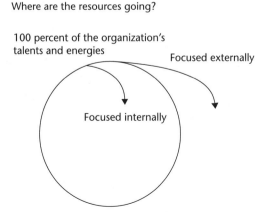

Figure 13-2 A technical visual aid.

being eroded away *internally* on office politics, unhappiness with the compensation system, resentment over executive perks, and so forth. I point out that the best companies manage a 90 percent external focus. Inevitably, the buyer admits that her organization is far below that. Sometimes, organization even have a preponderance of their energy focused internally.

Let me present two more process visual aids to whet your appetite for creating and using them yourself. Figure 13-3 is "market gravity" from Chapter 2, and Figure 13-4 is an example of the filters that must be overcome to reach an economic buyer. These are examples of low technology, perhaps, in that they are relatively simple graphic representations, but they are extremely powerful in conveying your message.

Technology can't make a sale, but its judicious use can enhance your value to the buyer. One obvious area for this potential is in visual aids at the outset to create value.

Once again, this visual aid can be adapted to the particular client, employ differing terms (that is, staff time, field time, executive time, and so on), and use various visual alternatives. I suggest that this relationship is the heart of productivity, as opposed to downsizing, training, or quality programs. This dynamic can be managed, but it has to start from the top. The buyer inevitably asks, "What would that look like in our case?" Bingo again.

Figure 13-3 Creating market gravity.

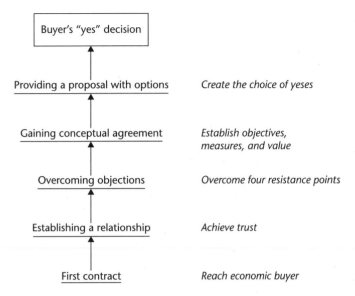

Figure 13-4 Filters that must be overcome to reach an economic buyer.

MANAGING THE BUYING DYNAMIC

It's up to you to manage the initial meeting with a buyer. Of course, it's important to practice reflective listening and to ensure that you hear the concerns that are on the buyer's mind. However, this alone is insufficient. You have to use what you've heard to demonstrate your value, and your value is never in the features and benefits of your product, service, or expertise. It's in your ability to *connect* with the buyer's desire and needs, and you often have to accentuate them far beyond the buyer's own words.

This is why a visual aid that creates involvement, agreement on principles, focus on results, and implied value is so important. This is a key step in *conceptual agreement*, and those of you who have read my work know that this is the centerpiece of acquiring large projects and enduring relationships.

Start with a half-dozen of these process visual aids using my SIGN criteria. Build others as your experiences and needs dictate. Carry them around at the outset so that you don't forget them. They'll become second nature soon enough. Practice how you'll introduce them; they have to be in smooth response to an issue raised by the buyer, not adding a jarring, discordant note to the conversation. If you draw your visual aid, ask the buyer if he would like you to send a copy along later or, preferably, bring it on the next visit or include it with your proposal. Using your technology, ask the buyer what form would be desirable: on a disk, as a sign, on a slide, with the company logo, and so on.

I've seen far too many consultants sit down at that precious initial meeting with the buyer and act as though they had never done it before. While it's true that they've never met this particular buyer before, they've certainly been in this position before. What good is experience if we don't learn from it? We can manage the buying dynamic, but only if we choose to. The default position takes this power away and puts it in the hands of someone whose inclination is not to buy. Use technology to prepare for, deliver on, and follow up on the value you can create through visuals.

Use technology and visuals to accelerate your pace with a prospect or client, and nothing more. That makes sense, doesn't it?

Or do I need to draw you a picture?

QUESTIONS AND ANSWERS

Q. *All of my friends are on LinkedIn and Plaxo and so forth. If I'm not there, won't I be missing something?*

A. Maybe socially, but we're talking business here. It's amazing how consistently people who love social networking confuse personal fulfillment (affiliations) with business utility (finding buyers).

Q. *I get too much e-mail. Won't I just be encouraging more time-wasting spam?*

A. You could if you're not careful. Use spam filters, rigorously remove your name from lists, and quickly delete the irrelevant. Never provide your e-mail address on networks and chat rooms unless you have thoroughly vetted them.

Q. *Are Webinars going to replace classroom training and speaking?*

A. No, not now, and not ever. The gifted, interactive instructor isn't going to lose that position to a remote image. People will always want to "press the flesh," especially if it means traveling to Rancho Santa Fe or the Bahamas to do so.

Q. *A lot of people are getting by with just a cell phone and no landline at all. Is that a good idea?*

A. Different strokes for different folks, but I find a long call is best done using a headset with my feet on the desk, so make sure you're able to do that in either case. Also, it's tough to do conferencing, speakerphone, and multiple lines on any cell I've ever seen. If you have a home office, why wouldn't you have a home office landline phone?

Q. *Is it even worth having physical materials?*

A. A great many buyers still prefer to sit in a comfortable chair, fold back pages, and read in the old-fashioned way. (And this is not age-related.) Also, they like to pass things around. Do you really want them to have to wait until they're near a computer to read about you or see your stuff?

Final Thought: Technology should be making your life and work easier, not more difficult. If you find yourself consumed with technology problems, bugs, repairs, and research, then consider changing your entire system to something, that's simpler to use and more supportive. Important criteria: Is your technology becoming cheaper, smaller, and easier to use? If not, get some nontechnological human help.

THE SELF-ACTUALIZATION OF THE MILLION DOLLAR CONSULTANT

THE MILLION DOLLAR PARTNERS

BORROW $1,000 AND THEY OWN YOU, BUT BORROW $1 MILLION AND . . .

ESTABLISHING CREDIT LINES

Once you've created what the accountants like to refer to as a "going concern," it's time to start acting like one. Treat your bankers as you would your clients— as partners in a relationship business.

The easiest and most practical credit source to tap for your growing firm is home equity. However, the credit lines you arrange should be business credit lines in the name of your business.[1] I'm very partial to this form of credit because

1. Most banks will allow for interest payments only, meaning that you can repay the principal at your leisure. This is a considerable cash-flow benefit during lean times.

2. The money is accessible immediately, either in the form of checks drawn against the credit line or through a phone call to transfer funds into the business account. This provides the flexibility to meet unanticipated short-term needs (for example, paying a subcontractor to help with an unexpected project even though the client won't pay you for at least 30 days).

3. As you borrow against and repay this line, your credit standing improves continually. Banks despise people who don't pay their debts, but they aren't enamored of people who never borrow, either. Their favorite people are *customers*—people who borrow money and faithfully pay it back with interest. This relationship has been in place for only about 2,000 years.

---

[1] If you need a personal credit line, too, that's fine. You can split the equity the bank allows you in your home between the two. For example, if the bank's appraisal provides for $200,000 in credit, you can allocate $150,000 for personal purposes and $50,000 for business purposes, or vice versa. However, don't regard them as interchangeable because business credit used for personal reasons must be allocated as some form of compensation or loan, both of which will increase your tax liability.

> ## Digression
>
> *We've all seen chaotic economic times. In some cases, credit is tough to obtain. Therefore, a cash reserve is critical. You should consider "tithing" to yourself, which means putting 10 percent of all your revenues aside in a separate account. Your priorities should be*
>
> 1. *Creating six months' reserve for living expenses*
> 2. *Fully funding retirement plans for the year*
> 3. *Creating reserves for college funds, future purchases of major impact (new car), vacations, and so forth*
> 4. *A "slush fund" for unanticipated expenses or impulse purchases*
>
> *Note that paying down debt is as important as saving, and you should try to reduce all credit card debt to zero monthly.*

4. It gives you peace of mind, and this is invaluable. If you are worried about how to pay the bills each day, you are spending that much less time developing the business. All professional firms have credit with banks. One absolute sign of your growth and professionalism is access to one or more bankers whom you can call at any time.

5. You are not surrendering any aspect of ownership or control of your business by borrowing and repaying in this manner. Assuming that you use the credit only as required and responsibly and that your overall personal money-management practices are sound (that is, you don't buy a new Mercedes after every sale), you will remain in complete control of your destiny.

An important precursor to the following system is to build credit references by acquiring the standard travel cards that rental car firms and airlines offer, as well as telephone and commercial credit cards, *billed to your business.* Even gasoline or store credit is useful. Also develop local credit accounts with the stationery stores, printers, office suppliers, and other vendors with whom you do regular business. These will all help with the bank. Use the credit—even if you don't need it—and pay it off promptly to establish a payment record.

I'm going to suggest a process to establish or increase your credit resources using your home and/or business asset equity. This should work for the professional who has no current credit lines with a bank, and it will also increase credit opportunities (perhaps even more dramatically) for those with modest arrangements already in place. (All the following assumes that the advice in the preceding two sections of this book has been taken to heart. That is, you are growing from a lone wolf to a thundering herd. If you haven't the confidence in yourself and your own business to use your home equity to fund your business, then you're in the wrong business.)

Step 1: Get Your Business Finances into Shape

You should arrange to have a monthly balance sheet and ledger. There are excellent computer programs that will turn out professional documents if you choose to do this yourself. I choose to use a bookkeeper on a monthly basis because

- She proactively suggests improvements in my reporting.
- She is another source to catch errors and reconcile problems.
- I can use her as an independent reference if needed.
- She is cost-effective because less than 30 minutes per month of my time is required. (My monthly cost is about $250.)
- She provides input to my financial firm for tax reporting and other audit purposes during the year (and it would be ridiculously expensive to ask that firm to perform these mundane tasks).

Shop around for bookkeepers, asking clients and colleagues for references. My bookkeeper picks up and delivers my paperwork each month. In my experience, you can acquire excellent help for as little as $30 an hour (although many charge $50 and over), and your affairs can probably be handled in 5 to 15 hours a month, depending on the number of employees and the complexity of your transactions.

Obtain a payroll service, such as Paychex or ADT, that will provide you with salary checks and tax notices and documentation. Even if you are the only one on the payroll, the ease and accuracy of the system make it a must. You'll be issued checks on your existing business account, be notified of tax bills due and amounts withheld, and have an excellent tie-in to your bookkeeper. These services are available around the country and can cost as little as $35 per month, which is more than paid for by your freed-up time. The services call you weekly or biweekly for payroll amounts and usually provide next-day check delivery, drawing on your existing accounts. Tax payments are withdrawn electronically to conform with Internal Revenue Service (IRS) requirements, and salary checks can be deposited automatically into your personal accounts.

Finally, find yourself an excellent financial advisor. By advisor, I mean someone who will sell you nothing other than his expertise (sound familiar?). Ideally, the advisor should have an array of diverse professional clients so that your circumstances are not pigeonholed into a model financial approach.[2] The advisor should not be a lone wolf; he should be part of a firm and, preferably, should be one of the principals. Such an advisor is in an empathetic position to your own! Your advisor should handle your firm's business taxes and affairs and your personal taxes and affairs because they are so intertwined when you own a personal services company. Ideally, in addition to an empathetic understanding of your business and your strategy, your advisor should have these attributes:

- Strong ties with local banks to assist you in obtaining credit lines
- Strong ties with local businesses to assist you in getting leads and publicity
- Sufficient staff so that your questions are answered immediately
- Computerized tax-reporting documents and planning guides
- A contemporary in-depth knowledge of small business tax regulations
- An inventive and innovative track record in sheltering income from taxes
- Peripheral benefits, for example, an empty office to use if you have to meet a client

---

One Percent Solution: In selecting a financial advisor, professional credentials are a secondary requirement. The primary requirement is the chemistry. Does the advisor appreciate your business and its intent and empathize with your growth plans and challenges?

If you are aggressive about taxes, find an advisor who is similarly disposed. If you are conservative, find a soul mate. Expect to pay anywhere from $3,000 to $10,000 a year for first-rate help, depending on your firm's size and your personal requirements.

---

[2] Consultants' businesses aren't readily understood by someone who specializes in medical practices or small law firms, for example. You need someone who understands the entrepreneurial nature of your business. Many consultants are getting lousy advice from lawyers and accountants who are family members and who do not comprehend this business.

The combination of a professional financial advisor, a bookkeeper, and a payroll service will create a financial picture of your company that is comprehensive and impressive. Figure 14-1 shows how they relate to each other and to your business.

> *Note: It's important that you choose someone who's providing advice and not selling products. Every single insurance professional I've ever met insists that life insurance is a key part of estate planning, annuities, savings, diversification, you name it. And for most of us, it's not.*

Step 2: Sweat the Financial Details Yourself

Once the system is in place, you must have high-quality data for it to polish. Consequently, keep careful records of receivables, contracts, prospects, and all other items that bear on your fiscal health. (The pipeline approach of Chapter 12 can be a key input.) These should be prepared by computer and updated weekly as required. There are excellent software programs available for this purpose (such as Quicken, or simple Excel spreadsheets that I create). The objective is to demonstrate that you have your business finances well managed and under control. Bankers don't like to do remedial work. They like to work with people who are already in excellent condition.

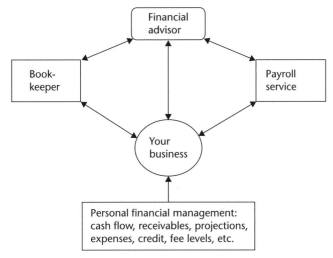

Figure 14-1. A financial management system; the financial professionalism of a going concern.

Use these documents to construct a rolling one-year forecast. The forecast includes booked business, advance payments, scheduled payments, proposals submitted, targets of opportunity, and probabilities of success with each of them. These aren't matters to delegate to your bookkeeper or advisor because they are qualitative assessments that rely on your knowledge of your client base and judgment about your prospects.

If your banker can see the financial documentation prepared by your advisor for the preceding year (or more, if available), she will be much more amenable to giving credence to your projections for the next year. Without this professional backup, however, and reasonable growth predicated on it, it's hard to convince anyone that forecasts are anything more than aspirations.

Finally, construct a personal financial statement that shows your current assets, liabilities, and net worth, including the worth of your business and its prospects. If done well, this can be the most powerful document in convincing a bank to provide credit. Banks love to see two things side by side: ability to pay, meaning strong cash flow and reasonable debts, and appropriate net worth, meaning sustenance in case cash flow suffers temporary interruptions.

> *One Percent Solution: Especially in a Subchapter S or LLC structure, where everything flows through your individual tax return, create as positive a net worth "picture" as possible. This is why reducing debt is so important.*

Step 3: Court the Banker as a Partner

Working with your advisor, references from colleagues, and knowledge of your business community, you should pursue those banks that

- Offer credit lines based on home and business equity
- Provide personalized services for key customers
- Have established similar relationships with professionals
- Are sound, stable, and convenient[3]

[3] If, for any reason, you are not familiar with the stability of local banks, use a bank rating service for an in-depth analysis of their strengths. The cost is modest—less than $100 in most cases—and in an era of closed banks and frozen funds, you will sleep much better at night. Note that at this writing, every bank account in an FDIC-insured institution is insured to $250,000. (This refers to each account with a different social security number or federal identification number, so Alan Weiss, Marie Weiss, and Summit Consulting Group are all separately insured).

- Offer a personalized relationship, such as "trust customer"
- Waive most fees for their best customers
- Provide access to officers readily in person and/or by phone

In a larger community, this is fairly easy. For example, in Providence, with a population of 400,000, I found three excellent candidates. In smaller communities, you may have to go farther afield and sacrifice the convenience aspect.

Approach the right person. This is usually a full vice president (everyone else in a bank is an assistant vice president, a title apparently given out in lieu of raises) in a department such as "personal banking," "professional lending," or the like. An introduction from your advisor will shortcut the process. If you don't have this luxury, find the specific name, write a letter explaining that you'd like to meet to discuss your business and a possible banking relationship, and follow up with a phone call for the appointment.

Your attitude should be that of a careful buyer. The bank will be lucky to have you, so you want to make sure that you choose the right bank. Provide the documentation from your advisor and your own rolling projections and financial statements. Make it clear that you intend to move *at least* your business accounts to the bank you select, and probably a great deal of your personal business as well.[4] Share your business strategy in detail, preferably in writing. Show the banker the articles you've published, the clients with whom you work, and examples of your projects. Provide specific client references and a press kit, just as you would for a prospect. And bring the last several years' tax returns for yourself and your business. Illustrate the growth you've achieved and the growth you've projected for the next few years, backed up by the figures and projections.

Then settle back and ask what the bank can do for you. Don't be anxious. Explain that you're exploring several alternatives. Ask about key services, such as overdraft protection, cashing foreign checks if and when you do business internationally, wiring funds, notarizing documents, and so on. *You are not looking for a loan. You are seeking a relationship that will support your growth.* Let the banker sell you.

You should work as hard at establishing this relationship as you would with any client. After you establish it, keep your banker on the mailing list you use for promotion. Have lunch together once every other month. Provide yearly tax returns and financial statements, as well as updates on your rolling projections, without being asked.

Depending on the size of your business and the nature of your collateral, try to begin with a minimum of $50,000 dedicated to your business credit line.

---

[4] Minor digression: you don't want all your business at one bank for pragmatic economic reasons. Maintain a small second business account elsewhere, and divide your personal accounts as well. Your financial advisor should provide an intelligent diversification of funds for you locally. I currently use three banks, one local, one regional, and one national, and am a special customer at each.

Always aim for the upper limit. Remember, you don't have to use it, but it's difficult to increase it under desperate circumstances. Every year, when you submit updated financials to your banker, explore the possibility of raising the limit.

When you are trying to borrow $1,000 at a time, bankers will regard you as a minor bureaucratic fact of life and demand that you jump through hoops. However, when you have the capability of borrowing hundreds of thousands of dollars of the bank's money, representing a sizable risk and a sizable piece of business, you and the bankers are in it together. Ironically, the more you borrow, the more you're in control.

The first thing I did when I received a $100,000 credit line was to borrow $25,000 against it for a month and pay it back along with the interest charge. I wanted my company and my banker to get used to the process.

Case Study

I had fallen into a rut in dealing with my principal bank over 10 years and assumed that I was receiving top-flight service. The inconveniences I experienced I tended to write off as unavoidable.

Finally, after one royal pain during a transaction, I asked my financial advisor to look around for me. He found a major bank that was eager to have my business. Not only did it give me a better business deal, but it refinanced my mortgage at a better rate, provided a better credit card deal, and supplied higher interest on my money market funds, both professionally and personally.

The moral: don't become complacent. Continue to search out better deals. Loyalty is fine, but profit is better.

THE HYDRODYNAMICS OF CASH FLOW

The rules of incoming cash flow are as follows:

Rule 1:   Cash must flow *in* at a rate in excess of cash flowing *out*, and this excess must represent sufficient funds to cover your total personal and professional needs, as detailed earlier, down to the "slush fund."

Rule 2:   If you adhere scrupulously to Rule 1, there are no other rules that mean a thing.

Are there any questions? Well, there must be, because small businesses fail at an alarming rate, and consulting businesses are no different. The most direct way to manage the flow-in portion of your equation is to monitor receivables meticulously. A *receivable* is, quite simply, a payment due from a client that has been billed but not yet paid. If it is never paid, it becomes a bad debt and disappears from your revenue column. In 23 years and millions of dollars of business dealing with the largest firms on the planet in long-term consulting relationships and with tiny businesses that purchase my books and downloads, I've never had one unpaid bill of any type or any amount. None. Not one. *Niente.*[5]

COLLECTING RECEIVABLES

Here is the time range for collecting receivables in order of priority:

- Prior to commencing work
- In full on commencement
- Part on commencement, balance in progress early
- In progress
- In progress and at conclusion
- At conclusion only
- Delayed after conclusion
- Contingent on certain results
- Never

Prior to Commencing Work

I've mentioned in earlier chapters the benefits of offering a discounted fee for early payments in full. If you are signing a contract that requires about nine months of elapsed time for implementation at $100,000, for example, a 10 percent discount nets you $90,000 thirty days prior to commencement. The compounded interest earned on this money over a year at even a 2 percent rate of return would be about $1,800, not to mention the far greater flexibility in your cash management and less

---

[5] My greatest challenge was a $50 bill for abstracts sent to a department at Rutgers University. After six months, I wrote directly to the president and got my money. The purchasing department hadn't appreciated that I am an alumnus and still had some connections.

administrative work in billing and follow-up.[6] Finally, if the money is in your bank account, no amount of client reorganization, buyer departure, or economic downturn can threaten your payments. *This is simply a wise move every time.*

Note: Many organizations have internal policies that demand that any discounted offer be accepted. You must offer such an option to trigger the system.

One Percent Solution: You won't be paid in advance if you don't ask. Suggest to your buyer that the project cannot be canceled if the funds are already committed and paid. And remember, if you're charging by the hour or some other time unit, you should put this book down and move away from it. You're an amateur, and you might get hurt here.

In Full on Commencement

This is a highly desirable arrangement that may be worth a 5 percent discount in your fee. You are losing a month's interest based on the preceding formula, and if the check isn't ready, you will probably have to begin implementation anyway because your time and resources are committed. (When you are paid prior to commencing, you have at least 30 days to communicate with the client that the fee has not been received as specified in the agreement, and the discount may be withdrawn.) There are some clients who pay in this manner without a discount because it's easier for their financial administration and because of excess budget remaining at year-end or canceled projects that have created a budget glut. You don't know unless you ask. I've often been requested to accept partial or full payments early as a favor to the client. I always manage to comply.

At fiscal year-end, many organizations have systems that force units to spend unallocated budgets or face a reduction in the following year's budget. In these cases, you can be paid well in advance without any discount because you are actually doing your buyer a favor. Always be cognizant of your client's fiscal year and remaining budget.

---

[6] Even if the full amount isn't banked for the entire term, its presence prevents you from having to use other funds—or worse, credit lines—that would cost you interest income or interest payments.

Partial on Commencement, Balance in Progress

This is by far the most common payment option. You should request at least 50 percent on commencement because your expenses will have to be borne by your cash flow (you won't be billing expenses until the end of each month, and the client will probably take at least an additional 30 days to pay them). I favor billing the remainder as one payment in 45 days, or alternatively as two portions of 25 percent each at 30 and 60 days or 45 and 90 days.

You want to avoid payment on completion whenever possible because too many events outside your control can interfere with completion. (I once had an entire operation burn to the ground.) Use *calendar* dates, not *activity* dates, to determine the payment schedule. Explain to the client that you have to manage cash flow just as the client does, that unanticipated events can occur, and that you're sure the client doesn't want to establish an incentive to finish rapidly rather than thoroughly.

In Progress

We now enter the portion of the range that represents danger in cash-flow management. If you collect your fees only in the course of the project's progress, then try to collect a healthy portion as soon as possible. Also, don't establish *relative* dates, such as "in 30 days." Always establish *absolute* dates: "due on or before July 9." Otherwise, someone in accounts payable inevitably will claim that the fee was due 30 days from some point 2 months later than you had meant. If you are forced to collect in progress, try to avoid any portion being paid on completion, for the reasons stated earlier. Keep the number of payments to a minimum (six payments of $20,000 each is far better than ten payments of $10,000 each), and always send your statements 30 days in advance of the due date.

In Progress and at Conclusion

This is a double whammy—the last payment is subject to the problems of determining completion. The danger with in progress and in progress and at conclusion is that too many variables can change within the client company that can jeopardize your outstanding payments. Try to establish calendar dates if you're stuck with this option.

At Conclusion Only

Never, ever accept such a contract for consulting work. Even if you trust the client implicitly, it is unprofessional and antithetical to the collaborative relationship-oriented business we've espoused. Such payments tend to actually become contingency contracts (see below), which have no place in intelligent cash-flow management. The only exception to this is when you are delivering a speech, workshop, seminar, or some similar short-duration service. In such cases, you may well bill after the fact, including your expenses in one statement with your fee. However, this is not consulting work, and I try to get paid in advance even for these brief assignments.[7] (The briefer the assignment, the easier it is for the client to cancel it owing to other priorities, which means that you've sacrificed several days of your time in preparation and allocation for delivery.) As a rule of thumb, if the assignment is over $5,000, it's worth arranging a favorable payment schedule.

Digression

There is the famous (and stupid) question, "What happens if you die?" (I call this the "beer truck question": What happens if you're hit by a beer truck?)

I usually respond, "What happens if you die?"

The fact is, your estate will take care of all claims against payment for work not performed. You have insurance. Why don't we focus on the future and not the improbable? (The person asking that question is usually lower level or someone with whom you haven't established much of a relationship.)

Delayed after Conclusion

This implies that the client either wants to see "how things are working" or has serious cash-flow problems of his own. Don't accept this for *any* kind of work. At best, it is a contingency agreement.

Contingent on Certain Results

Contingency fees have become more popular of late. The proponents claim that such a fee is simply payment for performance. I believe that it's the result of desperation. Essentially, a contingency fee means that you get paid if certain mutually agreed-upon measures are met. This can be something as objective and measurable as a written performance evaluation system or as subjective and nebulous as a reduction in controllable turnover. Although there are those who

[7] I demand full payment on acceptance to secure a speaking date. Period.

claim that contingency fees are higher than typical fees because they enable the consultant to have a piece of the action, I think that they are inevitably lower and harder to collect and that they seriously undermine cash flow. The acceptance of a contingency fee really means that the consultant has never made the conceptual sale and has never demonstrated how the client's condition can be improved. However, the client is certainly willing to take a "flyer" that may not cost anything, and the consultant badly wants the work. Hence you have not a collaboration but a potential confrontation. Not only must you show that the results have been achieved, but you also must convince the client that you alone were responsible ("Come on, it would have happened anyway!"). Whenever I see lawyers advertising about taking on personal accident claims with no payment "unless they win" (because value-based fees are alien to these hourly billers), I picture mercenary soldiers. This is not the business I'm in.

Case Study

The worst part of contingency (or performance) fees is that they invariably present conflicts of interest and ethical quandaries. A colleague faced this problem: removing a vice president of sales becomes an obvious long-term need, but keeping him in place for another six months would take care of the period on which my friend's contingency was largely based, so what do you do?

The client's long term inevitably will suffer for the consultant's short term in contingency billing. This is why contingency lawyers often pursue hopeless cases and/or try to discourage their clients from agreeing to a settlement early in the process.

Stay away from contingency billing, especially early in your career.

Never

If you are not getting paid and your billing arrangements call for advance payment or in-progress payments, you certainly have the leverage to stop the project and resolve the situation. You're better off losing the assignment than losing both the assignment and your time and contributions. However, when you are not scheduled to be paid until late in the game or after it's over, you may find that you're at risk of losing everything. (If your payment is 90 days late, assume that you're not going to get paid at all. This is not a harsh assessment. You are being treated unprofessionally.) Since you have nothing further to lose, fire your heavy guns:

- Give the buyer one last chance by making it clear that you're going to the chief executive officer (CEO) the next day.
- Approach the CEO of the entire organization directly by phone and by certified mail. Request an immediate response, and let the CEO know that you intend to seek legal recourse and publicize the difficulty.
- If the contract is large enough to warrant it, have your attorney at least "fire a shot across the bow" to the client's legal department and again to the CEO.
- If the contract warrants it, sue. In my opinion, if you can sue for an amount in excess of the unpaid bill, do so. If the client wishes to settle merely for the actual amount due, accept but insist that the client pay for legal fees.

I have never been in any litigation with clients at all. This is mainly due to the quality of my clients and the quality of my work. However, in a couple of instances, at least a partial reason for this was my clear, written billing procedures and payment schedules.

If you arrange intelligent billing options and work with the client in a partnership orientation, you can avoid the major pitfalls that endanger cash flow. The way you establish the relationship will determine how much money you collect and how early. Most consultants are their own worst enemy. The only thing worse than having no business is having business that doesn't pay the bills.

A few words about retainers. Unlike legal retainers, which are really deposits against future hourly billing, consulting retainers represent access to your smarts. They should not represent projects, merely access. As we've previously discussed, there are three key variables:

1. Who has access (the buyer, the buyer's team, or others)?
2. What is the duration (a month, a quarter, or a year)?
3. What is the scope (phone only, availability during eastern and western business hours, unlimited e-mail, personal meetings)?

Once you know the answers, develop a monthly retainer to be paid on the first of each quarter. In other words, with a $10,000 monthly retainer, $30,000 should be paid on the first day of that quarter. You may discount that for longer agreements, for example, six months for $50,000. Remember, this is access to your smarts. Don't start feeling guilty if you're not called! No one feels guilty when she doesn't have to use her insurance policy.

Remember, you don't develop the business by reducing expenses; you develop it by maximizing income. The velocity or speed at which you receive income is as important as the volume that you generate. Never tolerate a client who owes you money beyond the agreed-upon terms, and always make those terms as favorable to you as possible. You are a consultant, not a banker.

Never listen to "hard times" excuses from clients. Your bank won't listen to yours.

TWELVE CASH KEYS

While you don't develop your business through Scrooge-like attention to expenses, you can increase your ability to invest in growth strategies by avoiding unnecessary drains on your capital. The best time to examine expense controls is in *good* times, from a position of strength, not in bad times, from a position of desperation. Here's the mantra: selling the conference table is never an appropriate decision.

I've assembled 12 techniques to help you build expense management into a source of growth funds for your business strategies. Some may seem old hat and others unreachable, but as you grow, all of them will apply at one time or another.

1. Maximize the Number of Bills You Pay on Credit Cards or Business Accounts

This enables you to refuse payment if goods or services were not delivered as promised or if charged items could not be used. The credit card laws of this country are excellent: you have a legal right not to pay American Express or Visa if the business that accepted your charge card did not provide its product or service to your satisfaction.

How dramatic can this be? Well, anyone who charged tickets on a defunct airline and was unable to use them when the company went under did not have to pay for them *if they were charged on a credit card.* However, those who paid cash, paid their travel agents, or used some other form of payment were stuck. I often return airline tickets that have already been billed to my credit card accounts because my plans change abruptly and it's easier to buy entirely new tickets. When the charge for the unused tickets appears on my bill, I simply ignore it (and inform the credit card company of the return). However, if I had paid for the tickets, I'd have to file for and await a return of the funds, which can take more than 90 days.

Don't let anyone talk you into the "wisdom" of paying cash unless you intend to sell consulting services from a pushcart in the street. Establish local accounts with printers, office supply stores, travel agents, and anyone else with whom you regularly do business, and keep at least three major credit cards. At year-end, most provide a complete summary of the year's expenses, which can be invaluable at tax time.

One Percent Solution: Any credit card charges in place that you don't pay in the current year are still tax deductible as expenses in the current year. Make sure you make these apparent to your tax people. This includes charges you can see on your Internet access to your account, even if you don't have the physical bill in hand.

---

2. Pay All Local Vendors Promptly

I talked about this earlier: if you find yourself in a cash squeeze, don't put off the local suppliers.

These are the people who can least afford disruptions in *their* cash flow and whom you will often need to provide last-minute frenzied help with a project. I'm often told that I'm a pleasure to do business with not because of any special charm but because I scrupulously pay bills on time. As a result, I've often been able to jump the line at the local printer to get a rush project out or get a special date from a video production house. Simply paying on time has become a sterling character asset these days. If you must, put off Hertz or pay only a portion of the Master-Card bill, but always pay quickly close to home. (And it doesn't hurt to send a present at the holidays, either.) This is why you have the bank credit lines, right? (*Caveat:* Make at least minimum payments on time so as not to endanger your credit scores.)[8]

---

[8] If you do receive a late charge, which are usurious, call the credit card customer service line. It will almost always waive the first transgression or even accept extenuating circumstances (you were on a three-week trip to Europe).

3. Make an Expense Budget, and Compare Your Actual Expenditures Quarterly

Use major categories such as travel, office supplies, insurance, telephone, memberships, and so on. After two or three quarters, you should be able to arrive at your average expenses in these areas. Subsequently, comparing your actual outgo with these averages can provide you with critical expense-management information. For example, you may well find that your renewal and membership category is inordinately high and realize that you've joined five airline clubs (which run about $300 to $500 apiece nowadays). How many of them have you used in the last six months? If you never fly two of the airlines, drop them. Similarly, you might find overlapping insurance coverage, travel expenses that you neglected to bill for reimbursement, or fax charges that aren't yours.[9]

If you don't have a budget, you're at a disadvantage when you try to compare the actual expenses against reasonable criteria. When you're growing, it's easy to overlook the "budget bloat," so make it a point to build such scrutiny into your quarterly activities. (I most frequently find errors in rental car bills, local limousine bills, and any billing that covers a period in excess of one month.) There are several excellent computer programs that allow you to track and compare expenses at minimum effort, often keyed to your checkbook.

Your bookkeeper should provide a monthly report on current income and expenses and compare them with last year's, both per month and year to date.

4. Use a Travel Agent, and Make Your Travel Preferences Clear

Don't waste $500 of your personal time trying to save $25 on a hotel rate. Tell the agent how you prefer to travel (first class, first class but only with free upgrades, best coach fare nonpenalty, best coach fare no matter what, or whatever you prefer) and where you prefer to stay (closest hotel to the client, only in Marriotts, in the least expensive place within five miles, or whatever). Give the agent all your club membership numbers, and sit back and run your business. The agent is being paid to be valuable to people like you. Not only should you be able to simply give the agent a general itinerary, but you should expect periodic perks that the agent is capable of providing, such as free upgrades, discounted travel opportunities, and so on. Use only one agent, and expect excellent service. Keep moving until you find one with whom the chemistry is perfect. My travel agent saves me tens of thousands of dollars of my time and money each year and gives me a gift at the holidays. (There were two owner's suites on the

---

[9] Certain credit cards, such as Amex Platinum or Black (by invitation only), provide access to airline clubs, making separate membership unnecessary and saving you sometimes thousands of dollars.

cruise ship *Norway*. I spent $4,000 less than the guy who had the other one because my travel agent knew enough to register me for free in the Norwegian Cruise Lines Club and take the instant discount that comes with membership.)

Travel agents are being squeezed badly by the airline and hospitality industry. They need consistent clients.

Digression

The Internet services such as Orbitz have proved to be less than ideal for finding good deals and are totally nonresponsive to problems and questions. Travel agents can generally do as well, and if you're worried about their $50 commission, you're not on the way to becoming a million dollar consultant.

Amex offers an excellent travel service that is available 24 hours a day, which is superb for emergency changes around the world.[10]

---

5. Pay Your Bills Twice a Month at Single Sittings

If you pay them more frequently—for example, as you receive them—you tend to lose track of the big picture in terms of total outgo each month. (Firms such as UPS and FedEx will bill you each time you use their service, so you might have several bills from each every 30 days. It's nice to know the *total* you're paying, and it's less hassle to pay twice instead of five or six times a month.) If you pay less often, you're likely to miss some due dates, especially if your travel schedule takes you away during your normal bill-paying time. Also, a single session can be onerous if a great many bills pile up.

Match up credit card receipts with the billing statement (I've found unauthorized use of a commercial credit card and telephone credit cards). Minimize your bill-paying legwork: if some firms accept direct bank transfers, you can reduce your paperwork; at least have address labels prepared for those that don't provide return mailers; the more you can arrange for expenses to appear on a

---

[10] While sailing in the Mediterranean from Naples to Capri, I received a message that my daughter had given birth three months prematurely. I made one call from our hotel on Capri to Amex Centaurian Black Card travel service. In 20 minutes, the remainder of our vacation had been canceled, and we had three limos, a ferry, two airplanes, and a New York hotel suite, where we arrived the next evening to see our new grandchildren the following morning, both of whom did just fine. You cannot put a price on that kind of service and peace of mind.

single or a few major credit cards, the easier it is to write a single check instead of dozens. Of course, many people pay directly on the Internet.

6. Try to Buy Equipment (rather than Lease or Rent It), and Pass Up Long-Term Service Contracts

If you buy your computer, fax machine, copier, phones, and other major equipment, you can take certain business deductions (or depreciation, depending on the amounts and your accountant) immediately and avoid long-term payments that eat into cash flow. (If you must, use your bank credit line to purchase that expensive copier that will increase your productivity, and pay it off as cash flow permits.)

Purchase service contracts or insurance only in those cases that make sense. For example, my postage scale calculates rates based on class of service, weight, and prevailing rates. I'm insured against rate changes in that Pitney Bowes will send me new software to reflect any changes in return for my yearly premium. Otherwise, the cost could be excessive in the case of multiple rate changes. However, I don't carry a maintenance contract on the postage meter because the chances of a problem are remote, in my experience, and the repair costs aren't excessive anyway.[11] Avoid a procession of monthly bills representing payoffs on a dozen pieces of office equipment.

7. Request Prepayment of Expenses as well as Fees

With certain set arrangements (for example, you are delivering six workshops a year at the same site in exactly the same manner), you can predetermine your expenses and request payment in advance. While airline fares can vary, an alert travel agent can usually protect you, and if the client pays in advance, you have the luxury of advance purchases or interest gathering in the bank. Unlike with fees, you can reach an agreement with the client that any project cancellation will generate a return of the prepaid expense reimbursement.

You have no idea what billing terms are acceptable to a client unless you ask. The answer may surprise you.

With such "set situation" work, over half of my clients will pay the fee and travel expenses in advance, especially if I make my reduced fee offer contingent

---

[11] As a general practice, find a high-quality rental source for key office equipment in the event of breakdowns. The time for this search is when you *aren't* experiencing breakdowns. Your computer printer will fail, as a rule, exactly when your most critical client report is due. You'll want to be able to access your phone directory and call the rental people immediately and not waste time trying to determine if such services exist. (I also use local Apple repair rather than sending the computers to Apple, which takes four times as long.)

on payment of full expenses in advance as well. You simply don't know what the client will accept unless you ask. (I recommend that you deposit all prepaid expenses that are not immediately expended on advance purchases into a separate, interest-bearing account that you do not otherwise access. Success in this technique has a pitfall, in that you can spend thousands of dollars in advance expense reimbursements months before you incur the actual debt, resulting in disproportionate outgo later on.[12])

8. Don't Forget to Ask, "What's the Absolutely Best Rate (or Deal) You Can Give Me?"

Not only do airlines, hotels, and rental car companies have bewildering hidden deals that you can mine with a good shovel, but local vendors also will often negotiate if you simply ask the question. In those cases where you don't use a travel agent, ask the reservations clerk what the absolute best rate is—not what you might qualify for. Then work with the clerk to determine how you can qualify for it. I've called the same airline four times, spoken to four different agents, and received—you guessed it—four different rates. I accepted the best offer.

If you merely ask the local printer or graphic artist or computer store manager, "How much?" he understandably will give you the best rate *for him*. However, if you ask, "What's the best you can do for me here?" he will tend to give you the best rate *for you*. The more you patronize the business, the better deal you should expect.

On one trip, I flew first class on American Airlines, stayed in a suite at a Hyatt Hotel, and drove a luxury Hertz car, all without coupons or frequent-traveler awards. The airfare and hotel cost me no more than full coach fare and full rate on a regular room. Only the car cost more than a smaller one, but it did come with a navigation system at no additional charge.

9. Don't Prepay Your Own Bills

Certain otherwise excellent institutions will bill you months in advance. While I admire their intent, I have no intention of helping them out.

For example, the American Management Association and the American Society for Training and Development will bill your renewal membership about

---

[12] I can calculate rental cars, hotels, and incidentals in addition to airfare with significant accuracy. If I'm $100 or so worse off, it's still worth it to have received early payment. If I'm $100 or so to the better, I return it to the client with a note of explanation. This generates substantial goodwill. Million dollar consultants don't concern themselves with a couple of hundred dollars one way or the other on expenses.

four months in advance. Either stick the bills in a tickler file for the appropriate month or throw them out. Rest assured that you'll receive others. Business publications also will bill far in advance to ensure "uninterrupted service." My experience is that even publications I drop keep sending me issues after the expiration date in an attempt to lure me back.

You might want to drop a membership (such as the excess airline clubs mentioned earlier) or change some provisions. It's tough to do this once the check has been cashed. Pay your bills on time, but not before time.

10. Establish a Clear, Written, and Signed Expense Policy with Your Employees and Subcontractors

Specify what you will pay for by type (Holiday Inn or equivalent lodging), amount (daily meal charges, a maximum of $60), and policy (taxis to and from airports and clients unless rental car rates are less). Demand that expenses be turned in monthly (or more frequently) with complete receipts, and promise reimbursement within a reasonable period. (I find 10 days to be reasonable and "when the client reimburses me" to be unreasonable.) While using your corporate credit card and travel agent is helpful, you also want to avoid inappropriate charges on those cards, so make sure that there are criteria for the card's use (always for air travel; never for incidentals). One subcontractor kept calling her lover on my credit card, and when they quarreled, my phone expenses tripled.

I find that subcontractors and employees are rarely dishonest, but that there can be large areas of misunderstanding. You are protecting all parties by specifying the policy on phone calls, local secretarial services, weekend travel, and so forth. My practice is to have anyone who travels on my behalf sign a brief statement of expense reimbursement policies and the person's agreement with them. In return, I pay promptly and always give the benefit of the doubt ("The personal calls were to my husband, whom I forgot to tell about the babysitter being rescheduled so that . . . ").

11. Use the "Envelope Approach"

As explained earlier, plan for funding your retirement, living expenses, impulse buys, and so on. That's often best done by establishing separate bank accounts into which you deposit the appropriate cash.

This isn't much different from the envelopes we used to put rent money or vacation funds in when we were very young, but it works on the same principle, and it will direct cash to the right purposes; it will also enable you to tell when you're shortchanging yourself in any one category.

12. Examine What You're Giving Away

I began my seven-figure Mentor Program in 1996 when it dawned on me that I was providing a lot of free help in the wake of the publication of the original version of this book! I wondered if people would pay. I tried it. They did. They still are. Some of you reading this will join my Mentor Program.

Review everything that you give away: advice, products, downloads, services, responses, and so on. Then ask yourself, "Would they pay cash for this?" The first sale is to yourself.

In managing capital, it's not what you make—it's what you keep. If you're successful in keeping most of it, you can invest in accelerating your growth to dramatic heights.

QUESTIONS AND ANSWERS

Q. Can I have a retainer arrangement and also charge for projects concurrently in the same account?

A. Of course. Just be clear that each represents different value, one is for access to you and the other for actual work with the client.

Q. Is it wise to invest in certificates of deposits or bonds that deliver a higher return but require minimum investment periods?

A. Only if you have no other use for the money. The difference in return is negligible in many cases unless you're talking about hundreds of thousands of dollars. You're not in the money-management business. Don't lose sleep just because someone else is making an additional $250 in interest.

Q. What if the client has policies about not paying until certain junctures?

A. You can have policies, too. Stress to your buyer that you are a small business that is highly dependent on cash flow, and guarantee the quality of your work (not the results, which depend on many independent variables).

Q. What do I do with clients who tend to balk at paying so much in advance, just because it's their nature not to do so?

A. You can always compromise on payment terms (but never on the fee itself), but if you begin with terms that are optimally beneficial to you, any compromise is likely to be very favorable in any case.

Q. Does it ever make sense to delay cash?

A. Yes, at year-end, if your financial advisor recommends it. In that case, ask your client to delay payments until January, since you don't want to have additional income in the current fiscal year. Be careful: if you have received the check but just don't cash it, it's still income.

Final Thought: Merely by being scrupulous about cash flow, you can add tens of thousands of dollars to your bottom line without attracting additional business. Don't be so happy that you obtained the business that you forget that you are in business. This means maximizing your payment terms and cash flow. The client won't do it for you.

CHAPTER 15

GRACEFUL GROWTH

GROWTH DOESN'T ALWAYS EQUAL EXPANSION

ENHANCE YOUR PRESENCE

A few people have taken me to task over the years for not writing the book that *they* wanted me to write—how to build a solo practice into a larger firm that ultimately can be sold to a still larger firm. The fact that such a model was never my intent didn't seem to influence the few benighted people who don't seem to "get it." (Just as a few readers always demand that I correct something in print "immediately." Sure, send me the book and I'll make the correction.)

I'm writing for solo practitioners to enable them to get to a critical point and a highly rarified one at that: $1 million and above in annual billings for their practice. It is no minor point that in this *fourth* iteration of this book, 17 years after the original, million dollar consulting is *still* a lofty goal, and I haven't had to rename the work *Two Million Dollar Consulting*.[1] It's also important to understand that a million dollars *is* what it used to be—a great living for a solo practitioner with little overhead. In fact, such an income will place you in the top 2 percent of the entire U.S. population in terms of income.

Unless you have a personal objective to build a large firm, surround yourself with the accoutrements of size and mass, and build the equity in the company to the point where you own a valuable business (or a share in one), there is no intrinsic personal financial benefit in linear growth. The highest revenue per professional I've seen on lists published by Kennedy Information's research arm was $760,000 from First Manhattan Consulting Group in the late 1990s. Many firms were under $200,000 per professional.

---

[1] In fact, for the first time, I've been able to convene a Million Dollar Club, which will be having it's third annual meeting around the time this book comes out. There are a dozen of us, and we're growing. When I was asked about doing this 10 years ago, I offered to hold the meetings in my Ferrari—a two-seater!

How do you adequately reward people for their talents at this level of productivity, let alone compensate them for unceasing travel and long hours, once overhead and related expenses are deducted? I have always been of the view that the sole reason to work for a major consulting firm was the opportunity for partnership and equity, and if this is your personal and professional goal, then go for it.

Be advised, however, that this is not my model, not the subject of this book, and not the best way to get rich.

One Percent Solution: If you agree that discretionary time is real wealth, then you can easily see that simply maximizing income, despite personal and family sacrifices, can actually decrease your wealth. Be careful about that.

If your objectives are to earn a high income while helping clients to improve their condition—in other words, to support your family and your aspirations while engaging in constructive and valuable work—then your chances of fulfilling this goal are immeasurably greater if you are running your own small firm (*small* meaning just you or with a few others). You don't have to wait years for a portion of the ownership because you already have all of it. You are not reliant on colleagues' productivity or management's strategic decisions, and you absolutely control how much money you keep.

Ask virtually any professional—doctor, attorney, accountant, architect, musical director, writer, and so on—and they will all tell you the same thing: it's far better to earn $100,000 working for yourself than it is to earn $150,000 working for someone else. And when you begin to earn $300,000 or $500,000 or $1,500,000 working for yourself, the opportunities increase geometrically because the discretionary income of your firm and yourself becomes so powerful.

Digression

As a solo practitioner, with expenses reimbursed by the client, your top line is really your bottom line. That is, except for some modest marketing and office expenses, you keep what you make. That's a tax problem, but it's a wonderful one, and it's better than a business problem.

If you don't look at your business in this manner, then why are you incurring the risks of a solo practice?

The general business community probably hasn't heard of you, but all you're interested in for the moment is growing to $2 or $3 million.[2] How can you intensify the firm's profile so that such revenue goals are realistic and your key prospective buyers begin to perceive you as a million dollar business?

Here are the major methods I've found to intensify your profile. Your perceived profile will inevitably be a diminution of what your firm actually is unless you actively manage and intensify that image. You may call this public relations, image building, marketing, or exposure. I call it Million Dollar Consulting Orchestration: if you don't blow your own horn, there is no music.

1. Author or Coauthor Scholarly Research

I've discussed in earlier chapters the merits of publishing articles. In this instance, I'm concerned more with academic work that will validate your approaches and sanction you as an authority. One of the methods I used was to pursue my doctorate in organizational psychology (late in life, it's not a direct marketing aid, but an indirect one), recruit several key clients as "laboratories," and keep all my clients abreast of my progress and my ultimate degree. Excerpts from my dissertation have been published or cited in the popular press, and I made copies of it available to any client or prospect who was interested (or whom I could make interested).[3]

There are other, somewhat less grueling methods to produce work in this arena. It is usually highly attractive to university professors to collaborate with consultants on research papers. In fact, it's often a marriage made in heaven. The professor must publish anyway, and she has a raft of theories and beliefs honed from years of reading, research, classroom discussions, and—heaven forfend—part-time consulting. You, on the other hand, aren't well versed in the rigors of scholarly research, but you have clients who can serve as laboratories or databases, as well as observations and theories based on pragmatic, real-life experiences and the time and motivation to collaborate with the professor. These collaborations

---

[2] I've found that 9 times out of 10, people to whom I've just been introduced who tell me that they've heard of Summit Consulting Group, Inc., either are confusing us with someone else or are under the impression that they ought to have heard of us and don't like to admit that they haven't.

[3] I'll be discussing international expansion in Chapter 18, but I want to mention here that advanced degrees—and particularly Ph.D.s—are not critical in obtaining work in the United States, but are very helpful in securing work in the Far East, some parts of Europe, and other places. I pursued a nontraditional course of work, which included three Fortune 500 clients in my research, a year on a suicide hotline, board work on a shelter for battered women, speeches to the American Psychological Association, and so forth. After all that, I had my dissertation rejected and had to resubmit, then got into an argument at my oral defense. My wife told me to stop whining and get things done.

often produce work that appears in refereed journals, which constitute one of the most serious and validated publishing outlets.

The purpose of such publishing, whether solo or in partnership, isn't to establish yourself as an academic. In fact, you don't want the profile to be one of monastic theory without practical application. It is, however, to establish you as a recognized, credible source within a community with strict standards for intellectual honesty and disciplined research. This kind of profile will attract and impress executives; it is also useful in winning over the occasional academic who happens to be a senior executive of a prospective client.

2. Present Papers, Theories, and Findings at Conferences

This too is different from the public speaking I advocated earlier. Those were paid speeches before groups that comprised high-potential buyers of your services. In this case, I am speaking about professional conferences that may not have a potential buyer within 50 miles.

There are thousands of major conferences held every year on behalf of every imaginable professional group.[4] They usually pay very little or nothing to most presenters, and you'll often have to foot the travel bill as well. However, the opportunity to present your firm's work on "Strategic Planning for the Commercial Banking Industry in Recessionary Times" or "Motivation of the Workforce through Nonparticipative Management" (remember contrarian consulting from Chapter 12) will enhance your profile significantly. These proceedings generally produce papers, recordings, reprints, summaries, new accounts, and similar summaries of their output.

You will have to appeal to the organizing committees of these affairs up to a year in advance. It's a good idea to put all of them that are relevant on your general mailing list (see Chapter 6) so that they can call you when they happen to see that your work lends itself to a future theme of their conference. The work is well worth it because it is highly credible to cite these presentations in your firm's materials and because the various summaries of your material can be reproduced and distributed as part and parcel of your press package as appropriate. Moreover, there is a centrifugal force at work that will tend to retain you within the orbit of these conferences once you have presented to strong response. You will find yourself on the groups' mailing lists, requesting papers and future presentations.

---

[4] I attended an awards banquet one year for exceptional service in the water treatment industry, and the top honoree of the evening, after acknowledging prolonged applause, began his acceptance speech by deadpanning, "It's true. Sludge is my life."

3. Appear on Radio Talk Shows (and Television if You Can)

Appear in this sense is a misleading term. There are public relations, media, and image-building firms in this land that can place you on radio talk shows with considerably more ease than you imagine. For a modest fee, which can range from as low as $200 for a local-exposure talk show to $2,500 or more for a syndicated, national show, the firm will arrange for a brief (5- to 20-minute) interview, which may also include some listener call-in questions. In most cases, you provide a synopsis of the type of work you do (that is, whatever you want to promote at the time: your strategy work with large companies, your motivation work with small firms, your newest book on leadership, and so on) and a list of a dozen or so questions that the host should ask you. This serves the dual purpose of making the talk show host appear to be knowledgeable about your business and approaches and focusing the conversation on your highest-profile potential.

And now the *appearance* part. Most of these shows conduct the interview—no matter where the station and the host are located—over the telephone, with you sitting in your office (or at the pool). Through the magic of modern communications, your interview and any questions and answers with listeners are completed without so much as a car ride being required. Although many of these shows may have only local appeal and/or poor demographics for your work, by choosing a good media firm, carefully selecting the shows, and being very patient, you can achieve some penetration of relevant markets.[5]

However, the most important benefit is the ability to cite your appearance on the *Minneapolis Today* radio show specifically to discuss your work in conducting customer focus groups or your interview by WWXR in Chicago that focused on your work in increasing sales force productivity. These are highly beneficial instances to include in your literature and to politely drop into conversations with prospects.

These firms can also place you on television talk shows. The investment is still less than you'd expect—perhaps around $1,000 per placement—but the key is that you must have a dramatic and unique story to tell. Don't despair. If you watch the TV talk shows during any given week, you'll find that they desperately need people with decent stories to tell, and there's no reason why yours can't be one of them.

[5] Or do it yourself, using a source such as *Radio and TV Interview Reporter* (RITR).

Warning: Let me state that you should not pay to "host" a TV show on cable, "host a radio talk show," or appear in a book with "big name authors." These are scams, often perpetrated with recognizable names. Steer clear. They are worthless except to the parasites who feed off the egos of those drawn to 10 seconds of "fame."

Case Study

I advertise every year in Expertclick.com, both online and in hard copy. I am interviewed frequently because these sources are accessed by assignment editors, producers, reporters, and so on.

After the original Survivor *television show in 2000, I was asked by a* New York Post *reporter, who found me in that resource, to comment on the management techniques that the winner, Richard Hatch (who called himself a "corporate trainer" and later went to jail for tax evasion on his Survivor prize money), had used to earn his million dollar prize.*

Not only was I liberally quoted in the Sunday edition, but I also was cited as "one of the most highly respected independent consultants in the country." Similarly, Success *magazine once called me "a worldwide expert on executive education." These citations went into my press kit in about nine seconds and are timeless in their applicability and credibility.*

This is how you can leapfrog any larger firm or competitor on the radar screens of buyers, becoming a bigger blip than you otherwise might appear.

Another excellent source is PRLeads.com, which allows you to tailor the kinds of reporters' inquiries you receive on a daily basis.

4. Place "Nonadvertisements"

I don't advocate advertising as a useful promotional tool for a consulting firm, although I do believe in appearing as an endorser or supporter. ("Summit Consulting Group, Inc., proudly supports the efforts of Save the Bay.") However, there are occasions when a "nonadvertising" advertisement can make sense.

I look at these as informative efforts, as opposed to promotional efforts. You are, in fact, informing readers that "this is the profile of my firm." One good instance occurs on anniversaries: "The Delpha Consulting Company wishes to thank all its clients and friends for their continuing support on this our tenth anniversary." A display ad of this type in magazines most relevant to your targeted demographics helps to create a perception about your profile. Such an ad is often accompanied by a client list and examples of projects completed or fields of expertise. You can include a photo of your staff or you at work on a client site.

Another appropriate reason for an ad is to announce something. You might announce

- That you are the recipient of a particular award or honor
- The addition of a notable professional to your firm
- An alliance you have formed with another organization
- A new toll-free number or additional office location
- Congratulations to a client for a certain achievement or honor
- An annual conference or meeting that your firm is hosting
- Sponsorship of a charitable or nonprofit undertaking
- A new or additional site on the Internet

These types of ads shouldn't be frequent, or they will be perceived as promotional advertisements despite their content. They are usually most effective when they are done once or twice a year and without pattern. You are simply being your own press agent in a low-key manner and influencing the perception of your firm.

5. Seek Out and Apply for Awards and Honors

If you actively inquire, you'll find that there are a plethora of awards and honors in our profession, ranging from client interventions to papers published. Outside of the famous MacArthur Awards ($500,000 grants to secretly nominated people in diverse fields), I know of no bestowing bodies that proactively canvass the field. Every award requires an application if the candidate is to be considered.

Thus, when you read of a call for papers in some journal, take the time to determine if your work might lend itself to such a paper. If you find a competition for "customer service quality," explore whether you might collaborate with a client to assemble an entry. After all, this is the ultimate win/win scenario.

Other practitioners of technique 4 probably will be "advertising" their winning efforts, so you need only be on the lookout for who won what under which conditions. How can you compete in the future? And winning isn't the only salutary outcome. Merely by competing, you will be able to examine your own practices, enhance your own standards, and increase your own profile in the process. You may win an "honorable mention" or a specialty award, which can be appropriately "advertised." You can publicize the mere act of *competing* for a prestigious honor. (For example, for several years my firm was nominated in *Inc.* magazine's "most dramatically growing small firms" category.)

There is no grand arbiter who examines all companies for all practices and makes bestowals and awards based on pure empirical evidence and absolute merit. Neither the Olympics (Have you ever watched the diving or skating judges?) nor the Oscars (How many comedies have won best movie?) are that impartial. You must enter, compete, and keep trying. If you're diligent and your work is worthwhile, eventually you will carry home an honor or two, and your "box office" value will be enhanced.

6. Diligently Send Out Press Releases

Press coverage of your activities is worth its weight in gold because an independent, objective source has seen fit to comment on you or your work. Keep a separate mailing list of newspaper and magazine editors (usually the business editor, but this may vary depending on your slant), and alert them whenever

- You are appearing as a speaker in their area.
- One of your clients has completed a dramatic project with your help.
- You have earned an award or honor.
- You have published something of note.
- You have an internal publication that is of relevance to their publication.
- You have a finding that is of relevance to their readership.
- There is a significant event in your firm's history (for example, your tenth anniversary).
- You produce a new product or offer a new service.
- One of your regular client mailings goes out.
- There's a new development on your Web pages.

Once you get to know the editors and the publications, you can begin to customize the material to better pertain to their personalities and their readership. For example, some might prefer scholarly reports, whereas others may print business surveys,[6] and some accentuate CEOs' observations. This technique requires perseverance; most such releases don't receive careful (or any) attention at most times. Eventually, however, because you've hit the right combination or because it's a slow news day (sometimes it's better to be lucky than good), you'll hit the print, and your profile will bask in the growth.

Hint: Include a photo with press releases. Photos can often serve to fill a "hole" in the copy or formatting, making the editor more inclined to use the piece. (The editor can always use the text and not the photo, so there's no harm done.)

The aforementioned Expertclick.com allows you to send out a free press release every day as a benefit of membership. It claims to have about 10,000 reporters, editors, assignment editors, talk show producers, and the like on its contact list, and you can track "hits" if you're particularly anal-retentive about these things.

7. Conduct Independent Surveys

This is a simple and grossly overlooked method to enhance repute. All you have to do is decide on an issue about which clients would appreciate some information, arrange for a suitable survey to obtain it, and disseminate the results.

Let's hypothesize that your clients and prospects are concerned about turnover among newly hired college graduates, believing that there is a decline in company loyalty among this group and that they must take extraordinary measures to retain these hires. You can send out a mail survey to your client base (and if it's not big enough, to similar organizations chosen at random) asking questions about their experience with new hires, their efforts or lack of efforts to retain them, comparisons with turnover among longer-tenured employees, and so on. This is not a scientific survey but an anecdotal one (unless you choose to use scientific rigor), and the results can be expressed as such.

In any case, you will be seen as a leading-edge factor in your field. Organizations will often cooperate if you offer to share your results with them in return for their participation and if you keep the survey simple, offering return mailers and professional documents. Many publications are eager to print such

---

[6] The *Wall Street Journal* is forever publishing items on its front page that begin, "A survey by Acme Consultants reports that. . . ."

results, and most organizations are happy to review them because they lend perspective to current approaches. You are the perfect intermediary to provide cross-organizational information of this type.

Surveys may cost you a few hundred dollars to create and interpret (and are often amenable to online, automated systems), but you are under no deadlines, and the work can be accommodated as time permits. This technique is superb for establishing repute and a profile that may be far greater than your actual previous work in the area. (For years I was familiar with the firm Wyatt Associates only because no less than the *Wall Street Journal* would excerpt a variety of its survey results on its front pages.)

8. Launch Yourself into Cyberspace

You must have a professional Web site, complete with graphics, text, e-mail links, and assorted bells and whistles, testimonials, audio, video, position papers, and so forth. This can cost from $3,500 to over $10,000. (The site can be maintained for a few hundred dollars a year on someone's server.) If you're a technological consultant, you can probably attend to this yourself and save the money. If you are not, pay someone to do it because trying to learn the ropes and do it yourself will cost $25,000 of your time. Besides, would you suggest to your clients that they do their consulting themselves? No; call in the expert.

Try to maintain two e-mail addresses, one for your corporate mail, which you put in your literature and business cards, and a personal address that you release to special people. This helps overcome the impersonality of e-mail and helps establish a priority for you when you're rushed.

Don't allow your Web presence to merely resemble everyone else's. (And by the way, no one likes to wade through pages of boring text on how good you are or wait for umpteen pages of graphics to download so that your smiling face can appear. Less is more.) For example, I have hundreds of free downloads on my site, which can be read and downloaded by anyone who visits. Past articles are archived and can be accessed readily.

My monthly newsletter, "Balancing Act", is also archived there. I want people to derive value from the visit, to have reason to return next month, and to spread the word. Some Web sites have self-scoring tests, others have book reviews, and still others contain puzzles.

If you'd like to visit my Web site for some examples or to order my newsletter, "Balancing Act: Blending Life, Work, and Relationships," I'm at http://www.summitconsulting.com. You can e-mail me at Alan@summitconsulting.com. My personal e-mail? Sorry, it really is for key clients and close friends only.

Digression

Blogs are very useful if you have a brand or some form of repute, even if in a narrow niche. However, most blogs are dreadful, poorly written, and poorly supported.

Social media platforms such as Twitter, LinkedIn, Facebook, or whatever are just that: social media. For consultants trying to reach corporate economic buyers, they are a waste of time.

As a test, I currently have 1.5 million contacts on my LinkedIn account (an experiment that I began six months ago), and 99.9 percent of the communication has been information about what people are doing, job hunts, silly questions, and attempts to get my help from those who have no intention of paying me for it. Worse, this can be a huge time dump, which detracts from real and important marketing gravity.

As we say in New York, fuggedaboudit.

ACTIVELY SEEKING PASSIVE INCOME

Multidimensional growth is a key component of financial success, which in turn supports the life goals that a career in consulting can sustain. Since we've reached a point in this book that deals with exploiting success and capitalizing on such growth, let's spend some time examining passive sources of income. I call them alternative sources because they are not a direct result of consulting engagements. For example, I've talked about the value of books and speeches and the fact that they are lucrative in and of themselves, beyond the more immediate marketing value. These are direct or active sources of income.

One growing source of passive income is from CDs, and even more from MP3 downloads, podcasts, and similar products. There is an iPod-devoted, enormous self-help market that gobbles up audio offerings in subject areas ranging from self-motivation and personal grooming to time management and managing cultural diversity. Consultants who deal in virtually any area of management—who have their clients as practical laboratories—and who may be publishing their approaches in various print media are ideally placed to create audio offerings, which are leveraged through the media noted earlier.

Here is a great way to leverage (and grow) your brand by leveraging audio and modern technology:

1. Schedule a teleconference. You can establish these inexpensively through sources such as http://telephonebridgeservices.com/. You can charge for this if you have a sufficient brand and mailing list, or do it for free if you are building your brand and mailing list (thus, this is a two-sided benefit, no matter where you are in your career).

2. Simultaneously record the teleconference as a podcast, using software such as GarageBand, which is included with most Macs.

3. Create a download (MP3) version of the teleconference and an MP4 version of the podcast.

4. Sell these on your Web site and/or blog.

5. Create CDs from them, and offer those for sale.

6. When you have a sufficient number (e.g., 6 to 12), offer the CDs in an album or the downloads as a set.

7. Augment the audio products with text, graphics, slides, coaching, e-mail access, or whatever. You can have a graphics designer create artwork for both the electronic and the hard-copy versions.

The podcasts can easily go onto iTunes or similar sites.

To be perfectly candid, here are some drawbacks to be aware of:

• Promotion is difficult. The business is highly competitive, and direct mail is a science that can drain your time, focus, and resources. Essentially, you need excellent databases of people who know you or your work.

• The creation of the programming can be difficult and time-consuming. You have to organize your ideas in writing and then hope that they translate well to recording. If you're not used to this, you need to practice it until it's conversational and smooth.

• Your topics can become dated quickly, rendering the album obsolete. Today's "empowerment" can easily become yesterday's "transactional analysis." Try to be timeless in your advice and examples.

• There is no endorsement other than your own credibility. No matter how sound your credentials, it is clear that you have published the work on your own behalf because you wanted to create and sell it. Therefore, be sure to pack it and promote it in terms of value to the buyer.

> *One Percent Solution: Always remember that you're in the consulting business, not the publishing or audio business. These passive income approaches are intended primarily to gain you more major consulting business. Don't focus on the tail and forget the dog.*

This brings us to my special recipe. I believe in synergies among your various focuses in the consulting business, and here is an example that has worked splendidly for me. Whenever you make a speech in front of a major audience, there is a 50–50 chance that it will be recorded. Associations and conventions, for example, almost always have an agreement with a professional taping service to record all sessions (even the smaller, concurrent ones) and then sell the tapes to participants during the convention itself.[7]

These firms create an excellent master even from wireless lavaliere microphones. At smaller conventions or in-house management conferences, there is often a sound engineer available to make professional recordings.

In your speaking contract with the client organization, always stipulate that you will allow your speech to be recorded at no additional fee, provided that you receive two complimentary copies of any recordings made. Many speakers prohibit the recording of their talks, and others charge stiff fees for the right to do so. Consequently, your trade-off is quite reasonable. After all, your speech is your proprietary work, and recordings have been known to wind up in other organizations' and even other speakers' material. No organization has ever contested this clause in my contract, and many times I've stimulated them into recording the session when they themselves hadn't considered it originally!

> *If the client isn't considering taping your presentation, then suggest that such a tape be made to leverage the client's investment. All you want in return for your permission is a copy of the tapes.*

---

[7] When I appeared as the general session speaker for the American Newspaper Classified Advertising Managers Association, for example, tapes of my speech were available for purchase in the lobby within 30 minutes of my saying "thank you" to the audience.

Note: All of this applies to video as well.

What you will walk away with is a live recording of your work and the reactions of a live audience. You have to ensure that you do the following:

- Provide the person who introduces you with a written introduction, and ask that it be read exactly as it appears. (Or, in the editing, dub in a professional voice-over.)
- Carefully prepare your material with the knowledge that it will appear on tape. (For example, if you generally use a visual aid at a key point, it won't be appreciated on tape unless you explain it or translate it into an oral example.)
- Investigate whether the audience reactions will be picked up on the recording equipment, and if not, see if you can make arrangements for better audience pickup. (This is especially important if questions and answers are a key part of your presentation—always make sure that you repeat questions before responding to them.)
- Remove all references that will date the tape (current events, television shows, movies, etc.)

For video:

- Have two cameras, one on the audience to splice in reaction shots.
- Be careful about your backdrop—I've critiqued videos of the speaker in front of a mirror, in front of an emergency exit, and in front of an indoor pool entrance complete with people in bathing suits.
- Wear clothing consistent with video—no loud stripes or checks, and blue is better than white for blouses and shirts. Consider using professional lighting and makeup people. And for goodness' sake, have your hair in place.

Read on in this chapter for still more video techniques.

I've found that spending 15 minutes with the technology engineers or top manager on-site from the recording company is time well spent. I tell her that a good recording will result in large-scale purchases from me and specify what I'm looking for. This always results in careful attention and excellent results.

Once the recording has been made, listen to it (watch it) and decide how to edit it. This may include all or some of the following:

- A professional voice-over introducing the tape, its subject matter, and the setting; for example, "You are about to hear management consultant, author, and speaker Alan Weiss deliver the keynote address to the annual convention of the National Auto Dealers Association, recorded live in Atlanta." (Omit when the speech was given because you don't want to date the tape.) For video, include a title screen. Consider generic background music, which you can purchase.[8]

- Editing out of the thumps and whacks that occur when you inadvertently pound the mike or drop a glass of water (or belch).
- Augmentation of the audience's applause, laughter, and/or questions, if needed.
- A professional voice-over with instructions to turn the tape over, if required, at the end of side one and concluding the tape, reminding the listener of who you are and providing the means to contact you for further information.
- Background music to precede and follow the voice-overs.

I then have my graphic artist or the tape company's artist prepare a simple label with my logo, and I select an off-the-shelf album box that accommodates the number of tapes I envision for that series. (They generally hold 2 to 12 tapes, CDs, DVDs, and so on.)

(My partner in The Odd Couple workshops on marketing for professional speakers, Pat Fripp, and I have a 12-CD, 100-page workbook album that we sell for $150.)

Using these live recordings greatly reduces risks. First, you have the audience reactions, which helps to shape the eventual listeners' reactions. Like the music accompanying a movie, the audience helps the listener to know when to laugh, when to "ooh and aah," and when to reflect. Second, the live nature helps to maintain the staying power, despite the topic. Third, the "recorded live" promotion adds tremendous credibility to the tapes. These are not tapes done by a guru who feels that the world should pay to hear the message, but recordings of a live speech made by an expert to people who paid to hear that message. You're simply doing prospective listeners a favor by making the message available to those who happened not to be present.[9]

Finally, these live recordings are among the most powerful of all the promotional tools you'll develop (and infinitely more so than self-published products).

---

[8] If you use someone else's music, you will need permission and must pay fees to ASCAP.

[9] Many professional speakers record their own speeches through the use of a cordless lapel microphone and a high-quality cassette recorder that operates automatically. The equipment is available under trade names such as Freedom Mike, and the recording costs about $500 to $800 complete.

You can have extras duplicated for very little money (as opposed to the entire album). These "singles" provide high credibility to prospects when they appear in the mail simply as a routine part of your press kit.

I knew that I was on the right track when a participant at a speech came up to me and told me that he was happy to finally hear me in person. "My predecessor," he said to my glee, "left one of your CDs in his desk, and I've listened to it a half-dozen times over the past year." The best part was that he kept telling that story to everyone around him.

BUILD YOUR BRAND OR BRANDS

It's never too early to begin thinking about brands and branding. A *brand* is simply that public perception with which potential (and current) customers identify you. [See my book *How to Establish a Unique Brand in the Consulting Profession* (San Francisco: Jossey-Bass/Pfeiffer, 2001) for details and specific strategies.]

One Percent Solution: A brand is a representation of uniform quality.

- A brand can be a name: "Get me McKinsey & Co."
- A brand can be an approach: "Get me the total management quality guy."
- A brand can be a trademarked identifier: "Get me The Telephone Doctor."
- A brand can be an attribute: "Get me the Million Dollar Consultant approach."

Brands can be many things, but the objective of all the techniques is to establish you as a particular value proposition in the eyes of the customer: reliable, experienced, relevant, consistent, and so forth. Think of the great brands: Google, Coca-Cola, Levis, Nike, Kleenex, Mercedes. They evoke confidence and quality. And the owners of these brands are also constantly reinforcing and protecting their brand.

Procter & Gamble, to name one famous example, has a multiplicity of brands (the parent company is not really a brand itself) that it actually allows to compete against each other for shelf space and sales. Mercedes-Benz is one of the great brand names ("We are the Mercedes-Benz of the florist business"), but virtually no one knows that the parent company was for many years Daimler-Benz. On the other hand, executives readily shout into their speakerphones, "Get me McKinsey!"

The moral of all this is that a brand is what you make it, and that brand can be you, your services, your attributes, or a combination of factors. No matter what your brand is or how many brands you develop, however, here are some important guidelines for effective branding.

Eleven Techniques to Make Your Brand Indelible and Memorable

1. *Use it repeatedly.* When you write an article, make a speech, converse with a prospect, create a Web site, and/or engage in any other form of business communication, always incorporate your brand. If your brand is "The Financial Strategist," casually write or comment that, "The reason I'm called 'The Financial Strategist' is because of my unique approach to. . . ." (If you don't blow your own horn, there is no music.)

2. *Make it visual.* Even if the brand is used only in words and type, include it prominently in your collateral and electronic materials. If it's conducive to a logo or graphic, then use this avenue to impress it in the mind of readers or viewers.

3. *Trademark or register it if possible.* Your name is, by definition, unique. However, if you are "The Conflict Resolver," explore a trademark or registration mark, and then use it constantly. The Telephone Doctor is such an example. The woman behind it is Nancy Friedman, but her moniker is her uniqueness.

4. *Use it as the title of a book or article.* Virtually nothing will solidify a brand like a book based on it. Just look at the "idiot" books on a variety of topics. Or my book, *The Million Dollar Consulting Toolkit.* It doesn't hurt to use it as a speech title either.

5. *Put it in your e-mail signature file.* This is automatic once it is set up and a no-brainer to sustain, but the volume of people associating the brand with you will grow exponentially.

6. *Create a product around the brand.* This could be a CD, pamphlet, booklet, manual, or even a game. I've seen people use mugs, T-shirts, and bumper stickers (although I hate this stuff).

7. *Have clients endorse it.* Obtain testimonial letters and blurbs that specifically say, "Winning Negotiations' was the finest experience our management team has ever been through together."

8. *Build a newsletter around it. Balancing act* is a public-domain term used by many people who work in the area of life balance and even the name of a book or two (you cannot copyright book titles in the United States). However, I've established a unique newsletter with that title that has become phenomenally popular, reinforcing that brand for me.

9. *Be outrageous.* My buddy Patricia Fripp, with whom I mentioned I conduct The Odd Couple marketing seminars, has been a great example for me of "over the top" marketing. As a result, I made it known that I drive Ferraris and Aston Martins and Bentleys and use those car names in my private e-mail addresses. As a result, I developed the "Ferrari brand" associated with my consulting: high quality and high performance (and very expensive). It has served me better than I ever could have imagined.

10. *Experiment and change brands.* Few brands last forever amid changing times, and new times create new needs. There is no scorecard on your success rate with brands. Keep trying them out and changing the ones that don't seem to grab attention. Procter & Gamble, Coca-Cola, and Mercedes-Benz (and I) all constantly introduce new brands. What do you have to lose?

11. *Use the Internet and search engines to promote the brand globally.* Use the phrase in every article, column, newsletter, posting, and other souce that you can. Use Google alerts to tell you how often your brand (and your name and company) are picked up and mentioned elsewhere (and to make sure no one else is infringing on you).

BECOMING A "STAH"

There is a logical progression from audio to video. For those of you who are about to skip this section because it is too far out, I would advise you to stay put. Twenty years ago it was unusual for a consultant to be on audiotape, 10 years ago it was unusual to do a videoconference, and 20 years from now it will be common for consultants to be on a variety of currently unknown media. If you can't view change as opportunity, how will you ever get your clients to do so?

Being on video (DVDs, streaming video on the Web, YouTube, and so on) serves several purposes, any one of which may apply to you:

- It is a marketing or "audition" device to acquire speaking engagements.
- It can be a passive income source: "Tom Jones on Leadership in the New Millennium."

- It can be a "leave behind" for appropriate consulting interventions.
- It can provide a skills-transfer medium for internal client consultants.
- It provides powerful credibility to refer to "my video on the subject of . . ."
- It can serve in place of a published book.
- It can create repeat and "cult" following and, therefore, viral word of mouth.

Convinced about the utility? If so, read on to learn how to be a star.

The best way to create a video is analogous to the creation of an audio: try to be taped in front of a live audience. I've encountered a few conventions or associations along the way that routinely videotape presenters, but many client organizations also have the capacity to do so. I've been taped by many different clients with facilities ranging from a company employee with a stationary camera in the rear of the room, to a production team brought in for the purpose, to a professional stage with video shot from a projection booth and projected on huge screens.[10]

Your best bet for video is to have a client tape a presentation. As with audio, many clients are willing and able to do it, but they simply haven't thought of it. It's your job to help them understand the value of creating such a tape to show to people who couldn't attend the session, people in distant locales, people who join the organization in the future, and as a later point of reference for those who do attend. You may be able to add more reasons, given the nature of your talk and/or consulting project. These simple but accurate justifications are usually highly influential.

You must prepare your presentation to take advantage of the video medium.

One Percent Solution: Videotape clients giving you testimonials and place these on your Web site home page. This is the most dramatic video marketing tool that I know of.

---

[10] One was at what was then the Golden Nugget Casino, a client in Atlantic City that is now known as Bally's Grand. On one such occasion, I addressed casino management from the stage, and several days later Frank Sinatra sang to the high rollers from the same spot. I was told to avoid the video screens set flush with the stage, which couldn't be seen by the audience. They were installed so that the song lyrics could scroll down while Mr. Sinatra sang, enabling him to glance down to find his place if he needed to. All I could envision was crashing through them in the middle of an anecdote.

Set up your talk to take advantage of the medium. This is much trickier than audio, although even there you had to make some adjustments (for example, no lengthy nonverbal demonstrations). The absolute worst video sin is the "talking head" syndrome. Nothing creates stupor faster than watching someone on the screen stand in one place and talk for 30 minutes or more. Closely allied to this horror is a person on video—a fairly sophisticated medium—using a flipchart or chalkboard—fairly primitive media—to illustrate points for the audience. Similar problems arise with slides and overhead transparencies because of lighting issues.

Work with the client to best exploit the video format. Since you've suggested (or even if the client has suggested) the videotaping, invest a few hours over the phone with the person who will be running the equipment. Find out how many cameras will be used, where they will be placed, whether they can zoom, if there are dead spots in the room, what the sound system will be, and so on. Inform the operator of your plans for movement, visuals, and audience participation, and carefully work out what can be covered effectively and what cannot. Here are some guidelines for videotaping effectiveness from the speaker's perspective:

- Arrange to have your introducer included in the taping, and prepare that person carefully for the introduction you want.
- Try to move across the front of the room and use physical gestures. This means that you can't be tied to notes, which must remain on the lectern. Make sure that the camera can be panned in this fashion and that the operator is prepared to move with you, not "catch up" with you. (Depending on lighting, you may need a follow spot.) Alternate close-up shots with long shots.
- Repeat any questions from the audience for the camera and sound system.
- Try to have sound pickups to capture audience reactions. Or use central mikes that they walk to (or circulate handheld mikes).
- Don't wear a white shirt or blouse or a patterned suit. Conservative dress comes across best because the medium somewhat exaggerates colors. Navy blue is always a safe choice. (Black is always stylish and it's slimming, plus all accessories go with it. What's not to like about black?)
- Practice until you are smooth, but *don't worry about perf*ection. Correct any errors in a natural, conversational way; don't harp on them or try ad lib humor. The benefit of a video of a live presentation is that the video audience is not surprised by minor,

MILLION DOLLAR CONSULTING

normal errors, but it will be distracted by someone obviously playing to the camera.

- Pretend the camera isn't there during your delivery. This will enhance the natural aspects of the presentation.

- Keep the session relatively short. My bias is for a 30 to 45-minute duration. It's tough to edit these down because later points are often dependent on earlier foundation.

- Keep the visual aids simple and sensitive to the medium. For example, holding up an item is ideal, provided that it's large enough for the camera to capture. Try to stay away from slides that require lighting adjustments. (It's often possible to edit in a picture or diagram specifically for the video later if something from the session doesn't show up well on tape.) PowerPoint will show up, but it's overdone and usually boring. Try to stay away from it.

- Review your notes to avoid making any references to timing or events that would indicate the date, and refrain from ad libs that do so.

- Offer to stay after the session to reshoot any segments that the technician feels may not have been captured well. Even with the room empty, you can deliver a five-minute example or restate something that was garbled earlier. In most instances, you'll be able to view the completed tape immediately.

Once you've obtained a master of the video, you can work with a production house to create whatever packaging you desire. I recommend the following essentials:

1. Include a voice-over at the beginning with generic background music.
2. Add a title graphic with the topic, your name, and the client or group. Don't include the date.
3. Edit out extraneous material (picking up dropped notes, an interruption at the rear of the room), and enhance the audience reactions if needed.
4. It's often best to end the tape during the applause and/or while the host is thanking you. Fade to a final graphic.
5. Conclude with a voice-over explaining what was just seen, accompanied by a graphic showing where to write for more information. This is the place for your 800 number if you have one. Use generic music to close.
6. Package the video in a simple box with a professional label, including your name, company, and logo and the title of the subject.

7. Also place the finished production on a DVD (just as inexpensive to duplicate and increasingly popular to use). Most of my current demonstration videos are requested on DVD.

These videos needn't be placed in albums; they can stand alone in their boxes. In volume (over 100) you can easily find sources that will duplicate them for less than $10 per disk and sometimes for as low as about $5 per disk. Production costs for editing and voice-overs generally run less than $300 depending on how elaborate your needs are. (My advice: keep it simple and professional.) Thus, for somewhere around $1,000, you could have 100 DVDs duplicated to your specifications, and I suspect that you might get that down closer to $500 if you investigate carefully. (Does the client have a production house it often uses that it could recommend to you?)

Finally, what if your clients don't videotape? The best alternative is to seek permission to have your own production company shoot the session. You can find local firms (that is, local to your presentation—you don't want to pay for travel expenses) easily, often from the client's suggestions, that professionally tape such sessions for reasonable fees. In my experience, you can have a presentation shot with two cameras by an outside group for under $1,000, and this often will include the subsequent editing. Be careful about minimum time requirements, however; some firms demand that you retain them for a day because they can't do anything else besides your job anyway. The advantage of an outside firm hired by you is that you know that the video will be done well and coordinated with your efforts because *you* are the client.

The only downside risk is the client's sensitivities about confidential matters, company policies, and so forth. If you want to bring in an outside firm, always offer to waive any fee you're getting for that particular speech or grant the client something—a reduction in the project fee, free copies of the video for distribution, an additional presentation at another site, and so on. Make it worth the client's while because it's certainly worth a great deal to you. Often, trade associations and conventions will agree most readily to your bringing in a video outfit, particularly if you waive your speaking fee for these budget-conscious groups.

Stay light on your feet. At an international management conference, I noticed that the camera projecting presenters onto large screens had a recording capability. The operators graciously agreed to tape my two-hour keynote speech, which benefited from sensational audience reaction. With the client's permission, I used this as my demo video, my bureau video, and a product that sold for $199. Appropriately, my theme that day was "Capturing Opportunity"! Always be prepared to seize the moment. (My current DVD is also a live keynote speech shot at a client site. I had zero production costs.)

Your firm is doing well, your growth is accelerating, and your personal profile is being enhanced. Yet we've established that this is a *relationship* business. Let's turn, then, to the ultimate relationships.

QUESTIONS AND ANSWERS

Q. *What is the key step in branding?*

A. There are three. First, establish a brand that makes sense, whether its your name, a trait (I've been "the contrarian"), or an analogy. Second, nurture it by using it constantly on the Internet, in conversation, in print, in introductions, and so forth. Finally, realize the equity of the brand by charging more for having "the contrarian" in person, or "the globally renowned Alan Weiss."

Q. *What if I really want to build a business with people and infrastructure?*

A. More power to you. Remember that you'll have to invest annually in your assets, in hopes of selling the business for its equity at some future point, so that you'll be taking far less out of the business personally Just don't get stuck between the two models, and don't create a "corporate welfare state" where you're supporting employees. They should be supporting *you*.

Q. *I can see professional speakers on audio and video, but does it make sense for a consultant?*

A. Marketing makes sense for everyone, and this is increasingly a visual age, especially on the Web. Think about videos of you working with a client and/or the client providing a testimonial.

Q. *Isn't it manipulative to paint my firm and my accomplishments too grandly?*

A. That depends on how much you feel you can deliver value to clients. If you're not convinced, enthused, and full of examples, they certainly won't be. I don't want a surgeon, an interviewer, an accountant, a designer, or a consultant who isn't captivated by the work and who doesn't feel he is great at what he does.

Q. *What's the most effective branding mechanism of all?*

A. Your name. After all, there is no other "you."

Final Thought: Perception is reality. Act like a "going concern" and a large firm, and others will regard you that way. Self-image becomes general image. The first sale is always to yourself.

THE MARKET GRAVITY RELATIONSHIPS

WHEN PROSPECTS CALL YOU SEEKING TO BECOME CLIENTS AND CLIENTS NEVER WANT YOU TO LEAVE

LONG-TERM CONTRACTS

Intelligently managed growth creates its own momentum. Gradually you will find that the breaks that never came your way when you were struggling begin to turn in your favor. "Where were they when I really needed them?" we are prone to ask. The fact is that we make our own breaks, and the mere act of developing your business creates a force that sweeps newer and better opportunities your way.

The great Brooklyn Dodgers general manager, Branch Rickey, responding to critics who said that he was merely lucky in finding the best players in the game, replied: "Luck is the residue of design." And master science-fiction writer Robert Heinlein, with scores of books and awards behind him, noted: " 'Luck' is the term used by the mediocre to explain away genius."

> *One Percent Solution: The very act of growing creates a momentum that generates additional opportunities that hadn't been anticipated.*

One such opportunity is that of long-term contracts. Although I've advocated finite, shorter-term projects with clear starts and finishes, I've also emphasized long-term relationships, from which such projects periodically arise. Occasionally, a client will have a legitimate and attractive situation that calls for ongoing collaboration. By long term, I mean consulting relationships that meet these two criteria:

- The agreed-upon period is at least one year.
- The objectives are dynamic, not fixed.

The one-year provision is my own arbitrary assessment of what constitutes long term. In most cases, this will involve two fiscal years for the client, even if all payment is made in only one of them.[1] It will involve the completion of a year's results to be compared against the plan and the creation of the next year's plan. And it will involve sufficient normal change in the operation—turnover, competitive actions, new products and services, acquired and lost customers, and so on—to provide a realistic opportunity to assess the impact of your assistance. In other words, you can tell quite clearly whether your presence is improving the client's condition.

The second criterion means that the client might say, "Let's meet twice a month to brainstorm what I should be doing to improve the operation in view of ongoing results. In the interim, wander around the business and tell me what you think I don't know or appreciate."

The client isn't looking for your participation in installing a system or procedure, in delivering a workshop, or in helping to redefine reporting relationships, although any of these activities might, in fact, occur if conditions warrant it. Your relationship is based on establishing objectives for improving the organization, not on meeting predefined ones. You are functioning as the "independent expert" on the chart of possible interventions from Chapter 1. (And this is ideal retainer work, as we've alluded to earlier: access to your "smarts.")

These types of contracts are the ultimate demonstration of trust. The client is not expecting specific tasks to be accomplished, nor is there a particular objective that needs to be met. Instead, the client is trusting you to provide the ongoing advice and assistance that will improve the organization and is trusting that it will be delivered with candor, accuracy, and pragmatism.

Firing all the vice presidents doesn't usually solve anything. Establishing written statements of accountability that all officers help to write, commit to, and agree to be evaluated against usually does.

In long-term retainer relationships, the client doesn't need to have specific objectives accomplished. The client needs ongoing access to your "smarts."

---

[1] In my experience, it is very difficult to secure fixed-fee consulting assignments that call for commitments from the client in more than two fiscal years. Many organizations have policies against such multiyear commitments, especially since tighter financial reporting rules were introduced in the wake of Sarbanes-Oxley.

I worked with the Calgon Corporation's water management division for five years. The newly appointed president and I agreed on a six-month assignment, which led to a second six-month assignment and four additional one-year assignments. During this extended period, I conducted workshops, facilitated meetings, shadowed the president, interviewed all the key executives and managers, visited field sites, participated in field service calls, designed programs, recommended personnel moves, evaluated outside programs, and helped establish key accountabilities.

None of these activities was specified at the outset. The need for them became apparent as the relationship continued. Most of the time the president and I agreed; sometimes we didn't. No matter. I served in the role of consultant to the management team and provided help as requested or as I thought needed to be initiated. Some of this work was on a project basis with clear objectives, measures, and value (e.g., designing programs), while some was purely access to me (e.g., sounding board for policy creation).

It remains one of the most rewarding consulting assignments I've ever had. Over the course of five years, I saw my recommendations implemented, observed the results in terms of the business goals of the organization, and was able to fine-tune as needed. I knew virtually every manager in the home office and the field, and there probably isn't one who would hesitate to call me if she thought I could be of help. I was part of the team.

After the first year, the division met (and exceeded) its plan for the first time in several years. This was when the group president noted, "You must be very pleased to have been a part of our success this past year." And that is exactly how I felt.

Long-term contracts[2] are extremely valuable because they provide the maximum opportunity for multidimensional growth. (See Figure 16-1 for the essentials of a long-term contract.) You are able to consistently test the envelope in a setting that is familiar, trusting, and accepting of change (or you wouldn't be there). These relationships are the exact opposite of what most people in the consulting profession seek.

Too frequently, external consultants help companies implement programmatic change. They design and staff corporate training programs, draft corporate mission statements, design gain-sharing programs, and implement quality circles. Such programs are ideally suited to the role of external consultants. They are easy to describe to potential customers. Precisely because they are programmatic, they can be replicated from one company to the next. Because customers

---

[2] When I speak of *long-term relationships*, I mean a continuing contact with a client over the years, which usually involves several fee-paying projects during that time period. By *long-term contract*, I mean a fee-paying project that lasts for at least a year.

A Long-Term Contract

- Is usually established with the CEO or business unit head.
- Requires extended time on-site and with client customers.
- Should never include competitors of your clients, since extensive confidential data are usually shared.
- Is usually established at the request of the client, not as a result of a proposal from you.
- Requires that you establish credibility and trust with management several layers down. (If you are seen as a threat or a "hatchet," your long-term value will be nil.)
- Requires a far greater amount of innovation and initiation on your part, since you must both react to and anticipate change for the clients. Your attitude must be not to *fix* but rather to *improve*.

Figure 16-1 A long-term contract has these six characteristics, in addition to the duration and dynamic objectives already cited.

are buying a known product, consultants can accurately estimate the time and cost of implementing the new program. Programs that do not require lasting changes in ongoing employee behavior are not usually threatening. However, while such programs are easy to sell to companies, they do not in and of themselves promote revitalization.

There are two basic methods of assessing fees in such contracts. The better of the two is consistent with the advice already provided in terms of fixed fees based on value (Chapter 9). What is the value to the client of your long-term personal help in understanding the operation and its people intimately and in providing specific assistance to improve the client's condition? How valuable is it for the client to have a priority call on your time?

My preference is to establish your fee for the year (or whatever the period is) and fix the payment terms, again providing a discount for one-time payment. (This is often highly attractive in such situations and provides you with a substantial sum of money at one time.) Alternatively, require your usual 50 percent deposit and establish periodic, calendar-date billing times. Expenses should be billed at the end of each calendar month.

The first method is a long-term retainer. It's important to accelerate the payment schedule because even with an ironclad contract, clients will tend to cancel consulting retainers when management changes, the economy suffers, and/or the organization suffers other kinds of trauma (even though the consultant is then needed more than ever). This is the tropism toward cost cutting that occurs in threatened organizations. And this is what makes the second alternative so dangerous to your cash flow.

> *Remember the retainer criteria for fees: who is involved in the relationship, what is the scope of the relationship, and what is the duration of the relationship?*

The second alternative is a monthly retainer. If the client prefers this, always establish in your contract one of two provisions (or both):

- The retainer is paid in advance, a quarter at a time.
- There is a contractual guarantee of six months.

In this manner, you have protected yourself, to the extent possible, from unforeseen events, such as falling victim to a bad sales month.

Long-term contracts ensure that you are a going concern. They also alleviate cash-flow worries and, most important, provide for the multidimensional growth that is that is vital to million dollar consultants.

In one $2^1/_2$-year retainer with a division of the Times Mirror Company that involved myriad linked projects, the client paid nearly a quarter of a million dollars in one lump sum on January 1. We both think we had a great deal. So did my bankers.

Since the client generally calls you for such contracts, how do you help make them happen? How do you create the gravity for long-term retainers?

Criteria for Successful Retainer Business

1. Establish the longest time frame possible.

2 Move all payments toward the front end, and encourage full payment in advance in return for a discount.

3 Ensure that there is two-way unlimited access: the client can reach you at any reasonable time, but you also must be able to reach the client in the same manner.

4 Severely limit the number of people who can access you, or dramatically increase the retainer amount as that number increases.

5 If the client insists on your not working for competitive businesses, accept this condition in return for a premium on your fee—the longer the noncompete provisions, the higher the premium.

6 Create separate proposals for specific projects the client may ask you to undertake that involve more than your advice. If you're asked for recommendations on an evaluation system, that's fine, but if you're asked to design and implement one, that's a separate project requiring a separate proposal and fee.

7 Meet with the buyer at least once a month and talk with the buyer by phone or fax at least once a week, but don't feel you must have an agenda or proactive advice. Just manifest your availability.

8 Provide an option to renew the retainer well before the current term expires, that is, in October for the following year if it's an annual retainer. You have to plan your time, and the client has to plan the budget.

9 Do not feel that you must show up to justify the retainer. The value here is your ongoing advice and counsel on call, not your appearances.

The latter will limit your business severely while providing no extra, discernible value to the client.

10 Offer provocative ideas. You're there to stimulate and break paradigms, not merely to reassure the client about a conservative course.

11 Never feel guilty if you're not used "often enough." Look at yourself as an insurance policy, if that helps.

ALLOWING THE BUYER TO BUY

Ultimate relationships mean that you merely need to make it simple and pleasurable for the buyer to buy. That's easier than you think, and here are some techniques to employ.

Client Conferences

A friend of mine specializes in strategy consulting, particularly in the formulation stage. He charges fees of $100,000 and up per assignment. He does virtually no advertising, he doesn't exhibit at trade shows, and I've never found him in any professional listings. Yet in the first half of most years alone, he books more than a dozen strategy assignments. For a long time he was selling, delivering, and following up on these projects by himself.

How does he achieve this rate of business? Well, in 1991, when he began (during the Gulf War, no less, a lesson for all of us dealing with these turbulent global times), he gave a client symposium. He invited some of his ongoing, satisfied strategy customers, some likely prospects, and some outside speakers to a couple of days at a posh resort. Spouses were encouraged to attend. There was no fee for the session, but everyone paid his own airfare and lodging.

The result? By June, he had sold a strategy formulation to all but one of the prospects that had attended the symposium.

He long ago learned the lesson of investing money to make money. He saw the symposium as a strategic marketing tool and employed a tactic that is one of the most powerful in our profession: peer influence. He did little selling during the course of the meeting. He let his current clients sell for him during cocktails, in the halls, and on the golf course.

These are examples of the ultimate relationships: clients selling to prospects through the communications channels you establish. He has never hesitated to spend $50,000 or more for a keynote speaker (Henry Kissenger appeared one year) because he knows that the investment will pay a huge return, and just one sale more recovers much more than the mere costs.

There is no greater influence, no more powerful sales stratagem, than arranging for one executive to have the opportunity and the motivation to say to another, "Use this consultant. I thank my stars that we did."

Client conferences are an excellent method for achieving the interaction that results in peer influence. The key factor in successful client conferences is ensuring that you invite more than just clients! If you are running a symposium, as my friend did, or a general conference on a particular management subject, then it makes sense to have a strong mix of people—clients and prospects alike.

> *One Percent Solution: The platinum standard in marketing is a peer-to-peer reference at buyer level recommending your services by name.*

If you are running a client-oriented conference, most of the attendees will be clients, but some should be high-priority, high-quality prospects. You might even want to pay for their transportation if their organizations don't forbid the practice. Every conference you hold is a marketing opportunity of enormous value.

Here is the checklist for successful conferences. (By *successful*, I mean that the participants find the time investment well spent, and the prospects are moved closer to a buying position.)

- Attendees notified at least two months in advance, and preferably more

- A ratio of at least three high-quality prospects to each client present (if it's not a purely client conference)
- One excellent outside speaker—a recognizable/prestigious name in the field—per day[3]
- The use of a superb facility with a wide variety of recreational opportunities
- A limited formal agenda (that is, mornings only or a full day off), with ample time for socializing
- Prearranged press coverage during the conference or publicizing via the press afterward
- Provision of complimentary copies of books, articles, or examples that are of use during the conference
- Provision of a postsession report and summary materials and an offer of ongoing help after the conference
- Online promotion and conference summary
- Provision for participants to remain in touch with others on their own initiative
- Special password-protected Web site or chat room for use postconference
- Electronic newsletter updates on the subjects discussed

Note that these conferences are intended for present and potential *buyers* of your services. Many firms hold *user-group meetings* that encompass the internal facilitators, instructors, and others who have been instrumental in implementing your project work. These are valuable undertakings that enhance the relationship you are trying to form with your clients, but they are not the significant, peer-influence marketing tool that buyer-level conferences and symposia are.

Moreover, the user-group meetings often can be held internally or regionally among several clients using client facilities. Their goal is enhancing the technical application of your project work. The buyer-level meeting is a marketing opportunity of tremendous value, which is why a significant investment is justified. However, don't confuse the two, and *never mix executives and implementers* at the same conference. Not only is their frame of reference going to be different, but your intent with them also will be radically different.

---

[3] Estimated cost is from about $15,000 for noncelebrities to over $25,000 for celebrities. Sometimes you can get a local politician or university professor for peanuts or an honorarium, however.

Case Study

Many of the consultants I've mentored have launched breakfast and lunch meetings as mini-conferences. They invite 25 local potential buyers, both clients and prospects, to a hotel conference room. Typically, about 15 to 20 actually attend, given last-minute emergencies.

The sessions last no more than 90 minutes so as not to impinge too much on the business day. The consultant pays for the conference room and meal and facilitates an informal discussion around a single theme: retention, global marketing, business regulation, inventory management, and so on. A guest speaker is often used, and this can be a local professor of economics or someone from a government agency.

The total cost is about $1,000, including the invitations. The key is that the invitation is nontransferable. (Executives do not like to mingle with those at subordinate levels at these events.)

Some colleagues have found these sessions so popular that they have created business roundtables, where the same group meets monthly to share common issues under the consultant's aegis. It's hard for these relationships not to lead to additional consulting business.

Client Advisory Groups

Client advisory groups are another technique used to build ultimate relationships. I have an insurance client whose chief executive officer asked four of us—all outside consultants—to participate in an informal advisory board. We met twice a year at resort locations for no fee, but with all expenses paid and spouses encouraged to attend. Typically, we spent one day on company business, advising the CEO on issues that were on his priority list and often arguing among ourselves about our advice. The result was that we explored every issue thoroughly, and the consultants learned as much as the CEO. The second day was spent socializing—at the beach, on a fishing boat, or whatever.

This CEO received a wealth of consulting help during these few days a year. It didn't replace what we did for him independently, working on clearly defined projects, but it augmented all our work and provided him with a valuable (and unique) sounding board that was unavailable within his organization. None of us held back, and no one ever said, "Wait a minute, this issue really should be addressed within a project arrangement!"

Commensurately, it's a good idea for you to form advisory groups from among your clients and nonclients (who may someday become clients). These informal outside advisors should *not* include your attorney or your financial advisor. Those people offer advice in narrow, important fields but should not be included in an advisory board. Keep your advisory board or group small—no more than eight members, but more than just a handful because schedules always will interfere with some individual participation at meetings—and meet infrequently. I think that twice a year is about right.

You don't have to fly everyone to Antigua, but you should foot the bill for two days at a decent place, with sufficient social time built in. This is to allow for that old peer influence to operate, among other benefits. Remember, consider including at least two or three nonclients who are key prospects in the group. And keep the membership at executive level only.

Among the issues you can ask your advisory group to discuss and consult with you on are these:

- Your strategy in the marketplace
- Major moves/investments: alliances, office expansion, new hires, and so on
- Major marketing plans
- Publishing plans
- Economic trends
- Pro bono work
- Emerging management priorities
- Competition
- Growth of the business and/or infrastructure
- Personal growth needs
- Relevant new technologies
- What to abandon
- Continuing utility of your business model

> *Client advisory groups serve to cement existing client relationships by forming a collaborative effort on behalf of your business. They also develop potential relationships among nonclient members and member contacts.*

Client advisory groups or boards are not boards of directors, which I would discourage you from forming. As long as you are taking the risks and providing the talent, a board of directors can serve no purpose that an advisory group cannot. Meanwhile, a board has certain significant drawbacks in terms of restrictions on your activities and divulgence of personal business affairs. The advisory board has all the supportive elements of a board of directors and none of the disadvantages. (It is also considerably easier to form, alter, and end when necessary.)

No matter what you call your efforts in creating special relationships and forums—symposia, conferences, meetings, boards, committees, gatherings, sessions, task forces, councils, or something else—your goal should be the same: to create opportunities for peer influence to sell your services to prospects and to create opportunities to solidify and extend the ongoing relationships you've formed with existing clients. These alternatives provide you with great leverage in these marketing pursuits.

THE VALUE-ADDED DISCOUNTING PRINCIPLE OF NEVER LOSING CLIENTS

Every book needs a clever acronym. Maybe this is mine: TV-ADPONLC. On second thought, I'd probably better explain.

The value-added discounting principle of never losing clients (TV-ADPONLC) is simply my way of emphasizing that the longer term the relationship, the longer term it is likely to be. No, this is not a truism. At birth, an individual's life expectancy may be 77 years. However, once that individual has reached 40 successfully, the life expectancy is probably about 80 years. And once you're 79, the odds are that you have a few more years left.

In other words, the longer you live, the longer you probably will live. Client relationships follow these actuarial realities very closely. But not for the same reasons.

As you have no doubt realized by now, my path to millions of dollars in business is through the establishment of long-term relationships. The creation of these relationships is, in turn, based on creating and implementing the value-added qualities that enable you to improve the client's condition.

The sustaining of these qualities and this improvement over time create a bond that is quite difficult to break because your worth to the client increases geometrically as you move from project to project. You are not merely the sum of the performance-evaluation system you implemented plus the customer survey you conducted plus the creation of educational strategies for the human resources area. As you've engaged in these projects, the client organization has imparted information to you that has made you wise in the organization's ways and culture. Your value added is no longer merely the talents that you bring to the client; it is also the wisdom that you can now apply through your intimate knowledge of the client.

And wisdom is critical because it isn't readily replaceable.

One Percent Solution: Once the client educates you about the client's culture and business, you are more valuable and can charge more, and are therefore harder to displace. It doesn't get much better than that.

Most consulting assignments begin with the gathering of information and the application of knowledge. These activities are replaceable and nondifferentiated. The attainment and use of wisdom are an intrinsic value that is difficult and time-consuming for anyone else to re-create.

Clients can find a great many alternatives to implement succession-planning systems, to design workshops on innovation, and even to assist in formulating strategy. In all these and myriad other consulting activities, there is a joint educational process occurring. The client learns processes, methods, and skills from the consultant that improve the client's condition.

However, preparatory to this result, the consultant must be educated about the client's organization. The less the consultant knows about the client and the client's industry, the more education is required, the longer the process of learning will be, and the greater the chances of early errors, misconceptions, and misjudgments.

The more the consultant knows about the client's organization and industry, the less remedial education is required, the shorter the process of learning will be, and the lower the chances for errors, misconceptions, and misjudgments.

Typically, when I begin an assignment for a new client, I include what I call *roaming time* in my plans. During my roaming, I try to

- Meet all key senior managers to learn their responsibilities and their perceptions of the organization.
- Meet a wide cross section of middle- and lower-level managers to learn their perceptions.
- Meet a wide variety of hourly and administrative people to learn their perceptions.

- Accompany field people on client calls and sales calls and attend field sales meetings.
- Observe the normal work routines, including the way complaints and crises are handled.
- Immerse myself in the organization's culture, mores, beliefs (real and perceived), and attitudes toward customers.
- Meet customers, if possible, on site or off site.
- Understand how knowledge is used (is it readily available at the point of need?).
- Learn how technology is used (does it tend to help or hinder?).

Case Study

While roaming through an organization that had assured me that it had a "fully diversified, interactive employment," I found the cafeteria voluntarily segregated into Hispanic, African American, and white, and even these groups were stratified by hierarchy.

My buyer told me that I "was not describing his company." I asked him when it was that he had last roamed around "his company."

This roaming never really ends, but it's most intense in the beginning of an assignment, when I try to gather this information in as little time as possible so that I can be as productive for the client as quickly as possible.[4]

On succeeding projects for that client, my primary education needs have been met, my knowledge is intact (although the continuing education never ends), and I begin to become a source of wisdom for that client. That is, my consulting help now has the added dimension of a thorough understanding of my client's beliefs, goals, culture, comfort zones, and unique problems. I am a wise man.

---

[4] Consultants who simply enter client organizations with canned approaches and off-the-shelf interventions don't do this and are never as potentially useful and powerful as true consultants who design interventions based on unique client needs and conditions. No one makes $1 million delivering workshops on time management, but you can make tens of millions showing organizations how to save time and increase productivity by changing their systems and procedures. When you see a consultant "selling" off-the-shelf testing instruments for any occasion, throw him out.

In Australia (my fifteenth trip is coming up), I've had a very warm reception, as do American consultants in general. We are cordially (I like to believe) referred to as "wise men from the East." I think there's more to this quotation than meets the ear.

Data can be exchanged. Information can be exchanged and communicated. Knowledge is readily shared. All these things are based on facts and circumstances that can easily be *instantiated*—moved from the abstract to the concrete via the written word, examples, discussions, and exchanges. This is one of the reasons why organizations hold so many meetings. They are frantically trying to share information so that their knowledge base can be increased.

Information alone isn't valuable. It is only a prerequisite for knowledge, which is the application of that information to improve the workings of the organization.[5]

For example, you may have data about turnover that include the fact that it is 5 percent in marketing, 7 percent in sales, 6 percent in administration, and 22 percent in production. As you investigate and gather more data, you learn that the general manager of production has a different compensation plan that is strictly oriented toward quarterly production goals. As you combine these data, you have information that suggests that employee turnover is unimportant to production management and that the reward system actually encourages turnover if production goals are met. If the company's objectives are to reduce the expenses of turnover and create long-term employees, your knowledge of the problem and of effective organizational interventions provides this solution: modify the reward system and educate the general manager about the organization's needs to reduce turnover as well as meet production goals.

So far you've applied information to create knowledge and improve the client's condition. Let's assume now that the client has asked for your advice about reorganization of the field force to reduce unnecessary layers of management. During this process, you advise the client (given your experience with production turnover) that the reorganization must include a restructuring of the field management performance evaluation and reward criteria because the organization has a propensity to manage tasks rather than results. In fact, the correct emphasis on long-term business goals for field management will be the key factor in the success of the sales force reorganization. The client leans back, ponders you for a moment in deepest respect, and says, "That's very wise. Tell me more."

---

[5] There is a school of thought that requires information to be gathered before the sale and prior to money changing hands. Let's be perfectly objective: that school gets a flunking grade.

> *I've heard many people sarcastically say, "Don't be so smart." But I've never heard any one say, "Don't be so wise."*

Once you've acquired the wisdom that comes with the successful implementation of several client projects, close relationships with key managers, exposure to the organization's "soul," and establishment of credibility and trust through your improvements, you are a wise person.

This wisdom is worth a great deal to the client because to replace it would cost a fortune. To replace your level of wisdom with a new consulting source would require that the new person engage in several successful projects, develop the necessary relationships, gain exposure to the inner workings of the organization, and build the credibility and trust you that have already acquired.

Even if another consultant charges fees that are less than yours, the cost of bringing that consultant up to your current level of wisdom would be prohibitive.

So now we have arrived at the ultimate relationship. You have become so valuable to the client—so wise in the client's ways—that replacing you is far more expensive than whatever your fees may be. And if you recall our discussion (in Chapter 9) on establishing fees, the best and most lucrative way to do so is to base fees on perceived value.

> *One Percent Solution: Your perceived value is never higher than when you have arrived at a long-term relationship in which the client sees your wisdom as irreplaceable.*

An executive at Merck told me a story about one of his most brilliant lieutenants who was clearly destined to become one of the very top people in the organization. However, one day the subordinate reported that he had made a huge error in judgment and that his bad decision would cost over $1 million to correct. After making a candid disclosure, the subordinate tendered his resignation.

"Why on earth do you think I'd accept that?" asked my client.

"After this disaster, you have no choice but to fire me, and I wanted to make it as easy as possible for you," responded the subordinate.

"Are you crazy?" said the boss. "I've just invested a million dollars in your education. You're much too valuable to lose after that. Now get back to work!"

Your job isn't to make million dollar mistakes, of course, but to make million dollar improvements and contributions. If you do this consistently, you become much too valuable to lose—in good times or bad—and your fees are literally not an issue. In tough economic times, it's easy to cut outside consulting expenses. If you are a little-known entity or simply implementing programs, your time to go has probably come. However, if the executive says, "We've got some tough decisions to make. Get Alan Weiss in here for our next meeting, and tell him we'll be needing a lot of his help . . . ," " there probably isn't too much to worry about other than making plane reservations.

You see, I'm not a consulting expense to my clients; I'm Alan Weiss, a person who has provided substantial assistance in the past and has the wisdom about the operation to continue to do so. In tough times, clients cut expenses, not wisdom.

The ultimate client relationships are those in which you are the wise person whose contributions are a synthesis of personal talents, organizational knowledge, and interpersonal relationships established with top management.

In these ultimate relationships, you are simply too valuable to lose, and the cost of replacing you is prohibitive because of the client's past investment in your education. Consequently:

1. You will not tend to lose clients in tough economic conditions.

2. Your fees can be value-based and will not be an important issue.

3. The client will call you regularly for assistance.

4. You will be immune to inroads from other consultants.

5. You will develop a priceless model and reference for other work.

What I've been calling ultimate relationships [see my book and series, *The Ultimate Consultant* (San Francisco: Jossey-Bass/Pfeiffer, 2001), for detailed discussions on these issues] are not purely a factor of longevity. Simply hanging around a client for a long time doesn't do it. You have to amass wisdom through continual learning about the client and the organization's business goals, and you must constantly learn about and consider new interventions. This is why a single consulting model, limited programmatic offerings, and a "flavor of the month," fad-type approach will never result in such relationships. They don't represent any unique synthesis between the client and you, and they are readily replaceable with other alternatives without great expense.

I've seen consultants thrown out of client organizations after five-year relationships because the one trick in their bag had finally worn out. (Workshops and seminars are famous for this. They identify you with a single, narrow intervention—decision making or negotiating, for example—and after you've trained everyone in the discipline, what do you do next—train them again?)

The value-added discounting principle of never losing clients simply means that

1. If you become sufficiently valuable in the client's eyes, you will be continually called on for assistance.

2. This value is based on your becoming wise in the ways of the client and combining this intimate relationship with your own talents and your never-ending search for new interventions and solutions to improve the client's condition.

LIFE BALANCE: TIAABB (THERE IS ALWAYS A BIGGER BOAT)

As my practice grew over the years, I realized that I needed to manage the trajectory of my business. In other words, getting on airplanes every week and having only the weekends for myself and my family was one thing when I was in my twenties but would be completely unacceptable when I was in my forties, and into my fifties and (yikes) beyond, I intended to be able to "write my own ticket."

I don't suggest that you adapt my model for your life, but I do recommend that you create *some* model for your life.

I've become intrigued by the issue of life balance as I've grown personally and professionally. What I've discovered is that a holistic and full life makes one a better consultant and that a narrow and business-focused life makes one, ironically, poorer at business.

> *One Percent Solution: Discretionary time is real wealth. Chasing too much money can actually erode your wealth.*

Case Study

I was conducting an evening workshop at Boston University for a select group of highly successful entrepreneurs under the auspices of the school's business department. Forty of us were discussing the merits of life balance and flexibility.

An attorney asked if he could demur. "I work probably 80 hours a week for my clients, but I love the work. I have no other interests," he said, "so why shouldn't I immerse myself in what I love? It provides a fine contribution to my family's lifestyle. So what if this is all I know, and I don't have varied pursuits with my family? They benefit financially better than most."

"I would only ask you," I said, "how much they are benefiting from a husband and father who is largely 'absent' in his work and who can't support them in anything other than financial underpinnings?"

Ultimately, the "workaholic" is a selfish position and a severely self-limiting one. This man was probably an adequate lawyer but not a great one because he allowed himself no time to learn and to grow. He simply did the same thing over and over again.

If you're successful on the road toward million dollar consulting, you're going to be afforded the opportunity to diversify your life through travel, recreation, personal interests, family, philanthropy, community service, continued formal and informal learning, and so on. I would suggest to you that these pursuits make you a better person, which also makes you a better consultant.

You have to help yourself if you are to be in a position to truly help others. (Put your own oxygen mask on first, as the airlines advise.) Aggressively pursue a well-rounded life. Don't compartmentalize your life into business and nonbusiness. There is nothing wrong with watching your kids play soccer at two in the afternoon and equally nothing wrong with taking a cell phone and a laptop on vacation to check in with clients for an hour each day. You don't need purity of purpose in your life—you need flexibility.

Nietzsche wrote, "A day has a hundred pockets if you know what to put in them." Since we're approaching the latter parts of this book, let me suggest some techniques to ensure that you use your good fortune and hard work to create a full and enriching life for you and for those around you.

Twelve Techniques for Million Dollar Life Balance

1. *Eliminate arbitrary time boundaries.* Do things when the spirit moves you (which also results in higher quality). If you want to go to the beach on Monday and complete a client document on Saturday afternoon, then do so.

2. *Accentuate continued external learning.* The noted psychologist Albert Bandura has conducted studies demonstrating that people who believe that they can acquire skills readily from external sources are resilient and tend to persevere through setbacks. Those who believe that skills are strictly innate are more easily defeated by setbacks because they have no other source of skill acquisition.

3. *Push the envelope.* Try new things. Learn to paint or play a musical instrument. Experiment with fine wines or cooking. Stretch your capabilities and explore new passions. Constantly reinvent yourself.

4. *Maintain perspective.* Nothing you do will affect the course of Western civilization tomorrow. Don't confuse yourself about priorities. We do important work, helping individuals and organizations improve. Nothing more, nothing less.

5. *Reward yourself regularly.* I've seen too many people promise themselves that a lifetime of sacrifice will lead to a joyous retirement, only to find that the sacrifice never ends. Buy the impulse gift for your family or yourself. Take a long weekend. As an entrepreneur, you have control over your time and your life. Don't sacrifice that control to an anthropomorphic little guy on your shoulder who shouts in your ear, "You don't deserve it!"

6. *Avoid isolation.* You'll need a "trusted other" in whom to confide your fears, your triumphs, and your uncertainties. This might be a spouse, a relative, a close friend, or a therapist (we need to get over the idea that we use therapy only when we have serious problems). You're a lone wolf only if you allow yourself to be one. Create your own pack.

7. *Help others.* You'll be amazed at how soon you can mentor and counsel others (who are where you were a year or two ago), and

how that help will rebound to assist in your own learning and growth. Make a contribution to the profession and the community.

8. *Employ healthy outrage.* There are times when you will be poorly treated. Do not neurotically search for where you went wrong. Sometimes we do everything right and still lose the business or miss the opportunity. Channel your frustration into healthy outlets.

9. *Stay fit.* I've become convinced that, physically, mentally, and emotionally, exercise and a proper diet can build confidence, sustain a diversity of interests, and combat life pressures. Stress is a killer. Take care of yourself, and make that your top priority.

10. *Never be afraid to fail.* Fear is a dampener of talent. If you're not failing, you're not trying.

11. *Money is a means, not an end.* It is fuel for our lives. There is always someone with a bigger boat. Don't let others control your life through your competing with them. Meet and exceed only your own aspirations, not someone else's.

12. *Rejoice.* Whether in loving relationships, spiritually, in nature, mediation, or whatever, energize yourself. You are an entrepreneur who has taken control of your life and your destiny. There are perils and risks, but also great rewards and fulfillment. Focus on the half-filled glass.

You need strong, long-term relationships with only a few clients to make—and keep—a million dollars a year. As I originally wrote the last page of this chapter—honest to goodness—I was interrupted by a call from a client with whom I've worked continuously for six years. He told me to "prepare my schedule and time allotment" for next year accordingly because the company had just submitted a budget calling for me to conduct a minimum of two major projects for one division alone. I had never submitted a proposal, and one of the projects was totally unknown to me.

The two projects will net about $200,000.

Digression

In 2008, my best year ever— well into seven figures— 75 percent or more of my income came from services and activities that I was not providing—that did not exist— three years ago.

> *You should constantly seek to reinvent yourself because times, technology, society, and economies have a funny way of constantly changing. If you get in the habit of doing that, you'll never have to play "catch-up" and you'll establish ultimate relationships that are constantly renewed.*

QUESTIONS AND ANSWERS

Q. What if a client mentions that he hasn't used me much on a retainer and would like to get some future credit?

A. The preventive action is to note in your agreement that there is no time use included and that the time period expires at a certain point, regardless of use. The contingent action is to say at that time, "You don't use your fire insurance policy if there is no emergency, and I didn't hear you shouting, 'Fire!' "

Q. What happens if the buyer learns something unpleasant at a joint meeting with prior clients, or wants a different deal?

A. Be careful whom you place in the room! But that's a buying signal, so deal with it. Just don't forget that *past* clients always get the best financial deals, not new ones.

Q. Are you saying that I shouldn't be aware of and competing against the standards set by other consultants I respect, like you?!

A. Yes, I am. I can't be you, you can't be me. Focus on the life goals that are important to you and your loved ones. This book is titled *Million Dollar Consulting*, but it's not mercenary. There is no subtitle, "At any cost." TIAABB, and I don't even own a boat!

Q. Won't clients be confused if I'm constantly offering new services?

A. This is evolutionary, not revolutionary, but offering new services (and products) to existing clients (with whom you already have a relationship) is a primary aspect of smart marketing. Don't your clients constantly try to improve their offerings to their customers?

Q. At what point should I anticipate that I've "enabled buyers to buy" and I can reduce my travel and labor?

A. At the point where your brand (or brands) is working extremely well, typically where market need, your competence, and your passion are all strongest, and/or where people are flocking to you!

Final Thought: Escape velocity is very tough to achieve and demands a huge expenditure of fuel. It is far more cost-effective and less wearing on your life to attract clients to you. As long as you're doing this, you might as well attract them for the long term. Turn your gravity into magnetism.

CHAPTER 17

ACCELERATING REPEAT AND REFERRAL BUSINESS

THINKING OF THE FOURTH SALE FIRST

THE VELOCITY FACTOR

One of the key factors in consistently growing practices is the ability to increase the velocity of sales. By *velocity*, I mean the speed at which you progress from a lead and a first meeting to a conceptual agreement and a signed proposal.

Think of the ability of a Toyota Camry to proceed from a standing start to 60 miles per hour in about 12 seconds, a BMW 650 to do the same thing in about 6 seconds, and a Bentley GTC to do the same thing in 4.4 seconds. The second car takes half the time, and the last one takes a third less than that. Yet they are all manufactured on production lines using strikingly similar technologies.

We're all consultants, part of the same profession. However, some of us have engineered our practices to move much faster and reach our targets much sooner. While you can argue that the time it takes to reach 60 miles per hour in an automobile is unimportant (although it seems to make a big difference in entering a freeway filled with other consultants), the time it takes you to close business is vitally important.

One Percent Solution: It's not what you make, it's what you keep. But in this business, if you follow sound fee policies, you should keep most of what you make.

The greater your velocity of closing business, the more your profit is, because what we make is generally close to what we keep.

The Twelve Factors of Lucrative High Closing Velocity

1. Money enters your bank account more quickly.
2. You spend less money on acquisition, so your margins will be higher.
3. Things are less likely to unexpectedly go wrong or awry.
4. You complete the project more quickly.
5. You can allocate your time more effectively (and with certainty).
6. Repeat business will occur more quickly.
7. Referrals and testimonials can be gained more rapidly.
8. There are fewer buyers involved and fewer potential naysayers.
9. When the client is prone to move quickly, commitment is usually higher.
10. You enter the account with much higher credibility (no "tough" calls).
11. You can plan much farther out in terms of both cash flow and time allocation.
12. You can withstand tough times more easily because you've been paid in advance for business yet to be delivered.

> *If you view a sale as a series of small consents from the client, you can examine which parts of the sequence tend to slow you up and how you can better handle the "car" on that "stretch of road."*

The fundamental fuel in accelerating your closing speed is to know the automobile and the road signs very well—in other words, to know your own business model intimately and exactly where you are in it at the moment. For example, here is my business model from first step to closure (details of these steps appear at various places earlier in this book):

1. Initial contact (phone call, inquiry, e-mail, letter, referral, etc.). This may be initiated by you (reach out) or by the prospect (market gravity).
2. Ascertain if the contact is the economic buyer.
3. If no, gain agreement for an introduction to the economic buyer.
4. If yes, gain agreement to meet in person.
5. Establish a trusting relationship with the economic buyer.

6. Gain conceptual agreement (objectives, measures, value to the organization and to the buyer personally).

7. Submit proposal.

8. Begin work on approval.

You may have a different model, with fewer steps or more steps. However, the point is that I always know where I am in my own model. For instance, I'm not going to submit a proposal to someone who is not the economic buyer. Period. I'm not even going to try to meet with someone who's not the economic buyer unless that is the sole way to gain access. I know I can't gain conceptual agreement unless I've first established a trusting relationship. (One of the great consulting marketing sins is wasting time with people who can't say yes but can say no. Just ending that bizarre habit boosts income dramatically.)

Consequently, my model is a series of yeses. Each yes is relatively minor—I don't enter a prospective client organization for the first time and expect to emerge with a signed contract. However, I do expect to make progress toward my next small yes. Thus my goal is to accelerate through this sequence, understanding the road signs and my own machine and how they interact. I want the car revving at full throttle for this trip, so I need great visibility—the clear knowledge of what my next step is and how to achieve my yes.

Digression

I advise all my Mentor Members to apply a "min/max" rule. This means that you should have a minimum expectation and a maximum expectation for every prospect call.

The minimum might be to ascertain that this is, indeed, the buyer, and the maximum to gain conceptual agreement, or whatever. After the call, you can assess whether you at least met your minimum objective and evaluate how well you're doing.

If you never meet the minimum, you may be too ambitious, or you may have a weak approach. If you always meet the maximum, you may have too low an expectation or you may just be an all-star!

The faster someone signs your proposal, the better off you are. However, if you believe in a sequence similar to the one I use, this means that your speed is actually a factor of making sure you hit the intermediate points correctly.

Ignoring them and blindly accelerating—sending a proposal after a perfunctory initial visit—will merely send you up a wrong alley or careening off a curve into a ditch.

Velocity is a function of *controlled* speed.

Most consultants I've worked with ignore the initial steps and speed happily off in the wrong direction, meaning either that they have to turn around and begin again or that they've wrecked their chances.

HOW TO HANDLE THE BENDS IN THE ROAD (OR THE BENZ ON THE ROAD)

Here are the biggest mistakes that consultants make in ignoring the proper sales sequence and hitting detours and potholes and how to avoid them.

Meeting with the Wrong People

Sometimes it's necessary to meet with gatekeepers and feasibility people (typically in human resources, training, purchasing, quality control, and other such departments) in order to gain access to the economic buyer. But not always. Don't accept this meeting by default. Ask who the economic buyer is (for example, "Who's sponsoring this project?" or, "Who is funding this initiative?"), and state that your procedure is to meet with that person to ascertain whether the project makes sense.

Meeting with the wrong people will have two adverse effects. First, you'll be delayed, perhaps fatally, by people who are unwilling to allow you to move forward. Second, you may well be regarded as a peer of those people even if you do meet the economic buyer, meaning that you'll be relegated to their status. Both conditions are fatal in terms of the life of a consulting assignment.

Fear of Hurting the Feelings of the Wrong People

This error is inexplicably chronic. The consultant, having met with lower-level people (perhaps out of necessity—it was the only way in the door at all)—now believes that alienating them by attempting to go to the next level is unethical, illegal, immoral, or some kind of athletic infraction.

Allow these people time during your initial meeting to indicate their willingness to make the proper introductions. If they are disinclined to do so, force the issue (for example, "I'm happy to work with you on the ongoing implementation of this project, but *ethically* I must meet the person who is actually approving the expenditure so that I can be sure that her expectations are realistic and that I have the resources to meet them").

I have seen more sales delayed and acceleration halted completely by the unwillingness—not inability, but unwillingness—of consultants to simply boldly move past gatekeepers than any other single reason.

Case Study

I was called by an event planner at Fleet Bank who had obtained my name from a colleague at another institution. She asked if I had expertise in a certain area. I told her I did.

"Fine," she said. "Could you submit materials for our review? We're searching for some consultants in this area."

"No," I replied, "but I would like to meet the person who is sponsoring this to determine mutually whether it makes sense for both of us."

She was incredulous. "No other consultant has requested that, and in any case, Martha is very busy."

"Well, that's why I might be your best choice, and I'm busy, too, but I'm sure we can both make time for a 20-minute initial meeting. Here are some dates I can be in Boston. Can you check her calendar while I'm on the phone?"

I was the only consultant to meet personally with Martha, who asked me for a proposal by the end of the meeting, after we had reached conceptual agreement. The total business over the next year was nearly $265,000.

I could have easily put material in the mail to the event planner and hoped for a $15,000 speech. But that was the slow road to nowhere.

By the way, the fear that a disgruntled subordinate will sidetrack your project later is just an excuse not to alienate the subordinate. In most healthy organizations, subordinates are jumping aboard the initiatives sponsored by their superiors. It's amazing how rapidly these people will support you once their boss does. Be bold.

Failing to Establish a Trusting Relationship

Most consultants (in fact, most salespeople) think that they are accelerating rapidly when they launch quickly into a features and benefits tirade, showering the buyer with a sound and light show. (A related detour is the amateur sales process of "finding the pain." Not only do many buyers not have pain—their operations are doing quite well—but seeking new levels, rather than fixing things, is much more valuable anyway.) In fact, such sales approaches mean that the salespeople are simply spinning their wheels in the mud they've created.

Demonstrate your business acumen to the buyer. Be prepared to discuss current events and their effects on the business environment. Know something about the competition. Determine what the buyer's personal interests might be (the office decor will often tell you). This trust building may take an hour or a month, but it's always the express lane to conceptual agreement. *Buyers will not share important and intimate needs if they don't trust you.* Period. That's why you have to be quite clear on the sequence of steps in your business model.

Failing to Move Zealously toward Conceptual Agreement

If trust has been established, then it's time to

- *Establish objectives.* What will the scope of the project be, and what results will delight the buyer?

- *Establish metrics.* How will the buyer know that progress is being made that can be specifically attributed to your work together on this project?

- *Establish the value to the organization.* If the metrics indicate that the objectives have been met, then what is the return for the organization and the buyer?

Once you have these answers, you can submit a proposal with a high probability of acceptance. My experience indicates about 80 percent probability, which is not chopped liver. [See my book *How to Write a Proposal That's Accepted Every Time*, 2nd ed. (Fitzwilliam, N.M.: Kennedy Information, 2002), which includes a disk and proposal examples that can be used as templates.]

Gaining conceptual agreement about the value of the project to the organization will virtually ensure that your fee will be seen as an intelligent investment (return on investment) and not as an unbudgeted cost. This is a nuance, but it is the equivalent of turbocharging the process because fee resistance will not impede progress.

Submitting a Poor Proposal

Finally, a great acceleration factor once you've traveled this far is to submit a lean and mean proposal. Most proposals suffer from bloat and weigh down the vehicle with their pomposity. If you have gained conceptual agreement, you don't need biographies of the consultants, lengthy descriptions of methodology, tables of data, and other esoterica that consultants use to generally gum up the works.

My proposals are $2^1/_2$ pages, no matter how large the project. This is so because a proposal based on a previously obtained conceptual agreement is a *summation, not an exploration.*

Million dollar consultants accelerate the speed from first contact to close. They also do one other thing to ensure low-cost, high-margin business.

THINKING OF THE FOURTH SALE FIRST

Whenever you are dealing with an economic buyer, consider the long-term relationship and not the immediate project. I know that this may sound counterintuitive (or downright crazy when there's a mortgage waiting to be paid), but hear me out.

A new client represents the following potential:

- The immediate project
- Successive projects for that buyer
- Projects for other buyers within the client
- Projects for the customer's customers
- Projects for the customer's vendors and suppliers
- Projects for the customer's trade and professional organizations
- Referrals to friends of the buyer in nonrelated organizations
- Referrals and testimonials to use with unrelated buyers
- The cachet and credibility to use unilaterally in your relationship with the client
- A transient buyer who leaves and brings you into his new organization

Thus the immediate project is merely one aspect of the full potential represented by this superb new relationship. I think that you get my drift.

Don't be overanxious to exploit merely the first one.

I don't believe that many consultants truly appreciate the dynamics of my list. A relationship with an economic buyer and the power that accrues from a project that is well implemented and results that are well documented (objectives/measures/value) represent vast potential.

When I suggest that you think of the fourth sale first, I mean that these projects create cumulative benefits that amass over time. It's always better to accept an initial $50,000 project that is unambiguous, discrete, and easily completed so as to build on the other steps (and their $400,000 of potential) than it is to try to stretch the initial opportunity to $70,000 (by promising too much or attempting something that you are not prepared for) and sacrificing $380,000 for sure.

In other words, $400,000 over three years always trumps $70,000 over six months. I want you to accelerate to the close of the sale, but then take your time by adopting a strategic view of the overall potential. These are compatible, not contradictory, notions. You speed your way through conceptual agreement and then formulate a proposal that's geared to maximize the full potential of the relationship.

Case Study

I was asked to help coach a division president on his delegation skills. When I met him for the first time, I was guessing that it would be a $15,000 to $25,000 project.

Once I had established a trusting relationship, he told me of the pains he had gone through to make delegation work, albeit unsuccessfully. He also shared the difficulties of his predecessor and why he had been replaced.

I used this trust to point out the real need: the culture was far too authoritarian and risk-averse for even the most adept delegator. We had to change the culture, the reward system, communications devices, and so on if delegation and empowerment were ever to work.

This took the burden from the CEO's shoulders, and he agreed to my approach, which resulted in a $65,000 project. When that worked beautifully, we entered into a series of five one-year retainers for $100,000 per year, attacking every issue that was appropriate through the ultimate sale of the company to a new parent.

By accelerating to the close but then looking at the larger picture, I increased the business from $15,000 in coaching to $565,000 in organizational development. As consultants—as drivers of our cars—we control this dynamic far more than we think or act on.

When you are at that profound moment of conceptual agreement and about to embark on your proposal, use this opportunity to take a strategic view of your long-term potential relationship, and act accordingly. What's immediately in front of you may be less than you and the client deserve to achieve.

Million dollar consulting is based on the premise that somewhere around 80 percent of your annual business will be repeat business. No one (whom I know) generates this kind of revenue from a standing start each year. Instead, you need the momentum of ongoing delighted clients who have moved quickly to the initial sale and who are constantly providing you with second, third, fourth, and even further business opportunities.

THE SECRET ART OF REFERRALS

I mentioned one of the basic sins of consultants earlier in this chapter: stabling relationships with gatekeepers and intermediaries. But the greatest sin, at least in terms of repeat business, is failing to ask for referrals.

I can trace about 90 percent of my business today to four common sources—which arose between 1985 and 1990! I can see the lineage better than any anthropologist trying to trace our ancestry. The DNA is quite clear.

That's because clients talk to prospects naturally enough, but you can accelerate this a thousandfold by amplifying the communications. Here is the wording to use with any client; adjust it for your own comfort and for the relationship: "Referrals are the coinage of my realm. We've both been pleased with the results this project has generated, and I wonder if you'd be kind enough to give me three or four names of colleagues or contacts whom you believe could benefit from similar value."

That's it. Then you shut up and wait. Here are some guidelines:

1. Set this up early in your relationship by mentioning to your client that you routinely ask for referrals when the project results begin to be manifest.

2. Anticipate company policy and individual preferences by offering three options:

   a. A personal introduction would be great.

   b. It would be wonderful to be able to use your name.

   c. I'll happily withhold your name if you can just suggest the best people for me to contact.

   Now your buyer can decide *how* best to do this for you, not *whether* to do this for you.

> *One Percent Solution: You need to ask everyone you know*
> *for referrals at least twice a year, and quarterly is fine.*

3. Use the approach and philosophy that this is a win/win/win. Your contact should be thrilled to be able to help others.

4. Use reciprocity. You probably refer people to your doctor, your accountant, your lawyer, and so forth. It's not unreasonable to expect them to refer people to you. (Which is why you should always attach your name to referral business to others and follow up.)

5. Practice doing this smoothly.

6. Don't be put off. If the other person says, "Give me some time to think about it," reply, "Of course, I'll give you a call tomorrow at 2."[1]

Hal Mapes was an insurance agent who visited me and my wife when I was 22 and first working at Prudential. He came by every six months, and he *always* asked for and received three referrals.

If he had 200 clients, that means that he made 400 visits and received 1,200 names annually. If he closed 10 percent, that would be 120 new clients at about $3,000 commission over the course of the policy. And the next year, of course, he had 320 clients to ask.

I still remember his name, and he retired a very successful man. Are you asking for three names?

THE TALENT IS YOU, SO CHARGE FOR IT

I didn't want to leave this topic without a reminder that *you* are the talent.

By that I mean that you shouldn't be charging more when you use other people or subcontractors, you should be charging more when you do everything yourself.

You are the talent.

Case Study

A Fortune 50 client asked me to propose how to launch a
new strategic communications initiative. I explained that
the overseas work could be done by the client's own people,

---

[1] Some people who don't have referral names are happy to serve as a reference, which is just as good. Don't abuse this, and provide their names only to serious potential buyers, never to gatekeepers.

> *but that was unacceptable to the client, because they*
> *wouldn't have credibility.*
> *I explained that I could use colleagues in key overseas*
> *cities, but the client felt that those sites would feel like "poor*
> *cousins," since I had personally launched the domestic work.*
> *I explained that I could do the global work, but that*
> *would be the most expensive option of all. The client said*
> *that was just fine.*
> *My wife and I then went around the world on a*
> *$350,000 project.*

One Percent Solution: Don't sell yourself short. Sell yourself
expensively.

If you can accept that you are the real talent, and are therefore worth a premium, you can

1. Reduce your labor intensity, or at least direct it to the most lucrative projects.
2. Guarantee repeat business through your promise of continued personal intervention.
3. Maximize referral business through "I can have her *personally* contact you and work with you."
4. Increase margins dramatically.
5. Build your brand emphatically.
6. Implement much more easily because you have achieved "expert" status.

Repeat after me: "I am the talent, and I'm worth a great deal. Which colleagues do you think would best appreciate and utilize my value?"

QUESTIONS AND ANSWERS

Q. What is the average time I should consider in terms of first contact to closing a sale?

A. I know of none. Sometimes you can gain agreement to accept a proposal in one meeting; sometimes you don't make much headway but the buyer calls you a year later and says that the timing is now perfect. The key is to have a lot of stuff in the pipeline, as discussed earlier.

Q. With those percentages of repeat business, does that mean that I'm working with clients for a long, long time?

A. It means that outside of small business, education, and government (though there are exceptions even there), you should reasonably hope to engage in several projects over several years with clients, assuming two things:

1. You've done excellent work.

2. You are diverse enough to be able to work on a variety of client issues.

Q. Isn't it a bit arrogant to think that I'm the talent and I deserve more than if I brought in other, excellent people?

A. Confidence is the honest belief that you're highly capable of helping others. Arrogance is the honest belief you have nothing more to learn yourself. It's a fine line, but walk right up to it. (Smugness is arrogance without the talent—these are the people "coaching" others who have never done what they're coaching.)

Q. Will some clients request or expect a referral fee or other remuneration for referrals or to serve as a reference?

A. Not corporate or organization clients, and you shouldn't ever offer one; it's unethical.

Q. Can I offer a referral fee to an independent third party?

A. Sure, and my formula is:

- 5–10 percent for a valid buyer's name
- 10–15 percent for an introduction to a buyer
- 15–20 percent for having made the sale and I just have to show up

Be careful: if this is someone working with or for that buyer, then you must make your financial relationship transparent lest the buyer think that this is an objective, arm's-length referral.

Final Thought: You need new business to keep you fresh and to replace business that inevitably will end. But the predominant percentage of your yearly revenues should come from existing clients. If you are completing only a single project for most clients, you probably have either been implementing poorly or, more likely, not associating yourself closely enough with the results (objectives/ measures/value).

BEYOND SUCCESS

MONEY IS ONLY A MEANS
TO AN END

ETHICAL ISSUES

As you achieve multidimensional growth and your firm prospers, the nature of the problems and challenges you face evolves. At the outset of your consulting career, you are typically concerned about cash flow, marketing, and developing the expertise required to complete more diverse assignments.

In midcareer, during the firm's dramatic growth, the issues become those of finding the right alliance partners, developing long-term relationships, and establishing proper fee levels. Once you are a going concern, the priorities become the unique issues related to your very success.

Million dollar consulting generates some million dollar ethical challenges. How would you respond to these 11?

1. Can I simply charge the highest fee possible and not even worry about perceived value? If I'm in demand, isn't the guideline "whatever the traffic will bear"?

2. I choose to travel first class, stay on the concierge floor of the best hotels, and take limos rather than taxis. That's my travel style, and I'm worth it. As long as I'm honest about it, shouldn't the client be billed for my normal travel preferences?

3. There is nothing new under the sun, and I'm a recognized name and a sought-after figure. There's nothing wrong with taking some ideas espoused by other consultants and authors and using them in my work or writing as long as I put my personal spin on them. You can't copyright ideas, so I can use what I wish to, right?

4. I'm seeing three clients on this trip. I know that if I attempt to prorate expenses, their accounting systems will question the charges. However, if I simply bill each one for the entire airfare and

lodging, there won't be a single question. Shouldn't I make it easier on myself and on them and bill each of them for 100 percent, since I have to visit each one anyway?

5. In doing my research within a client organization, I'm told by a midlevel manager *on a strictly confidential basis* about an internal leak to competitors and ongoing employee theft. If I divulge this to the president, it will be clear that I was the source, and my value to the client within the organization may suffer. Isn't it better—and even ethically necessary—to maintain the confidentiality and continue to be a valuable resource within the organization for the client?

6. A client offers me first-class airfare to visit its European offices. I can use my free airline mileage to take my entire family and, by cashing in the first-class tickets, pay for all our food, lodging, and recreation. There's no reason to explain all this to the client, is there, since it's my personal business?

7. A competitor of one of my largest clients wants to hire me because my reputation has been associated with my client's success. Is there any problem with taking on competitive organizations?

8. A client asks me to conduct an anonymous employee survey by mail, but asks me to use a hidden code to differentiate by unit—though not by person—the source of the feedback. This is because the client is sincerely interested in the quality of the unit managers and wants to isolate those whose people are unhappy with their treatment. Is this a legitimate goal to justify the subterfuge?

9. I am asked to write speeches and articles for the president of the organization, who is my client. He confers with me on topics and critiques the final work, but the actual writing is totally mine. The president gives no attribution whatsoever, publishes some of the articles in the trade press, and gives the speeches at business conferences to great acclaim. Is this a service that I should continue to provide?

10. Through an alliance partner, I develop a client contact with the alliance partner's blessing. After a three-month, highly successful assignment, the client asks me to take on a long-term project in place of the alliance partner, with whom the client has been unhappy for some time. Can I ethically accept this project?

11. The prospect is the antithesis of "green" and environmentally friendly. The firms observes the laws in theory, but not in practice. Can I use my opposition to its wasteful ways as justification not to do business with this firm?

> ***One Percent Solution: Always ask yourself, "Would I be proud
> of this if it appeared all over the Internet tomorrow?"***

Most of these situations have happened to me, and the rest have happened
to colleagues. There are no magic answers to ethical dilemmas. Ernest Hemingway observed, "What is moral is what you feel good after, and what is immoral
is what you feel bad after." Of course, no one ever recorded that Hemingway
tried his hand at consulting; otherwise, *For Whom the Bell Tolls* might have
been called *An Analytic Report on Bell Cacophony, Causation, and Demographic
Probabilities.*

You can't do much better than to try to do the right thing consistently.

I'd rather go with the credo that I've heard virtually all managers at Merck
& Co. articulate when they are asked what to do in ambiguous situations when
policy and precedent don't apply: do the right thing. Here's what I consider the
right thing to do in each instance.

1. Should You Charge the Highest Fees You Can Get Away With?

There is certainly no moral prohibition that I know of to discourage you from
charging what the traffic will bear. If you are charging on a fee basis and
the client is aware of and accepts the fee, the client obviously has determined
that the value is worth the investment. However, I would emphasize two
caveats:

- It is never advisable to overpromise and underdeliver. Consequently, if
  you are justifying the high investment through extravagant promises
  and providing only marginal delivery, you are certainly not building
  long-term potential. Which is better: a single $150,000 project that
  results in no further work or an ongoing series of $75,000 projects the
  results of which send the client into fits of ecstasy?
- If you are charging a per diem or a fee based on some other fixed
  standard, despite the strictures of Chapter 9,[1] there is never an excuse
  to charge for anything other than actual hours performed, on-site or
  off-site. Padding days goes beyond an ethical transgression—it's theft.

---

[1] Frankly, if you are charging by the day, I doubt that you'll ever need the advice in this chapter, and I wonder why you've even read this far.

2. Should You Travel First Class and Bill the Client?

You can make a case for the fact that if the client approves of a sybaritic travel style, there is no problem. However, your primary charter is to improve the client's condition. Do you help fiscally through this kind of expense (which has nothing to do with your value or expertise), and do you help your credibility with the client's people through this kind of image?

I doubt it. There are some high-flying organizations in which this mode of travel is the status quo, and in such circumstances, the luxury makes sense. I've also found that most clients offer first-class transportation overseas, and many do so for domestic coast-to-coast trips. (However, these tend to be terminated quickly in a poor economy.)

Nevertheless, my rule of thumb is simple: if the client doesn't offer it, I don't abuse it. I travel first class and use limos and the best hotels, but I charge clients for coach, taxis, and standard Marriott-type rates. And I won't use limos or other frills if their visibility raises questions about the "high-priced outside help," even if I am paying for it myself. And don't pull a fast one: take the difference in the cost of luxury travel out of your pocket as a decreased margin; don't pad the fee to make up the difference.

3. Should You Borrow Others' Ideas and Present Them as Your Own?

It's true that you cannot copyright concepts (you cannot even copyright book titles) and that there are few breakthrough ideas. Most of the really good ones are merely old ideas reapplied in new ways. However, your clients are smart. People recognize ideas that were formulated by others. Since it's your *application* of the idea for your client that is novel, why not give credit where credit is due? It's the mark of a successful, self-confident consultant to say, "This is a technique developed by Sally Smith and written about in the *McGoo Review of Management*. I've developed an adaptation for your situation that I believe we should implement."

You are not expected to be a rocket scientist or the director of a research and development factory. You are hired to provide pragmatic consulting interventions using the best ideas in existence. Since this is what you are being paid for, it makes sense to reveal the sources of all ideas and techniques.

4. Should You Bill More than One Client for the Same Basic Expenses?

Never double-bill (or, in this case, triple-bill). I've seen every excuse under the sun for doing this, and none of them passes muster as "doing the right thing."

Send a cover letter with your expense statement explaining why you are charging the client only one-third of the full amount on some of the receipts (for example, airfare) and the full amount on others (for example, meals during the days you are working exclusively for that client). Turn the procedure into an opportunity to demonstrate your fiscal responsibility toward that client.[2]

5. Should You Pass on to the Client Confidential Information Given You in the Course of Your Assignment?

Who is the client's here? You were brought onboard to help improve the client's condition, and it's up to the client to determine what the most useful role is. In this case, you're ethically bound to inform the client about what you've discovered and allow the client to decide whether to take action immediately or to preserve your current role by not taking action.

You cannot make these moral decisions *for* the client, only in collaboration *with* the client, and only *with* the client, reserving the decision-making prerogative.

By the way, I never ask for information in return for a promise not to reveal it, and I *never* agree to accept information on the condition that I not reveal it. Once you do this, you are ethically compromised on the spot. When someone tells you, "This is confidential, but . . . , " you are free to listen and use the information as long as you haven't acknowledged that you will respect the confidentiality. Good consultants find out what they need to through intelligent questioning and keen observation. Relying on informants isn't consulting— it's spying.

Case Study

I was asked to coach the president of a bank's retail lending division. One of his direct subordinates had sent alarming reports about his behavior to the president's corporate boss.

---

[2] I once had two clients whose accounts-payable bureaucrats both demanded the single, original receipt for the airfare. Since there was only a single original (which I like to keep for my records), I gave them each a choice: I would send the original to whichever wanted to pay the entire air bill and a copy to the one who would pay a 50 percent share. Both quickly accepted copies, and I had examples of internal policies that, when followed blindly, create waste to show to my buyer.

> *As I conducted my work, the subordinate continued to send confidential messages to the corporate officer and to me, reporting transgressions but demanding that the information and source not be revealed. I quickly ended this by telling the corporate officer and the subordinate that he was compromising the organization. You can't say, "I know where we're losing money, but you can't do anything about it."*
>
> *The subordinate was furious at having been "sold out," but I merely pointed out that his behavior was as destructive as his boss's and maybe worse because his was with premeditation. Confidences are not more important than the health of the organization. Period.*

6. Should You Use Tickets Supplied by Your Client to Bring Your Spouse Along?

This might be your personal business, but the tickets are the client's. There's nothing wrong with this practice if you inform the client of your plans. You can never be too candid or err on the side of excessive honesty.

I've taken my wife on many trips using the tons of free air mileage we all acquire, and I tell the client what I'm doing and that I'll simply charge the equivalent of coach airfare. I also pay any difference in the room rate.

I've never had a client say anything other than, "It's always a good idea to take along your spouse whenever you can; I always try to myself."

As for "it's only my personal business," here's what happened to my own personal physician, who consults on medical/computer applications. The client provided a first-class ticket to Paris on British Air. The doctor cashed it in to pay for two business-class tickets for a subsequent European vacation with his wife, and he booked a coach fare on another carrier. Just before his departure, he received a fax informing him that the client's limo would meet him at the special first-class arrivals area!

> *"Innocent" falsehoods can develop into complicated and unnecessary questions about your ethical standards. Either tell the client what you're doing, or don't do it. (If you're uncomfortable telling the client, the chances are strong that what you're doing is unacceptable.)*

As for my doctor, he had to fess up, which is why he's a full-time physician and only an occasional consultant.

7. Should You Accept an Assignment from a Client's Competitor?

This is a tricky one, and I've found the following criteria to be sound in determining whether to accept or decline an assignment:

- I will not do anything that reveals confidential information, directly or indirectly. A direct revelation: "Tell us how they plan to promote in region X." An indirect revelation: "Design a succession-planning process that is similar to theirs." Acceptable conditions: "Evaluate our field-force management personnel and tell us what developmental work is needed in light of our business goals." (No competitive revelation is necessary at all.)
- I will try to assign different personnel to each project. If I am personally demanded, I will make the provisions in the first criterion clear at the outset.
- I will inform my present client of the competitor's request and the tentative project and ask if the client wishes me to decline.
- If the new assignment is accepted under the preceding criteria, I will not divulge anything learned to the current client either.

There is nothing intrinsically wrong with working for several clients within the same industry. After all, many buyers use "experience in our industry" as a hiring condition. The critical ethical consideration is this: are you being hired for your expertise and your ability to improve the client's condition, or are you being hired for what you happen to know about the competition? Revealing confidential data is never itself a confidential process, and once it is inevitably discovered, it will propel you back to a nine-to-five job very rapidly.

8. Should You Agree to Use Secret Identifying Codes on a Confidential Survey?

Sorry, but ends do not justify means. Despite the client's pure thoughts on the matter, the action is unethical. Anonymous surveys are supposed to be exactly that. You are committing an unethical act as soon as you tell people that their responses are confidential and then provide a document that exposes them by area.

If the client's need for information makes sense, as it does in this case, there are other options. You could tell people that the responses are sorted by unit. Or you could provide a place for the unit to be recorded at the respondent's option. Or you could suggest other alternatives altogether, such as focus groups or direct observations.

There are always pragmatic reasons for doing the right thing. I've found that any attempt to disclose respondents' feedback by unit or person, despite promises to the contrary, is always found out by the rank and file. There are no secrets in organizations. There are simply some facts that take longer to surface than others.

9. Should You Continue to Write for a Client Who Passes Off Your Work as His Own?

No problem here. The president is paying you for your expertise, you have agreed to the arrangement, and the president is acting with your permission. (Presumably, this service is also specified in your consulting contract with the client.) The only trouble with plagiarism arises when permission is not obtained. If you don't like someone else taking credit for your pearls of wisdom, don't open the clam by accepting such assignments.

10. Should You Agree to Supplant an Alliance Partner Who Introduced You to the Client?

Well, yes and no. Improving the client's condition certainly justifies the project, since the client, having worked both with the partner and with you, is convinced that you can better meet current needs. However, you also have an obligation to anyone who has introduced you to a client that you won't steal her revenue.

In these cases, I tell the client's that I can accept only after I speak to the partner, explaining my obligations and my ethical concerns. This usually raises my esteem in the eyes of the client. I'll then explain the situation to my alliance partner, encourage the partner to contact the client to talk about it, and offer assurances that this initiative was the client's, not mine. Having done all this, I will accept the assignment. The client has made an objective choice, my expertise is deemed appropriate, and I've been honest with the partner organization.

Of course, engaging in any action whatsoever to supplant a partner at your initiative is unqualifiedly unethical. If you feel comfortable informing your partner of the situation and inviting the partner to discuss it with the client, you probably have acted well. If you accept without providing this opportunity, you have no doubt acted badly.[3]

11. Am I Justified in Turning Down Business from a Firm Whose Practices Are Reprehensible to Me?

Absolutely. There is no law requiring you to take on all prospects. You are neither a public conveyance nor a public accommodation. You can refuse to work with people to your heart's content, providing

a. You're not being capricious or biased ("I'm not working with men!").
b. Your whims don't adversely affect your income. (Whims are not values.)

One of the benefits of building a successful consulting firm is the opportunity—and the necessity—to ponder on, develop criteria for, and take action on ethical issues with clients and colleagues. I've described composites of 11 of the more common ones that I've encountered, but you'll undoubtedly be faced with some unique quandaries of your own.

Therefore, in conclusion, here are the guidelines that I find useful in determining whether I am doing the right thing:

1. Does the activity improve the client's condition or merely my own?
2. Is the activity something that I am comfortable explaining to the client?
3. Is the activity something that I am proud of and would publicize as a trait?
4. Is there harm being done to anyone without his knowing it and/or being able to respond?
5. Is this treatment something that I would willingly subject myself to?

There are no simple yes or no answers. In fact, the very act of putting the question to the client often may be sufficient to help you avoid ethical compromise. Ultimately, the client will be thankful that you asked.

---

[3] I have a short list of consultants whom I would never use as subcontractors because I have seen evidence of their theft of business from former employers or other consultants. I freely tell my partners and colleagues about them. A pox on their houses.

THE GLOBAL COMMUNITY

The only reasons not to pursue foreign clients early in your career are the problems of lack of focus and lack of funds. It takes more time and certainly more of an investment to develop relationships abroad. However, I've found that foreign organizations are very receptive to consulting help, particularly if you target your efforts carefully. Once your firm is well established, with both its repute and its resources in larger supply, international expansion is a logical and practical consideration.[4]

There is a hierarchy of requirements when picking targets for foreign concentration (see Figure 18-1). These criteria apply irrespective of whether you are pursuing a target of opportunity or an organization is pursuing you. I've seen many situations in which what appeared to be a lucrative overseas consulting assignment turned out to be just the opposite because funds couldn't be taken

---

Language

1. English-speaking as a first language (e.g., U.K. Australia)

2. English-speaking as business language (e.g., Hong Kong, Singapore)

3. English-speaking capability common (e.g., Germany, Switzerland)

4. English spoken by elite only (e.g., Spain, Thailand)

Sophistication

1. Information-based, knowledge-oriented society (e.g., Japan, France)

2. Emerging from manufacturing base to knowledge (e.g., Brazil, Korea)

3. Labor-intensive manufacturing (e.g., Indonesia, Nigeria)

Currency policy

1. Stable and relatively easy to covert and exchange (e.g., Germany)

2. Somewhat unstable, easy to convert and exchange (e.g., Italy)

3. Diffcult to exchange (e.g., Philippines, Brazil)

4. Highly unstable (e.g., Eastern Europe)

Figure 18-1. Priorities to bear in mind when choosing a foreign target for concentration.

---

[4] If this is an area of interest, for a full book discussing it, see the author's *The Global Consultant* (with Omar Kahn) (Hoboken, N. J.: Wiley, 2008).

out of the country (one poor soul wound up investing his consulting fee in local baskets, which he tried to import and sell in the States), or because a key client manager demanded a bribe (they're often listed on the books as "commissions" in Latin America), or because the client, after hearing all the consultant's ideas during the proposal process, decided to handle the issue internally.[5]

The best way to acquire overseas clients is through strategic alliances. I've worked with people in Singapore and the United Kingdom whose skills and approaches are complemented by my own. They will often underwrite a trip for me, during which we make joint sales calls after I help them on a particular project. In this manner, I've developed work with Shell Singapore, Citibank in Singapore, and the *Singapore Straits Times*, and with Case Communications, Lucas Engineering, and the British Standards Institute in the United Kingdom. These alliances are extremely productive because they combine current, fee-paying projects with the opportunity to develop new business.

One Percent Solution: The globalization of economies combined with ever-advancing technology makes this the best and easiest time ever to work globally, whether in person or remotely.

A second effective method is to pursue international work through existing multinational clients based in the United States (or based elsewhere, with a U.S. operation as your primary client). Through an international division of Merck, I've had the opportunity to work and develop a reputation in the United Kingdom, Costa Rica, Hong Kong, and Brazil. (Note that when you pursue this avenue, some of the difficulties involved with the lower-priority targets are mitigated. For example, I don't worry about currency restrictions or instability in Brazil because I'm paid in the United States by the parent company.)

State Street Bank sent me around the world, first class, because it didn't want to give its global management team the perception that it was getting anything less than what the home office got (me).

Still another way to market internationally is to write for international publications. There are management journals in most countries, and they will

---

[5] In the Republic of China, all management ideas are considered the property of mankind, and thus belong to everyone. In Indonesia and the Philippines, plagiarism of published work from even major authors and publishers is widespread and tolerated, and copyright laws are virtually unenforceable. I'm finding entire books made available free online through "clubs" you can subscribe to run by people around the world.

usually accept articles written in English. (Many publish in English as well.) I've generated many contacts from writing for such publications in the United Kingdom, Brazil, Mexico, Singapore, Switzerland, Germany, and Hong Kong. As a rule, foreign clients place a much higher value on written papers and research than do Americans. I've recently published in a major German-language publication based in Switzerland. I was sought over the Internet and wrote and submitted the article via e-mail.

Finally, you can market overseas by seeking speaking opportunities at international conferences. This is no different from seeking domestic speaking assignments, except that you will often be asked to pay your own way. This is one reason why I advocate such tactics only after you have established yourself. The greater your reputation, the more likely it is that your expenses and fee will be covered, but even if they are not, the greater your growth, the more you are able to underwrite such marketing opportunities yourself.

Case Study

Perhaps the most effective way to acquire overseas clients is through a commercially published book, even when that book is solely in English. My books on sales acquisition, proposals, and fee structure have attracted clients in 20 countries in the last five years alone.

Several of my books have also been translated into German, Italian, Spanish, Korean, Arabic, Japanese, Russian, and Chinese.

As noted earlier in this book, there are few marketing devices as powerful as a book that promotes your consulting (and/or speaking) business through the force of your authority as an expert. The allure of having the author work with a client in person overcomes any problems in terms of expense, currency translation, fees, and so on.

Given the increasing globalization of business, there may well be more opportunity for dramatic growth abroad than at home for entrepreneurial consultants. Million dollar consulting is just as lucrative when the components are pounds, euro, yen, and pesos. And once you've worked internationally, you have a tremendous marketing opportunity at home for your business literature, proposals, interviews, speeches, and articles.

You are now an international consultant who has worked in x number of countries. If you don't think that this carries instant credibility, try it out yourself. The first time a client asked me what I could possibly contribute to its benchmarking plans and I replied, "Let me give you an example from my work on innovation with the British Standards Institute, anticipating the plans of the European Union," there wasn't a sound in the room other than the client's pen sliding out of his pocket to sign the contract.

Digression

The Internet and it's peripherals—online communities, cell phones, Skype, e-mail, Webinars, teleconferences, discussion groups, and so forth—have made global consulting not merely available, but mandatory.

In diversifying your client portfolio, international business now is a virtual "must." Make yourself known through publishing articles, blogs, newsletters, interviews, and so on.

No consultant who aspires to seven-figure status—anywhere in the world—should be focusing merely on domestic prospects.

DESIGNING YOUR OWN FUTURE

My experiences in the consulting profession have led me to establish a very simple philosophy:

1. This is a relationship business.
2. Multidimensional growth provides for high-quality, enduring relationships.
3. There is no limit to the firm's—or your own—income from those relationships, and you must help yourself if you are to help others.

At this point, you may be asking, "How can it be that simple? After all, if everyone is trying to establish those relationships, aren't we all back in the old competitive-commodity ball game, trying to prove that a relationship with me is somehow superior to one with the other consultants?

"What about all the people reading this book? Won't we all look the same going out there to try to do the same thing?"

One Percent Solution: It's not what life deals you, it's how you deal with life.

I'd like to respond to these concerns by drawing on a consulting assignment as an avatar. I had been working with a large specialty chemicals firm that found itself a diminishing "number three" among its competitors. Whereas it had once had hopes of overtaking its two much larger rivals, it found itself facing the possibility of smaller organizations chipping away at some of its traditional business. The firm's strategy team was divided: do we invest the substantial resources needed to make a run at the leaders, or do we solidify our position as number three, fighting off challenges to that spot? Neither position was terribly attractive. After all, overtaking the leaders would take years, flawless performance, and a great deal of luck. However, to remain number three was to manage an "also ran," and it's hard to attract, retain, and motivate people in an acknowledged "loser."

The answer, of course, was breathtakingly simple: to be number one on the company's own terms. The company redefined itself in terms of what it did better than anyone else in the industry—including its larger competitors—and established a vision and mission of being number one in the market and under the conditions it had defined for itself.

I call this "taking a sharp right."

Strategically, it's quite simple: you don't allow the competition to define the playing field or to write the rules. You redefine and reinvent yourself.

When I began my own practice leading up to my current firm, I was told unequivocally that I couldn't generate over $300,000 in income and that I would have to add people and facilities, probably using outside investors. I was also advised that I would be swallowed whole unless I specialized in some market segment as protection against "the big guys."

It's extraordinarily difficult, if not impossible, to break the paradigms when someone else is defining the paradigms.

Now listen up: those pieces of advice probably were accurate for someone who chose to play by the existing, conventional rules. However, I defined what I wanted to become. Under my rules, such as the three listed at the beginning of this section, traditional conditions didn't apply. I wasn't competing with anyone because I was going to be *numero uno* as a unique, boutique-type consulting firm that did business with Fortune 1000 organizations and their brethren.

If you use the other person's equipment, play on his field, use his rules, and employ his officials, you're going to lose the game.

The key is *not* to outthink your competitors, because doing so is unlikely and overwhelmingly tiring. The key is to *have* no competitors because you have defined your own playing field and written your own rules (taken the sharp right). The specialty chemical firm did this, avoiding the suffering of myriad organizations in similar straits that have vainly tried to play by others' rules.

I did it, made a fortune, and emerged to write this book because I determined how I would play the game. However, the idea itself isn't mine. It's practiced by the most successful businesspeople and entrepreneurs in the world.

> Don't worry about being smarter than your competitors, because any competent competitor will be working just as hard to be smarter than you. The trick is to have no competitors.
>
> —Warren Buffett, CEO, Berkshire Hathaway[6]

Once you've established who you are and how you'll play, concerns about the competition and "Isn't everyone doing this?" evaporate. You'll always need to be cognizant of what your competitors are doing, but you'll never need to be *concerned* about what they're doing.

Another consultant and I were with the CEO of a company that is a client of both our firms. We were returning from a day-long fishing trip off Montauk, Long Island, with two of our kids. There were five tuna in the hold, and Bob and I were very contentedly reflecting on the lives we had carved out in this business.

I remarked that client relationships didn't get much better than this. He pointed out something that never ceases to astonish me: "The relationship is one thing," he said, "but it's exploiting the opportunity it presents that sets people like us apart. Most consultants I know are pretty good at scrambling around and overcoming setbacks, enabling them to survive. But very, very few know how to exploit success, and know how to prosper."

---

[6] An "oldie but goodie," quoted in *Emory Business Magazine*, Emory University, Atlanta, GA 30322, and cited in *Boardroom Reports* 20(16) (August 15, 1991), p. 2.

Maybe out there off the continental shelf we were suffering terminal male bonding. However, Bob's observation makes just as much sense to me here on dry land.

Each of us has to transcend the mere survival reflex and understand that surviving is not the point. *Prospering*, to me, is the ability to meet personal and family goals through the income, wisdom, and experiences generated by a thriving business. The multidimensional growth I've been espousing doesn't pertain only to your professional life, which is why I advocated life balance so strongly in Chapter 16. As you grow personally, you grow professionally, and as you grow professionally, you grow personally. This is why this business is so wonderful.

As you prosper, you will begin to create what I call a *body of work*.[7] By this I merely mean that the combination of the types of projects you are best known for, your publishing and/or speeches, your pro bono efforts, and your general visibility will represent those facets of your business at which you have become most adept. Nearer to the beginning of your career, you will have had to deliberately establish your unique, number-one-in-the-field brand and strategy. As your career blossoms, your body of work will speak for you. By the very nature of what you've accomplished, you will be considered the best at what you do, and your clients and prospects will see you in this distinguishing light.

The future of the firm then becomes whatever you wish it to be. What will become of Summit Consulting Group, Inc.? I'm still not sure. My kids won't be going into the business, apparently, because one is an Emmy Award–nominated producer at MTV after majoring in broadcast journalism, and one is headed for the stage after majoring in drama and gaining a Master of Fine Arts to teach, as well.

I don't plan to retire because I can do what I'm doing—consulting, speaking, writing—without age constraints, although I can become more selective, into the indefinite future.

Will a larger firm buy me out? Possibly—I'm sure there's an amount of money somewhere that constitutes an offer I can't refuse. Perhaps people with whom I work or even clients will take over the firm. Frankly, it's a matter of no great importance to me.

My firm is and always has been a means to an end. That end has been the well-being of my family, the pursuit of our interests, and what Maslow cryptically termed "self-actualization." You see, the future of the firm isn't so important; it's the future of the founder that's crucial! Your body of work defines more than your company's projects and positioning. It defines your values and your

---

[7] When a different publisher expressed interest in this book, the acquisitions editor told me that I had "a nice shelf." After a stunned moment, I learned that she was referring to the solid sales of my other books. I didn't know whether to be disappointed or relieved. I'll try not to be so obscure here.

contribution to the environment around you. I have since completely lost the source, but I remember Peter Drucker saying once, "An organization is not like a tree or an animal, successful merely by dint of perpetuating the species. An organization is successful based on the contribution it makes to the outside environment."

> *One Percent Solution: Remember that money is fuel for life and that the real wealth is discretionary time.*

For an individual to establish a consulting firm that contributes to the improvement of its clients' conditions, to the enhanced productivity and quality of their people, to the increased profitability of their operations, and therefore to the increased well-being of their customers and stockholders is an ultimate contribution to the outside environment. And if, in so doing, you personally achieve success through the realization of your personal life goals, then you are in rarefied air indeed.

How many of us are in a position to meet our personal and professional goals—and to amass true wealth—through a constant process of helping others to meet *their* personal and professional goals and enhance *their* wealth?

Professional consulting isn't just a wonderful profession; it's a wonderful way of life. And if, in that pursuit, you make millions, who can object?

TIPS FROM THE MILLION DOLLAR CONSULTING COMMUNITY

Instead of questions and answers, I'm ending with tips garnered from the Million Dollar Consulting Colleges, the Grad Schools, the Million Dollar Club, and the members of the Mentor Hall of Fame (many of whom you've seen contribute throughout the book).

About Us as Consultants and Self-Esteem:

1. A large proportion of attendees (about 75 percent) felt "alone" when they were very young, either because they perceived themselves to be different from others or because they were somehow not in a "traditional," loving family. And where are we now? In a profession that requires a certain strength in being alone!

2. "Lone wolves" don't have much opportunity for exploring emotional issues with trusted peers. Life and work revolve solely around work to too great a degree, and most conversation is centered on work challenges, not personal issues.

3. What doesn't kill you makes you stronger. Most successful people have learned from setbacks and turned them into sources of strength and self-worth.

4. Forgiveness is critical. If you don't forgive those whom you perceive as having hurt you, you become permanently enslaved to them (even though they might not realize it). If you allow real and perceived slights to fester, your self-worth will suffer.

5. Efficacy and self-worth are separate. You can be excellent at a given pursuit but not feel good about yourself, and vice versa.

6. Personal relationships are a key foundation of self-worth. If you can positively and constructively engage in your personal relationships, your self-worth improves. Hence, poor relationships have to be improved or abandoned, not merely maintained as poor relationships.

7. You can look at self-esteem as a *verb*— an action, leading to a condition—or as a *noun*—self-confidence.

8. People carry far too much old "baggage" around, and it's insufficient merely to drop it. You must throw it "off the train" so that it isn't merely at your feet traveling in the same direction and at the same speed that you are. However, don't jettison everything. Some of the positive baggage makes sense for the trip.

9. Positive self-talk is one of the most powerful tools to build self-worth. Stop apologizing and be honest about your own talent and abilities. Don't generalize from a specific: just because you didn't understand a play doesn't mean you're ignorant about art.

10. It's not about what life deals you; it's about how you deal with life.

About the Business of Growing in Consulting

If you don't understand something, do two things. First, question it immediately, because otherwise the ensuing structure will have a weak foundation. Second, try to apply it in your circumstances to integrate the learning.

People learn in different ways, so notes, recordings, mind maps, and holographic telepathy are all fine with me. But if you don't have three things (or less) to move forward on at the end of the day, you may have quantity but not quality.

"The 1% Solution: Tools for Change" says that if you improve by 1 percent a day, in 70 days, you'll be twice as good. But if you don't learn carefully and instead become confused, the opposite can actually occur. People can get dumber.

When creating pragmatic representations of conceptual images, whether brands or graphics or process visuals, it is *always* better to work with a small team that you trust for quicker and higher-quality results.

Failing, and learning as a result, among peers is better than mindlessly succeeding among inferiors.

Emotion is as important as intellect in integrating learning.

The female advantage in learning: less ego investment and more openness. The male advantage: less tendency to take disagreement personally and more tendency to focus on the issue, not the person.

Groups don't bond through dumb icebreaking exercises. They bond through sharing challenge, contributions, disagreements, and socializing.

All groups claim that they want to stay in touch and reconnect. The ones that do so most successfully always have an organizer or organizers who take on that responsibility.

If the facilitator isn't learning constantly, she should go into another line of work. Simply doing something well and receiving plaudits for it is like watching people applaud a movie you made years ago.

About the Most Frequent Organizational Issues

Leadership is inept in that key people are not serving as avatars of the behavior they are seeking in others.

Team building is sought when, in actuality, the organization has committees and needs committees, not teams.

There are silos headed by powerful people who are defending their turf.

Problem solving is prized over innovation, and "black belt nine delta" nonsense takes over people's minds like a bad science fiction movie from the 1950s.

There is excessive staff interference instead of support, typically from HR, finance, IT, and/or legal.

There are too many meetings that take too long and are overwhelmingly focused on sharing information—the worst possible reason to have a meeting. The organization's talent and energy are being squandered internally instead of being applied externally.

The customer's perceptions of the organization's products, services, and relationships are different from the organization's perceptions.

The reward and feedback systems are not aligned with strategy and are not encouraging the appropriate behaviors and not discouraging the inappropriate.

Strategy and planning are mistaken for each other.

Career development and succession planning are not wedded.

The organization is bureaucratic, in that it focuses on means and not ends.

The Very Final Thought: I've found that about 10 percent of people who voluntarily expose themselves to new thinking—in a book or a workshop—actually take affirmative action quickly. Yet you need only 1 percent improvement a day to continually double your effectiveness. As you reach this final word, you'll understand the driving force required to become a million dollar consultant: you.

INDEX